Open Access and copyediting funded by the European Union project IMPACT,
Number: 621672-EPP-1-2020-1-DE-EPPKA2-KA,
Project Duration: January 2021–December 2023
Companion page: www.uxberlin.com/sustainable-innovation-cultures
Contact: contact@uxberlin.com

ISBN 978-3-11-137528-1
e-ISBN [PDF] 978-3-11-137570-0
e-ISBN [EPUB] 978-3-11-137572-4
DOI https://doi.org/10.1515/9783111375700

Library of Congress Control Number: 2025945709

Bibliographic information published by the Deutsche Nationalbibliothek
The Deutsche Nationalbibliothek lists this publication in the Deutsche National-
bibliografie; detailed bibliographic data are available on the Internet at
http://dnb.dnb.de.

The book is published open access at www.degruyterbrill.com.

Copyediting: Paul Lauer

Layout, typesetting and cover design: Done by People, Elmar Birk
Illustrations: Henning Breuer, Vincent Beck and Elmar Birk

www.degruyterbrill.com

Questions regarding general product safety:
productsafety@degruyterbrill.com

For Inho Anton, Jun Robert, and Su Hyeon
Henning Breuer

For Uta and Chika
Kiril Ivanov

Henning Breuer
Kiril Ivanov

Sustainable Innovation Cultures

Overview

Table of Contents

List of Boxes

List of Tables and Figures

Preface

Facing the Greatest Challenge of Our Time

It is the greatest challenge of our time. Keeping the impact of our activities within safe and just boundaries, regenerating our natural and social ecosystems, and working towards desirable futures.

In business, efforts to meet this challenge have been driven for quite some time by idealistic entrepreneurs and mission-driven companies who voluntarily aligned their organisations with environmental, social and ethical values. With the European Sustainability Strategy of 2001 and the first non-financial reporting directive of 2014, new regulations, international agreements and stakeholder expectations are compelling more companies to take action. Today, despite a temporary 'sustainability recession',[1] sustainable development is no longer a visionary pursuit or a matter of tick-box compliance. It is becoming a non-negotiable requirement for companies of all sizes, in all sectors of the economy, in countries around the world. Failure to transform a business is now not only ethically irresponsible, but also carries significant legal, financial and reputational risks.

Many companies have already succeeded in replacing individual processes, products or services with green alternatives. For economic reasons alone, most of them are already masters of efficiency – only by maximising their output with scarce resources can they compete on fierce markets. Some find it relatively easy to extend an economically proven approach to protect the environment or benefit social groups, for example, by introducing energy-saving processes, closing material loops, or providing access to vital services. Some companies have followed up on their initial successes and have already taken the next step, creating sustainable business models that prioritise environmental and social value creation alongside economic profitability.

However, for most companies and organisations, the more fundamental challenge remains unsolved. They must not only redesign individual products, services or business models in a socially and environmentally responsible way. They also need to develop a culture that enables them to repeatedly drive innovation in processes, products, services and business models with sustainability in mind and in hands. Only by establishing a sustainable innovation culture that reliably creates economic, social and environmental value can they contribute to sustainable and regenerative development.

Innovation itself is a demanding business, finding viable paths between utopian sounding promises on the one side, and the need to solve existential problems on the other. It's success is part of the definition, while it comes with great risks, and a need for continuous learning and investment goes hand in hand with uncertain outcomes. Learning by failure is inevitable if you want to succeed.

Sustainable innovation is an even higher art. It is not simply about realising an idea in an organisation or a market. It requires you to establish a culture that produces innovations that qualify as sustainable, consistently. Many companies and organisations invested in regenerative development, some (chapter 7) brought sustainability into the core values of their organisational strategy and innovation activities. However, many are also still struggling to establish a shared sense of direction, to engage diverse stakeholders, to translate their aspirations into daily practices, or to achieve desired results. To do so, they need to conceive their current culture, its activity patterns, its tensions and gaps between values and action, they need to create local interventions, and they need to cultivate new innovation-related practices in a long-term perspective.

This book will show you how to conceptualise sustainable innovation cultures and how to facilitate their development. It serves as a practical guide for innovation managers and entrepreneurs, consultants and trainers, educators and students in the fields of innovation, sustainability and human resource management – all those who seek to mainstream or foster sustainable innovation in their organisations. Based on years of collaborative research across Europe and global business consulting, it combines theoretical rigour with empirical evidence to provide a comprehensive and practical resource for those seeking to create a sustainable innovation culture in their own organisation: Those who are ready to face the greatest challenge of our time, to engage in the great transformation.

Approach and Outline of this Book

'Sustainable Innovation Cultures' provides the first comprehensive overview on this topic. Insights, practices and methods described are grounded in scientific research, including a comprehensive literature review on the web of science, empirical field studies in diverse European companies and interviews with recognised experts. It can help readers and their organisations in pursuit of sustainable innovation, but it is up to each organisation and its participants to select and gain experience with the methods and practices that best suit their needs and goals.

We conceptualise sustainable innovation cultures as generative systems that translate human values into desirable outcomes and impact. We introduce 3C activities and exemplify the practices and methods for conceiving, co-creating and cultivating sustainable innovation. Years of study turned the sentence into an insight: It takes a whole culture to understand and bring about desired change.

We focus on the how to create a sustainable innovation culture and not on the why. We pursue a concept of sustainability, where natural capital cannot be traded off against human-made manufactured capital for economic benefits, and where resource thresholds and allocations are integral to sustainability. We encourage high ambition, but our goal is to help organisations, innovation managers and business leaders realise their deliberate goals and aspirations, whatever their level of ambition.

On the higher levels of sustainability strategy, ambitions of different organisations tend to resemble one another. However, when it comes down to an organisation's cultural notions, practices and artefacts, the sustainability-related challenges and innovation efforts they face are unique. Each organisation has to understand where it stands and which sustainability-related values and goals it is striving to implement.

Part I of the book covers the conceptual foundations of sustainable innovation cultures. Following an overview in the first chapter, we review the relevant literature to develop a framework for sustainable innovation cultures that translates human values into desirable outcomes and generate sustainable innovation in a repeatable and reliable manner. Part II spells out how an existing culture can be conceived and how co-creating and cultivating can redirect innovation efforts towards a desired impact on sustainable development. Part III features case studies from European firms describing their efforts to turn sustainability strategies into practices, documenting how they applied some of the practices and methods described in this book to increase their sustainable innovation maturity. Part IV presents implications for developing sustainable innovation cultures during mergers and acquisitions and looks at the financing practices of mature sustainable innovation cultures. We conclude with a future outlook. A glossary of key terms, information about the authors and the project behind this research, as well as acknowledgements to contributors are available in an appendix.

IMAGINE

Imagine you have just started a new position in innovation or sustainability management in a mid-sized company. You do not need to be convinced about the need for sustainable development, nor that boosting competitiveness can be well aligned with sustainable value creation. You want to get going – and you are wondering where to start. You could read the research reports and ask experts for advice, but that would take forever.

The good news is we have already done that and created a framework of practices and methods that will help you understand, create and cultivate sustainable innovation in your organisation. This framework will enable you to better perceive the status quo, the starting points for interventions and how to approach the desired changes. The practices, methods and cases in this book, illustrated by experiences made in other companies and organisations, will help you to transform your organisation into a sustainable innovation culture.

We wrote this book for those who want to see the forest and the trees, who want the big picture and the details. In other words, for those who dare to tackle cultural change in order to implement their goals for sustainable value creation. These are our guiding questions:

> How can organisations and the people running them translate what they care about into high-impact strategies? How can sustainability strategies be embedded in an organisation's everyday culture? How can we conceive our innovation culture, and how can we recreate and cultivate it to deliver sustainable innovation on a regular and reliable basis?

PART I

FRAMEWORK /
It Takes a
Whole Culture

Across political orientations, regional contexts and economic situations, innovation is widely acknowledged as a powerful lever for gaining a competitive edge and transforming products and services, companies and even whole economies towards sustainable development. However, given the multitude of existential challenges facing humankind, it will require more than incremental improvements to meet the urgent need for transformation towards sustainable development.

Part I begins in chapter 1 by introducing the three basic concepts of culture, innovation and sustainability. In chapter 2 we examine the conceptual underpinnings of sustainable innovation cultures, and in chapter 3 we introduce a framework for establishing your own sustainable innovation culture. Our goal is to facilitate a shared understanding our readers regardless of their professional background or functional area of expertise, before we go into the practices and methods you will need to create sustainable innovation cultures.

There is a well-known saying that it takes a whole village to raise a child.

> For sustainable development, it takes a whole culture to make it happen. It takes sustainable innovation cultures to bring about desired changes towards sustainability on a reliable basis.

Chapter 1 /
It Takes a Whole
Culture

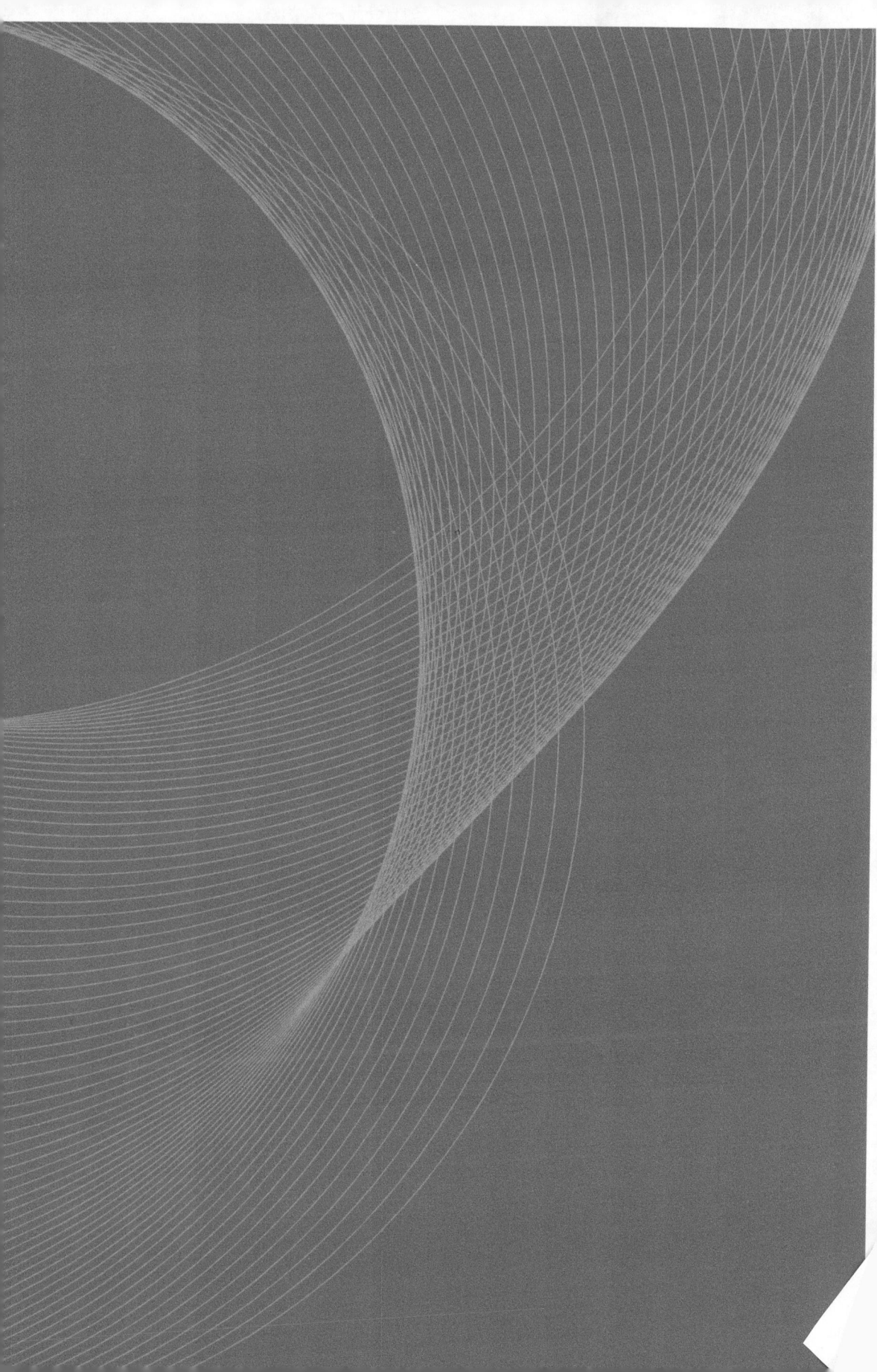

First off, what is an organisational culture? Culture in business has long been treated as something that operates at a subconscious level and escapes rational planning. However, just as our subconscious still influences our lives (psychoanalysis refers to the 'return of the repressed'), the subconscious 'organisational mind' can cause all rational efforts at management to fail. This is what Peter Drucker was getting at when he said that 'culture eats strategy for breakfast'. However, there's another important side to the story. We should not just blame culture for destroying our strategic choices before the day even begins. Culture can also turn strategies into reality and make innovation succeed.

> Culture plays the decisive role in enabling sustainability and innovation strategies to succeed. Therefore, this is about the generative aspects of culture.

Culture is not just a bundle of implicit beliefs, ill-perceived practices and off-the-shelf methods. It's a production site for innovation, a place where strategy can be turned into practice. It begins with shared notions of what is desirable – such as sustainability, equity or well-being – but it also needs appropriate practices and artefacts. A good cultural fit for an organisation means aligning fundamental notions with practices and artefacts. In other words, it means aligning mindsets and skillsets with toolsets and datasets.

The second concept, innovation, is defined by the International Standards Organisation as an outcome that creates or redistributes value. That outcome needn't be a new product or service. It can be a change how things are done. In the context of sustainability, that value is not only economic, but also social and environmental.

> Innovation and its management generate novel outcomes that are environmentally, socially and economically valuable.

The third concept, sustainability, is complex. And the confusion around how it can be best interpreted already poses a major barrier to sustainable transformation. For many organisations, a beginning is found in their efforts to comply with more rigorous reporting requirements by collecting environmental, social and governmental (ESG) information. Indeed, reporting directives have promoted sustainability from a concern for the few to a mandatory practice for large companies. Still, some companies and organisations are slow to understand that profound cultural change is necessary if they are to have something substantive to report or keep ahead of regulation. However, slowly but surely, companies are coming around to embracing more far-reaching change and transforming their business models to cultivate sustainable innovation.

> Ambitious approaches to organisational sustainability address sustainability-related challenges and promote competitiveness in the long, mid and short-term.

Forward-looking companies are already taking a bold approach that doesn't shy away from Context-Based Reporting and Sustainability Foresight (practices, marked with ☐ and methods, marked with ○ described in chapters 3–6 of the book are capitalised and highlighted with italics). They use real data and normative future scenarios rather than estimates and hindsight. They rely on science-based thresholds and values-based norms to support sustainable development and compete to find the best solutions to meet recurring challenges. They do not just report ESG data in order to be in compliance, but actively manage sustainable innovation.

This proactive approach enables companies and other organisations (such as non-profit or community-based entities) to transform themselves over the long term with an innovation culture oriented towards values of sustainability. In the mid-term, these cultural pioneers gain a competitive edge, not only by competing for the best solutions, but also by finding new markets for sustainable value creation.

> Sustainable innovation culture is a dynamic configuration of values, practices and artefacts that generate environmentally, socially and economically valuable outcomes. Culture translates values into added value.

By identifying values of sustainability and embedding them deeply in the fabric of the organisation, a company can drive sustainable innovation in a reliable and repeatable manner.

If this is what a sustainable innovation culture can do, what does it take to establish one? Sustainable innovation cultures do not come into existence by accident, nor can they be implemented by top-down directives from management. The first step is to understand what constitutes a given culture. There are three dimensions to culture: its notions (in particular values as notions of the desirable as well as other relevant terms used colloquially), its practices (how people get things done) and its artefacts (media and material resources). These three dimensions must be aligned with each other in a way that engages all of a company's stakeholders. If they are not – if there are serious tensions or gaps between values and actions – the company will fail to achieve its goal. In our case, it will fail to create a sustainable innovation culture that gains competitive edge and impact.

Imagine the entry hall of a company's office building is decorated with high-flying statements that everyone knows do not guide its everyday decision-making and practice, the employees will experience discomfort at this contradiction between rhetoric and reality. Some might leave the company (a phenomenon HR professionals call 'climate quitting'), while others will stay, but become demotivated or cynical. Or imagine top managers proclaim the benefits of informal collaboration in a talk to their employees, but the only space for casual meetings is in the cramped lunchroom, which doubles as a stockroom for office supplies. Something will seem wrong. Likewise, if the company website announces a sustainable AI initiative, but fails to ensure that its employees have the needed skills, software tools and datasets. They will feel little more than frustration.

> Sustainable innovation requires a company to align its values, practices and artefacts.

Many things can go wrong here, leading to ineffective, unintended or undesirable results. Values might not be well articulated in guiding principles and policies, or not well communicated by leadership. Ever received a call for more personal eye-level relations and informal communication via email? Contradictions between implicit and explicit values and conflicting values of different stakeholders may cause tensions and distract the workforce from realising its capabilities. Values-action gaps can undermine the espoused values and commitment of employees or other stakeholders who promote or get in the way of turning ideas into innovation. Missing tools or data or other poorly designed artefacts can get in the way of practices unfolding their innovative and regenerative potential. Understanding both misalignments and conducive practices is key to cultivating sustainable innovation.

Based on comprehensive literature reviews, expert interviews and empirical studies in European companies, we have identified 32 documented practices and 36 standardised methods that help companies establish their own sustainable innovation cultures. Each practice comes with a title, description and related methods. Each method bears a title, subtitle and a description of the challenge it responds to, an approach and an example. Each practice and each method is presented with references in the chapters 3–6. Together they provide a menu of options for companies and other organisations to consider on their journey to becoming sustainable innovation cultures. Some practices are overarching. Other practices and associated methods are particularly useful to supporting one of the three stages of cultural development, namely the conceiving, co-creating and cultivating activities that are part of the journey towards a sustainable innovation culture.

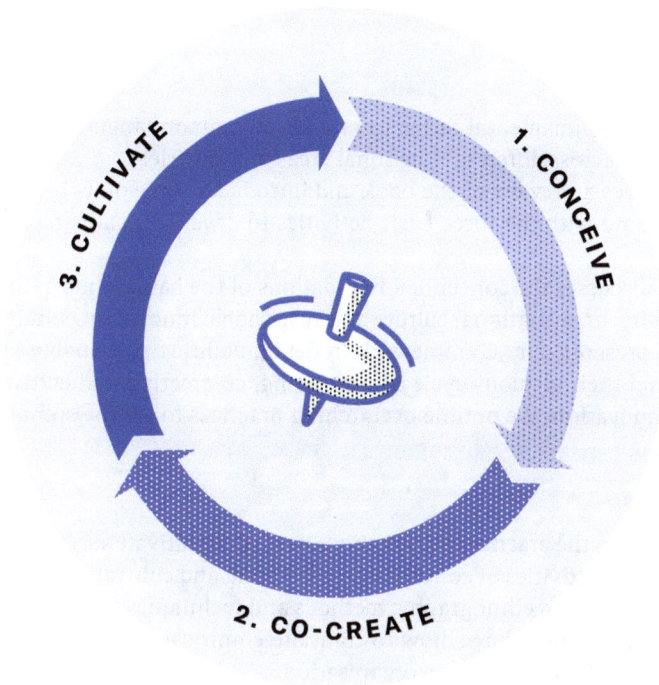

FIGURE 1. 3C framework for creating sustainable innovation cultures with three stages of basic activities: conceiving, co-creating and cultivating

Conceiving: First, we need to understand our current organisational culture.

> How can we conceive our cultural practices to understand our values, their tensions and the gaps between values and action?

Co-creating: The second step is to address specific tensions and gaps as well as to build existing strengths for sustainable innovation.

> How can we co-create sustainable innovation practices – and strengthen existing ones – with targeted interventions?

Cultivating: The third step is to embed the values, practices, tools and data deeply in the organisation's daily practices.

> How can we cultivate virtuous circles that lead to new sustainable value as outcome and ultimately achieve the desired impact?

Preview

PART I clarifies fundamental terms to provide a common language and facilitate collaboration across different functional areas or industries.

CHAPTER 1 gives a preview of the book and introduces some of its basic ideas and concepts along with the three basic activities to develop sustainable innovation cultures.[1]

CHAPTER 2 discusses the conceptual foundations of the basic terms of innovation, sustainability, organisational culture and sustainable innovation culture.

CHAPTER 3 presents our 3C framework in detail, defining sustainable innovation cultures and their virtuous cycle of conceiving, co-creating and cultivating sustainable innovation. We outline overarching practices to get the spinning top up and running.

PART II identifies the practices and methods needed to cultivate sustainable innovation across the activities of conceiving, co-creating and cultivating.

CHAPTER 4 focuses on ethnographic methods and techniques to conceive an innovation culture. It also shows how to translate empirical insights and challenges into actionable task areas for an organisation.

CHAPTER 5 introduces practices and methods to co-create targeted interventions that advance an innovation culture and explore opportunities for sustainable innovation.

CHAPTER 6 shows how to cultivate values, practices and artefacts in order to ensure desirable outcomes in the development of sustainable innovation cultures.

PART III dives into cases from European companies who took up the challenge to conceive and co-create their own innovation cultures to get on a high-impact, sustainability-oriented track.

CHAPTER 7 presents the case of a German inspection company that was founded on the premise of ensuring safety. It successfully adopted sustainability was adopted as a core value, but still faces challenges in turning this strategy into practice until it mainstreamed its sustainable innovation culture across the ecosystems it is engaged in.

CHAPTER 8 reviews the development of sustainable innovation cultures in the energy technology industry in Italy. This case shows how a company's IT division introduced strategic sustainability innovations that could serve as a model for the industry.

CHAPTER 9 zooms into the case of a Polish engineering company in the cleantech sector. It highlights the pivotal roles of a qualified workforce, technological development and management by values for the development of sustainable innovation cultures.

CHAPTER 10 focuses on the communication challenges facing science-based companies in Spain. It shows how consistent communication strategies, overcoming silos and cross-functional coordination are crucial for establishing sustainable innovation cultures.

PART IV looks into specialised disciplines and the roles of facilitation and finance for the development of sustainable innovation cultures and concludes with a future outlook into emerging challenges.

CHAPTER 11 shows how values and identity drive organisational transformation. It builds on the case of a Slovenian brewery acquired by an international brand to map out a viable journey for sustainability-oriented transformations.

CHAPTER 12 shows how to finance sustainable innovation and specifies the implications for the accounting and finance functions in organisations. The case of a sustainability-oriented investment management company illustrates good practices in financing sustainability-oriented transformations.

CHAPTER 13 provides an outlook into future challenges and discusses how forward-looking companies gain a competitive edge and create sustainable value by driving transformation, fostering collaborative innovation ecosystems and leveraging intelligent systems to enhance sustainable innovation cultures.

How to Read This Book

The hurried reader might jump ahead now, browse through the 3C framework in chapter 3 and then dive into some of the practices and methods in part II. Readers with more academic interests will look at the conceptual distinctions explored in chapter 2, whereas practitioners seeking to create or develop their own sustainable innovation cultures will focus on chapters 3–6 that show how to conceive, create and cultivate sustainable innovation. They might also appreciate the focus of chapter 12 on the financial side of the transformation journey. Cases in chapters 7–11 provide deeper insights into the real-world struggles of individual companies to find a viable approach. If you are interested in where we feel this journey is headed read the final chapter for an outlook. For most of us, this journey is just beginning.

Chapter 2 / Conceptual Foundations

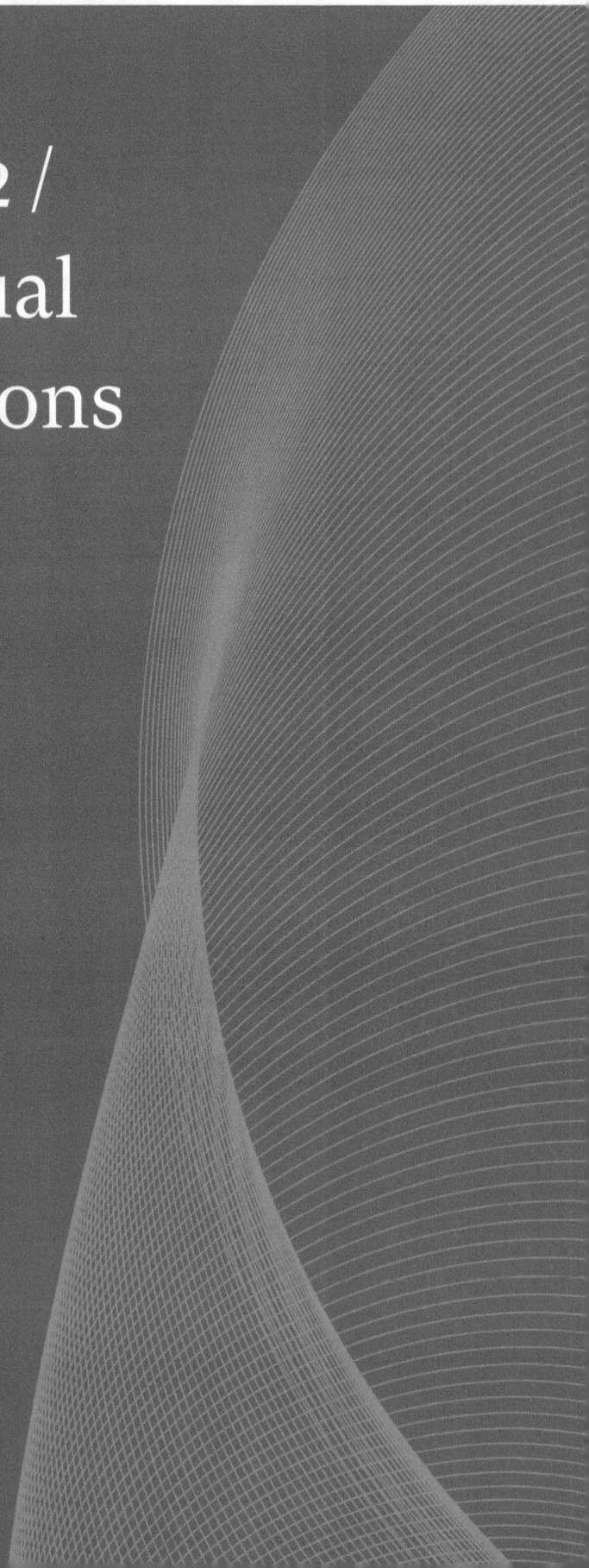

In order to understand how sustainable innovation cultures work and how they can be established, we must first clarify some basic terms and concepts, not just for the sake of establishing a shared language, but to facilitate a common understanding for readers with different professional backgrounds and who occupy different functional roles in an organisation. Our own studies have shown that basic terms – such as innovation, impact or sustainability – can be understood in different ways, posing a major obstacle to efforts to promote sustainable innovation and cultural development. By clarifying these terms, we can take a crucial first step towards establishing sustainable innovation cultures.

In fact, writings on sustainability, innovation, culture (together with their combinations sustainable innovation and innovation culture) already fill a library. We have developed a new conceptual framework by doing our own systematic literature reviews, empirical studies and panel discussions with experts. We focus on approaches that share three main characteristics. First, they show an ambitious understanding of sustainability, not as a constraint, but as a lever for innovation. Second, they pursue a values-based and future-oriented approach to innovation. And third they share an understanding of culture not as a soft, nice-to-have factor, but as a complex generative system that translates human values into new forms of sustainable value creation.

Forward-looking approaches create sustainable innovation cultures as generative systems that turn sustainability challenges into opportunities for innovation and system-wide value creation.

We start with a brief review of the concepts of sustainability, innovation and sustainable innovation (section 2.1). We then highlight major insights into organisational culture and its development (section 2.2), followed by a discussion of recent works on sustainability and innovation culture that identify good practices and barriers to cultivating sustainable innovation (section 2.3). We then present a 3C framework of basic activities for conceiving and co-creating innovation culture and cultivating sustainable innovation (chapter 3). Note that the terms in capitalised italics refer to the 68 practices and methods of the 3C framework discussed in chapters 3–6.

2.1   Sustainability, Innovation and Sustainable Innovation

Sustainability management has evolved from a niche pursuit of a few pioneering entrepreneurs to a strategic imperative for established businesses throughout the economy to grow their business and contribute to environmental and social sustainability. Early initiatives focused on efficiency and regulatory compliance, but a more holistic approach is now emerging. By embracing sustainability, companies are building competitive advantage through sustainable innovation practices and methods, while creating greater value for a wider range of stakeholders – that is, anyone affected by or contributing to the success or failure of organisational activities.[1] This shift marks a departure from 'tick-box' compliance, as companies prioritise forward-looking strategizing aligned with evidence-based targets, local thresholds and broader societal goals.

Innovation itself has the potential to create not only economic benefits but also positive outcomes for society and the environment. Sustainable innovation embraces values of sustainability to generate new products, services, processes and business models. Driven by external pressures and internal motivation, it aims for long-term impact across operational, strategic and normative management levels of organisations.

2.1.1 Sustainability

We are facing enormous challenges to keep human impact on the planet and our natural and social ecosystems within safe and just boundaries to achieve desirable futures.[2] Sustainability is not just about doing the minimum to secure a satisfactory lifestyle or to run an eco-friendly business, it is an existential issue for humankind and indeed for all species on the planet Earth. The research results and the sometimes controversial discussions on how sustainable development can and should be shaped are correspondingly extensive. Rather than trying to cover every aspect, we highlight some historical accounts, current market-based approaches and more ambitious calls to transformative actions.

CONCEPT 1. Sustained Yield Management

The concept of sustainability dates back more than 300 years when Hans Carl von Carlowitz wrote *Sylvicultura oeconomica*, a comprehensive treatise on forest management. Logging to provide timber for the silver mines in Saxony had decimated whole forests. Carlowitz, as the chief mining administrator, called for sustainable forestry and introduced the principle of sustainability as living off the yield of the resource (the harvest) rather than depleting the resource itself. Timber was to be harvested at a rate not exceeding the ability of the forest to regrow naturally.

In the 18th and 19th century, 'sustained yield management' was operationalised by 'normalising' the planting of different tree species.[3] Monocultures of Norwegian spruce and Scottish pine were planted in blocks. The undergrowth was cleared to prevent insects from feeding on the trees and retain the nutrients in the soil. This scientific approach facilitated forest maintenance and experimentation, harvesting and yield calculation, and it was soon copied by other countries.

Inevitably, the detrimental effects became visible, such as the spreading of diseases, increased vulnerability to storms and the loss of nutrients from the undergrowth. The mathematical normalisation of forest yield in the pursuit of sustainability is now understood to illustrate 'the dangers of dismembering an exceptionally complex and poorly understood set of relations and processes in order to isolate a single element of instrumental value'.[4]

Sustainability and Sustainable Development

In the 20th century, the catastrophic effects of industrial exploitation of nature became apparent. Over time, sustainability emerged as a key concept, broadly defined as 'intergenerational ethics in which the environmental and economic actions taken by present persons do not diminish the opportunities of future persons to enjoy similar levels of wealth, utility, or welfare'.[5] In 1987 the Brundtland Report brought concerns of sustainability to a wider audience and argued for intergenerational and intragenerational justice and equity of opportunities as essential values for 'our common future'.[6]

This definition of sustainable development became a basis for initiatives in the political and the private sector: 'Humanity has the ability to make development sustainable to ensure that it meets the needs of the present without compromising the ability of future generations to meet their own needs.'[7] The report also contained a second, less well-known definition of sustainable development: 'A process of change in which the exploitation of resources, the direction of investments, the orientation of technological development; and institutional change are all in harmony and enhance both current and future potential to meet human needs and aspirations.'[8]

The concept of sustainable development has since gained widespread recognition. It has helped to raise awareness of the interconnectedness between environmental, social and economic systems, promoting a more holistic approach to economic and organisational development. In 2015 the Paris Agreement was adopted by the UN to strengthen the world's response to climate change. The UN's Sustainable Development Goals (SDGs) were primarily aimed at governments and political entities, but have been taken up by organisations in the private sector in order to take responsibility, fulfil regulatory requirements, convince investors, meet changing customer expectations and gain a competitive edge in the search for novel and viable ways to meet the pressing economic, social and environmental challenges.

Sustainability Management and System Value Creation

Initial successes have been achieved. Technological innovations in resource efficiency, renewable energy and sustainable agriculture have begun to mitigate environmental degradation. Efforts are increasingly being made to address issues such as climate change, biodiversity loss and social inequality. However, unsustainable consumption patterns, disparities in global development and inadequate policy implementations persist.

These challenges will not be met by technical solutions alone, as sustainable development is not subject to natural laws. It is an ethical and societal choice based on the values of intra- and intergenerational equity.[9] While most companies manage sustainability to comply with regulatory requirements, a growing awareness of the multiple threats of environmental crisis and collapse has increased societal expectations on business to take responsibility for their actions and contribute to sustainable development beyond their legal obligations.

Sustainability management is defined as an organisation's concerted efforts to contribute to sustainable development. It operationalises sustainability by formulating, implementing and evaluating environmental and socioeconom-ic sustainability-related decisions and actions.[10] Sustainability management is evolving into an ethical and strategic imperative that is integral to the long-term viability of any business. In fact, an increasing number of companies are seeking to leverage their unique strengths with sustainability management and gain a competitive edge.

A competitive edge can be achieved by adopting the best approaches to solv-ing sustainability challenges and to meeting economic priorities.[11] The search for a business case of sustainability revolves around the potential of sustain-ability management to create a strategic business advantage. This approach plays a crucial role in mitigating risks from regulatory changes, reputational damage or physical threats to infrastructure due to climate change. By adopting sustainability management practices, companies can capitalise on business op-portunities such as long-term profitability, social acceptance and a motivated workforce.[12]

However, reducing sustainability to an instrumental lever could lead to unethi-cal behaviour.[13] As a call to responsible action, values of sustainability push man-agement efforts towards an extended concept of value creation and beyond the pursuit of instrumental goals to embrace a stakeholder-oriented and values-based business case *for* sustainability.[14]

Economics and management theory have long defined value creation in eco-nomic terms,[15] whether direct benefits through shareholder value, employee com-pensation or the customer value of a product or service or indirect benefits for society through taxes and employment. This narrow understanding of value cre-ation is now being extended to include the social and environmental benefits a company can provide. The former includes social inclusion and participation in the labour market and access to essential services and products, while the latter includes the reduction of greenhouse gas emissions and positive contributions to the strengthening of environmental ecosystems.

Along with sustainability orientation, stakeholder integration and systemic thinking, expanded value creation is therefore one of four guiding principles for the design of sustainable business models (see concept 2 below).[16]

> **CONCEPT 2. Principles for the Design and Development of Sustainable Business Models**
>
> Sustainability management defines a company's sustainable business model as how it 'proposes, delivers, captures, maintains, unlocks and shares value with and for its stakeholders'.[17]
>
> *Sustainability orientation* in a company is crucial to the development of sustainable business models. It is grounded in the prioritisation of sustaina-bility-related values at the core of business aspirations, strategic decisions and operational practices. It provides clear 'directional certainty' (see also concept 3: section 2.1.3) against a background of market, technological and political uncertainties. Moreover, companies seek to identify and resolve

tensions with other participants in the business ecosystem, aligning interests and encouraging cooperation and shared responsibility.

A striking example is Unilever's transformation under the leadership of Paul Polman,[18] who stepped in as CEO in 2009. Polman used strategic foresight to identify four megatrends that would transform the consumer goods market by 2020: shifts in markets, lifestyles, the environment and stakeholder empowerment. Acknowledging that traditional profit-oriented strategies would not work, in 2010 the company launched the Unilever Sustainable Living Plan. It mandated a *Roadmapping* to achieve ambitious goals by 2020, such as helping over one billion people improve health and well-being, halving the environmental footprint of its products and sourcing 100 percent of agricultural raw materials sustainably.

Extended value creation broadens the profit-oriented understanding of how value is delivered to customers and how value in terms of revenues is captured to include multiple economic, social and environmental outcomes. It includes non-monetary values such as workplace satisfaction or employee turnover. It is about the maintenance, unlocking and sharing of value.[19]

Maintaining value also refers to the preservation of existing resources and systems, both natural and man-made. Unilever maintains value by optimising its business model to reduce water use and waste reduction in factories and increase sustainable sourcing of agricultural produce. Unlocking value means that companies utilise untapped potential for creating sustainable value, for instance, by addressing unmet needs or inefficiencies in current market systems.

Unilever has done this by shifting away from simply selling products and moving towards encouraging behaviour change. For instance, the Help a Child Reach Five[20] campaign teaches rural communities the health benefits of washing hands. Echoing this campaign, Unilever's Lifebuoy antibacterial soap has created long-term brand loyalty in new markets. Lastly, value sharing refers to ensuring the equitable and responsible distribution of value among stakeholders. Unilever's Shakti programme has trained over 200,000 women in Indian rural areas to become micro-entrepreneurs selling the company's products.[21]

Systemic thinking recognises the interdependence of business activities and the need to adopt a holistic perspective. By considering the entire life cycle of their products, businesses can integrate them in product-service systems. They also design their business models to generate sustainable value for multiple stakeholders, while avoiding potential negative outcomes for other social groups or the environment. Unilever's Domestos Toilet Academy[22] educates consumers and communities to apply sanitation practices while also training entrepreneurs to form businesses that supply, install and maintain hygienic toilets.

Stakeholder integration in sustainable business models negotiates the diverse and sometimes conflicting interests and values of those individuals and groups who have a stake in a company's work. The systematic management of stakeholder relationships enables a company to access and acquire resources (e.g. finance) and capacities through other market participants (e.g. investors) and non-market-actors (e.g. training local communities to engage in micro-entrepreneurship as in Unilever's Shakti and Toilet Academy programmes) and to address conflicting interests and navigate complex challenges.

The expanded concept of value creation invites companies to take a holistic perspective and rethink the kinds of outcomes they create, not only economic benefits but also social and environmental harms. So-called 'weak sustainability' calculates whether a negative environmental impact can be outweighed by positive economic and social impacts. It assumes substitutability between natural and human-made capital (e.g. the loss of biodiversity is compensated by the recreational benefits of a park built when a forest is cut down).

A holistic approach to sustainability is not about making trade-offs between its different dimensions. 'Strong sustainability' knows that many natural assets cannot be traded off against human-made alternatives. They provide limited resources and provide an irreplaceable foundation for regenerative development. In the strong sustainability approach, companies create value not just for themselves, but for the systems they constitute and are a part of.[23]

> System value aligns economic, social and environmental value creation to meet human needs within the Earth's planetary boundaries.

Different organisations follow different frameworks. Some companies take the SDGs of the United Nations to prioritise the desired outcomes of their business activities. Others follow European regulations including the Corporate Sustainability Reporting Directive, EU Taxonomy and Corporate Sustainability Due Diligence Directive or international initiatives such as the Business Roundtable, which require companies to formulate and fulfil social and environmental objectives. Both reflect an expanded understanding of sustainability.[24]

Moreover, companies seeking to redirect their business activity towards sustainable value creation engage in *Guiding Principles Review* to revisit their guidelines and values and reprioritise their business goals. This involves translating the EU Taxonomy's six environmental goals, the UN's 17 SDGs (with 169 targets and numerous indicators) into guiding principles such as vision, mission and purpose. These principles are then incorporated into daily practices, achieving multidimensional economic, social and environmental value creation.

Sustainability Reporting: From Today's Standards to Forward-Looking Approaches
Regulatory and stakeholder demands to avert a 'tragedy of the commons',[25] or the overexploitation of shared, finite resources like clean air and water, public healthcare systems and stable financial infrastructure continue to grow. As a result, sustainable value creation has evolved from a voluntary ambition of a few idealistic entrepreneurs and business leaders to an indispensable requirement for

companies in every economic sector. To provide transparency and allow stakeholders to assess the extent to which they are fulfilling their societal responsibilities, companies are now disclosing sustainability-related information and expanding its scope. Initially seen as a burden, reporting is now becoming a hub for innovation and strategic development. Not only does it provide stakeholders with extensive insights into a company's practices and impacts, reporting indicators and results help the company identify challenges and prioritise levers for sustainable innovation.

Integrated reporting requires companies to compile and disclose information on their economic, environmental and social performance using indicators such as greenhouse gas emissions, energy consumption, labour practices and community engagement. Several reporting standards have been established, for example, the Global Reporting Initiative or the Sustainability Accounting Standards Board.[26] However, reporting efforts focusing on ESG progress (i.e. the integration of environmental, social and governance criteria) have faced severe criticism. Their focus on investor relations and their outside-in, retrospective and decontextualised approach emphasises the impact of the environment on companies rather than their own inside-out impact on the environment, and it uses historical or relative benchmarks rather than references to environmental carrying capacities and social caring capacities.

The call for double materiality reporting requires that companies not only consider the outside-in effect of sustainability-related risks and opportunities on financial performance. They must also report inside-out how a company's activities impact society and the environment. Regional contextual factors – sometime referred to as triple materiality – provide the necessary baseline.

Without the contexts of safe and just Earth system boundaries[27] and a fair allocation of common resources, ESG reporting remains detached from its scientific and ethical baselines. Reporting can become a more delusive than helpful exercise if it relies on competitor or historical benchmarks rather than on references to the carrying capacity of the planet and the region they are located in. In fact, a negative correlation has been shown between high ESG scores and real environmental impact, raising the suspicion that high scoring companies are engaging in greenwashing.[28] *Context-Based Reporting* and forward-looking approaches address some of these shortcomings.

First, Context-Based Reporting grounds sustainability goals and practices in science-based limits, human needs and local thresholds.[29] For instance, a context-based company report on the reduction of water usage needs to consider regional water resources and their fair allocation among stakeholders (other companies, utilities, communities) and rightsholders (rivers, domesticated animals and wildlife). This creates a baseline and global sustainability norms for negotiating and allocating available resources to different actors in a region. Such an approach already involves looking beyond the present to possible future developments. Climate transition planning – which involves mapping out concrete steps, future roadmaps and risk management measures for decarbonisation – has already been adopted as a requirement by several reporting standards.

Second, forward-looking approaches such as *Sustainability Foresight* comple-ment retrospective reporting by directing innovation efforts towards achieving desirable outcomes.[30] Both outside-in assessment of financial risks for the com-pany and inside-out assessment of value and damage creation through business activities focus on the present state of affairs. Foresight focuses on possible, probable and desirable future developments, usually with the help of explora-tory and normative scenarios. Exploratory scenarios explore external (social, technological, economic, environmental and political) developments to de-scribe possible futures to prepare for. They answer the question: *What external developments do we need to prepare for?* However, they lack normative objectives and a goalsetting function, especially in relation to normative frameworks such as the SDGs.

Normative scenarios envision desirable future outcomes and serve as guides for planning, policy-making and strategic decision-making to achieve specific goals. They answer the questions: *What kind of future do we want? How do different stake-holders envision a desirable future?* However, they easily lose their connection to reality, and it is difficult to anchor them concretely in everyday practice.

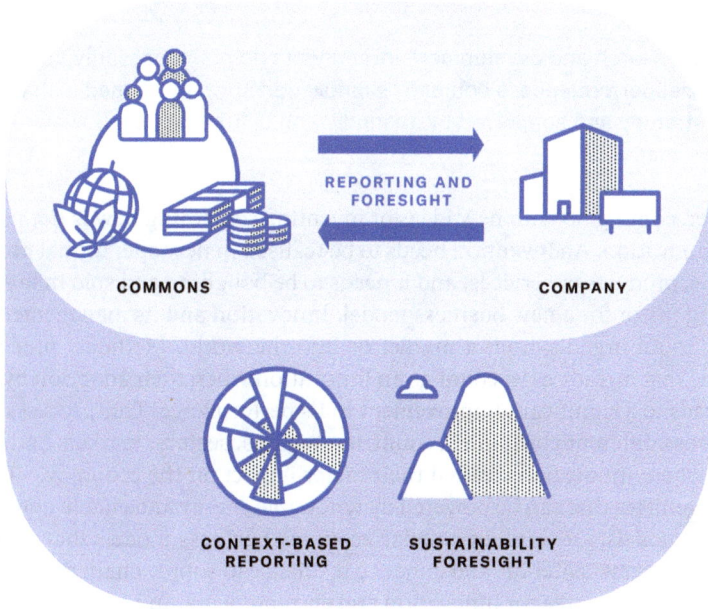

FIGURE 2. Forward-looking approaches complement retrospective reporting and help to direct sustainable innovation efforts

Both approaches can be combined. For instance, the European Environment Agency developed four scenarios for desirable European futures, each one accounting for different external conditions, each one prioritising different SDGs of the United Nations.[31] Likewise, sustainability foresight in companies combines the exploratory and normative outlooks with the values and goals of sustainable development to deal with emerging challenges. Here we ask questions like: *What economic, social and environmental value do we seek to create in the future? How can we contribute to sustainable development?* Figure 2 illustrates these approaches to sustainability reporting and foresight.

2.1.2 Innovation

Innovation takes us from the present state of affairs to new ways of doing things. Different definitions stress different aspects of such renewal. Innovation has been simply described as 'significant positive change'[32] or, more academically, as resulting 'from creative processes involving different actors to establish new means–end combinations' and altering 'our capabilities to act'.[33] Innovation and its management have been recently added to the body of global norms agreed upon within the International Standards Organisation. The standard defines innovation as an outcome of innovation activities or processes, as a 'new or changed entity, realising or redistributing value'.[34]

> While research and development investments do not necessarily improve financial performance, a company's innovation strategy aligned with corporate strategy and supported by an innovation culture has been shown to be key to success.[35]

However, coming up with new ideas or inventing something new is not necessarily an innovation. An invention needs to be realised in new operational processes, methods, products or services, and it needs to be bought to and sold in markets as a driving factor for a new business model. Innovation and its management bring novelty to an organisation, a market or into the world. Methods, processes or products that already exist count as an innovation when their adoption by a company leads to a significant improvement in its performance. This process of diffusion across different consumers, countries, regions, sectors, markets and companies is where innovations unfold their major impact on the economy.[36] Think of electric vehicles that can be powered by renewable energy and enable new sharing business models. Or think of circular economy business models that reduce dependency on raw materials and enhance resilience to supply chain disruptions.

Several frameworks for innovation and entrepreneurship have been developed and adopted by business schools and practitioners. Some like user-driven innovation,[37] open innovation,[38] disruptive innovation[39] or blue ocean strategy[40] have played an important role in innovation projects in large and mid-sized organisations. Others such as business modelling[41] or the lean start-up[42] have also inspired entrepreneurs. However, most of these frameworks, developed in the 1990s and 2000s, highlight the search for new market opportunities and strategic differentiation from specific competitors.

The values-based innovation management framework complements 'opportunistic' approaches to innovation and entrepreneurship by the central role it places on understanding and applying 'individual, organisational, societal and global values, and corresponding normative orientations as a basis for innovation'.[43] This approach is illustrated through numerous cases from large and smaller companies and start-ups, which demonstrate how values function as an integrative source, serve directive orientation and (heuristically) lever innovation.[44]

Over the past decade, values and related ethical guidelines have been more widely acknowledged as drivers and pivotal factors in innovation management, as well as fruitful resources for entrepreneurship.[45] A wide range of methods is available to implement values-based innovation. Several practices and methods to establish and maintain sustainable innovation cultures can be drawn from cases discussed from the perspective of values-based innovation management.[46]

2.1.3 Sustainable Innovation

Sustainable innovation serves as an overarching term in this book. There has been some debate about how to best formulate this concept, with related terms being eco-innovation, frugal innovation, sustainability innovation or sustainability-oriented innovation. All these terms are relatively new, starting with eco-innovation in the mid-90s. With its focus on reducing environmental impact, eco-innovation has given way to a more holistic approaches that integrate economic, social and environmental aspects. Frugal innovation is a term often associated with a positive impact on sustainability by addressing resource-constrained customers in emerging markets. However, like eco-innovation, frugal innovation offers an incomplete perspective on sustainability and has been criticised for creating rebound effects.[47]

We distinguish between sustainability innovation, sustainability-oriented innovation and sustainable innovation. 'Sustainability innovation' highlights dedicated efforts to enhance the sustainability of organisational processes, products, services or business models. Examples include reducing waste or introducing carbon-neutral technologies. 'Sustainability-oriented innovation' is widely understood to involve 'intentional changes to an organization's philosophy and values, as well as to its products, processes or practices to serve the specific purpose of creating and realising social and environmental value in addition to economic returns'.[48] It refers to an ongoing transformation[49] and widely overlaps with our understanding of sustainable innovation.

We use the term 'sustainability-oriented innovation' to highlight the purpose and direction involved in an innovation process. 'Sustainable innovation' has been defined 'as a process where sustainability considerations (environmental, social and economic) are integrated into company systems from idea generation through to research and development and commercialisation. This applies to products, services and technologies, as well as new business and organisation models'.[50]

> We understand sustainable innovation as an overarching term for the systematic integration of sustainability-related values and considerations into innovation activities. Sustainable innovations create or redistribute economic, social and environmental value through new or changed entities (such as products, services, business models or ecosystems) or processes for an organisation and its stakeholders.

Push and Pull Driving Factors

Factors driving sustainable innovation can be classified into push and pull factors. Their importance varies depending on industry, societal expectations and sustainability topic. Together, they shape the way companies approach sustainable innovation.[51]

Push factors compel companies to adapt their practices to external pressures, such as governmental and international regulations or standards for emissions, product safety, social inclusion or environmental protection. For example, the need to comply with regulatory targets to reduce CO_2, SO_2 and NOx emissions, as well as mandates on recyclability, are increasingly pushing companies across industries to innovate.[52] Anticipating regulations acts as a catalyst for companies seeking to stay ahead of stricter requirements.

Costs are another push factor, as rising raw material and energy prices encourage businesses to adopt environmentally protective practices to reduce expenses. For instance, investments in energy-efficient processes not only serve compliance goals but also save costs. Civil society also pushes – driven by activists, scientists and the media – and adds further ethical pressure to avoid pollution, resource depletion and unsafe or unhealthy materials. Public scrutiny thus pushes companies to innovate and adopt more sustainable practices to maintain their reputation.

Pull factors, by contrast, incentivise voluntary engagement in sustainable innovation. Regulatory pull includes government incentives encouraging businesses to innovate – such as tax reductions, grants or research funding into greener technologies. *Sustainable Finance and Investment* instruments in both the public and private sector help to reduce investment costs for sustainable innovation. Market pull is driven by evolving customer demands and consumers that prioritise products with improved environmental performance, as well as process innovations that increase material efficiency, reduce energy consumption, minimise waste and avoid hazardous substances. Visionary pull drives sustainable innovation under the direction of forward-thinking leaders (see case 7, section 3.1.4) or sustainability frameworks and agendas, such as the SDGs (see case 3, section 3.1.1).

These push and pull factors often work interdependently. For instance, regulatory standards on emissions, cost pressures from rising energy prices and heightened customer demand for emission-free mobility choices – taken together – foster product, service and business model innovations in electromobility. The cumulative effects of regulatory pressures, cost-saving considerations and increasing market demand are propelling the production and adoption of electric vehicles.[53]

A Values-Based Approach to Sustainable Innovation

The call for sustainable development and innovation was initially guided by values of inter- and intragenerational equity, as formulated in the Brundtland Report. And values continue to play a key role in sustainable innovation. In the values-based approach 'values are the wellspring of innovation and value creation'.[54] Values such as quality of life, social security, safety from natural disasters and social upheaval or simply peace of mind have taken on an existential meaning as the consequences of unsustainable living and economic activity have reached catastrophic proportions. Values cannot be directly translated into action. They must first be mainstreamed and established as practices to target qualitatively and quantitatively defined outcomes.

In stakeholder theory,[55] the values at stake in sustainable innovation are those of the people who implement or are affected by an organisation's activities. These are not only customers and employees, but also the communities and others that benefit from or influence an organisation. For instance, an organic foods company will align itself with the values of its customers, who prioritise healthy, naturally sourced and environmentally friendly products. Employees who share these values will find pride in their work.

Moreover, as organic production methods protect local ecosystems, the company's reputation will be enhanced in the local community and potentially lead to stronger partnerships and support from local stakeholders. Investors and suppliers also profit from the economic stability, resilience and growth driven by organic production. An emergent stakeholder network based on values of sustainability can lead to joint innovation efforts by establishing official certification or labels confirming the quality of the company's organic produce.[56]

Values-based approaches to sustainable innovation go beyond the standard success criteria for innovation. We have mentioned that an idea or a prototype must be translated into a daily practice in order to count as an innovation – that it must become a new process that is actually used in a company, adopted as a new product or service on a market or implemented as a business model. However, for values-based innovations, this reality check is not enough. They must also deliver on their values. A safety innovation must increase safety,[57] a health innovation improve health or cure diseases, and a sustainable innovation enhance equity and contribute to sustainable development through sustainable value creation. This means that sustainability-oriented organisations formulate their guiding principles and policies with reference to the desired outcomes of their innovation activities.

'A sustainable organization expresses its purpose, vision and mission in terms of social, environmental and economic outcomes.'[58]

Normative, strategic and operational dimensions of sustainable innovation

Innovation is often thought of as something that entrepreneurs do when tapping into new markets, but it also plays a critical role in renewing business operations, strategic business models and guiding principles towards sustainable development. It works across different dimensions of management – that is, it coordinates activities that direct and control the innovation process.[59] These dimensions include operational, strategic and normative management.[60]

On an operational management level, companies need to track and report their economic performance as well as the social and environmental value they create, neglect or destroy.[61] Practices like *Values-Based Ideation and Assessment* and methods like *Materiality Assessment*, *Context-Based Reporting* and *Innovation Impact Assessment* provide the baselines for process innovation and optimised performance, for instance, with respect to resource efficiency or waste management. Sustainability-oriented product and service innovations are achieved with new, eco-designed products or waste management services.

On the operational level, typically only individual business model components are affected. But transformation towards sustainability requires renewal on the strategic level if it is to lead to new sustainable business designs – such as moving from products to services, from product ownership to sharing or providing unserved communities with essential goods. Methods such as *Values-Based Business Modelling* and *Values-Based Ecosystem Modelling* enable 'systems building' and radical business model innovation that reach beyond the boundaries of a single organisation.[62] Circular economy business model patterns[63] and examples like the Danish Kalundborg industrial ecosystem[64] are at this level where business design activities are guided from the outset by the search for new environmental, social and economic value.

On the normative management level, organisations establish principles and policies that guide innovation management in response to growing sustainability-related risks, competitor actions, customer demands, regulations, and shifts in societal values and legal frameworks. They provide their own ethical orientation by embedding sustainability-related notions within their core values, vision, mission and purpose. This approach goes beyond economic considerations and articulates values that define the organisation's identity and aspirations to generate a specific sustainable impact.

One key task of normative management is to review the organisation's implicit values. By integrating the priorities of stakeholder groups and codifying them into guiding principles and policies for innovation management, normative management provides 'directional certainty'.[65] It increases the company's capability to develop and implement sustainable innovations while addressing potential rebound effects and negative unintended outcomes.

CONCEPT 3. Directional Certainty through Process Design, Risk Reduction Criteria, Timing and Methodology

Niko Paech coined the term 'directional certainty' to account for the inherent uncertainty of innovation and highlight the essential factors needed to ensure innovation projects support sustainable development.[66] These factors are process design, risk reduction criteria, timing and methodology.

PROCESS DESIGN sets guardrails for the management of innovation projects. Internal guardrails are established through the influence of internal stakeholders and the practices that operationalise innovation management. External guardrails are established through the engagement of external stakeholders, who provide feedback on the legitimacy of innovation projects, for example, in *Stakeholder Advisory Boards*. Both internal and external guardrails rely on guiding principles and policies that outline the direction and desired impact of innovation projects.

RISK REDUCTION mitigates the economic and environmental risks associated with innovation. Economic risk mitigation includes avoiding supply-side and demand-side lock-ins, such as making product-specific investments that lead to inflexibility on the supply side or binding customers to a particular technical solution on the demand side. Environmental risk mitigation focuses on avoiding innovation projects that could have an extreme impact on environmental degradation, such as biodiversity loss or the release of harmful emissions. Directional certainty also acknowledges the need for error leeway to allow for the correction of unintended consequences occurring after market introduction.

TIMING refers to managing the innovation process before, during and after a project's start. In the ex-ante phase, normative management formulates a vision and a clear set of values that define desirable future outcomes and set the boundaries for defining an innovation strategy. Decisions follow a stage-gate sequence during development to maximise learning opportunities and allow for continuous adjustments to the project's guardrails. In the ex-post phase, outcomes are closely monitored and evaluated to ensure they meet desired objectives and can be optimised before irreversible harm can occur.

METHODOLOGY provides a structured approach to the innovation process, from ex-ante planning to ex-post monitoring. The project's guardrails and risk reduction criteria guide the selection of suitable methods – such as *Stakeholder Advisory Boards* and *Innovation Impact Assessments* – for project development and evaluation.

Responsible Innovation Practices

The unintended consequences of innovation has increasingly become a concern for innovation managers, researchers and regulators. In response, an international policy framework based on the concept of responsible innovation was introduced for governments, funding bodies and organisations with the goal of taking care 'of the future through collective stewardship of science and innovation in the present'.[67] Research is now being conducted to deepen our understanding of responsible innovation practices in companies.

There is considerable overlap between the concepts of responsible innovation and sustainable innovation. Responsible innovation seeks to prevent unintended consequences, ensure a democratic and transparent innovation process, and account for the values enshrined in the European Union Treaties, such as social justice, equality and sustainable economic growth.[68] Central to the responsible innovation framework are four dimensions of overarching innovation practices: inclusive deliberation, reflexivity, anticipation and responsiveness (see also section 3.4.1).[69]

- Practices of INCLUSIVE DELIBERATION engage diverse stakeholders in discussion about 'visions, purposes, questions and dilemmas'.[70] For example, involving stakeholders at different stages of the innovation process and facilitating an exchange of views and opinions among them provides the basis for *Envisioning* desirable futures and *Backcasting* innovation strategies for their achievement.[71]
- Practices of REFLEXIVITY focus on 'uncertainties, risks, areas of ignorance, assumptions, questions and dilemmas'.[72] For instance, employees engage in critical thinking about their actions and values[73] or about the 'value-ladenness' of technological solutions they are working on,[74] such as the alignment problem in new artificial intelligence applications.[75]
- Practices of ANTICIPATION seek to identify the intended and unintended outcomes of innovation by systematically assessing potential problems and available alternatives.[76]
- Practices of RESPONSIVENESS build and apply capabilities to flexibly adapt the innovation process when adverse outcomes are anticipated or have become evident.[77]

In sum, the four dimensions of responsible innovation practices help organisations to identify, integrate and address sustainability values and concerns across every stage of the innovation process.

2.1.4 Key Takeaways

Sustainability-related values are not just factors limiting the scope of a company's potential strategies and operations, they are drivers and levers for innovation. Some companies are already pursuing ambitious approaches involving *Context-Based Reporting* and forward-looking transformation and system building in order to gain a competitive edge through extended value creation. On an operational level, sustainability-oriented innovation in processes, products and services is facilitated by practices like *Values-Based Ideation* and *Assessment* and methods like *Innovation Impact Assessment*. On a strategic level, methods like *Values-Based Business Modelling* and *Values-Based Ecosystem Modelling* contribute to extended value creation for multiple stakeholders and systemic transformations within business ecosystems. Values-based normative management strengthens these efforts by embedding sustainability values within an organisation's core identity and ensuring directional certainty about the long-term positive impact of innovations.

2.2   Organisational Culture and Its Development

Albert Einstein reputedly said that 'problems cannot be solved with the same mindset that created them'. Sustainable development and innovation are not just a matter of business strategies or tweaking business models, services or processes or reporting thresholds. Instead, a fundamental overhaul of values and culture is indispensable to bring about the required and desired changes. It takes a whole culture!

In this section we review widely adopted theories about organisational culture to identify practices and methods that are relevant for developing sustainable innovation cultures. Anthropology provides us with a way of understanding organisational culture as the shared notions (in particular values as notions of the desirable as well as understandings of related terms used colloquially), practices and artefacts of an organisation. Psychology and the social sciences provide us with ways of classifying different types of cultures and understanding misalignments as entry points for interventions.

Traditionally, organisational culture has been understood with respect to internal practices and relations within the organisation, as 'how we do things around here,'[78] rather than as the things we make. Our view of sustainable innovation cultures is distinctive in seeing culture as generative and productive, rather than only representational.

2.2.1 The Lenses of Anthropology and Social Sciences

For empirical studies 'culture' serves as a construct to identify shared values, meaning-making practices and related phenomena that distinguish coherent groups of people from one another, even though the boundaries of their 'webs of significance' are permeable and flexible rather than well defined.[79] Based on different epistemologies and research paradigms, business anthropology and social sciences provide complementary lenses for understanding organisational cultures.

Four Characteristics
In her foundational textbook on business anthropology, Ann Jordan identifies four characteristics of culture in a business context:[80]
1. Culture is founded on shared patterns of ideas and behaviours. In this regard, anthropologists are experts 'on the patterned aspects of group behaviour'.[81]

2. Culture is learned through processes of socialisation that begin in infancy and continue throughout an individual's life. In an organisation this includes formal training programmes and more informal participation in common practices and narratives.
3. Culture is symbolic. Patterns of behaviour or artefacts need interpretation. For instance, using first names across hierarchical levels does not signify equal standing.[82] New members of an organisation must learn its symbolic language to understand its organisational culture.
4. Culture is constantly changing. Culture must adapt to changing market environments and shifting societal values.

Anthropology as Framing for Psychological, Sociological and Systemic Insights

From an anthropological perspective, culture is 'an integrated system of shared ideas, behaviours and artefacts that characterise a group'.[83] Jordan contrasts her anthropological approach to culture with psychological and sociological categories of the individual (personality and motivation), group (formation and relationships, structures, norms or conflicts) and organisational (purpose, structure, technology, environmental fit) levels. In the classic psychological or sociological perspective, culture is studied at the organisational level, and it is conceived as largely intangible and therefore difficult to define or measure.

An important contribution of these social science approaches to culture is their focus on the 'unwritten feeling'[84] and tacit rules of the organisation, which might otherwise be overlooked. Similarly, systemic approaches tend to treat culture as a residual category, stressing its tacit and deviant aspects. For instance, a pattern of deviance from established safety standards can be explained by more fundamental values guiding behaviour, for instance, the belief that one must deliver the expected results despite all adverse circumstances and despite a blatant lack of time.[85] Following the anthropological tradition as a basic framing for our understanding of culture and its empirical inquiry, we still draw on psychological, sociological and systemic insights as far as these are helpful to empirically study, explain or create sustainable innovation cultures.

Subject-Oriented and Object-Oriented Approaches

Two further ways of studying organisational cultures are the subject-oriented and object-oriented methodologies,[86] each of which rests on very different assumptions about culture, yet provide complementary insights. The subject-oriented approach is closely related to the anthropological perspective, as it treats organisations as cultures and analyses them from the subjective viewpoints of their participants. In contrast, the object-oriented approach is associated with (natural) scientific, psychological and sociological science views on culture, which treat it as an object that the organisation possesses rather than what it is. The subject-oriented approach uses qualitative research methods, while the object-oriented approach, on the other hand, uses quantitative methods.

Subject-oriented approaches focus on the lived experiences and perceptions of organisational members that quantifying methods cannot capture. By working with qualitative data from observations, narratives and personal accounts, subject-oriented approaches provide a nuanced and holistic understanding of the dynamics of organisational culture. In this view, culture is not a function of management but the organisation itself.

Likewise, but arguing from an economic viewpoint, Gorton and Zentefis use the concept of corporate culture to create a theory of the firm, with group formation and cooperation as essential elements.[87] They argue that without understanding corporate culture, it is impossible to understand how companies operate and how they succeed. They write, 'Companies exist because, at times, corporate culture fulfils production more efficiently than detailed contracts would.' In the words the former IBM chairman and CEO Louis Gerstner:[88]

| 'Culture is not just one aspect of the game, it is the game.'

We should not mistake culture for what senior management thinks it ought to be. Culture is also not just a function of a company's official values or of its codes of conduct. This distinction has implications for the alignment of innovation activities and outcomes with shared cultural values, customs and norms. Subject-oriented approaches to organisational culture recognise this distinction and explore the actual values, situated practices and mediating artefacts that bring about more or less desirable results. This approach also acknowledges the conflicts and tensions that can arise between individual, subcultural and overarching cultural values and actions, providing insights into how these issues can be addressed and resolved.

In contrast, the object-oriented approach emphasises organisational culture's functionality, which is something that can be managed and controlled.[89] It assumes that the cultural characteristics promoted by organisational leaders are adopted and practiced by the organisation's employees. The degree to which this is achieved is measured through predefined variables, which are then interpreted as an indication of the culture's contribution to organisational objectives. In this perspective, conflicts or divergent perspectives are seen as cultural malfunctions that require intervention.

Object-oriented approaches also rely on theoretical frameworks to derive predefined variables, which are assumed to be universal characteristics shared by all organisational cultures. This approach often utilises dimension-based theories of culture, which breaks down complex cultural phenomena into measurable variables, such as levels of employee engagement, values fit or communication effectiveness. Standardised questionnaires measure these predefined variables and their relations, allowing a comparison of different cultures.

2.2.2 Dimension-Based Theories

Several theories use mainly quantifying methods to analyse different dimensions of culture and use them to distinguish between different types of organisational cultures. The concepts developed in dimension-based theories are useful to understanding different 'aspects of the game'. They identify potential entry points for interventions, facilitating, for instance, mergers and acquisitions (see chapter 11) as well as sustainability-oriented transformations.

Clan, Adhocracy, Market and Hierarchy

Kim Cameron and Robert Quinn's competing values framework uses two dimensions – internal versus external focus and flexibility versus control – to classify organisational culture into the four archetypes of hierarchy, clan, market and adhocracy.[90] These four archetypes relate to factors that influence organisational performance[91] and to specific dimensions of corporate sustainability.[92]

Hierarchical cultures are thought to emphasise economic performance, growth and long-term profitability; clan cultures to prioritise social outcomes such as staff development and capacity building; market cultures to focus on environmental efficiency; and adhocracy cultures to balance the economic, social and environmental dimensions of corporate sustainability. More recent research suggests that organisational cultures rarely fit into a single archetype.[93] Instead, cultures consist of multiple and often contradictory values that are subject to situational interpretations and reprioritisation.[94]

There is, however, firm evidence that highly flexible and externally oriented adhocracy cultures are more conducive to the adoption of sustainable innovation practices.[95] Their flexible and less formalised structures promote *Experimentation* and encourage employees to pursue unconventional ideas, making it easier to integrate new sustainability priorities into an established innovation management process. Furthermore, adhocracies are more open to stakeholder input and adapt more quickly to evolving sustainability needs and market demands.

Power Distribution and Cooperation Level

In Charles Handy's model,[96] the two cultural dimensions of power distribution and cooperation determine four different types of culture. Power cultures feature low power distribution and high cooperation and are often seen in small businesses with strong leadership. Task cultures have high power distribution and cooperation levels, fitting project-based organisations that thrive on teamwork and adaptability. Person cultures, with high power distribution and low cooperation, prioritise individual work and professional growth and are common in fields like law and medicine. Lastly, role cultures have clear hierarchies and procedures, which are typical of large organisations where job positions are defined by qualifications and expertise.

Each of these cultural types has specific advantages for promoting a cultivating of sustainable innovation. Power cultures can speed up adoption by leveraging strong leadership, task cultures can foster collaborative efforts, person cultures can encourage individual initiatives and *Experimentation* with new practices, while role cultures can establish well-defined procedures and systems for operationalising sustainability values and goals.

Six Dimensions of National and Organisational Cultures

Geert Hofstede's model of national and organisational cultures is based on six dimensions derived from multiple statistical factor analyses.[97] Hofstede outlines six dimensions to assess the values that make up national cultures, including power distance, uncertainty avoidance, motivation towards achievement and success, individualism versus collectivism, long-term versus short-term orientation and indulgence versus restraint. These dimensions provide valuable background information when trying to understand national differences in, for example, multinational collaboration. They can also be used to apply practices that challenge established power dynamics through practices of *Inclusive Deliberation*, *Participative Decision Making* and *Decentralisation*.[98]

Pathological, Bureaucratic and Generative Cultures

According to Ron Westrum, organisational cultures play a crucial role in enabling effective communication, cooperation, innovation as well as problem-solving. Communication should be relevant, timely and clear.[99] Depending on the degree to which they enable and constrain information flow, his model distinguishes between three types of organisational safety cultures: pathological, bureaucratic and generative. In pathological cultures, information flows are limited by fear and self-preservation, with individuals hoarding or distorting information to serve political purposes rather than the organisation's values and goals.

Bureaucratic cultures also hinder information flows, but because of rigid adherence to rules and departmental boundaries. Information is shared in a way that adheres to protocol rather than prioritising the needs of the recipient, resulting in delayed and fragmented information flows. In contrast, generative cultures are characterised by a strong commitment to the organisational values and goals, which organisational members prioritise over their personal and departmental concerns.

> Generative cultures enable relevant, timely and clear information flows because they translate the organisational values and goals into shared criteria.

These shared criteria are not based on isolated individual or departmental priorities but foster the sharing of responsibilities, risks, competencies, innovations and lessons learned from failure throughout the entire organisation. This emphasis on overarching values and goals contributes to a seamless and performance-oriented flow of information. While generative cultures in this sense are conducive to organisational performance, they are not enough to establish sustainable innovation cultures as systems that generate sustainable outcomes.

2.2.3 Frameworks for Cultural Development

'Culture is the deeper level of basic assumptions and beliefs that are shared by members of an organization, that operate unconsciously and define in a basic "taken for granted" fashion an organization's view of its self and its environment.'[100] Edgar Schein's organisational culture model applies a dynamic definition of culture as 'accumulated shared learning'.[101] It views culture as shaped by its historical development and by the norms and values established by the leadership teams. Schein's model conceptualises the different layers of culture according to degrees of visibility and psychological insight.

Organisational values are shared on three levels: implicitly as basic underlying assumptions (or unconscious, unspoken beliefs), explicitly as verbal statements (such as missions, goals, value statements and social contracts) and materially as artefacts (that is, as visible behaviours, rituals, physical environments, documents, language and other tangible cultural phenomena). Alignment between these levels fosters organisational performance and cultural (or sustainable) development, just as misalignment impedes them.

Leaders take on a central role in mainstreaming and embedding values in culture. For cultural transformation to be successful, they must address all three layers of culture, with a particular focus on the deepest layer of assumptions and implicit beliefs. They must recognise that while artefacts and espoused values can be altered relatively quickly, changing underlying assumptions requires a much more extensive effort.

Building on Kurt Lewin's three-stage model of change, Schein proposes a three-stage process of cultural development:[102] 'Unfreezing' creates a sense of urgency and awareness about the need for change, then 'cognitive restructuring' introduces new ways of thinking that challenge existing assumptions. Finally, 'refreezing' involves developing a new cultural identity and establishing new behaviours in interpersonal relationships and practices.

We adopt Schein's model in acknowledging the three layers of culture and the need for 'humble inquiry'[103] to make hidden beliefs, assumptions, underlying values and cultural misalignments visible. However, we take a more holistic approach and place practices on the second level as behavioural elements of culture and artefacts on the third level as material elements of culture[104] that mediate the performance of practices.

Other frameworks provide further insights into how cultural development takes place and how it can be supported.[105] Unfortunately, many of them lack empirical evidence and are based on unchallenged assumptions.[106] Attempts to create a robust framework of cultural development have so far been unsuccessful.[107] And there is still a need for a transformational framework that would bring practices in line with the unspoken values of an organisation.[108]

2.2.4 Values, Artefacts and Practices for Cultural Development

As representations of organisational culture, values play an essential role in its transformation.

❚ Values define what is important and prioritised within an organisation.

In Shalom Schwartz's cultural value theory, values are:[109]
- beliefs linked to emotions,
- desirable goals that motivate action,
- transcendent, meaning they apply to a wide range of actions and situations,
- standards for evaluating actions, policies, people and events,
- elements of a hierarchical system ordered by importance, and
- guides to actions and attitudes, requiring trade-offs among multiple, competing values.

Values can be both terminal, consisting of beliefs about desirable end-states (e.g. carbon neutrality) and instrumental, shaped by beliefs about modes of conduct that contribute to reaching those end-states (e.g. collaboration).[110] Values thus provide an orientation for future-oriented decision-making and decision-making under uncertainty.[111]

❚ 'Defining values and norms, turning these into shared rules for behaviour, is de facto creating and managing culture.'[112]

In Schein's model of organisational culture, implicit and espoused values are realised through artefacts such as individual behaviours, formal statements and the physical environment. Senior managers have a key role in establishing norms in practices and artefacts to support innovation performance.[113] The clear communication of values is obviously an essential lever for managing organisational culture. However, communicating values and norms is only one side of the story – their enactment in daily practices and their embodiment in artefacts is the other, indispensable, side of the story.

❚ Values influence the adoption of practices. But they are also influenced by practices and can be reinterpreted in relation to them, creating a cycle of mutual influence that predetermines cultural development.

Schein's model of organisational culture, we have seen, does not consider practices as a distinct component of culture. Other models and theories highlight their importance. One of the best known theorists is Pierre Bourdieu, who places practice at the heart of his theory, which views culture as generated by the dynamic interactions between social actors and societal structures.[114] These interactions involve different forms of capital (economic, social, cultural and symbolic), habitus (a collective system of dispositions such as conventions, rules and values) and the field (a structured social space in which people enact their dispositions.[115]

Echoing Bourdieu's emphasis on the key role of practices in shaping cultures, recent research has challenged the conventional assumption that values must shift before new practices can be established and lead to positive impact on sustainable development.[116] While this unidirectional view has become widespread in the past decades, it has not produced the desired positive impact on socio-ecological change. A more reciprocal and dynamic understanding of the relationship between values and practices is needed. This view would frame practices not merely as outcomes of cultural development, but as levers to mainstream values and drive cultural change. For example, substituting unsustainable procurement practices with local sourcing alternatives can shift employee interpretations of sustainability values, while fostering new skills and expectations among them. As new practices become established, they gradually influence other related practices, values, social interactions and organisational artefacts, paving the way for holistic cultural transformation.

2.2.5 Key Takeaways

There is broad agreement in the literature that organisational culture 'refers to something that is holistic, historically determined (by founders or leaders), related to things that anthropologists study (like rituals and symbols), socially constructed (created and preserved by the group of people who together form the organization)'.[117]

These definitions of organisational culture share certain basic features. First, they include the concept of sharing within groups. Second, they highlight the foundational role of values in shaping culture. For instance, the European Sustainability Reporting Standard (ESRS) defines organisational culture as expressing goals through values and beliefs and 'guiding the undertaking's activities through shared assumptions and group norms such as values or mission statements or a code of conduct'.[118] Third, they model culture as made up of different layers, which can be aligned, for instance Schein's[119] underlying assumptions, espoused values and material artefacts or the anthropological focus on ideas, practices and artefacts.

We understand organisational culture as a multifaceted phenomenon that can be analysed through various lenses. Object-oriented approaches and dimension-based theories enable a comparative assessment of cultural variables using quantitative methods. In subject-driven approaches, using mainly qualitative and interpretative methods, subjectivity is a crucial resource for a more nuanced understanding of cultural dynamics. Concepts and methods from both types of approaches contribute to understanding the practices needed to create sustainable innovation cultures.

2.3 Sustainable Innovation Cultures

Growing awareness of environmental and social challenges have made sustainability a high-standing priority for organisations worldwide, compelling them to rethink and transform their cultures. However, a significant share of companies and other organisations face little to no accountability for translating their sustainability strategies into practice. For example, a recent study reports that of 1,041 global companies which set greenhouse gas emission reduction targets for the year 2020, nine percent officially failed their goals and 31 percent had quietly abandoned them.[120]

This discrepancy indicates that formal commitments alone are insufficient unless supported by a holistic cultural transformation that translates sustainability values and strategies into daily practice.[121] Strategic alignment between corporate strategy, innovation strategy and a culture that supports innovation is key not only to economic success[122] but also to sustainable value creation.

This section builds on the concept of organisational culture by introducing innovation culture as the shared notions, practices and artefacts that foster innovation within an organisation. Making an innovation culture sustainable means aligning notions, practices and artefacts to generate beneficial outcomes for the environment, society and the economy. This approach contributes to the foundation of a regenerative economy, allowing companies and other organisations to reproduce themselves while sustaining the social and environmental systems they are part of.

2.3.1 Sustainability Cultures and Transformations

The need to understand and close the gap between sustainability strategies and cultures has fuelled two bodies of research: one on sustainability cultures and another on sustainability culture transformations. Research on sustainability cultures focuses on the characteristics and components of organisational cultures that support sustainability management, such as beliefs, norms, values, practices and artefacts. Closely related is a growing body of work on sustainability culture transformations. Such transformations unfold within a complex network of individual actors, competing priorities and power dynamics. This is why they are regarded as the greatest challenge of contemporary change management.[123]

Beyond the Adoption of New Practices and Methods
The limited focus on profit and shareholder value leaves many organisational cultures ill-equipped to address the complex and multifaceted challenges of sustainability.[124] To effectively respond to social and environmental challenges, organisations must undergo a profound cultural transformation that goes beyond a superficial adoption of new practices and methods. They need to fundamentally revise their values and practices to place sustainable development at the core of their business strategy.

Several frameworks provide theoretical insights and practical approaches for the holistic transformation of organisational cultures, highlighting the need for consistent efforts to embed shared goals, values and corporate identity across all functions and hierarchical levels.[125] One such framework is Managing by Sustainable Innovational Values[126], which emphasises the integration of economic, social and emotional values as drivers of sustainable innovation. These frameworks stress the essential role of normative management in presenting sustainability not just as an add-on but as a fundamental part of the organisation's identity, strategy, policy and operations.

Once underlying values are identified and made explicit, it is not enough to simply tell employees what they mean.[127] Practices such as *Policy Communication*, *Human Resource Development* and *Gamification* help employees reflect on and apply these values in their work. By systematically adopting practices and methods that support the overarching notions defined by normative management, organisations foster cultural alignment and facilitate cultural change.

Enablers and Barriers in Sustainability Transformations

For cultural change to be effective it must address both enablers and barriers within basic assumptions, espoused values and artefacts.[128] There are five strategies for achieving this.[129] First, orchestrated and iterative change involves continuously addressing change drivers, enablers and barriers at the organisational levels of individual, group and the overall organisation. Second, simultaneous and holistic change addresses barriers concurrently across the individual, group and organisational levels and Schein's three cultural levels of basic assumptions, espoused values and artefacts.

The third and fourth strategy establish congruence between informational (what is learned), emotional (what is thought) and behavioural attitudes (what is done) across the organisational and cultural levels respectively. Finally, organisational learning facilitates interpersonal and intergroup interactions to shift deeply rooted mental models and informational, emotional and behavioural attitudes. These five strategies not only highlight the elements necessary for cultural change but also suggest systematic approaches for overcoming the psychological barriers that often impede cultural transformations.

These five strategies identify the elements necessary for cultural change and can be combined in a systematic approach to overcome the psychological barriers that often impede cultural transformations.

2.3.2 Innovation Culture

Organisational culture is a major factor in both driving and inhibiting innovation.[130] An innovation culture is defined as a social environment that enables its members to develop novel ideas and implement innovations.[131] One way to establish an innovation culture is to identify its constitutive elements and ensure they are embedded in the organisation.[132] These elements include innovative mission and vision statements, democratic communication, safe spaces, flexibility, collaboration, boundary-spanning individuals, incentives and leadership.[133]

Other cultural elements that support innovation efforts include risk-taking, Experimentation, teamwork, employee autonomy and *Empowerment*, *Knowledge Sharing*, open communication, customer orientation and networking.[134] However, although the importance of culture for innovation is widely acknowledged, executive leaders often try to improve innovation performance through standardised structural and institutional interventions, rather than addressing the fundamental values, beliefs and patterns of behaviour[135] that make up organisational cultures.[136]

The role of values as drivers of innovation is in fact too often overlooked. Until recently, major textbooks on innovation management were missing an entry on values in their indices. In light of the growing interest in ethical aspects of business and sustainability transformation over the past decade, a values-based approach to developing innovation cultures is gaining increased recognition. This approach involves companies placing values-based visions, missions and goals at the core of their innovation efforts. They develop values-based innovation cultures by introducing new values or reinforcing existing values, turning them into heuristics and directives for innovation practice.

2.3.3 Challenges and Practices: Establishing Sustainable Innovation Cultures

In this section we provide an overview of insights into how organisations can navigate through their transformation processes to developing a sustainable innovation culture. To do this, we addressed four guiding questions by means of three systematic literature reviews together with expert interviews and panels:[137]
- *What is the current state of knowledge about sustainable innovation cultures?*
- *What is the role of values in sustainable innovation?*
- *What are the barriers to sustainable innovation?*
- *What are good practices and methods that lead to sustainable outcomes?*

In the following sections we present the insights we gathered and spell out some of the major challenges, best practices and preconditions that characterise the transformative journey towards a sustainable innovation culture.

Values-based Innovation Practices and Functions
Values fulfil three key functions in the management of innovations: integrating stakeholders, informing guidelines for generating ideas, and anticipating threats and directing organisations towards desirable futures.[138] We use these functions to categorise and model five types of barriers and nine types of practices that had been identified in research.[139] We then show how the model can be used to introduce and refine sustainable innovation practices. Examples include creating mechanisms for continuous feedback and adaptation, implementing change initi-

atives and interventions to address barriers, and using existing methods or developing new ones to practice sustainable innovation.

For example, values can be a source of conflict between the organisation and its stakeholders or within an organisation determining its strategic agenda. These result in tensions and ethical dilemmas that force executive leaders to choose between multiple lines of action, each of which seems right.[140] Although sustainability-related dilemmas can undoubtedly be highly complex and difficult to address, when they are systematically examined they can trigger organisational change towards a more mature sustainable innovation culture.[141] When conflicting values and dilemmas are reframed to accommodate the concerns of all of the relevant stakeholders, they can reveal opportunities for new forms of value creation.[142]

This potential can be harnessed through practices such as *Engaging in Open Innovation*, practices of *Reflexivity* and practices of *Inclusive Deliberation* as well as methods like *Empathising*. These practices and methods leverage the integrative function of values to establish common ground between conflicting stakeholder values and co-create sustainable innovation based on overarching shared values.

Sustainable Innovation Practices and Methods

Sustainable innovation practices can be classified in several ways to show how they contribute to cultural development. One framework is provided by Geradts and Bocken, who interviewed managers of multinational companies and described how they contribute to sustainable innovation and cultivate entrepreneurial thinking and behaviours[143] by such methods as *Incentivisation Schemes* or *Mandatory Training* for new employees. They make three recommendations: managers should communicate the company's purpose and the role of sustainability, they should provide resources and opportunities for collaboration, and they should incentivise participation through performance management and sustainability reporting.[144]

Another useful framework classifies five types of sustainable innovation practices and explores their impact on production performance.[145] These practices include creating and projecting new sustainable consumption needs as well as integrating with local communities and other stakeholders to enhance social and environmental benefits (see also *Sustainable Market Creation* and *Engaging in Innovation Ecosystems* in chapter 5). Sustainable innovation practices in smaller organisations[146] include a 'hub and spoke' framework to create an integrated innovation culture. The hub stands for the manager's strategic selection and bundling of practices for implementation, and the spokes represent the active involvement of employees in the decision-making and implementation of these practices.

In chapters 3–6 we present a 'first of its kind' framework for transforming corporate culture to support sustainable innovation, accompanied by a comprehensive list of 68 evidence-based sustainable innovation practices and methods (see pages 96 to 103 for an overview). Research on developing sustainable innovation cultures is still in its early stages and there are multiple specificities and intricacies distinguishing sustainability cultures that can generate sustainable innovations, beginning with those that only support general compliance with corporate sustainability standards and ambitions. The lack of an approach to cultivating a sustainable innovation is particularly critical, given its pivotal role in driving sustainability transformations.

Expert Insights on Values-Based Transformation Towards Sustainable Innovation Cultures

In the following chapters, we provide guidance on how to transform sustainable innovation cultures.[147] First, we share insights from a panel discussion with innovation researchers and professionals on what they consider most important for a deep values-based transformation towards sustainable innovation cultures, a transformation that goes beyond simply introducing new practices and artefacts.

CASE 1. Expert Insights on Four Critical Factors to Develop Sustainable Innovation Cultures

Sixty innovation experts shared insights from their research and practice in developing sustainable innovation cultures in three conference events. We have identified four emerging themes as critical factors for a successful cultural change.

1. Overcoming short-termism: Ensuring a long-term perspective to prevent sustainable innovation projects from being abandoned prematurely.
Large organisations sometimes abandon sustainable innovation projects early due to a lack of strategic vision, but invest once competitors adopt similar initiatives. SMEs, on the other hand, hesitate to invest their limited resources in sustainable innovation unless they are assured of tangible benefits.

Many organisations try to counteract short-termism by communicating long-term strategies, managerial commitments and values or by assessing innovation projects using sustainability key performance indicators (KPIs). However, these approaches fail to integrate sustainability dimensions holistically, as the implicit values of an organisation, such as efficiency and profitability, lead to superficial compliance. Sustainability KPIs are simply tweaked to meet formal requirements rather than driving real change.

Sustainability frameworks, such as the SDGs, can operationalise forward-looking sustainable innovation efforts by encouraging the adoption of long-term KPIs for innovation project assessment and screening (see also *Innovation Impact Assessment* in chapter 6). Bottom-up initiatives also help introduce a long-term perspective on innovation, provided employees feel genuine ownership of long-term sustainability goals and are empowered to reflect and act upon shared values in formats like peer-to-peer coaching, mentorship or *Employee Resource Groups*.

2. Ensuring cultural fit: Aligning sustainability initiatives and practices with an organisation's existing culture ensures their relevance and impact.

Some companies introduce sustainability practices primarily to attract new hires and clients and so fail to embed these changes in daily operations. Employees often see sustainability as an 'add-on', with unclear relevance. Without clarity on why a sustainability practice is important, how it relates to the company's values, and how it benefits different functions, employees quickly become disengaged. For example, if an engineer routinely replaces equipment instead of implementing preventative maintenance routines, the company needs to clarify who is accountable for sustainable innovation.

Cultural alignment requires that an organisation's members understand how sustainability is relevant to their day-to-day work, and they are provided with the necessary incentives and resources so that they commit to sustainable innovation. Asking questions like *Why is this practice important for us?*, *How does it relate to our culture?*, *How does it benefit us?*, *What is its relevance for employees in different roles and positions?* or *What does sustainability mean for different functions and departments?* fosters a shared sense of purpose and reduces the risk of sustainability being dismissed as an add-on imposition.

3. Aligning sustainability strategies with local contexts: Innovation strategies must be adapted to local values and practices to prevent mission drift.

In some countries, low living standards have delayed local engagement for sustainable innovation. However, that is changing. In Bangladesh focused efforts have brought about new, local narratives that are shifting perspectives. Now more entrepreneurs and companies recognise business cases for sustainability and are beginning sustainable innovation projects. Such business actors, however, still struggle to reconcile their ambitions for sustainable innovation with local economic constraints and profit-driven priorities.

Big corporations can rely on leveraging economies of scale to meet regulatory requirements or customer demands for corporate sustainability, while smaller enterprises must resort to more localised approaches. This proves to be an advantage, as sustainable innovation in small enterprises can focus on reasonable growth within the community through circular processes and services, like reusing resources and promoting their communal use. This approach to sustainable innovation can respect local needs, cultural norms and economic realities.

Context-specific strategies and narratives can reconcile tensions between short-term profitability and values of sustainability. Localised or bioregional approaches can also foster more sustainable economies that remain within a manageable scale. Small-scale community enterprises can thus serve as role models for larger players seeking to enhance their sustainable impact through circularity and reasonable growth rates – or even degrowth.

Underrepresented groups, such as women or ethnic minorities, bring fresh perspectives to the management of sustainable innovation. However, even in companies that value diversity, integrating these groups can be challenging. One expert related how a German engineering company was struggling to hire female engineers and reported that women who had enrolled in engineering degree programmes were switching to business studies after feeling isolated among their male classmates. Competitive labour markets are intensifying the challenge of fostering workforce diversity. Employees are increasingly seeking to align their own personal values to engage in meaningful work with their employer's values. Practices of *Attracting the Right Talent* and green *Human Resource Development* must be aligned with an organisational culture that values diversity. When successful, attracting employees with prosocial and environmental attitudes and gaining reputation as a sustainability-oriented employer are two key strategic benefits that go hand in hand.

2.3.4 Key Takeaways

Organisations worldwide are aspiring to embed sustainable innovation into their cultures, yet many of them are struggling to translate their ambitious strategies into daily practice. Our review of research on sustainable innovation cultures suggests that to bridge this gap organisations must undergo a profound transformation. They need to prioritise sustainability values in their corporate and innovation strategies as core elements of their identities and as blueprints for cultural development, while ensuring that these values remain consistent with practices and artefacts. If these efforts turn out to be successful, cultures can become generative systems that translate sustainability-related values into sustainable value creation. Sustainable innovation cultures are generative systems of shared notions, practices and artefacts (figure 3).

Cultural development not only aligns the cultural layers of notions, practices and artefacts – it also translates values into criteria that guide value creation and organisational performance.

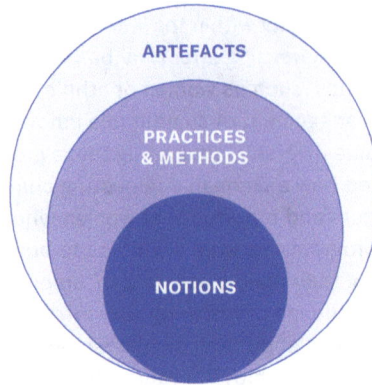

FIGURE 3. Three layers of organisational culture: notions, practices and methods, and artefacts

We use the term 'notion' to refer to concepts and terms that are used colloquially and are often vague. We focus on values as notions of the desirable, as well as notions of what is technically feasible and economically viable. They provide the basis of organisational culture. We focus on the potential of values to define priorities and guiding principles for an organisation, creating its identity. These values are shared among small teams, in departments or throughout the organisation as ideals, beliefs, attitudes and unspoken assumptions. They serve as motivation and are enacted in the organisation's policies and practices, managerial decisions and day-to-day operations.

Practices are the actions, behaviours and rituals that employees perform on a more or less regular basis. Formal practices are supported or sanctioned by the company's official policies or procedures. Informal practices include individual initiatives, workarounds and information sharing, promoting flexible work by individuals and among teams. They co-exist with the organisation's formal practices and can either support or compromise them. Just like the formal practices, methods are usually introduced as purposeful and replicable interventions to address a particular challenge to cultural development and are endorsed by the official management structures. When such methods are systematically applied over time and adapted to the needs of the organisation, they can turn into regular formal practices.

Artefacts are things like official statements, documents, reports, software tools, physical environments and other material media. They reflect written or unwritten values and can facilitate or limit their translation into practices. For example, a company that values internal collaboration may implement the practice of *Inviting for Informal Exchange*, which focuses on the exchange of ideas, knowledge and emotions among employees. An artefact that mediates this practice would be a collaborative workspace. If the workspace is suitably equipped, it facilitates collaboration. If it is not, it limits the potential of collaboration as a cultural practice. In other words, artefacts provide the toolset and dataset for operationalising the sustainable innovation mindset (notions) and the skill set (practices) of a company's culture. Their alignment establishes more sustainable work cultures.[148]

While sustainability cultures support compliance with corporate sustainability standards and ambitions, sustainable innovation cultures go beyond that. They seek challenges to sustainability as opportunities for innovation. They commit their resources to coming up with novel processes, products, services and business models that disrupt business as usual. And they ensure their long-term positive impact and guard against unintended consequences. Achieving cultural transformation oriented towards sustainability requires more than superficially adopting new practices and methods to support the innovation process.

Moving from a sole focus on economic outcomes to prioritising sustainable value creation and impact means that organisations must fundamentally shift their spoken and unspoken values. Despite their importance, these deeper levels of change are often neglected. A more holistic understanding of culture and its transformation is urgently needed, one that aligns all three cultural levels – notions, observable practices and artefacts – in the service of sustainable innovation.[149] Only a holistic view of culture and its development can ensure that sustainable innovation strategies are translated into positive impact, not 'one-off' or 'add-on' but on a repeatable and reliable basis.

Chapter 3 /
A Framework for Sustainable Innovation Cultures

Sustainable innovation cultures turn sustainability-related principles and strategy into practice. They generate outcomes that are economically, socially and environmentally beneficial both for companies and for their different stakeholder groups.

3.1 Establishing Sustainable Innovation Cultures

In this chapter we build on our discussion of the basic concepts of sustainability, innovation and culture and our review of research into sustainable innovation culture in chapter 2. We begin by defining sustainable innovation culture and then describe the three defining characteristics that ensure the reliable translation of sustainability values and strategies into daily organisational practices.

> First, sustainable innovation cultures are generative systems made up of shared notions, practices and artefacts that turn values of sustainability into novel regenerative outcomes that are economically, socially and environmentally beneficial.

> Second, a sustainable innovation culture is created by establishing sustainability as a priority and then aligning notions, practices and artefacts to resolve tensions between competing values and bridge gaps between values of sustainability and current practices.

> Third, values provide the ethical foundation and directional certainty that allows such cultures to create sustainable value repeatedly and reliably, against the odds of unforeseen challenges and unintended, consequences.

We will first describe the elements of this definition and then lay out how sustainable innovation cultures can be established through virtuous cycles of conceiving a culture, co-creating interventions and cultivating practices.

3.1.1 A Generative System

Sustainable innovation cultures are generative systems that turn values of sustainability into novel economically, socially and environmentally beneficial outcomes. Organisational cultures are not static constellations. They are dynamic systems[1] of patterned notions (values and other ideas of what is desirable, feasible and viable), practices and artefacts. Rather than being imposed from the top to the bottom of the hierarchy, its properties emerge and evolve from stakeholder interactions and learning in dealing with – foreseeable and unexpected – challenges.[2] This makes room for non-linear cultural shifts and organisational innovations arising from seemingly insignificant interactions.

Industry-Specific Organisational Values

Many organisations share the ambition to contribute to sustainable development. When reviewing their priorities to specify sustainable policies, some can build on their history. For example, the German technical inspection agency (case 9), since its founding 150 years ago, has always been a company that stood for one core value: safety. With the protection of human life already at the centre of their business, in 2018 they added sustainability as another core value. Their first step was on an organisational level. The next one was to develop sustainability-related policies and make them actionable for their business fields. *Innovation Impact Assessment* led to their developing video-based remote inspection services. Michelin (case 11) envisioned how their sustainability-related ambitions could have a positive impact on the mobility ecosystems in their hometown, which were then able to use sustainable business models to turn their visions into reality.

Depending on the industry and its social and environmental challenges, but also on their unique expertise and capabilities, different organisations will be able to make different contributions to sustainable development. 'Healthcare companies, in contrast to semiconductor or mining companies, have special duties to defend the basic value that defines their industry, "health".'[3]

CASE 2. The Role of Healthcare Companies in the Global Sustainability Transformation

To establish the criteria that define the role of healthcare organisations in sustainable development, the World Health Organisation has introduced a concept of a sustainable healthcare system as 'a system that improves, maintains or restores health, while minimising negative impacts on the environment and leveraging opportunities to restore and improve it, to the benefit of the health and well-being of current and future generations'.[4] Healthcare companies face these complex challenges by prioritising different strategies to generate a positive impact and to maintain their reputation.

The German Merck Group is the world's oldest pharmaceutical company and it is continuing to serve the industry as a role model. Merck has become a leader in sustainability transformation by aiming to dramatically increase its impact on health in low- and middle-income countries. Through equitable pricing and increasing the availability of its products for underserved populations and fast-track product launches in the Global South, it is seeking to generate deeper, wider and faster healthcare access.[5] A major pharma company from the United Kingdom, GSK, has led the way to greater transparency by publishing information on the design, methods and results of its clinical trials.[6]

Other large pharmaceutical companies have faced criticism for failing to balance financial and ethical priorities during the COVID-19 global health crisis by prioritising intellectual property rights over equitable healthcare.[7]

An alternative to building on a unique identity and established corporate values is for a company to drive sustainable innovation by catering to the values of its wider stakeholder network. This includes not only all the organisation's direct stakeholders but also those in the socio-ecological systems that the organisation affects with its activities. This broader view of values makes translating them into an equitable distribution of resources, opportunities and respect among all relevant stakeholder groups a challenge. Methods like *Materiality Assessment* and practices like *Stakeholder Values Integration* help identify and prioritise stakeholder values, integrating them with the espoused values of the organisation.

Political and Management Frameworks

Some organisations and companies adopt sustainability frameworks to specify their guiding principles, which can complement other approaches. Frameworks are ethical to the extent that they provide 'a set of assumptions, concepts, values and practices that constitute the way of viewing the specific reality'.[8] Global political frameworks – such as the UN's SDGs, the European Green Deal or the Paris Agreement – also give shape and substance to the ethical aspirations and innovation strategies of private firms. The SDG agenda embodies its vision of providing 'a shared blueprint for peace and prosperity for people and the planet, now and into the future' with 17 goals, 169 targets and 231 indicators. Although it was primarily conceived to address governments, it often finds its way into the ethical statements and strategic agendas of private companies

Management frameworks translate sustainability values into evaluation criteria for managing sustainable innovation and practices, for instance the frameworks of system value creation,[9] triple-bottom line,[10] the natural step,[11] responsible innovation,[12] and many others.[13] An innovation management system following ISO norms provides a common language and a framework for collaboration within companies and across ecosystems.[14] However, neither political nor management frameworks can be adopted as generic, off-the-shelf principles. Both need to be specified as priorities for each organisation.

CASE 3. **How Companies Integrate the SDGs into their Impact Strategies**

Companies can use the UN's Sustainable Development Goals as an ethical framework to create system value. Selected goals and targets are integrated into their impact strategy and monitored by appropriate indicators. For example, a fashion company seeking positive environmental impact focuses on sustainable consumption and production (SDG 12) to reduce waste through prevention, reduction, recycling and reuse (SDG target 12.5). Zooming in on circular business models, it formulates the ambition to use a large percentage of recycled material to produce fully recyclable or biodegradable clothes within the next five years. The percentage of recycled materials and clothes serves as a key performance indicator. The company also targets 'productive employment and decent work for all women and men, including for young people and persons with disabilities, and equal pay' (SDG target 8.5). It seeks to ensure ethical labour standards with fair wages, safe working conditions and equal opportunities throughout the supply chain within two years and tracks the number of workers benefiting from a fair-wage programme as an indicator.

Organisational Values Expressed by Intended Outcomes and Impact

Organisational values are crucial for defining and prioritising sustainability goals and the environmental, social and economic impact an organisation aims to achieve. Indeed, the intended outcomes and positive impact that an organisation pursues can be seen as an expression of its sustainability-related values. Some organisations foster values of environmental stewardship by trying to mitigate negative impact (e.g. of mobility) and to enhance positive impact by conserving biodiversity, preventing pollution or regenerating resources. Others embed values of social responsibility such as equity, diversity and community welfare into their business models and operations, striving for a positive impact on fair labour conditions, community development and social well-being, fostering inclusive mobility and reducing social disparities. Likewise, positive economic impact can consist in contributions to ethical labour standards, employment, fair trade and economic development.

A company in the mobility sector could plan to achieve green and inclusive mobility in 15 years' time by drawing on its own values – such as respect for the environment and its customers – to define its desired impact as contributions to visionary scenarios (see case 11 of Michelin). These can then be realised by specifying desirable outcomes in terms of environmental, social and economic value creation through innovation projects that introduce sustainable products, services, processes and business models, such as vehicle sharing or green pricing for intermodal mobility.

Outcomes and impact seem easier to handle in innovation using methods like *Result Chains* and *Innovation Impact Assessment* than the underlying values that articulate who we are and aspire to be as an organisation. However, while sustainability-oriented organisations are impact-oriented in this sense, the desired impact of an organisation is only one, although crucial, articulation of its values.

Equally important are the ideas of value created or destroyed and the ways in which values are enacted in daily practices. *Result Chains* refer to the outputs, outcomes and impact of business activities on economic, social and environmental systems. It is the customer or other stakeholders who determine whether these results involve value creation or value destruction.[15] Furthermore, values can be examined as they are enacted in daily practices, for example, by using *Rapid Ethnography*. This allows you to see where practiced values correspond with or diverge from one another – and with strategic choices or outputs of innovation initiatives.

Once a unique set of values and a desirable future have been formulated, ethical principles and norms can be established. Strategic management then decides which markets to target and how to succeed in them. As Roger Martin[16] puts it, strategies should not be confused with plans for action. They specify an integrated set of choices that position the organisation to achieve its aspirations. They do this by providing the guardrails for operational management and everyday practice. However, the example below (case 4) illustrates that establishing practices and artefacts to support a sustainable innovation strategy can be a difficult task.

CASE 4. Cultural Challenges to Translating Normative Guidelines into Practices and Artefacts

A large technical inspection company[17] used the SDGs to develop a normative guideline that informs its sustainable innovation aspirations, policies and practices. *Innovation Impact Assessments* were introduced to evaluate the expected sustainability impact of innovation projects. However, at first the company struggled to clarify which SDGs and indicators were most relevant to its business, to what extent and whether relevant indicators were missing.

Another discussion emerged from the introduction of an *Innovation Impact Assessment* to consider the long-term viability of new services or business models. The head of innovation management proposed weighting the ratings of sustainability impact for each project using the Fibonacci sequence of 1, 2, 3, 5, 8, 13, 21, which prevents estimates from being so similar that they become irrelevant. Low scores reflecting poor sustainability would prompt the team to address shortcomings in the project within a set timeframe. If those shortcomings remained unresolved, the project's rating would drop further, potentially leading to termination. However, some business units objected to this approach, arguing it would lead to irreconcilable differences at the expense of lower scoring projects. After extensive negotiation, they agreed to use the weighted rating approach, provided that the scores would not be excessively negative (reducing the spread between the rating results by just using 0 for unacceptable and 1, 2, 3, 5 and 8 to assess the projects).

Cultivating sustainable innovation relies on the continuous translation of human values and strategic choices into actionable practices that lead to the desired outputs, outcomes and impact. This process can be slowed down or halted by a culture that is permeated by ill-defined priorities, hidden conflicts or tensions, and values-action gaps. It takes a deliberate approach to addressing these challenges and to continuously generating ideas, practices and artefacts that result in new regenerative processes, products, services or business models with economic, social and environmental added value.

3.1.2 A Deliberate Approach

Sustainable innovation cultures do not come into existence by accident or chance. It takes a deliberate approach to establish organisational values, follow up with strategic choices and turn them into daily practices. It means not only spelling out guiding principles (in mission, vision or purpose statements) and strategies but also aligning ethical and strategic guidelines with the skills, tools and datasets needed to facilitate daily practices. This alignment process involves identifying and resolving tensions and gaps between values and actions.

Establishing Espoused Values

In new organisations the values of their founders and leaders shape the culture and provide shared rules for behaviour.[18] As companies mature, other stakeholder values gain relevance for the culture's different layers.[19] Executive leaders must consistently articulate values top-down to establish and maintain the organisation's culture, also in official statements and documents. They also need to align these values with those actually held and practiced by the organisation's members. Moreover, to establish a sustainable innovation culture, leaders need to align the organisation's espoused values with those of its wider stakeholder network, including local communities and the natural environment (sections 2.1.3. and 2.3.1).

APPROACH 1. Guiding Questions to Formulate Guiding Principles for an Organisation

In a moderated workshop setting, a range of facilitation methods (such as *Envisioning* or laddering techniques) helps to redefine organisational values, purpose, mission and vision. Questions often used in *Guiding Principles Review* (see section 4.3) include:

VALUES: *What is most important to you? What do you care about? How would you specify values expressing equity within and across generations? How are they relevant to your organisation?*

PURPOSE: *What is the reason for your organisation, your company, or your project to exist? How does it contribute over the long term to human wellbeing and planetary stability?*

MISSION: *What does your company or your project seek to achieve within the next five years, ten years, twenty years?*

VISION: *How would you depict a desirable, common future for our organisation in a vivid description?*

Push and pull factors can trigger an organisation to reformulate its values and other guiding principles found in its vision, mission or purpose statements. A vision describes a desirable future, whereas a mission shows the path to get there. Statements about purpose express the reason for organisation's existence and its motivation to contribute to human well-being and planetary stability[20] (approach 1).

Espoused values and associated mission, purpose and vision statements serve to integrate organisational members, subcultures and other stakeholders under an overarching frame of reference that prioritises ideas of sustainability. They also provide a reference for the design of artefacts such as assessment tools, incentive schemes or facilities for sustainable innovation projects.

Finally, they provide an orientation for the organisation's future ambitions. Values allow a company to go beyond profit orientation and the opportunistic search for short-term competitive advantages and market trends. They are about what matters most to a company's stakeholders and about addressing sustainability challenges. And they are levers for business development. However, when a company's actual values diverge from its espoused values, such misalignments are the usual suspects causing the organisational culture to 'eat' even well-defined normative and strategic management efforts. Identifying tensions and values-action gaps that contradict the espoused values is a crucial step.

Addressing Tensions

Tensions become more severe and conflict-laden when sustainability-oriented organisations mature and try to accommodate the values of a broader range of stakeholders. Resolving these tensions becomes more urgent when operating in highly competitive markets that impact profit margins.[21] Instead of recommending that divergent stakeholder values be aligned, recent research into management focuses on leveraging inevitable tensions to build synergies.

> Tensions between different ideas about how to deal with challenges, about which values and goals to pursue and about how to drive innovation are ubiquitous in organisations.

Defining tensions as the presence of 'two phenomena in a dynamic relationship that involves both competition and complementarity',[22] allows us to view them in a different light. Whereas competition between ideas provokes trade-offs that lead to win-lose outcomes, complementarity encourages synergies leading to a win-win outcome.[23] This suggests that understanding and leveraging tensions can help organisations to rise above trade-offs involving their management priorities and identify synergies that contribute to sustainable innovation.[24]

Sustainability tensions often arise from conflicts between personal values and organisational values or between a sole focus on shareholder values as opposed to broader societal and planetary interests. These tensions can be reconciled through *Aspirational Narratives* that use 'and' to reconcile profit *and* purpose, shareholders *and* stakeholders, markets and society, business *and* ethics.[25]

Synergies can be found in the tensions between different stakeholder values by using methods such as *Empathising*,[26] which encourage stakeholders to deliberate on the differences between their values. Instead of seeing these differences as conflicts that require a middle-ground compromise, they are harnessed to find innovative solutions from a more holistic perspective. For instance, despite different sets of values and cultures, *Empathising* between corporate and non-profit organisations in the United Kingdom has led to sustainable innovation outcomes in nine well-documented cases.[27] These include a retailer's new product line of lingerie for breast cancer operation patients, an energy supplier's new communication protocol to address vulnerable customers, and a TV broadcaster's new call centre dedicated to serving viewers with disabilities.

Addressing Values-Action Gaps

The term values-action gap refers to the difference between what people claim they believe and what they actually do. This gap between espoused values and daily practices is often unconscious. It plays a key role in understanding how culture can inadvertently hinder sustainable innovation.

> Values-action gaps are the discrepancies between the espoused values of an individual or an organisation and their actions.[28]

Values-action gaps often originate in unconscious misinterpretations. We can better understand the phenomenon by examining Kurt Lewin's concept of change resistance.

CONCEPT 4. The Evolution of the Change Resistance Concept

Kurt Lewin used the term 'resistance to change' to describe obstacles that impede change-driving forces.[29] He stressed that lasting transformation could only be brought about by weakening these obstacles, rather than amplifying change drivers. For example, in his work with Margaret Mead during the Second World War, Lewin sought to broaden the food choices of American housewives by first addressing aversions and misconceptions, recognising that failing to remove such underlying obstacles would negate any subsequent encouragement.[30]

Later, positivist views on organisational change became prominent and shifted attention away from Lewin's original ideas. Resistance was defined as an obstructive force and often attributed to employees who resisted employer-led changes. This perspective led to misconceptions, such as blaming subordinates for resistance and assuming that managers could 'overcome' it without addressing its root causes.[31]

An interpretivist approach offers an alternative way to understanding resistance, seeing it not as a fixed obstacle to be overcome but as a sign of differing perspectives that need to be explored.[32] This is exemplified by the case of a food processing facility[33] that sought to improve mutual respect between management and operational employees through *Participative Decision Making*. Interpretative analysis revealed that management and operational employees had conflicting interpretations of the notion of respect.

Management saw respect as leading to increased employee productivity, greater initiative and ownership of problem-solving without relying on managerial intervention. Employees, on the other hand, expected respect to mean that management would give them things they wanted, such as better pay, new equipment, more comfortable facilities or better parking lot security. These misunderstandings led to the intervention's failure. This case portrays a situation that could have been mistakenly framed by management as resistance by employees. The interpretivist lens revealed the deeper, conflicting interpretations of the notion of respect between the two groups, which resulted in unconscious values-action gaps.

Even though a company's espoused values can serve to orient its cultural development, values-action gaps can perpetuate existing practices and artefacts. For example, an organisation may claim its strong commitment to values of collaboration and emphasise practices of *Knowledge Management* and *Knowledge Sharing* to enhance sustainable innovation. However, although such practices might take place on a sporadic basis, the same organisation could cling to practices and artefacts that limit regular interactions between its employees by incentivising individual performance or only providing office space in cubicles or separate rooms.

When an organisation first adopts sustainability values, the gaps between these values and its practices may not be immediately apparent. Moreover, as the organisation grows and changes these gaps can evolve in unexpected ways and lead to severe problems in sustainable innovation. If values-action gaps are left unaddressed, they can provoke severe crises, tarnishing the organisation's reputation and calling into question its commitment to sustainability values.

The detrimental consequences that can result when officially espoused values are not lived by an organisation's members is illustrated in the Volkswagen diesel emissions scandal[34] and the Apple Batterygate scandal.[35] Through product development practices that contradicted sustainability regulations as well as their own organisational values, both companies inflicted harm on their customers and the environment as well as incurring significant financial and reputation losses themselves. To systematically identify and address values-action gaps, an organisation can and should use methods of field observation and interpretative analysis, such as *Rapid Ethnography* or *Sensemaking* of critical incidents.

3.1.3 Creating Sustainable Value Repeatedly and Reliably

Values provide the ethical foundation, orientation and directional certainty (see section 2.1.3) for creating sustainable value in a repeatable and reliable manner. As opposed to easily negotiable interests, short-lived attitudes or restrictive norms, values serve as enduring sources of orientation and intrinsic motivation throughout the innovation process.[36] They also provide criteria to validate the intermediary results of innovation efforts, ensuring the reliability and repeatability of sustainable innovation outcomes. Key value indicators, operating like key performance indicators, provide specific, measurable and realistic criteria to gauge the impact of innovation projects on values.

> **CASE 5. Key Value Indicators for Gauging the Impact of Information and Communication Technology Solutions**
>
> In a use case scenario that conceived the design, development and implementation of 6G technologies in smart cities, key value indicators helped to identify and estimate how future ICT technologies can lead to positive outcomes, such as increasing the quality of inclusive and safe mobility ser-

vices or improving urban health.[37] The implementation of key value indicators proceeded in five steps.

1. DESCRIBE THE SCENARIO by providing the context of stakeholders and their interactions, the physical environment and a high-level objective to be achieved. Then describe the use case by identifying the technology used to gain a specific result in the scenario. For instance, a scenario defined for European smart cities in the year 2050 addresses problems such as rising traffic congestion, air pollution and inadequate transport inclusivity. The use case involves 6G connectivity solutions, such as dynamic sensor networks, real-time data monitoring and autonomous vehicle integration.

2. IDENTIFY KEY VALUES associated with the use case as criteria and outcomes. Values as criteria represent overarching human or organisational values (e.g. sustainability, health or public safety) that guide project development and decision-making. Values as outcomes stand for actual benefits or drawbacks (e.g. cleaner air, better mobility or potential privacy risks) resulting from how the technology is used.

3. TRANSLATE EACH KEY VALUE into measurable key value indicators. For example, a key value to 'maintain air quality to levels at which human life is not endangered' can be translated into an indicator that measures the 'number of pollution-related health incidents'. Other indicators could involve tracking the availability of green transport options, improvements in process efficiency or how widely a service reaches a given population.

4. ANALYSE THE OUTCOME of technical solutions and system design using key value indicators. For example, a use case aiming to reduce CO_2 emissions might implement a network of transport sensors that improve energy efficiency, but it must also consider whether the energy used by those sensors cancels out some of the potential carbon savings. This step analyses the availability of enabling systems, such as data monitoring or governance systems, that are necessary for the achievement of the key value indicators.

5. ASSESS THE KEY VALUE INDICATORS through expert assessments, simulations or digital twins that model the use case implementation. For instance, the impact of an air pollution monitoring system on the 'number of pollution-related health incidents' might first be estimated using simulations or expert assessments, then assessed with a digital twin against real-world data once the system is in place. Such assessments reveal if indicators need adjusting or if new indicators are required to keep the project progress on track.

Achieving sustainable innovation requires consistency between organisational actions and sustainability values, though values should evolve to meet emerging stakeholder demands. If external or internal stakeholder values shift, organisations may also need to reprioritise or redefine their values to ensure alignment and reliable innovation outcomes.[38]

Maturity Levels of Values-Based Innovation Cultures

Different levels of maturity – implicit, defined, differentiated, managed and proactive – characterise the extent to which an organisation manages its espoused values, integrates stakeholder values and translates them into formal criteria and practices that lead to desirable outcomes.

> Maturity levels progress from minimal integration of espoused values into innovation practices to higher levels of integration and continuous revision of the espoused values in response to evolving stakeholder values.[39]

1. IMPLICIT: Both organisational values in general and values towards sustainable innovation initiatives in particular remain implicit.

A company that doesn't explicitly refer to the values that define its corporate identity or doesn't prioritise values of sustainability may still generate sustainable innovations. For example, a small manufacturing company might introduce an eco-friendly product line or adopt more sustainable production processes to meet new environmental regulations. This doesn't mean that values are not motivating the company's innovation efforts, but only that these values remain implicit and that the role of culture as a driver for innovation is being neglected.

The need to review implicit values arises from external demand or from internal developmental challenges. External parties may require the company conduct an ISO 9001 certification, which then leads to it clarifying basic policies and a reflection on underlying values, purpose and mission. Internal challenges can result from the need to improve the relationship between owners and shareholders or during a generation change in a family business. It can also result from the need to consolidate the core business after a period of rapid growth and diversification or the need for reorientation following a crisis.

2. DEFINED: Organisational values are defined on a global level. They are known and, to some extent, shared by employees.

Well-defined values provide a basic framework for sustainable innovation practices. However, there is a risk that these values may become meaningless once initial enthusiasm fades. The need for further differentiation and formalisation often arises when existing practices are given priority over the adoption of new sustainable innovation practices. Existing practices are motivated by the ideas held by individual employees, teams or departments rather than the espoused values of the whole organisation. Employees stick to these practices because they have been proven over time and by their own experiences.

An example could be a large consumer goods company that proclaims a corporate-wide sustainability strategy yet struggles to mainstream sustainability practices across its various departments, with some teams reverting to established practices that conflict with the new sustainability values and goals, such as re-source-intensive manufacturing or overpackaging. This leads to isolated green products or campaigns rather than a holistic, organisation-wide shift towards sustainable innovation.

3. DIFFERENTIATED: Values are defined globally, involving diverse stakeholders, but also with respect to organisational subcultures or innovation projects.

Different values of sustainability and preestablished practices that characterise departmental subcultures or innovation teams might call for a more dynamic handling of global and department or project-specific values.

For example, in an inspection company, an innovation team with an entrepreneurial mindset informally practices stakeholder analysis and small-scale *Experimentation* to develop concepts. Although these practices diverge from official strategy, the company encourages them to allow greater flexibility. If successful in driving sustainability outcomes, these practices may eventually be formalised and mainstreamed throughout the whole organisation.

4. MANAGED: Values are actively managed with measurable indicators and stakeholder feedback and used as a shortcut (e.g. for ideation) and as evaluation criteria for innovation projects.

Ambitious goals include moving beyond organisational transformation to eco-system building[40] but also advanced understanding and sensitivity of collaborators in pursuit of values-based objectives. These goals can motivate management and lead to the integration of values in daily practices throughout the organisation. Sustainability-related values are also actively adapted in response to new insights arising from, for example, the unintended consequences of innovation outcomes.

For example, a tech company that defines sustainability as one of its core values may begin to assess all innovation projects using key value indicators, tracking their potential to reduce their carbon footprint or enhance knowledge building and equity. As data, feedback and insights are gathered from field tests and stakeholders, the key value indicators are updated and reprioritised to ensure long-term positive outcomes.

5. PROACTIVE: Prospective management of stakeholder values becomes an integral part of innovation management and a constitutive moment of organisational culture and learning.

On this level, organisations foster a culture of continuous learning and adaptation by responding to changing stakeholder values and emerging sustainability challenges. The 'associative networks'[41] that values represent are proactively refined and translated into practices and artefacts that help to generate sustainable innovation in a repeated and reliable manner.

For instance, the case of the green search engine Ecosia exemplifies the iterative renegotiation and reprioritisation of values in response to internal and external stakeholders to drive sustainable business model development. Ecosia's values-based approach enables the company to deliver on its core values even at the expense of short-term financial returns (see case 6 below[42] and case 14 in chapter 6).

CASE 6. **Ecosia Considers Partnering with a Petrol Company**

Ecosia, the search engine that plants trees, was founded in 2009 by the German entrepreneur Christian Kroll. The start-up entered the fiercely contested search engine market with an innovative business model. Ecosia reinvests profits it makes from advertisements to support tree planting projects around the world. By 2024, the green search engine had already planted over 220 million trees, has over 20 million active users and is widely adopted as a default search engine option by Android and iOS users. Driven by values of environmentalism, sustainability and integrity, Ecosia stands as a role model for innovators and entrepreneurs wanting to reconcile financial success with social and environmental impact on a global scale. The company has six core values: [43]

- *Impact:* Think big and prioritise what will have the greatest impact.
- *Integrity:* Be honest, authentic and open.
- *Sustainability:* Seek long-term, sustainable solutions.
- *Leadership:* Lead the way to a sustainable future.
- *User focus:* Honour the user.
- *Happiness:* Make it an enjoyable ride.

These six values serve as a basis for Ecosia to develop its business. The company's former product manager, Philipp Baumann, gave an example of how their internal consideration of core values affected partnering decisions. In one case a 'big petrol corporation' approached the search engine with an offer to use its product, but, as Baumann concludes: 'One of our core values is "integrity", which also means not just being transparent about what we think and do, but also making sure that people can trust us ... because maybe if you have a partner and that allows you to reach five million people that would be a lot of trees ... but if you compromise too much then you start losing integrity. And so, this is really a challenging balance to find sometimes and, in that case, we were also like: No, the cost for our integrity would be too high.'

This incident shows how Ecosia's values guide decision-making by providing a shared reference for the evaluation of strategic choices, without closing off options. When invited to partner with a large but unsustainable firm, Ecosia prioritised integrity over impact in terms of outreach expansion and mid-term financial returns, leading to a decision against the collaboration. This approach to making decisions, rather than following a strict ethical code, reflects a conscious value prioritisation to prevent mission drift and protect long-term social impact.

Working Against Unintended Consequences and Potential Rebound Effects

Although innovation is considered a key driver of sustainable development, the polycrisis that endangers today's economic, social and environmental ecosystems is largely attributed to innovation-induced industrial activities and rebound effects. Innovation has been long considered an act of 'creative destruction' that contributes to economic growth at the price of destroying existing jobs, firms and whole industries.[44]

But technological breakthroughs have not only upturned economic systems, the three consecutive industrial revolutions were accompanied by destructive consequences for society and the environment: exploitation of workers, mental health deterioration, the pollution of air, water and land leading to climate change and species loss. In part this is due to so-called rebound effects, where improvements in technological efficiency result in increases in consumption that cause even more harm. For instance, drivers upgrading to fuel-efficient vehicles can be tempted to drive more frequently and cover longer distances due to the lower fuel costs.[45]

Digital innovation and the fourth industrial revolution are praised for their potential to alleviate the global polycrisis. However, digital technologies also have unpredictable and scalable impacts on ecosystems, leading to unprecedented challenges. Generative AI systems infringe on others' intellectual property by recreating copyrighted designs or text, raising complex legal and ethical concerns. Anticipating these outcomes calls for a nuanced approach considering factors on the interface between physical and digital realms, like identity ownership, data safety, digital waste and employment distribution.[46] Companies are facing ever increasing challenges to innovate meaningful products and services while avoiding unintended, negative consequences.

Cultural factors can cause innovation activities to have unintended consequences when employees remain entrenched in routines and notions without reflecting on how the innovations they are developing could contribute to negative sustainability outcomes in the future. But culture also holds the potential to steer developments into more desirable directions.

CONCEPT 5. How Organisational Cultures Create Unintended Consequences

The term 'unintended consequences' had already been proposed in the 1930s by the American sociologist Robert K. Merton. He identified five factors that limit the competence of social groups to anticipate the consequences of their actions.[47]

1. **'LACK OF FOREKNOWLEDGE'** refers to the general inability to foresee all of the potential consequences of an action. This inability becomes greater with the introduction of new, potentially disruptive technologies.

2. **'ASSESSMENT ERRORS'** cause organisations to assume that actions which had previously achieved the desired outcome will continue to be do so. For exam-

ple, renewable energy companies might assume that their past success in sustainable value creation will continue, without anticipating negative outcomes such as the environmental impact of battery disposal and resource extraction.

3. 'IMPERVIOUS IMMEDIACY OF INTEREST' refers to an overemphasis on the potential beneficial consequences of an action, which overshadows the ability to anticipate its negative outcomes. For example, an organisation may believe that the positive impacts of sustainable innovations will offset their potential negative impacts.

4. 'BASIC VALUES', rigidly followed, limit the ability of social actors to consider negative consequences of their purposive actions. Strict accordance with these values ensures individuals and organisations that they are doing the right thing, but narrows their focus to ignore foreseeable unintended consequences and alternative courses of actions. For instance, organisations committed to reducing their greenhouse gas emissions by adopting biofuels have reportedly perpetuated rebound effects such as inflated cooking oil prices and worldwide deforestation.[48]

5. 'SELF-DEFEATING PROPHECIES'[49] are exemplified by employees who doubt the potential of a sustainable innovation initiative to generate positive outcomes and therefore do not support it, causing it to fail or lead to unintended consequences.

Increasingly, the unintended consequences of innovation and their antecedent factors have become a topic of concern for innovation managers and regulatory agencies. And several practices and methods have been proposed to work against such consequences. The practice of *Sustainability Foresight* prepares organisations for alternative developments through the iterative assessment of future scenarios. This practice can be reinforced through methods such as *Envisioning*, which specifies desirable outcomes to detect unintended deviations early on. Iterative validation of intermediate results and outcomes in values-based approaches to innovation are designed to avoid unintended consequences. Likewise, responsible innovation practices of *Anticipation* and *Responsiveness* are aimed at avoiding and eliminating unintended consequences. practices of *Anticipation* systematically evaluate potential issues and available alternatives to capture both the intended and unintended outcomes of innovation on sustainable development. Practices of *Responsiveness* involve adjusting the innovation process if negative outcomes are predicted or observed.

Three Components of Sustainable Innovation Cultures
Together, the three components of sustainable innovation cultures discussed in this chapter make up the generative systems deliberately aligned to ensure sustainable value creation.

- GENERATIVE SYSTEMS consist of shared values, practices and artefacts that drive sustainable, regenerative outcomes.
- DELIBERATE ALIGNMENT clarifies ideas of sustainability as part of the organisation's priorities, promoting them through practices and artefacts while addressing tensions and values-action gaps.
- DIRECTIONAL CERTAINTY ensures sustainable value creation.

Each component can be illustrated in the now classic case of Interface.

3.1.4 Sustainable Innovation Culture at Work: The Case of Interface

Pioneers in sustainable innovation such as Interface took decades to deliberately translate their values and mission into an organisational culture that repeatedly and reliably generated sustainable innovation despite unforeseen challenges and against the odds of unintended or unexpected consequences. Interface, the global manufacturer of commercial flooring, is an outstanding case. Interface improved the energy and resource efficiency of its supply chain and production, it reinvented its business model, and it is now steering the whole organisation to working towards climate take back. Over the last 30 years, its sustainable innovation culture has become a role model for industrial transformation towards sustainable development.

CASE 7. Interface and its Outstanding Journey Towards Sustainable Innovation Culture

Founded in the United States in 1973, Interface has grown into the largest carpet-tile maker worldwide. In 1994, motivated by concerns of employees[50] and his own epiphany[51] after reading *The Ecology of Commerce*,[52] founder and CEO Ray Anderson set the course for a deliberate approach to creating a sustainable innovation culture and transforming the company into a sustainable and 'restorative enterprise worldwide'.[53]

An 'eco dream team' of environmental experts was set up to drive what became known as the company's Mission Zero to eliminate all negative environmental impacts by the year 2020. In a keynote speech held in 1994, Anderson outlined his strategy: 'reclaim, reuse, recycle, conserve, adopt and advance best practices ... feel free to take each of these, massage them, develop them, then come back to me with your version of each.'

An impressive list of innovations in engineering, sourcing and manufacturing, design and business models led to the sustainable outcomes the company has since delivered, most prominently by reaching the Mission Zero targets ahead of time.[54] Repeated and reliable delivery of sustainability innovations have paved the road for the company's journey. Already in 1995, a ReEntry programme was launched to reclaim and recycle used tiles. The same year, an

---

Evergreen Service Agreement offered clients the opportunity to lease rather than purchase carpets, extending the company's business model from selling products to offering services.

Engineers examined the manufacturing facilities and achieved impressive reductions in energy consumption simply by implementing pipes that are fatter, shorter and straighter.[55] Investments in new technologies and products in the late 1990s and early 2000s enabled the manufacturer to use recycled nylon fibres and backings. Since 2003, nature-inspired aesthetic designs have pushed product innovation. The world's first biomimetic carpet tile was introduced under the name Entropy. The design reflects the randomness found in nature and helps to extend product lifetime by saving materials during installation and on-site local fixes.[56]

In 2012, a Net-Works programme was launched in partnership with the Zoological Society of London to recover and recycle discarded fishing nets in the Philippines, also creating economically added value for the coastal communities. In 2014, a Carbon Neutral Floors initiative was launched committing the company to carbon neutrality across its product range. By 2018 this goal was achieved through offsetting and leadership in low-carbon manufacturing.[57]

Once Mission Zero was accomplished, a new Climate Take Back mission raised the bar even higher, dedicating the company to become a carbon-negative enterprise by 2040. In 2019 one of the first milestones was the introduction of carbon-negative products to help reverse global warming by using carbon as a resource. In 2020 the world's first carbon-negative carpet tiles were introduced to the market, with a tile collection branded as Embodied Beauty in 2020. Bio-composite so-called CQuest carpet backings were made from plants and organic materials that retain their carbon dioxide.

These remarkable sustainable innovation initiatives are backed up with internal measures to embed sustainability in the organisational culture and ensure that skills and practices are in place. In 1999 biomimicry workshops were conducted to inspire employees from different departments to go beyond traditional tile design. Since 2018, new hires have received *Mandatory Training* on sustainability through a global onboarding programme, briefing them about ongoing activities and lessons learned, building awareness for the mission and encouraging a sustainable innovation mindset. Advanced training is also offered to selected employees to enhance societal problem-solving skills or implement their own sustainable innovation programmes.[58]

This impressive list of milestone initiatives may appear like an unbroken success story, but there have been serious tensions and struggles along the way. Already when the new ethical guidelines were announced in 1994, employees expressed their doubts and Wall Street investors dumped their stock, doubting the sanity of the chairman.[59] In fact, upfront investment costs eat up short-term returns and may financially stress the whole endeavour, whereas passing on costs to clients may lead to loss in market share. In the case of Interface, clients also hesitated to adopt the new carpet-as-a-service model with Evergreen Service Agreements, shying away turning capital investment costs into operational costs.[60] In spite of limited customer acceptance, Interface kept the model for its contribution to a circular economy.

'What drives us? A positive vision of the future and the determination to make it come true. The moral courage to do what is right, despite all obstacles. An abiding commitment to show that sustainability is better for business. We believe that change starts with us and is transforming Interface from a plunderer of the Earth to an agent of its restoration. Through this process of redesigning ourselves, we hope to be a catalyst for the redesign of global industry.'[61]

The vision also provides a clear sense of direction that allows Interface to deal with unintended consequences. In 2008 a new product line of grass and bamboo woven floor tiles made by Indian weavers failed, but this experience improved the company's capacity to network and collaborate with non-traditional business partners and prepared the way for Interface to create a community-based supply chain. Interface's initial efforts at carbon offsetting to reach carbon neutrality also failed,[62] but they persevered and went on to pioneer carbon reduction when the company started its offset programme Cool Carpet in the 2000s. However, it doesn't come as a surprise that sustainability-oriented companies such as Interface do not rely short-term returns on investment, but see sustainability challenges as the core of their innovation efforts.

At Interface, the alignment of guiding principles, strategies and innovation in processes, products and services has contributed to create a 'corporate culture with strong shared values of community and sustainability'.[63] Today, the company can proudly announce that 'sustainability is in our DNA'.[64] The case tells a story of determination in facing internal and external challenges to create a unique sustainable innovation culture and become an iconic role model for a whole industry that once relied on high-carbon, petroleum-soaked and everlasting polymer products.

Sustainable innovation culture at Interface is hard to mistake for a peripheral or residual factor that escapes rational management. On the contrary, its case shows that culture doesn't eat strategy for breakfast, but nourishes a 'constant cycle of reinvention'[65] and innovation, forming a *machine désirante*, a productive assemblage that is not driven by a negative absence or external regulation but by positive desires and values.

3.2 The 3C Framework for Establishing Sustainable Innovation Cultures

Having reviewed the essential components of sustainable innovation cultures, we now turn to how they can be deliberately created, maintained and developed.

Based on an extensive literature review and empirical inquiry in European firms,[66] we have developed a framework of three basic activities:

> Sustainable innovation cultures can be developed through virtuous cycles of conceiving culture, co-creating interventions and cultivating new practices.

The 3C framework[67] provides practices and methods to diagnose and develop sustainable innovation cultures. By iterating through these activities, organisations can continuously evolve their sustainable innovation cultures as they incorporate new practices and methods to bring about the desired outcomes. While a lack of shared values, as well as tensions and values-action gaps, can keep an organisation from realising its full potential, these practices and methods can be used to facilitate the development of sustainable innovation cultures.

No single person can create an organisational culture, and even the most active members are usually not fully aware of their role in shaping a culture. Often employees are caught up in their daily work, with little or no time to think about the culture they are a part of. Many executive leaders also take culture for granted, ignoring divergent viewpoints and levels of commitment until problems surface. Even where there is a will, the path forward is not obvious. Understanding cultures is not a trivial task. It is not enough to understand the shared, or divergent, ideas of sustainability, the innovation process and its desired impact, nor to formulate ethical guidelines and generic policies.

Just as each of its members, every culture is unique. Rather than using off-the-shelf criteria to understand culture, we advocate an idiosyncratic approach that works with subjective interpretations in a continuous 'search for meaning'.[68] As 'all meaning is context-dependent and therefore unstable', our interpretative analysis of cultures follows a dynamic approach of conceiving.[69]

This approach acknowledges that the interpretation of culture is a dynamic process that takes place (*is conceived*) in the minds of those conducting the analysis. By conceiving a culture's characteristic notions, practices and artefacts, as well as the tensions and values-action gaps that hinder sustainable innovation, we can initiate a virtuous circle of cultural evolution. Only after gaining an understanding of the specific challenges to sustainable innovation that a particular culture faces can we devise and implement targeted interventions.

Organisational cultures are social systems that need to be addressed systematically. While it is rarely possible to get the whole system 'into one room',[70] it is important to get stakeholder contributions and buy-in from different hierarchical and experience levels as well as different departments, functions and locations. This co-creating approach to organisational development is based on engaging and empowering diverse stakeholders. Their engagement ensures that the designed interventions are comprehensive, well-informed and capable of overcoming resistance.

This approach empowers stakeholders to tap into their collaborative creativity and achieve experiential and practical outcomes.[71] Co-creating does not ask for complete consensus, which would in most cases be unfeasible, but instead leverages the different perspectives to tackle challenges. This bottom-up approach is in contrast with top-down methods that typically fall short in shaping organisational values into daily practices.[72] Through co-creating, organisations are able to design and validate novel interventions to resolve tensions and values-action gaps, advancing their sustainable innovation practices.

Conducting targeted interventions is necessary but usually not sufficient to trigger the sustainability-oriented transformation of an innovation culture. Instead, methods work together as a bundle of strategic choices to establish and sustain new practices. These build on inherent strengths and address specific challenges, contributing towards goals of sustainable development or of resilience in post-collapse scenarios. Following the pragmatist tradition in cultural studies, this process of cultural development is one of cultivation, which is characterised by 'interpretation and self-control motivated by goals rather than by origins'.[73] Cultivation becomes possible when individuals are able to interpret cultural values and goals and selectively redirect their attention and efforts towards realising them.[74] Cultivation thus leverages the potential of individuals to work towards shared goals and values through practices and methods, involving collaboration, capacity building and the benchmarking of progress towards the targeted outcomes.

Conceiving, co-creating and cultivating feed into one another. When cultural agents better understand the existing sustainability-related values of an organisation (conceiving) and when employees and promoters experiment with new practices and methods to address tensions and values-action gaps and to enhance sustainable value creation (co-creating), then an organisation can revise its values, practices and methods and design new artefacts, tools and datasets that empower sustainable innovation (cultivating). By iteratively working through these three basic activities, virtuous cycles evolve that allow the organisation to gain competitive edge and positively impact sustainable development.

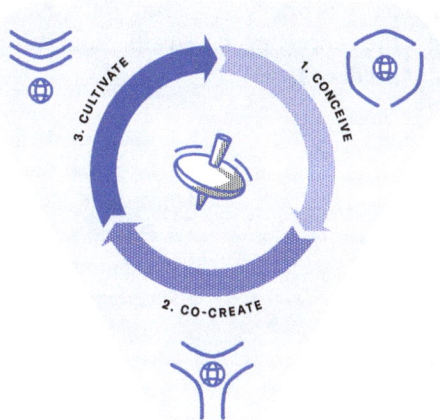

FIGURE 4. Spinning top illustrating the 3C framework activities of conceiving, co-creating and cultivating in a virtuous cycle of cultural development

3.3 Overarching Practices for Conceiving, Co-creating and Cultivating in Sustainable Innovation

Research has identified several practices and methods that contribute to the development of sustainable innovation cultures. Methods are well-defined, replicable approaches for purposeful interventions that address recurring challenges. Regular application, context-specific appropriation and iterative refinement of a method turns it into a practice. That is, it becomes a recurring action, observable behaviour and established way of doing things (section 2.3.4).

Examples for methods in the development of innovation cultures are *Envisioning* desirable futures or introducing *Incentivisation Schemes* to overcome short-termism.[75] Examples for related practices are *Sustainability Foresight* and *Incentivisation*. Some of these practices play a pivotal role across different activities of sustainable innovation management and cultural change. We call them overarching practices. Other practices are relevant to one of the 3C activities of conceiving and co-creating sustainable innovation cultures and cultivating sustainable innovation. We refer to them as activity-specific practices.

3.3.1 Overarching Practices

> Overarching practices facilitate the transformation towards a sustainable innovation culture, paving the grounds for activity-specific practices and methods to unfold.

Before we take a closer look at the different activity-specific practices and related methods with examples (in chapters 4–6), we give an overview of fourteen overarching practices that span all three basic activities in the 3C framework of cultural development. Each practice is briefly described, followed by guidance on how it can be applied across the conceiving, co-creating and cultivating activities. The fourteen overarching practices are:

1. Resilience Development
2. Moderation
3. Knowledge Sharing
4. Knowledge Management
5. Inclusive Deliberation
6. Reflexivity
7. Anticipation
8. Responsiveness
9. Empowerment
10. Decentralisation
11. Symbolic Ethical Leadership
12. Experimentation
13. Gamification
14. Human–Systems Collaboration

Resilience Development, Moderation and Knowledge Sharing
The first three overarching practices are derived from an extensive review of studies of sustainability culture by Ketprapakorn and Kantabutra.[76]

1. RESILIENCE DEVELOPMENT

Resilience Development involves continuous monitoring and investment to prepare organisations for dealing with new sustainability challenges and mastering cultural change. This practice ensures that organisations remain adaptable and forward-looking.

In conceiving, engage in direct investment towards triggering cultural change and *Stakeholder Values Integration*. In co-creating, anticipate future sustainability challenges and address them through innovation in products, services or business models (see *Sustainable Market Creation*). In cultivating, introduce policies, guidelines and sustainability-oriented *Management Systems*.

2. MODERATION

Moderation balances the inherent tension between short-term and long-term performance objectives. It helps organisations to make prudent decisions that align operational performance with sustainability strategy and values-based goals.

In conceiving, apply *Moderation* to balance cultural tensions between short and long-term performance as well as the stakeholder needs and values that give rise to them. In co-creating, use *Moderation* to assess and anticipate the benefits and risks of short versus long-term performance and explore approaches to reconcile or synergise these competing demands. In cultivating, establish a reference point for the criteria used by methods and artefacts to evaluate the impact of innovation efforts. For instance, integrate both short-term and long-term indicators in *Innovation Impact Assessments* to evaluate the expected contributions to achieving values-based goals.

3. KNOWLEDGE SHARING

Knowledge Sharing fosters the exchange of insights and expertise with both internal and external stakeholders. It enables organisations to build a culture of collaborative learning and co-creating.

In conceiving, engage cultural members in sharing their understandings of values, practices, tensions and values-action gaps. In co-creating, promote *Knowledge Sharing* among a wide range of stakeholders. In cultivating, promote formal *Knowledge Sharing* practices, artefacts and methods, such as a *Cultural Dictionary*.

Responsible Innovation Dimensions and Practices of Inclusive Deliberation, Reflexivity, Anticipation and Responsiveness

The 3C framework encompasses four dimensions for overarching practices that align innovation outcomes with societal needs and values of sustainability: 1) Practices of *Inclusive Deliberation*, 2) *Reflexivity*, 3) *Anticipation* and 4) *Responsiveness*[77] (see section 2.1.3). *Knowledge Management* has been recognised as an additional, fifth dimension of responsible innovation.[78]

4. KNOWLEDGE MANAGEMENT

While a successful project can be a big step forward, in order to repeat its success and go further, organisations need to understand exactly what they did and how they did it. This is where practices of *Knowledge Management* – such as knowledge creation, development, assimilation and synthesising – come into play, enabling the systematic sharing of experience-based knowledge regarding new sustainable technologies, processes and innovation practices. For example, a company developing new methods for recycling plastics must capture and share technical knowledge across departments to obtain the desired innovation outcome.[79]

In conceiving, coordinate practices of *Knowledge Management* to understand cultural weaknesses due to knowledge gaps and uncertainty. In co-creating, take proactive steps to address these challenges, for example, by *Engaging in Open Innovation* or in *Innovation Ecosystems*. In cultivating, introduce artefacts (e.g. frameworks, scorecards, tools or software) to incorporate sustainability concerns across all organisational operations and strategic decisions.

5. INCLUSIVE DELIBERATION

These practices engage stakeholders, such as employees, customers, communities and partners to inform innovation-related decision-making.[80] They allow firms to capture stakeholder requirements, address them with appropriate solutions and establish a new basis for collaboration.

In conceiving, leverage methods such as Focus Groups and *Values Jams* to integrate internal stakeholders and elicit employee values, needs and tensions. In co-creating, discuss sustainability values with internal and external stakeholders and translate them into new innovation practices and projects. In cultivating, introduce *Participatory Decision Making* or *Stakeholder Advisory Boards* to ensure that organisational and stakeholder values are embedded across all operations and strategic decisions.

6. REFLEXIVITY

These practices involve 'critically thinking about one's own actions and responsibilities, values and motivations, knowledge and perceived realities, and how each of these have an effect on the management of the innovation process.'[81] Practices of *Reflexivity* help to avoid unintended consequences of innovation by raising awareness of how values and other notions shape employees' decisions and actions.

In conceiving, engage employees in critical reflection, *Sensemaking* and retrospective thinking on what worked well and what are persisting challenges, tensions and values-action gaps. In co-creating, involve participants in critically assessing contributions and results, ensuring new initiatives are well-informed. In cultivating, enhance reflexivity to foster sustainable innovation by ensuring that efforts remain aligned with the espoused values and no mission drift occurs.

7. ANTICIPATION

Anticipation practices address stakeholder needs and values to describe and analyse intended and unintended consequences of innovation activities on sustainable development. They help to capture opportunities, minimise risks and prepare for future developments.

In conceiving, co-creating and cultivating practices and methods such as *Sensemaking*, *Sustainability Foresight*, *Envisioning* or *Results Chains*, ensure that not only positive future outcomes, but also potential unintended consequences of innovation are considered.

8. RESPONSIVENESS

Practices of *Responsiveness* change the direction, trajectory and pace of innovation 'in response to stakeholder and public values and changing circumstances'.[82] They help ensure that innovation activities and projects align with values of sustainability.

In conceiving stakeholder values and co-creating initiatives, manage innovation by responding to stakeholder concerns. In cultivating new practices and artefacts, ensure alignment between innovation efforts and stakeholder values and needs, for example, by leveraging *Participative Decision Making* or sustainability-oriented *Management Systems*.

Empowerment, Decentralisation and Ethical Leadership

This set of overarching practices is widely recognised for its role in developing conventional innovation cultures and, more recently, as critical for cultivating sustainable innovation.

9. EMPOWERMENT

Empowerment[83] gives employees the authority and resources to take ownership of sustainability initiatives. It is a critical practice for driving cultural change from the bottom of organisational hierarchies.

In conceiving, empower employees to influence how a given culture is understood, for example, by organising a *Values Jam*. In co-creating, ensure that diverse voices are heard, leading to more innovative and inclusive solutions. In cultivating sustainable innovation in the long term, empower employees to take ownership of sustainability projects and sustain their engagement.

10. DECENTRALISATION

Decentralisation[84] empowers local teams to make decisions tailored to their specific context. Rather than relying on one-size-fits-all approaches to sustainable innovation, they can draw on their unique expertise to address local challenges.

In conceiving, understand the subcultures of individual teams, departments or regions where tensions and values-action gaps prevail and where new opportunities emerge. In co-creating, empower local teams to generate sustainability initiatives that are context-specific and aligned with their needs. In cultivating, enable sustainable innovation on a local level, for instance, through *Tailored Communication* and artefacts.

11. SYMBOLIC ETHICAL LEADERSHIP

Symbolic Ethical Leadership[85] involves the active engagement of organisational leaders in fostering ethical values, integrating these in their own behaviour and communicating them across the organisation. This sets the tone for employees at all levels to adopt ethical values and uphold them in their daily practice.

In conceiving, understand the sustainability-related priorities and values of the leadership team and how it conveys the espoused organisational values through symbolic gestures and rituals. In the subsequent co-creating and cultivating activities, employ methods like a *Guiding Principles Review* or an *Identity and Policy Review* to provide a foundation to improve alignment across hierarchical levels and to ensure consistent ethical leadership with new interventions and strategies.

Experimentation, Gamification and Human-Systems Collaboration
The final set of overarching practices creates an inclusive and flexible culture for organisations to experiment, learn and embed sustainable innovation throughout the 3C framework activities.

12. EXPERIMENTATION

Experimentation[86] supports the testing of innovative solutions through small-scale trials, ensuring ideas are tested before scaling. It provides benefits such as discovery, rapid learning and low-cost, data-based validation of assumptions.

In conceiving, experiment with methods and practices on a small scale before scaling up those that prove effective throughout the entire organisation. In co-creating, promote employee *Experimentation* through methods such as *Ideation Contests and Markets* or *Values-Based Intrapreneurship*. In cultivating, foster sustainable innovation by establishing successful practices that originate from employee-led experiments.

13. GAMIFICATION

Gamification is an 'application of game design elements in nongame contexts'.[87] In an innovation management context, it creates transformative experiences that enhance employee awareness or capabilities or enable idea generation and experimentation to tackle grand challenges.[88]

In conceiving, help employees to understand their culture by having them interpret and apply otherwise abstract values in direct interaction, as in *Dilemma Games*. For instance, the Corporate Sustainability Dilemma game was designed to sensitise Deutsche Telekom employees to their corporate sustainability strategy by having them represent different stakeholder values in situations characterised by difficult decisions.[89]

In co-creating, stimulate the engagement of stakeholders, for instance, in *Ideation Contests and Markets*, such as the CEC Shoe Design Contest to co-design a shoe made of 100% biodegradable materials.[90]

In cultivating, integrate gamified formats into cultural artefacts, like physical environments, training and development materials or rituals. An example of that is the game Cool Choices, which engages employees in a six-month programme to gain points and badges for practicing sustainability-oriented behaviours.[91]

14. HUMAN-SYSTEMS COLLABORATION

This practice refers to new forms of collaboration and co-creating between humans and systems that mimic or simulate human intelligence, such as artificial intelligence, machine learning, natural language processing or robotics. A new culture of collaboration between humans and non-human artefacts emerges.

In conceiving, leverage *Human-Systems Collaboration* to understand status quo sustainability data and communication in relation to industry benchmarks. In co-creating, source a wide range of potential responses to challenges and unlock new forms of creativity in cultivating new approaches to drive sustainable innovation.

3.3.2 Digital Artefacts and Artificial Intelligence

Digital tools, media and platforms are powerful artefacts and levers not just to cultivate, but also to conceive and co-create sustainable innovation. Business intelligence and ESG software (designed to track and report environmental, social and governance data and initiatives) already provide indispensable tools for data collection and reporting as well as for forward-looking transformation planning and data-driven sustainability management.

New developments in generative language models and AI are able to enhance human learning and decision-making. A 2022 study by IBM reported that almost half of executive leaders were convinced AI would be an important lever for enhancing their sustainability performance and that companies with mature sustainability data capabilities outperformed competitors in financial figures of profitability, revenue growth and return on investment.[92]

AI is able to augment several practices and methods in the three stages of developing sustainability-oriented cultures.[93] We can expect that rapid developments in the digital modelling of practices will add to the following examples.

Conceiving current practices, AI can help to provide benchmarks and to spot inconsistencies in communication. AI-powered benchmarking platforms enable organisations to compare their sustainability practices against industry standards and good practices. Natural language processing can help to assess internal and external communications to gauge their alignment with sustainability goals. For instance, IBM's Watson (an AI that originated from innovation initiatives sparked by a *Values Jam*) can analyse sustainability reports and environmental metrics to help companies prioritise areas for improvement.[94]

Co-creating targeted interventions, generative AI and simulations like digital twins can generate a range of potential solutions before or as part of workshop settings, enriching results. From our own experiences, AI is already able to help design alternative workshop formats by drawing on *Gamification* design patterns,[95] and fine-tune exercises by helping anticipate potential stakeholder personas and their contributions and assessments. However, it is the expertise of an experienced workshop designer and facilitator that is required to select artificially generated options and to design an engaging flow that generates desirables outcomes and justifies the investment of human time and budget.

Cultivating practices, AI can be used in learning platforms to engage employees in *Mandatory Training* of sustainable innovation practices and methods. For instance, AI-driven solutions are used to capture knowledge from the workforce and transform it into engaging video, audio and text-based training programmes.[96]

Another example is Siemens's approach to preserve and systematise employee knowledge about corporate sustainability through AI-based semantic mapping.[97] *Innovation Impact Assessment* and *Result Chains* can be enhanced by tracking sustainability-related data and trends to ensure their alignment with long-term goals. For example, Microsoft uses AI to monitor its sustainability goals, automate reporting and refine long-term strategies through real-time analytics.[98]

Beyond the instrumental use of intelligent systems (which some would say are exploitative), new practices of collaboration and co-creating using artificial intelligence are just beginning to emerge.[99] A new culture of collaboration may evolve, one that recognises that the contributions of both sides are indispensable and lead to new forms of creativity and sustainability-oriented innovation practices and processes.

IN SUM

Several practices and methods are conducive to deliberately designing and developing a sustainable innovation culture. Methods provide formally described, replicable approaches to tackle recurring challenges, whereas practices refer to recurring, empirically observable actions that are performed by practitioners and constitute organisational culture. Overarching practices facilitate sustainable innovation across a range of activities, whereas more specific practices and methods can be associated with one of the three basic challenges in developing sustainable innovation culture: conceiving a culture, co-creating targeted interventions and cultivating new practices.

> Digital tools and media, collaborative platforms and intelligent systems provide mediating artefacts to enhance sustainability-oriented practices and methods.

In part II of the book we describe how to create virtuous cycles of 3C framework activities.

PART II

PRACTICES AND METHODS /
How to Create Sustainable Innovation Cultures

The 3C activities of conceiving, co-creating and cultivating make up a comprehensive framework of how to develop sustainable innovation cultures. Chapters 4–6 delve into each of these 3C activities, providing guidance on how to apply them using proven practices and methods. The choice of which practices and methods are most appropriate for an organisation depends on the challenges it is facing and on its own cultural makeup of values, practices and artefacts.

From the conceptual framework (section 3.1), we know that an organisation's culture is made up of three layers: shared notions, practices and artefacts. These layers of culture need to be aligned around values of sustainability if a sustainable innovation culture is to create economically, socially and environmentally regenerative outcomes in a repeatable and reliable manner.

These conceptual foundations now provide the main objectives for the 3C framework activities. Taken together, they also convey the conceptual model of what is essential in order to create a sustainable innovation culture. To simplify this overview, we distinguish between four dimensions that apply to each of the three 3C framework activities: notions (including the clarification of values and related tensions), practices (including the adoption of methods), artefacts (including the leveraging of official documents, software tools and physical environments) and consideration of outcomes in terms of sustainable innovation. The table below (table 1) provides an overview of the 3C activities and their objectives in terms of notions, practices, artefacts and outcomes.

	1. Conceiving (understanding) and reviewing the current culture	2. Co-Creating and validating interventions to redesign and transform culture	3. Cultivating and mainstreaming new practices across the organisation
NOTIONS	Understand prevalent values, how they are managed for innovation (maturity), and unresolved tensions between (stakehoder) values	Specify values, guiding principles and policies; resolve tensions and raise awareness	Mainstream values, principles and policies, and derive specify new business implications and innovation
PRACTICES	Identify values-action gaps	Explore new practices and methods to close values-action gaps	Establish new pract
ARTEFACTS	Identify existing and missing artefacts that mediate the mainstreaming of sustainability values and practices	Co-create new or improve existing artefacts	Introduce new artefacts
OUTCOMES	Translate insights on sustainable innovation challenges into task domains	Explore opportunities for sustainable innovation	Tap opportunities and drive sustainable innovation

TABLE 1. 3C framework activities and objectives in terms of notions, practices, artefacts and outcomes

To conceive an existing innovation culture, which more or less drives sustainable innovation, we need to understand what notions are considered desirable (values) and thought to be feasible and viable by important stakeholders. Conceiving a values-based innovation culture can start with reviewing guiding principles and policies, while attending to implicit tensions within the organisation's systems of priorities, between the values of different stakeholders and how values are managed for innovation (see maturity levels in section 3.1.3). With respect to practices, conceiving means identifying gaps between espoused values and innovation practices. On the level of artefacts, it means understanding which artefacts, either existing or needed, facilitate or hinder attempts to align practices with organisational values. Regarding desired outcomes, generating insights into values and related notions, practices and artefacts helps to identify challenges for sustainable innovation, which can then be translated into task domains for developing a sustainable innovation culture.

To co-create and validate interventions to transform a culture into a sustainable innovation culture, it is crucial to specify in detail and prioritise challenges and task domains. Depending on the findings of the conceiving activities in the first stage, notions, practices, artefacts and outcomes can be addressed with targeted interventions. Basic notions and values may have to be specified and guiding principles and policies revised. If major tensions stand in the way of effective collaboration for sustainable innovation, they need to be addressed and, if possible, further developed or reframed to inform cultural development. New practices can be explored by experimenting with new methods, and new artefacts can be created or existing ones improved to support the sustainability-oriented transformation. New opportunities for sustainable innovation can be explored to generate novel outcomes.

To cultivate sustainable innovation, the values and related notions, guiding principles and policies are then mainstreamed across the organisation, raising awareness and specifying implications for organisational management and innovation management. New practices are established that integrate proven methods and make use of new artefacts to foster sustainable innovation in a repeatable and reliable manner. Cultivating outcomes means professionalising sustainable innovation management in order to systematically tap new opportunities for sustainable value creation. Sustainable innovation culture is turned into a competitive advantage and a driver of positive impact, even beyond the boundaries of the organisation.

Practices and Methods Overview

**OVERARCHING PRACTICES TO DEVELOP
SUSTAINABLE INNOVATION CULTURES:**

(01) Resilience Development

(02) Moderation

(03) Knowledge Sharing

(04) Knowledge Management

(05) Inclusive Deliberation

(06) Reflexivity

(07) Anticipation

(08) Responsiveness

(09) Empowerment

(10) Decentralisation

(11) Symbolic Ethical Leadership

(12) Experimentation

(13) Gamification

(14) Human-System Collaboration

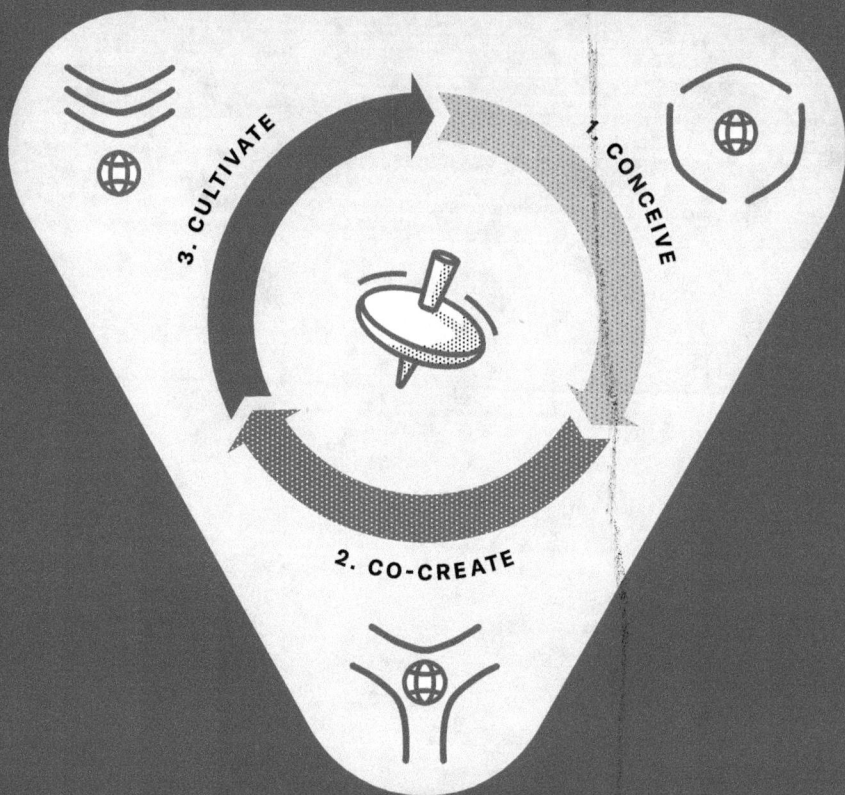

3. CULTIVATE

1. CONCEIVE

2. CO-CREATE

Conceiving

How can we conceive our existing culture – its basic notions and values, practices, and artefacts – as challenges for developing a sustainable innovation culture?

PRACTICES AND METHODS:

(15) Contextual Inquiry

(16) Cultural Surveys

(17) Mapping Competing Values

(18) Rapid Ethnography

(19) Memetics

(20) Focus Groups

(21) Sensemaking

(22) From Failure to Success

(23) Awareness Raising

(24) Appreciative Inquiry

(25) Dilemma Games

(26) Empathising

(27) Stakeholder Values Integration

(28) Co-construction

(29) Values Jam

(30) Identity and Policy Review

(31) Guiding Principles Review

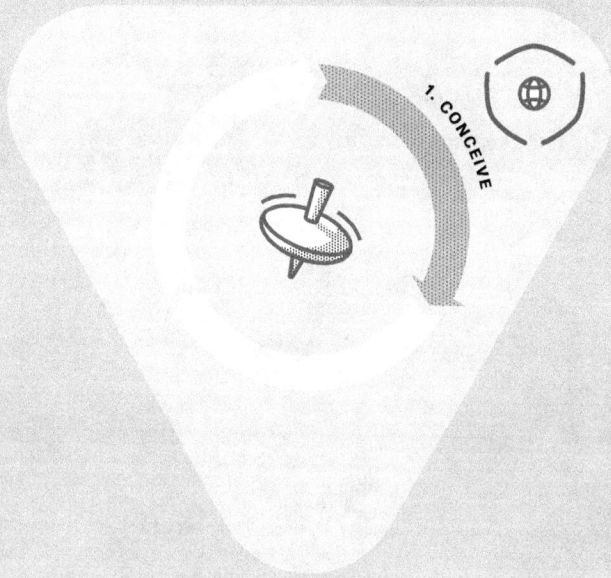

1. CONCEIVE

How can we identify implicit notions and values, practices, and artefacts to explain tensions and values-action gaps?

How can we reflect on and become more sensitive to proven practices and reoccurring challenges?

How can we review our values to better align them with changing stake-holder priorities and emerging sustainability challenges?

Co-creating

How can we use targeted interventions to address
sustainable innovation challenges, introduce new
practices, and explore opportunities?

PRACTICES AND METHODS:

(32) Values-Based Ideation and Assessment

(33) Facilitating Idea Management

(34) Sustainable Innovation Time

(35) Values-Based Intrapreneurship

(36) Ideation Contests and Markets

(37) Engaging in Open Innovation

(38) Lead User Integration

(39) Sustainable Market Creation

(40) Values-Based Business Modelling

(41) Engaging in Innovation Ecosystems

(42) Values-Based Ecosystem Modelling

(43) Sustainability Foresight

(44) Envisioning

(45) Backcasting

(46) Roadmapping

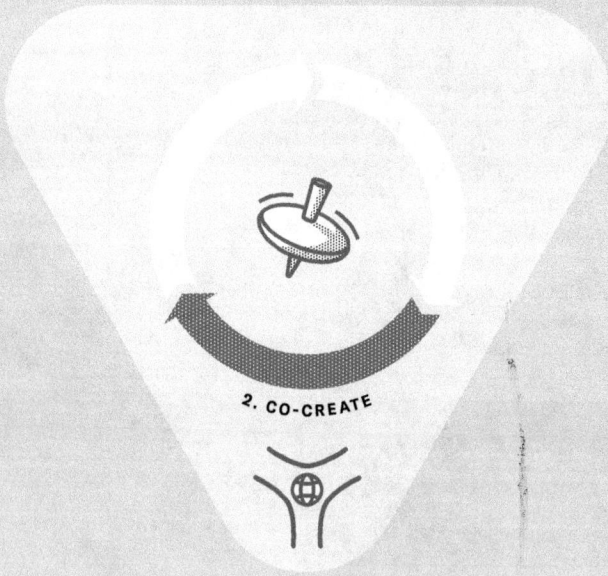

2. CO-CREATE

How can we engage employees to collaboratively drive sustainable innovation by experimenting with new methods and artefacts?

How can we engage external stakeholders in collaborative idea generation
and exploration of sustainable innovation practices?

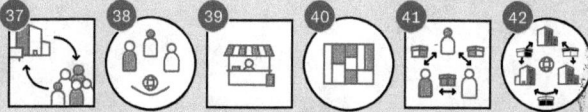

How can we proactively explore opportunities for sustainable innovation,
avoid unintended consequences, and enhance our resilience?

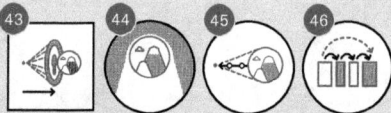

Cultivating

How can we cultivate virtuous circles that repeatedly
and reliably generate sustainable innovation as an
outcome and ultimately achieve the desired impact?

PRACTICES AND METHODS:

(47) Policy Communication

(48) Cultural Dictionary

(49) Tailored Communication

(50) Incentivisation

(51) Incentivisation Schemes

(52) Attracting the Right Talent

(53) Aspirational Narratives

(54) Human Resource Development

(55) Mandatory Training

(56) Inviting for Informal Exchange

(57) Off-Site Events

(58) Employee Resource Groups

(59) Participative Decision Making

(60) Stakeholder Advisory Board

(61) Management Systems

(62) Materiality Assessment

(63) Context-Based Reporting

(64) Results Chain

(65) Innovation Impact Assessment

(66) Sustainable Finance and Investment

(67) Life Cycle Cost Analysis

(68) Sustainable Innovation Financing

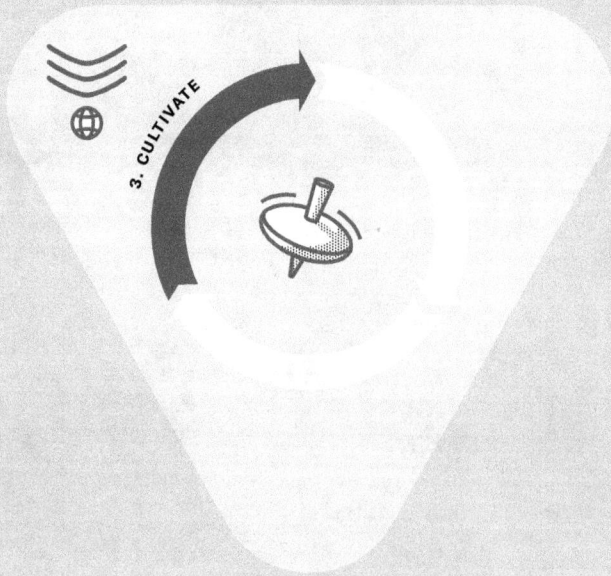

3. CULTIVATE

How can we mainstream values and related notions to promote sustainable innovation literacy and develop human resources to turn strategies into practice?

How can we promote sustainability-oriented collaboration, knowledge exchange and stakeholder engagement?

How can we professionalize practices and introduce artefacts that ensure the positive impact of innovation efforts?

Chapter 4 /
Conceiving Innovation
Cultures

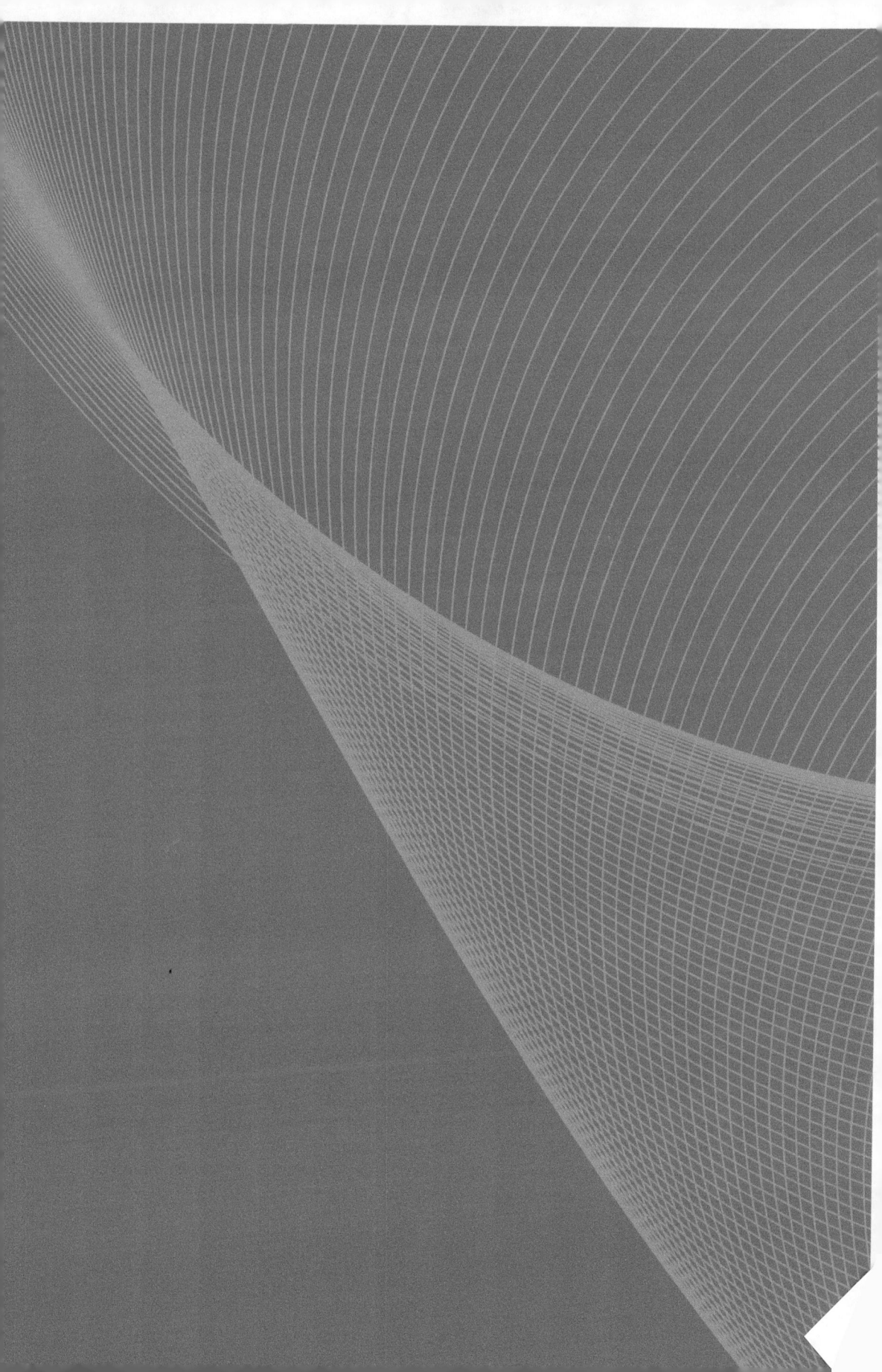

It is said that culture eats strategy for breakfast. But culture can also make innovation happen – and do it in a repeatable and reliable manner. Often enough an organisation's culture can both foster sustainable innovation and hinder it at the same time. Management's challenge is to enhance its contributions, while also raising awareness about the barriers keeping the existing culture from turning into a sustainable innovation culture. Its transformation starts with conceiving the existing innovation culture. This is the guiding question for this chapter.

> How can we conceive our existing culture – its basic notions and values, practices and artefacts – as challenges for developing a sustainable innovation culture?

For those that are a part of it, culture comes so naturally that it has been called our second nature. Yet we have to gain a fresh perspective on its guiding values, its embodied practices and material components so that we can see how it contributes to sustainable development and how it resists transformation. The term 'participatory observation' captures this approach nicely. Stay immersed and engaged in the ongoing flows of practices, but also take an observational distance, stepping back from the ordinary stream of consciousness and activity to reflect on what is going on. In this sense, participatory observation is not reserved for trained ethnographers, it also provides a basic approach for more lightweight methods to understand culture.[1]

In this chapter, we describe how ethnography is the most comprehensive methodology for conceiving sustainable innovation cultures (section 4.1). We share insights from our studies of European companies, summing up recurrent challenges and task domains for companies trying to put their sustainability strategies into practice when establishing a sustainable innovation culture. We explain in detail the ethnographic approach (section 4.2) and present proven practices and methods to understand sustainability-related notions, practices and artefacts as well as task domains for the development of a sustainable innovation culture.

4.1 Ethnographic Inquiry to Understand Values, Tensions and Gaps

Conceiving an organisational culture is not an easy task. Culture reveals itself in countless ways – for instance in official statements on websites and along the hallways of office buildings. Yet culture is not only about what people say or write. It is also about what people do in their daily work practices and how they respond to unforeseen developments. Culture is not self-evident, as people usually do not consciously experience their own culture as a culture. They know 'how things are done around here', but they often lack the reflective distance to perceive what makes up their particular organisational culture. This makes an external perspective invaluable to conceiving organisational culture.

4.1.1 Challenges in Conceiving Cultures

Although an external perspective can reveal otherwise hidden insights, outside researchers are not easily allowed to look below the surface of cultural performance and phenomena. Without a clear research strategy and appropriate methods, they will not be able to provide a reliable account of the organisational culture. In part this is due to an awareness that outsiders are visiting the organisation, which often causes its members to behave in line with social expectations rather simply proceed with their customary work practices. In other words, the exploration of an organisation's culture is already an intervention into its practices as it conveys expectations about what is desirable, often the organisations officially espoused values and goals.

Self-report methods are susceptible to other distorting factors such as social desirability and confirmation biases. Participants might, for example, exaggerate their organisation's commitment to values of sustainability because they believe that is what the researcher expects to hear. Or they feel obliged to comply with the organisation's official aspirations. Even if informants are conscious of social desirability biases and try their best to avoid them, their personal statements will provide only a limited perspective of the organisational culture. Sometimes, informants emphasise the importance of superficial cultural aspects because they seem interesting and overlook key aspects they regard as trivial.

For example, they might draw attention to a sporadic corporate event, such as a charitable fundraiser, while ignoring deeper norms about decision-making or collaboration that truly shape their culture. Sometimes, informants misinterpret characteristics of their department's or team's subculture as representative for the organisation's culture. For example, one team's highly competitive dynamic is generalised to the entire organisation. Moreover, informants will refrain from sharing their personal experiences and interpretations if the research situation makes them feel insecure. If they feel judged or worry about being seen as overly critical, they will avoid bringing up conflicts in the organisation, such as inconsistent sustainability efforts.

To overcome such challenges, researchers and practitioners need to follow a comprehensive and adaptable research strategy. The research design should comply with quality criteria for qualitative research to ensure comprehensibility, empirical grounding and reflected subjectivity.[2] Your own subjectivity serves as a resource for understanding culture, but you also need to critically reflect on your initial assumptions and potential biases. Building trust and ensuring informants feel at ease are essential to obtaining authentic and in-depth responses.

An accurate and nuanced understanding of cultural phenomena is facilitated by triangulating your sources of data, your methods of investigation and also researchers. This involves having empirical material collected and interpreted by different researchers. Methodological triangulation means combining, for instance, interviews with observations, with secondary data and analysis of artefacts.[3] Likewise, attention to values, practices and artefacts together with their challenges is key to conceiving organisational cultures. It involves understanding how employees interpret the publicly espoused values of the organisation as well as how they enact these values in daily practices. By exploring the conflicts or tensions they experience, we can understand how a culture can subvert efforts to attain a certain objective, such as achieving desirable outcomes from sustainable innovation efforts.

A fundamental challenge in conceiving cultures lays in identifying values-action gaps while recognising the boundaries for an organisation's sustainability performance. Environmental, social and economic thresholds set the boundaries, and a fair allocation of resources define the design space for innovation initiatives (see the *Context-Based Reporting* method and section 2.1.1). Gaining a contextual perspective on the company's degree of sustainability performance delivers a baseline against which the relevance and severity of values-action gaps can be understood, highlighting some for immediate intervention.

Authentic and transparent communication about the company's social and environmental impact creates awareness and a sense of urgency for the need to take corrective action. For instance, a company subscribing to values of sustainability needs to know its ecological thresholds so that it can determine what is a fair share of water resources for its factory. If there is a values-action gap in excessive water consumption, innovation initiatives can help the company reduce, replace or recycle water usage or regenerate the resource through wetlands or rainwater harvesting.

4.1.2 Ethnography as a Practice-Based Approach to Conceiving Values

Ethnography is an especially effective approach to understanding values, cultural tensions and values-action gaps together with their challenges for sustainable innovation. This is because ethnography sees values as intertwined with organisational practices and mediating artefacts. This approach differs from substantive and procedural approaches to analysing sustainability values in viewing values as interactive and dynamic 'lived realities' and not as 'ready-made entities' that can be found in policy agreements or self-reports.[4]

APPROACH 2. Substantive, Procedural and Practice-Based Approaches to Analysing Sustainability Values

Research into responsible and sustainable innovation management distinguishes between substantive, procedural and practice-based approaches to working with sustainability-related values, tensions and values-action gaps.[5] The *substantive approach* takes predefined values (e.g. the United Nations' Sustainable Development Goals) and applies them as criteria to assess how sustainable something is. There is a tension in the substantive approach

---

between treating values as entities that are stable or as adapting to changing societal conditions. The advantage to this approach for companies is that they can readily adopt values with broad political support as guidelines for sustainable innovation.

However, they still face the challenge of interpreting and realising these values in ways that are appropriate to their situation. For example, to safeguard public safety, businesses in sectors such as retail, aviation, event management and banking are increasingly adopting facial recognition systems.[6] However, they face serious difficulties in interpreting the right to privacy when applying such technologies.

The *procedural approach* identifies values and addresses the tensions between different interpretations of values by integrating the perspectives of a wide range of stakeholders and experts to find common ground. Instead of adopting predefined values, it endorses practices of *Inclusive Deliberation* and *Participatory Decision Making* or methods like *Co-construction* and *Stakeholder Advisory Boards* to determine which values should guide sustainable innovation. The procedural approach relies on the ability of stakeholders to reflect on their own values, articulate them openly and make compromises if they conflict.

Both the substantive and procedural approaches 'invite a conceptualisation of values as ready-made entities, at once knowable and available for deliberation. Whether they can be found in political documents or by interrogating stakeholders ... the moral hermeneutics of identifying values is ignored'.[7] *Practice-based approaches* recognise that values are dynamically realised in specific practices and can only be understood in interaction with their material, social and cultural environments. They cannot be simply drawn from policy agreements or found in the self-reports of stakeholders. Instead, values should be understood 'in action'[8] through interpretive methods such as case studies, *Focus Groups* or ethnographic inquiry.

4.1.3 Ethnographic Approaches

Ethnography is a method to describe and interpret a cultural or social group or system.[9] But it is more than just a methodology, it is a perspective that builds on particular commitments. As the British anthropologist Daniel Miller put it:

> 'Ethnography implies a commitment, first, to the people being studied; second, to understanding what people actually do, not just what they say they do; third, to study people in the context of their regular lives, not just a circumstance created by the researchers and, fourth, to understand people within the larger context of their lives, not just the context of the transaction under study.'[10]

Holism, the field as a unit of study, multi-method data collection and interpretative analysis requiring reflexivity on behalf of the researchers are all indispensable features of the ethnographic approach (see approach 3). This means it studies complex issues within their broader context, uses multi-method strategies like interviews, observation and analysis of secondary materials to explore environments, interpret patterns and symbols and reflect on the researcher's influence. With ethnographic methods, the researcher can uncover layers of cultural meaning that may not be obvious to the informants, exploring values, practices and experiences, artefacts and symbolic forms. They provide insights into otherwise latent or implicit values, tensions and values-action gaps.

APPROACH 3. Key Features of the Ethnographic Approach

- *Holism* refers to the ability to pull back from a specific problem, event or situation under study and address questions in a larger context. It focuses on a *field* of study and allows the researcher to unbundle complex, connected issues. Field research studies 'people in naturally occurring settings ... [to] capture their social meanings and ordinary activities, involving the researcher participating directly in the setting'.[11]
- *A multi-method research strategy* or 'style'[12] typically combines interviews with observation and attention to artefacts. Qualitative interviews with open questions and narrative stimuli to uncover the respondents' point of view are essential interview techniques. Participatory observation, as established by Kasper Malinowski[13] and William Whyte,[14] is the main data-collection technique. This means that observed activities unfold over time – even if the time span has been radically reduced from years and months (in ethnological studies) to hours or even minutes (in focused ethnography attending to specific courses of action). The technique requires researchers to gain an insider perspective by immersing themselves in the cultural environment.
- *Interpretation* conveys a deeper understanding of what has been observed by looking for patterns and generating insights from the field material. The language of informants and materials is studied to uncover the notions and practices of organisational culture, especially its insider slang, jargon, acronyms and specialised terms 'that are illustrative of the kinds of communities that organizations inhabit'.[15] Rituals, organisational symbols and artefacts such as architecture, furniture, tradition, meetings, images, events and clothing are also studied to make sense of the often unconscious enactments of cultural values.[16] Here, *Sensemaking* refers to the 'practise of cultural inquiry, a process based on a set of values'.[17]
- *Reflexivity* explores 'the ways in which [the] researcher's involvement with a particular study influence, acts upon and informs such research'.[18] The researcher's own experience in the field setting and their self-reflection are seen as an essential resource to generate insights.

Ethnography is now considered to be a valuable approach to new product development, as it 'provides perhaps the greatest insights and depth of knowledge into users' unmet and unarticulated needs, applications and problems. But the cost and time of conducting such research – essentially cultural anthropology – is considerable, while the skill set of the researchers must be high'.[19] These limitations have long hindered the expert use of ethnographic methods to analyse a company's innovation culture and draw conclusions about its strengths and weaknesses.

Moreover, in a case of organisational failure or a mismanaged sustainable innovation strategy, when quick actions are needed, there will not be enough time for extensive ethnographic research. In less time-sensitive situations, a deep dive into values and culture remains indispensable for organisations seeking to effectively deal with cultural tensions and values-action gaps and enhance their sustainable innovation performance. This raises the question how the ethnographic approach can be streamlined and still remain effective.

4.1.4 Rapid Ethnography

Rapid Ethnography[20] refocuses and standardises established ethnographic methods by providing templates and best practice examples[21] to help consultants and in-house practitioners quickly and effectively understand an organisation's culture. It enables organisations to accelerate their analysis while maintaining its quality, making it an ideal solution for smaller organisations or companies with a modest budget or time constraints. Companies can forgo extensive on-site visits and instead use qualitative interviews and interactive workshops with the leadership team to gather key insights for cultural development (see case 8 below). Larger organisations with more ambitious goals for sustainable innovation can implement *Rapid Ethnography* with the help of researchers, consultants or dedicated staff to draw on their experience in qualitative research.

> **CASE 8. Shortcut to Understanding and Reviving Brand Values in Mid-Sized Companies**
>
> *Rapid Ethnography* can be effectively used to review the business strategy of mid-sized companies. In one case we advised a family business preparing for a generational transition. The mid-sized company was losing its identity and brand values under the constraints of its operational business. We studied the company's history, values and purpose together with the challenges and potential for its future development as a company and its brands. Individual field interviews with shareholders and top executives were documented as profiles and prepared the ground for a collaborative redefinition of the company's core values and mission.
>
> In a two-day co-creating workshop, we discussed the profiles and the different assumptions about the values and passion, the potential and the business model of the firm.[22] We were then able to help the company realign

its diverse values among the key decision-makers and redefine its mission and mid-term innovation strategy. Field interviews and the individual profiles helped us find common ground and commitment. Feedback from the participants was unanimous that a greater awareness and shared understanding about the fundamental notions and values of the firm was created as well as an actionable framework for mid-term innovation development. As a result, a new innovation strategy was consolidated with revised priorities for new product, brand and business model development.

4.1.5 Ethnographic Insights

Before we provide an overview of *Rapid Ethnography* and its techniques, we will sum up the overarching insights into sustainable innovation cultures that we found in a large-scale comparative European study involving companies from Germany, Italy, Poland and Spain. In each of the four countries we identified values and practices as well as tensions and values-action gaps that helped or hindered turning sustainable innovation strategies into daily practice. These insights indicate recurring challenges that European companies are facing today and the task domains needed for establishing values-based and sustainable innovation cultures (chapters 7–10 present the country-specific cases).

CASE 9. Insights into Sustainable Innovation Challenges and Practices from a Comparative European Study

The project IMPACT: Establishing Values-Based Innovation Cultures for Sustainable Business brought together academic and industrial partners from Germany, Italy, Poland and Spain to explore the intricate dynamics of the ongoing sustainability transformation in European firms. Universities from Berlin, Florence, Kraków and Madrid joined forces and worked with eleven sustainability-oriented companies to delve deep into their values-based and sustainability-related cultural development.

Through 36 extensive field interviews, a wealth of ethnographic data was generated, including audio and film recordings, photographs and online materials and transcripts. Its iterative aggregation, analysis and interpretation yielded insights into recurring challenges, tensions and values-action gaps in mastering sustainability transformation. We also found promising practices to address these challenges. Six overarching insights challenged our initial assumptions about how companies develop a sustainable innovation culture.

1. SUSTAINABLE INNOVATION LITERACY:
We *thought* that sustainable innovation practices would be purposely built into the organisational culture step-by-step, based on shared values and

goals. But we *found* that existing notions and practices and an unevenly shared sustainable innovation literacy often stand in the way of bold collaboration around shared values and goals. In some companies, a strategic orientation towards sustainability was just beginning to emerge.

For instance, sustainability impact was first assessed after innovation projects showed profitability or conventional projects with higher returns were prioritised over sustainability-focused initiatives. Companies from Germany and Spain recognised the need to enhance sustainable innovation literacy by shifting from their solution-oriented engineering mindset towards a problem-focused, human-centric approach to innovation. However, their employees struggled to shift from a risk-averse, hard science-driven research and development towards learning from failure. *Experimentation* with sustainability values and criteria was used to drive ideation and innovation development and improve sensitivity in dealing with diverse stakeholders.

In each company, we noticed that terms like sustainability were interpreted in diverse ways, with some respondents equating it with ecology, while others focused on social issues or favoured a triple-bottom line framework and still others opposed such balancing approaches and highlighted system value creation within the Earth's carrying capacities.

Addressing the challenge of differing degrees of sustainability literacy requires organisations to cultivate a sustainability orientation, an innovation mindset and shared knowledge of key concepts and skills. In some cases, promising measures to mainstream sustainable innovation literacy and foster effective collaboration were already in place. For instance, a German company (chapter 7) offering inspection services and certification in domains such as mobility, training, IT, engineering, mining and aerospace, among others conducted *Awareness Raising* events to better learn from failure. *Mandatory Trainings* trained employees with an engineering background in soft skills and analytical techniques to expand the pool of solutions. In an Italian firm we saw a *Cultural Dictionary* that defined fundamental concepts and showcased their implications and the desired behaviours needed to promote core values and ambitions.

2. VERTICAL INTEGRATION:

We *thought* that bottom-up initiatives would be encouraged to feed into an actionable strategy and a clear normative framing. But we *found* deep divides between hierarchical levels, with the base often unaware of strategic goals and the top disregarding bottom-up initiatives.

Misalignments between hierarchical levels can desynchronise efforts to advance sustainable innovation. In several cases, sustainability-related values and innovation strategies were promoted by senior management, while operational staff were not fully aware or interpreted them in their own idiosyncratic ways in daily practices. Conversely, innovative sustainability initiatives from the operational levels struggled to gain recognition and support from senior and middle-level managers. For instance, proposals to adopt local sources of regenerative energy or improve the resource and energy efficiency of IT system were lost in administrative proceedings.

Vertical integration enables sustainability values and strategies to flow seamlessly from leadership to operational levels, while also encouraging grassroots initiatives to enrich sustainable innovation strategy. For example, *Employee Resource Groups* promote vertical integration by engaging employees from different hierarchical levels in regular meetings on sustainability issues. We found examples of such resource groups in Spain, Germany and Italy.

3. HORIZONTAL INTEGRATION:

We *thought* that expertise would be shared across a broad range of functions and departments to empower sustainability transformation. But we *found* that divergent interests and interpretations of values hamper multilateral collaboration and knowledge exchange.

Companies operating across multiple industries, regions, markets or types of expertise can empower different organisational units to synergise their competencies to more comprehensively address sustainability challenges. However, internal boundaries in large firms in Germany, Spain and Italy challenged sustainability-oriented collaboration and innovation management. In Germany, subsidiaries were incentivised to achieve short-term goals rather than find opportunities to collaboratively engage towards shared values and common goals. In Spain, science-based companies struggled with their internal specialisation that had led to departments working in silos, each focusing on a specific part of research and development. This resulted in diverging interpretations and objectives, making it harder to collaborate across teams and achieve sustainability goals.

Horizontal collaboration and communication require systematic approaches that foster interdisciplinary, consensus-based and community-inspired interactions. The German inspection company, for example, initiated peer-to-peer sustainability reviews on *Innovation Impact Assessments* to dismantle silos and promote *Knowledge Sharing*. In Spain, the two science-based companies initiated online communities for sustainability *Knowledge Sharing*, some officially supported by the organisation and others initiated by motivated employees on corporate social media platforms.

4. ECOSYSTEM ENGAGEMENT:

We thought that sustainability-oriented companies would lead transformation efforts across corporate and institutional ecosystems. But we found that engagement in sustainable innovation networks is left to local or personal initiatives – rather than being pursued as a unified strategy.

Conflicting stakeholder interests, untapped collaboration opportunities with market and non-market actors and the need to enhance legitimacy pose significant challenges to advancing sustainable innovation at the ecosystem level. In Poland, we found conflicts between contractors and subcontractors

that prevented efficient collaboration for the development of water management innovations, for example, when subcontractors tried to complete the
project as quickly and as cheaply as possible. In Germany and Italy, companies hoped to enhance their legitimacy with customers and suppliers by drawing on shared values. However, we found numerous occasions of untapped
potential to exchange benefits and leverage opportunities with partners from
academia, public institutions or non-governmental organisations.

While these challenges were widespread, companies in our study also
demonstrated dynamic capabilities by introducing practices and methods
for ecosystem engagement. For instance, the German inspection company
adopted practices like *Engaging in Open Innovation* to strategically select
B2B customers whose sustainability strategies align with its own. This helped
to strengthen the company's legitimacy as a sustainability-oriented organisation.[23] Together with selected managers, we engaged in *Values-Based
Ecosystem Modelling* and reviewed trends, desirable stakeholder relations
and sustainability drivers to envision sustainability-oriented ecosystems (see
chapter 7).

5. PRACTICES AND METHODS:

We *thought* that new practices and methods would be continuously tried,
evaluated and adapted to drive sustainable innovation. But we *found* that
mainstreaming new approaches is a conflictual process needing careful moderation, as is clarifying normative and conceptual frameworks for sustainable
innovation.

To establish effective practices and methods, companies need to provide
backing from *Human Resource Development*. Companies need to recognise
and formalise effective informal or local practices. However, in the inspection company we found that several tools and techniques were only used by
individual experts to promote their own sustainability agenda. Local experiments with peer-reviewing findings from formal *Innovation Impact Assessments* were awaiting approval for wider adoption. Likewise, we saw that the
Employee Resource Groups, originally introduced by a project manager in a
large Spanish science-based conglomerate, had been successfully integrated
across several departments.

To mainstream methods, practices and associated artefacts such as key
value indicators (see case 5: section 3.1.3) or other assessment criteria, companies need to tailor them to specific functions.

6. HIDDEN TREASURES:

We *thought* that the personal motivation of employees would be translated
into effective contributions to corporate strategic and normative goals. But we
found that strong values-based motivations of employees were not leveraged
for driving sustainable innovation and cultural transformation.

Unrecognised generational differences, personal values and informal
relationships can create challenges to sustainable innovation. Yet these same

factors often conceal the hidden treasures of a diverse workforce personally motivated to promote sustainability.

For example, at the German inspection company, we noticed that several of our respondents had joined the organisation with an idealistic desire to become part of the solution rather than part of the problem. These employees brought up several initiatives, for instance, to implement emission-free infrastructure (such as solar panels on facility rooftops or energy-efficient IT systems) or used informal communication to promote, for instance, the system value approach (see section 2.1.1). However, the sustainability-oriented engagement of such employees often outpaced the organisation's ability to implement their innovative solutions.

By celebrating employee ideas and success stories in sustainable innovation and by engaging employees in co-creating workshops and fostering their participation, organisations can unlock the hidden treasure of a strongly motivated workforce. New practices and methods can help tap into this resource, generating sustainable innovation and even leading to 'climate staying', where employees choose to remain with companies that demonstrate strong environmental values, sustainable practices and a commitment to addressing climate change.[24]

4.2   How to Understand One's Own Culture

There are a number of reasons to believe that a more systematic approach to questions of innovation culture is worth the effort. Many organisations think ahead and invest in sustainable development before they are driven by external factors. Some simply want to increase their sustainability impact and competitiveness. Sometimes requests from important customers or clients, employee surveys or reports point to neglected opportunities for innovation and increased competitiveness. Sometimes failed innovation projects, unpromising market conditions a generational change or a merger force a company to act. Or the initiative can come from the executive board or from individual departments for strategy, innovation, research and development, HR or corporate social responsibility. As a rule, when a new project is first discussed, there is a realisation that it will also entail difficulties. Even if the project has potential, it may be better not to commit to it prematurely and thereby miss out on an opportunity for a more profound transformation.

A critical view of culture begins with the realisation that no one yet sufficiently understands the innovation culture and its challenges, nor the alignment between sustainability-related notions, practices and artefacts.

Understanding a culture is not a trivial matter and requires dedicated effort with expert approaches before setting up a project and appointing a lead team. Their first step is to clarify the status quo, understand the actual values of the organisation in everyday practice and identify tensions between values and interest groups together with values-action gaps. They must also recognise the value of what is already in place if the desired transformation is to become a more resilient and sustainable organisation.

Once the need for inquiry into the current, sustainability-related innovation culture has been recognised, the project has to be defined, specifying the necessary steps and methodological options available and then funding them. *Rapid Ethnography* provides a structured approach to understanding innovation cultures, comprising four tasks or steps: framing, accessing, investigating and interpreting. These steps are also applicable to other methods of understanding culture, such as *Mapping Competing Values, Memetics, Focus Groups, Cultural Surveys* and *Sensemaking* (see section 4.3).

By following these four steps (figure 5), you can gain reliable insights into an innovation culture, along with its challenges and proven practices. A toolbox with templates, techniques and a card-based set of instructions are available online to support this process.[25]

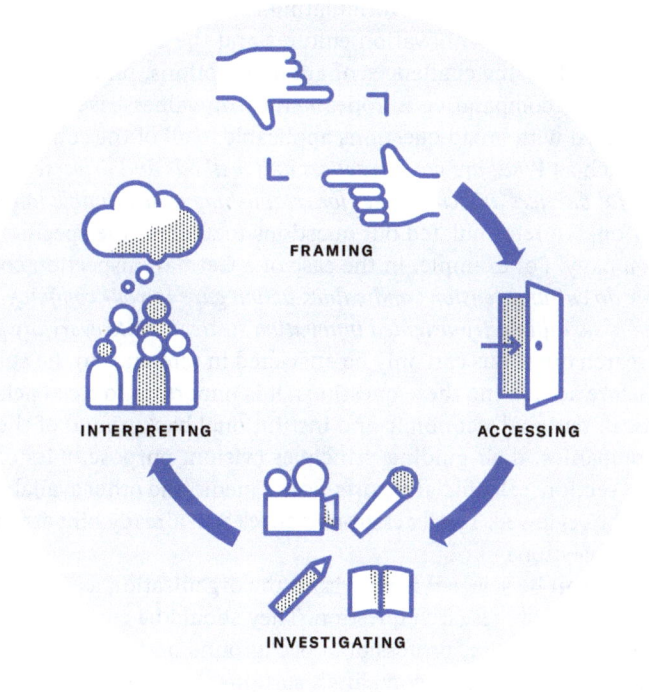

FRAMING

ACCESSING

INVESTIGATING

INTERPRETING

FIGURE 5. Four steps to understanding culture

4.2.1 Framing Culture

An ethnographic inquiry starts with framing a research question to define the project and its purpose, providing both researchers and their informants with direction, focus and coherence. The research question should be grounded in the ethnographic approach and relate to the holistic nature of organisational culture. Research questions are not questions put to informants, but the basis of a research plan. Usually, there are one or two primary research questions, which are subdivided into further questions. They should be increasingly specific yet have enough detail so they can be clearly understood. They should not exceed the time and resources available.

Qualitative research allows for questions to develop or even change over the course of the study.[26] In a business setting, managers often articulate rather narrow questions that will need to be translated by the researcher into broader terms to address the viewpoints of stakeholders. For example, in one study the consultants went from their customers' questions *How do we sell sports equipment?* to *What are sports?* and from *What toys do kids want?* to *What is the role of play?*[27] Elizabeth Briody, working at General Motors, went from *How can GM's effectiveness be improved?* to *What issues do its workers face? How can their work lives be made better?*[28] In other cases, as the project progresses broad questions that allow informants to address a wide range of topics are narrowed down to capture specific levers for cultural development.

Initial points of reference for formulating research questions are provided by the focus on sustainable innovation cultures and the conceptual 3C framework (chapter 3) as well as the challenges of aligning notions, practices, artefacts and outcomes. In our comparative European study on values-based innovation cultures, we started with broad questions applicable to all of the companies in a generic way, such as *What are good practices and methods and drivers? And what are organisational barriers and challenges for establishing a sustainable innovation culture?* Later on, we reformulated our questions to address the specific challenges of each company. For example, in the case of a German inspection company we asked: *How do cultural tensions and values-action gaps in your company impede the translation of sustainability-oriented innovation strategies into everyday practice?*

The research questions can only be answered in reference to the culture being studied. Before addressing these questions, it is important to step back and grasp the historical, national, economic and institutional background of the organisation. In companies, their guiding principles (vision, purpose, mission and core values – see section 3.1), official reports, social media and other available information should be reviewed. This background check will already hint at who can best answer your questions.

Informants can be selected from within the organisation as well as from outside depending on the research question. They should be chosen carefully to ensure diversity of expertise, professional background and areas of responsibility. In our study of an inspection company's sustainable innovation culture, we had a number of criteria for selecting informants. They had to be sufficiently knowledgeable about the subject matter, based on their first-hand experiences; innovation and sustainability had to be part of their job profile; and they needed to represent diverse perspectives from different hierarchical levels, business units, innovation-related functions and locations and length of employment. We complemented personal recommendations from our primary contacts in management with snowball sampling.[29] A total of nine informants allowed us to get a nuanced view of their sustainability-related innovation culture.

The final framing task consists in developing interview, observation and data-collection guides as well as templates for documenting the data in brief profiles for each informant. A semi-structured interview guide ensures that key research questions are addressed. For example, for our analysis of the inspection company's culture we designed an interview guide for 2–4-hour field interview sessions, with top-level questions that were mandatory and sub-questions that were optional. They covered the following five main topics: 1) personal background and history in the company, 2) interpretation and prioritisation of corporate values, 3) practices and experiences with innovation projects, 4) relationship between sustainability-related values and innovation management and 5) future outlook.

We included interactive exercises and staged activities in the interview guide that streamlined the process of understanding the culture within a limited time in the field (see approach 5 below). We used the structure of the interview guide to create a guide to conducting observations that would supplement the verbal material from the interviews. This guide also focused on identifying artefacts such as working tools and media as well as illustrations, visualisations, templates, presentations and site-specific installations. The structure of the interview and observation guides was used as a template to document informant profiles.

4.2.2 Accessing Culture

Thorough planning is essential before accessing the field, including determining when, where and how informants will be contacted, interviewed and observed as well as how interactions will be recorded. Good preparation optimises field time and enables open-ended and exploratory follow-up questions to be asked. Reviewing online information and making a preparatory call provide information on your informant's position and responsibilities in the company. Preparatory tasks can also be given to informants to help them mentally prepare for the interview.

A key challenge when accessing the field is to reassure respondents about the process and objectives of the study so they are willing to share information, including personal stories and points of view, without fear of judgement or negative consequences. Whether consciously or unconsciously, they may conceal their personal thoughts and feelings, negative interpretations of the organisation's espoused values or illustrative stories from their own work experience. It is therefore essential to inform them before the interview that their personal viewpoints are sought and that their contributions will be anonymised and used only for research purposes. A mutual non-disclosure agreement should also be signed, documenting their consent to audio and video recording. Moreover, guidelines and techniques can be employed to help informants feel more comfortable sharing their subjective feelings, desires and needs, which they might otherwise hide behind a mask of objectivity and corporate jargon[30] (see approach 4 below).

Not every research design requires extensive field observation, nor must every informant be observed. As work practices and findings move online, ethnographic observers are following.[31] Going online reduces time and costs and facilitates reviewing digital materials such as company reports or strategy presentations. However, online observation has significant limitations. The observer can only see what their respondent shows and non-verbal cues such as body language and changes in the environment are often hard to see or blended out.

Building rapport is difficult if it has not already been established in a previous personal meeting. Online interviews also require suitable devices and software, with substantial preparation to ensure good audio and video quality. Hands-on activities can be conducted using well-prepared templates on collaboration platforms (like Mural or Miro). In any case, in an online setting, the quality of data – and your findings – depends to a greater extent on your and your respondent's skills in using digital media.

APPROACH 4. Guidelines and Techniques for Ethnographic Observers

YOUR INFORMANT IS IN CHARGE: Follow what your informants mention as relevant. When you are asked to delete, show or filter sensitive information, do so.

BLEND IN: When people feel observed they tend to behave unnaturally. When interviewing, keep busy (e.g. taking notes or dealing with the camera), make eye contact and use an open body language to put your informants at ease. Dressing appropriately allows you to avoid attracting attention to yourself.

LOOK AT THE BIG PICTURE: Do not focus exclusively on your research questions. Look at your respondents' workplace and working habits, how they have arranged their desk and office furniture, what tools and software they use, how they spend their breaks and what clothing they wear.

MOVE ABOUT: Change physical and social settings to prompt different associations that help your informant share relevant information and break away from superficial conversations.[32] For instance, start the interview in your respondent's office, take a tour through the facilities and end the conversation in a meeting room or cafeteria. Another strategy is to accompany your informant during a working day or a project, moving with them between locations.

KEEP IT SIMPLE: Formulate clear and simple questions that your informants can relate to. Avoid complicated sentences and expert terminology or packing different questions into one.

PARAPHRASE AND SUMMARISE: After the field interview, summarise the key takeaways from the conversation and ask your respondent to correct you and share any additional thoughts.

RECORD: When accompanying your respondent in the firm, take close-up shots of the things and objects they use or show them along with other relevant items in the work environment. Do not be shy about taking pictures or video of the respondent and their workspace. It becomes natural if it is done casually during the conversation. Keep an audio recorder running throughout the whole interview.

4.2.3 Investigating Culture

Field interviews are the key methodology of *Rapid Ethnography*. They are conducted with the help of semi-structured interview and observation guides and are recorded through audio, video and field notes. Conducting field interviews demands flexibility rather than rigid scripts. Interview guides serve as frameworks to ensure that key topics are covered, allowing to let the conversation flow naturally and respondents to share their perspectives freely. Structured questionnaires narrow the range of possible answers the respondent can give, while open-ended questions encourage them to share their perspectives and experiences, thereby making their world accessible to researchers. As participants in the situation, the researcher also observes the situated actions and behaviour of their respondent.[33]

Several techniques help to streamline the field interview approach to uncover insights into values, tensions, practices and values-action gaps. These include structured observations, diaries for self-observation, open-ended questions, specification questions, tour questions, laddering, meeting protocols, protocols of thinking aloud, mapping tools, roleplay, card sorting, 'heaven and hell' and evocative objects (approach 5).

APPROACH 5. Techniques to Streamline Field Interviews and Observations

STRUCTURED OBSERVATIONS: Direct your attention to emotional reactions, tone of voice, insider jargon, body language, untypical behaviours and interactions with artefacts. Use an observation guide and make notes. For example: *Are there any artefacts (e.g. office layout, posters, documents) or other items of interest in your respondent's environment that are relevant to your research questions? What is their significance? How does your respondent relate to them or interact with them?*

DIARIES FOR SELF-OBSERVATION: Provide respondents with materials like diaries, physical or online templates and ask them to document their experiences and reflections related to sustainable innovation over a period at regular intervals or when prompted through a messaging app or in hindsight. For example: *Each day, please take a picture of something that you associate with sustainable innovation. Please comment on how far it facilitates or hinders your daily work.*

GENERATIVE QUESTIONS: Take some time to familiarise yourself with your informant. Clarify the goals of the interview and start with open-ended questions to understand your respondent's viewpoint. Ask clear questions for detailed information, for instance, on their career biography. These questions act as 'narrative stimuli', prompting informants to share an equally detailed personal story. For example: *Please tell me the whole story of your career in the company. How did you start, what were your first assignments and what were some of the milestones in your career? What are some challenges that you have been facing and what successes have you experienced?*

SPECIFICATION: Gradually move from general to specific questions about sustainable innovation practices and cultural tensions. *What is important to you in your professional life? What else do you care about with respect to your work? How would others characterise you? What matters to you?* followed by *What are typical practices in your organisation that further sustainable innovation? Why do you think that is? Can you give me an example?*

EXEMPLIFICATION: Ask respondents to provide specific examples and stories that illustrate key notions such as the official values. This clarifies how values are revealed in practice and how their interpretations converge or diverge. Ask about times when values were violated, as that is often when a value first becomes evident. For example: *Can you describe a situation where the company's values influenced a project you worked on?* or *Have you experienced a situation where you felt your organisation's values were challenged?*

TOUR QUESTIONS: Ask your respondent to give you a tour of the most important places around their work area.[34] Draw attention to spaces and artefacts somehow related to the values they mentioned in the interview to learn about how sustainability-related values find their way into everyday practices or face obstacles. For example: *Could you please show me where you discuss or work on innovation with others?*

LADDERING: Elicit values and decision-making structures by probing deeper into your respondents' answers. For instance, start by asking about a specific work situation. Then follow up by referring to key aspects of their story to ask why they consider them important. Keep probing with why-questions to uncover a hierarchy of implicit motives and basic values. For example: *Please tell me about a sustainable innovation project you were involved in. What were, from your perspective, the main criteria to determine the project's success? Do you consider these criteria important? And if so, why?*

MEETING PROTOCOLS: Ask permission to join meetings where innovation is discussed. Meetings provide a structured environment to observe social interactions and decision-making processes, revealing how sustainable innovation topics are prioritised and addressed. They also often provide structured outputs, such as notes on whiteboards, to complement your notes. For example: *During its weekly meeting, the team spent significant time discussing the new eco-friendly packaging initiative. The enthusiasm of the project lead was at odds with the finance department's concerns about costs. This revealed cultural tensions between departments prioritising the environmental impact of innovations and those focused on financial pragmatism. Several negotiation strategies were used to find common ground, such as phased implementation and less costly materials.*

THINKING ALOUD PROTOCOLS: Ask respondents to verbalise their thoughts, reasoning and decision-making processes while interacting with specific artefacts, such as guiding principles and policy statements, reports and documents or software tools related to sustainable innovation. By articulating their thoughts, respondents reveal part of their mental processes and personal interpretations. For example: *Please think aloud while you review this excerpt from a sustainability report. Tell me what comes to mind, why certain parts stand out and how you interpret the information.* or *Please fill in this sustainability assessment form for this new innovation project and think aloud while you are doing it.*

MAPPING TOOLS: Visual templates like onion diagrams or mood curves help you understand the emotion-laden nature of values and the obstacles and turn them into reality. For instance, mood curves provide information on what mattered to your respondent in the past. For example: *Can you point out critical moments – highlights and lowlights – in your experience with sustainability initiatives in your organisation? From the settling-in period, your work in different positions, up to your future expectations? Map these critical moments on the template and link them together with a line.*[35] *You can also ask respondents to draw an inventory map of the artefacts most relevant for their work on sustainable innovation.*

ROLEPLAY: Ask your respondent to enact the values of stakeholders. Provide them with cards or other cues that indicate typical characteristics of these roles, such as typical behaviours, values, needs or other characteristics. Roles can represent internal or external stakeholder groups, stereotypes like a good and bad cop or conceptual roles like the dreamer, realist or spoiler (in the Disney brainstorming method).[36] Roleplay can assign a devil's advocate role to your informant and ask for a critical response to officially espoused values. For example: *Let's roleplay a situation where you are a climate activist who publicly criticises your company for greenwashing. Roleplay and responses can reveal inconsistencies that respondents perceive in their organisation's* *sustainable innovation strategy, as well as their ideas for addressing such challenges. They can also convey how your respondent interprets their organisation's values when assuming a critical perspective.*

CARD SORTING: Card sorting builds on spatial perceptions of proximity, distance and direction to convey relations between different items. Your informants can put the cards into different contexts, interact with them and move them around. Cards make abstract statements more tangible. For example: *Here are some cards with the official, sustainability-related values of your company and other values that you've mentioned so far. Can you sort them in order of relative importance to your work from top to bottom and keep those that you see as related close to each other. Please explain why you've put each card where it is and how it relates to the others.*

HEAVEN AND HELL: This exercise asks respondents to imagine extreme, exaggerated developments in their company to tap into deep concerns, fears and far-reaching hopes. It usually starts with 'hell', when respondents are asked to share their thoughts about how the current situation (e.g., previously identified value-action gaps) could significantly worsen and what would be the absolute worst thing that could happen. Then they are asked to imagine 'heaven' on Earth as a state in which all challenges and constraints no longer exist – in terms of power, time, budget and anything else you can think of. For example: *What would be the worst-case scenario if current issues are not addressed? and What things look like if your organisation's values were all implemented? No matter how ideal or radical?*

EVOCATIVE OBJECTS: This technique can be used to close the session. Give your respondent an object that encourages imaginative thinking about innovation and change. Follow up with questions to clarify the relation between the object and your respondent's desires or concerns. For example: *Take this magic wand. It gives you the power to make your wish come true. Take some time to think about it and then tell me what you would wish to change in your company to make it more innovative. If there is anything here that is related to that wish, hold the magic wand over it.*

In addition to interview and observational data, secondary materials (such as internal documents) can be collected in the field or from publicly available sources. These materials can reveal information about an organisation's espoused values. They can be sourced from the company's official website, social media channels, scientific and journalistic publications, job postings, advertisements, podcasts and so on. Internal documents include presentations, strategic roadmaps, scorecards, innovation assessments and much more.

This secondary material can then be triangulated with interview and observational material to provide different perspectives on something of interest in your research. It can be used to reveal and compensate for unconscious or self-serving biases that may arise when informants try to cover up tensions between espoused values and values enacted in organisational practices.

In our comparative European study on values-based innovation cultures, we collected over 60 hours of field interview video and audio recordings, hundreds of photos and extensive field notes, which we systematically organised into 36 informant profiles. Coding techniques for content analysis, such as discourse analysis or historical analysis, were used to analyse and compare these materials. Qualitative data analysis software such as Atlas.ti, MaxQDA or NVivo[37] is available to document and analyse empirical findings.

4.2.4 Interpreting Culture

The final step in ethnographic inquiry consists in the systematic interpretation of empirical materials. Four tasks build on one another: storytelling sessions, pattern recognition, insight synthesis and ethnographic writing. Together they ensure that your understanding of a culture is grounded in empirical evidence, allowing the researcher to identify and prioritise critical issues that facilitate or hinder the cultivating of sustainable innovation.

STORYTELLING SESSION

A storytelling session kicks off the collaborative process of interpretation. Field researchers, and sometimes stakeholder representatives, work together to analyse the data and code relevant findings. The storytelling session enables triangulation, validation of individual findings and the establishment of an empirically based common ground within the research team. As a preparation, printouts of the informants' profiles are put up on the wall or in an online collaboration platform. Researchers take turns presenting the profiles, sharing empirical material collected in the field. Each researcher highlights particular observations, drawing on informant stories, visual recordings or quotes from secondary material such as internal documents.

The focus is on how the material relates to notions, tensions or values-action gaps (see examples in table 2 below). During the presentations, the rest of the team codes findings into brief, self-explanatory sticky notes. The notes address questions such as *What do you find interesting, new or surprising about each profile? What did you learn from this informant? What motivates him or her? and What is he or she struggling with?*

After each presentation, the sticky notes are attached to the profiles for discussion and further questioning. A facilitator keeps time and ensures that the notes provide diverse perspectives but remain empirically grounded. This process enriches the profiles with the researcher highlighting relevant aspects and focusing attention on subsequent steps. Collaborative coding and the subsequent clustering and analysis of material can be done online using software tools.

PATTERN RECOGNITION

The next step is pattern recognition. It involves identifying recurring issues and themes in the documented data and across the profiles. This step is based on a process called 'formal indication', which involves creative and analytical conversations to interpret the findings and cluster them into overarching topics.[38] Researchers organise all of the sticky notes into clusters, naming each cluster to reflect the pattern it contains. Together these clusters address questions such as: *What is interesting or surprising? What happens again and again? What are the main differences and similarities between the findings?* (see examples in table 2 below). These patterns serve as the basis for developing overarching insights in the next step.

INSIGHT SYNTHESIS

Insight synthesis explores and prioritises the resulting patterns in terms of shared desires and values together with the tensions or values-action gaps experienced by the informants. *Sensemaking* helps to streamline the ethnographic interpretation towards identifying overarching insights and determining which aspects are subordinate. Each overarching insight describes a fundamental tension between desires and values on the one hand and opportunities for fulfilment on the other. The session participants address questions such as: *What underlies each pattern? What is of overarching importance for the informants? What contributes to answering our research questions?*

To generate meaningful insights, researchers analyse the sticky notes and patterns to identify interrelated findings that are highly relevant to the research question. For a finding to qualify as an overarching insight, it must combine three key attributes:

1. *Subjective relevance:* It must describe fundamental characteristics of the informant's emotions and behaviours from their point of view.
2. *Explanatory power:* It must explain the underlying reasons behind the patterned aspects of their statements and behaviours.
3. *Tensions:* It must articulate tensions between the informants' desires and values on one hand and adverse circumstances on the other.

In our projects, we formulate ethnographic insights as configurations of the desires, values and tensions found in the field material. A useful formula is: '*I want to* do something *so that* some underlying values, *but* another party or an adverse circumstance is not allowing me to do so.' Desires represent a situated wish to do, be or have something. They create compelling motivations for actions that are not central to one's identity.[39] Values, on the other hand, as 'second order desires',[40] stand for persistent and identity-relevant notions of the desirable. They relate situated desires to personal ideals and cultural norms. Such values act as the foundation and motivating force for action. Finally, tensions arise when one's desires or values are at odds with other values or external factors that prevent the person from fulfilling a desire or acting in accordance with his or her values.

Researchers must identify a sufficient number of insights to capture the major tensions and values-action gaps from the informants' perspectives, yet without overwhelming the analysis with too many insights to be managed or communicated. Typically, insights are distilled into a concise statement that informants could have used to articulate the insight. A sentence structure that highlights the desire, values and tension at play is: We want ... so that ... but ... Each insight captures a major overarching challenge for developing a sustainable innovation culture (see table 2).

ETHNOGRAPHIC WRITING

Ethnographic writing is the final step in interpreting the material collected in the field. It results in 'thick descriptions'[41] of the observed phenomena. Thick descriptions are detailed accounts of fieldwork that make the contextualised patterns of cultural and social relations explicit.[42] In our case, researchers usually focus on three to six insights to explain the key innovation challenges together with related values, tensions and values-action gaps. Each insight is illustrated with descriptive quotes and stories from the data. Further details integrate additional interpretations, visualisations and references to related findings from research literature.

> Insights into sustainable innovation challenges are translated into task domains for cultural development. Using spatial metaphors, we also speak of design spaces or sustainable innovation territories.

In projects with large to mid-sized companies, the professional writing up and presenting of research findings can become a project of its own. Expertise may be needed to generate compelling graphics, illustrations and management summaries to ensure that the findings can be communicated effectively. The table below illustrates exemplary findings for each of the four steps of rapid ethnographic inquiry.

Research Tasks	Output	Exemplary Results	
1. Storytelling	Clustered findings with illustrative quotes and materials from field interviews, or secondary data	*Developing a constructive attitude towards mistakes:* 'Things simply go wrong, and we should develop a constructive attitude to it and always strive to draw something positive from these mistakes' (Theo). *Problems as sources of learning:* 'You want big enough problems so that failing gives you either a big gain or a big learning experience' (Ronald). *Resistance to change:* Observation of an informant commenting on a poster found in the meeting room calling for experimentation. He comments that many colleagues still resist experimental approaches (Mark).	*Teams avoid failure at early-stage development:* 'When you try new stuff you fail all the time ... Don't build the login mechanism that works perfectly ... Move on [to] the new stuff' (Mark). *Leadership struggles to accept learning from failure:* 'When I explained this "learning from failure" concept to my boss ... he struggled ... He said: "We must then also do learning from success"' (Theo). *Blaming others falls back on the speaker:* A photo shows the hand of an informant commenting on failure and blaming others. His index finger points one way, while three fingers point back to the person blaming (Theo).
2. Pattern Recognition	Patterns	Recognising the need for experimentation and failure tolerance	Fear of failure and being blamed
3. Insight Synthesis	Overarching insights	*'We want* to experiment and learn from failure *so that* we can rapidly advance towards our ambitions for sustainability-oriented innovation, but we also fear failure and finger-pointing and so we identify with the risk aversity that characterises the traditional inspection business.'	
4. Ethnographic Writing	Ethnographic descriptions of insights and task domains	Insight 1: A failure-tolerant and inclusive sustainable innovation culture presented in a one-sentence summary, an illustrative statement, short description and empirical evidence supporting the insight and task domains *(Fostering an Innovation Mindset and Promoting Sustainability Literacy)*, lessons learned from the insight and discussion of implications with reference to research.	

TABLE 2. From findings to insights in a rapid ethnography study of an inspection company

4.3 Practices and Methods: Conceiving One's Own Innovation Culture

Substantial time, effort and skills are required to conduct a full-fledged ethnographic inquiry, even if a rapid and streamlined approach is applied. While the ethnographic approach has proven to be a valuable method to generate insights, this path may not be feasible for smaller or mid-sized organisations with high operational pressures and limited budgets. Still, taking a step back from daily routines is essential for identifying effective entry points and efficient levers for creating a sustainability-oriented innovation culture.

In this section we outline proven practices and related methods with examples of conceiving an innovation culture together with its notions and values, practices and artefacts as well as challenges that must be addressed to generate desirable outcomes. Some of the methods can be easily implemented within a limited timeframe and effort, such as *Mapping Competing Values, Cultural Surveys, Focus Groups* or *Awareness Raising* workshops. Others require more time and effort and expert facilitation, such as *Rapid Ethnography, Appreciative Inquiry, Dilemma Games* or a *Values Jam*. Based on the current state of research (see section 2.3.3, endnote 137), the practices and methods presented here cover the full range of possibilities for a methodologically sound understanding of sustainable innovation culture. The following approaches address three guiding questions for understanding a given innovation culture.

4.3.1 Practices and Methods: Contextual Inquiry

The first set of practices (marked with □) and methods (marked with ○) digs beneath the surface of officially espoused values and prescribed practices to uncover implicit notions, values, tensions and values-action gaps. It addresses the question:

> How can we identify implicit notions and values, practices and artefacts to explain tensions and values-action gaps?

**15.
CONTEXTUAL
INQUIRY**

**16.
CULTURAL
SURVEYS**

Contextual Inquiry[43] is a practice that encompasses a range of methods to help the researcher conceive the unique culture of an organisation. This includes easily scalable and off-the-shelf methods, like *Cultural Surveys* and *Mapping Competing Values*, to more in-depth, interpretative methods that focus on particular contexts of work, subcultures, events or material artefacts. When applied regularly, these methods become a habitual practice of Contextual Inquiry, providing a nuanced understanding of the organisation's culture over time.

CHALLENGE: Self-reports and one-off empirical studies do not capture the nuanced notions, interactive practices and artefacts of organisational culture. *How can we gain a holistic understanding of an organisation's innovation culture?*

APPROACH: Understand an organisation's culture by having researchers immerse themselves in their informants' everyday work environments and collaborate with them to uncover and interpret cultural practices and implicit notions in real-time.

RELATED METHODS: *Rapid Ethnography, Mapping Competing Values, Memetics, Focus Groups, Cultural Survey, Sensemaking*

Cultural Surveys[44] assess an organisation's culture in relation to specific variables derived from theoretical frameworks or the organisation's unique aspirations for cultural development. For instance, surveys based on the Competing Values Framework can help organisations identify which values are dominant in their cultures and which of them should be reinforced or deemphasised to enhance sustainable innovation performance.

CHALLENGE: Cultural differences between an organisation and its subcultures need to be analysed efficiently. *How can we identify starting points for interventions and transformation with limited effort?*

APPROACH: Reach a large sample of informants (anonymised to ensure confidentiality) and conduct comparative analysis of cultural variables based on dimensional models of culture. Employ custom-made surveys to compare specific notions, values and practices.

EXAMPLE: A survey of innovation and executive managers from 85 Austrian firms examined the relationship between competing dimensions of cultural values and sustainable innovation performance.[45] The findings indicate that values emphasising internal orientation can hinder sustainable innovation, whereas values that prioritise external orientation towards stakeholders are positively linked to sustainable innovation performance.

17. MAPPING COMPETING VALUES

18. RAPID ETHNOGRAPHY

Mapping Competing Values[46] can be used as a stand-alone method for uncovering implicit values that help shape the development of a sustainable innovation culture. This method reveals discrepancies by comparing between the values prioritised by key stakeholder groups. Respondents characterise a fictious 'star employee' who represents the organisation's key values and behaviours and 'not so hot employees' that do not fit into the organisation and the leadership team's values and typical behaviours.

CHALLENGE: Organisational values are often implicit and conceal cultural conflicts and tensions. *How can we uncover competing values and tensions with limited effort?*

APPROACH: Reveal employees' implicit values to map typical values and behaviours across three groups of employees. 'Star employees' and the 'leadership team' represent the most highly valued values in the organisation. 'Not so hot' employees provide greater context and insights into values that hinder an innovation culture.

EXAMPLE: This method helped to reveal tensions between guiding values for sustainable innovation in an inspection firm:[47] *Experimentation* and failure tolerance of star employees contrasted with risk aversion and performance orientation valued by the leadership team.

Ethnography has a proven record in exploring stakeholder values, practices and artefacts as well as cultural tensions and values-action gaps in organisations,[48] paving the way for meaningful change in organisational strategy and innovation.[49] However, this method has not yet been widely adopted, as it requires substantial time, skill and effort. *Rapid Ethnography*[50] streamlines the traditional ethnographic approach, making it more accessible for companies that want to conceive their sustainable innovation cultures with limited resources or on an ongoing basis.

CHALLENGE: Ethnographic exploration is required to achieve a holistic understanding of stakeholder values, practices and artefacts together with related tensions and values-action gaps. *How can we make it easier for organisations to do ethnographic research?*

APPROACH: Use interactive exercises and staged activities to streamline the participatory observation of everyday practices. Interpret field material through storytelling, pattern recognition and insight synthesis from multiple perspectives.

EXAMPLE: Ethnographic research was used to analyse how unsustainable practices are reproduced in the multinational clothing company H&M and how processes of reformation and change towards sustainable practices take place.[51] Ethnography was selected for this research because it allowed the analysis of both micro (individual) and macro (social) perspectives on sustainable innovation practices and values-action gaps.

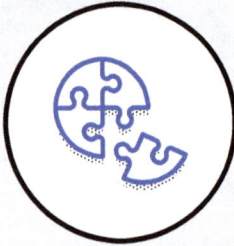

19.
MEMETICS

Analogous to the role of genes in biological evolution, *Memetics*[52] offers a framework to analyse cultural change. Just as genes are the basic units of biological inheritance, memes are understood as discrete units of cultural transmission. These units include notions, informal practices and artefacts that evolve through three key processes: imitation (how they are copied), variation (how they are adapted) and selection (how some are retained over others).

Memetics research at the Dutch coffee company Jacobs Douwe Egberts identified clusters of memes that affected employee engagement with the company's sustainability transformation.[53] Research revealed four so-called memeplexes: inner values (personal views on sustainability-related topics), working area (notions about how sustainability practices should be implemented), company operations (notions about the impact of corporate operations) and global impact (notions about the impact of the whole value chain).

Research also identified memeplexes that supported or blocked cultural change. Supportive memeplexes included increased employee awareness about sustainability, new incentives promoting sustainable behaviour and increased requirements for sustainability from customers and regulators. Blocking memeplexes consisted in values-action gaps such as 'doing the bare minimum regarding sustainability' or a 'wait-and-see attitude'. Recognising these memeplexes informed a *Tailored Communication* strategy targeting individual employees, aligning messages with the memes they found most important.

CHALLENGE: Cultural change is a complex process that is influenced by a wide range of cultural aspects, many of which are difficult to identify. *How can we effectively analyse and address different aspects of culture, including those that are informal and implicit?*

APPROACH: Break down cultural elements into memes to understand how they spread and how they influence cultural transformation. Memes are cultural elements (such as notions, practices and artefacts) that evolve over time through processes of imitation, variation and selection.

EXAMPLE: *Memetics* helped researchers understand how individual employees of Jacobs Douwe Egberts prioritised memes of sustainability and cultural change and how these priorities could be effectively addressed with *Tailored Communication* by resonating with their priorities.

20. FOCUS GROUPS

Focus Groups[54] engage heterogenous participants in discussing values and other notions together with their tensions, conflicts and synergies. For example, the Ploutos H2020 project engaged multiple actors across the agrifood value chain to discuss conflicts and synergies between their values and how they impact collaborative sustainable innovations. While shared values were seen as essential for actors to share resources for ecosystem innovations, conflicting values were related with challenges such as reverting to habitual patterns of consumption, maintaining unrealistic expectations about the price of products and triggering distrust between actors.

CHALLENGE: One-on-one interviews and standardised surveys do not capture important aspects of culture. *How can we reveal implicit assumptions, subjective meanings, group dynamics and shared interpretations when studying organisational culture?*

APPROACH: Stage social interactions, collaborative reflections and group dynamics to reveal where participants share common ground or differ in their viewpoints and clarify vague notions or implicit meanings.

EXAMPLE: The Ploutos H2020 project facilitated focus groups to identify values, enablers and obstacles for sustainable innovation in the agrifood sector. Participants discussed sustainable innovation scenarios dominated by conflicting values and multi-actor alliances based on shared values.

21. SENSE-MAKING

Sensemaking[55] is a process in which individuals and groups give meaning to their experiences[56] by bridging the gap between individual assumptions and shared interpretations of notions (e.g. concepts of sustainability), practices or artefacts. This method is essential for qualitative researchers, who use *Sensemaking* to develop their 'sensitivity toward meaningful differences – what matters to other people as well as to themselves'.[57] They seek to make sense of diverse clues and generate insights into tensions (e.g. between implicit and espoused values), gaps (between strategy and practices or values and action) or misalignments.

For instance, in a study of a Finnish financial firm and an energy company, *Sensemaking* was used to uncover tensions in how employees interpret sustainability reporting. The researchers identified three key frames: individualistic reporting focused on organisational self-interest, relational reporting as meeting stakeholder transparency expectations, and decoupled reporting as lacking clear purpose or alignment with the internal sustainability transformations. The findings suggest pathways for connecting reporting practices with tangible actions, enhancing the credibility of business reporting and aligning sustainability reports with stakeholder expectations through *Tailored Communication*.[58]

CHALLENGE: Unrelated clues are combined when interpreting complex and ambiguous phenomena or seeking to understand the foundations of a culture. *How can we understand sustainability-related cultural notions, practices, artefacts and their alignment?*

APPROACH: Engage stakeholders in deliberation on subjective experiences, interpretations of critical incidents and meanings of values, practices and artefacts to reveal tensions, values-action gaps and misleading communication. Understand how individuals and groups interpret sustainability-related notions, values, narratives, practices, artefacts and events in the organisation to derive targeted interventions.

EXAMPLE: In a Finnish financial firm and an energy company, different sensemaking frames revealed how employees' views on sustainability reporting were shaped during their companies' transformations.

4.3.2 Practices and Methods: Reviewing Practices and Challenges

The second set of practices and related methods enhances understanding of an innovation culture by engaging employees in structured and collaborative reflection. This approach encourages them to adopt a mindset of managing risks and learning from failure. Methods range from staging events and adjusting routines to raise awareness about sustainability-related issues, creating opportunities for systematic inquiries into slumbering developments and exploring alternative courses of action to reconcile diverging perspectives. The guiding question:

> How can we reflect on and become more sensitive to proven practices and recurring challenges?

22.
FROM FAILURE TO SUCCESS

23.
AWARENESS RAISING

Recognising and actively reflecting on failures and cultural tensions reveal valuable insights into an organisation's culture and its dynamics, providing opportunities for learning and better-informed decision-making. Similarly, successes are opportunities to explore and harness the underlying factors that contributed to them. This practice and related methods facilitate organisational learning and empower employees to navigate the journey *From Failure to Success*.[59]

CHALLENGE: Both failure and success are often taken for granted without learning about their underlying causes. *How can we facilitate organisational and individual learning from experiences in sustainable innovation management?*

APPROACH: Have employees draw on institutional knowledge and their own experiences in order to learn from failure and build on past achievements. Individuals who contribute to sustainable innovation are given both formal and informal recognition for their efforts.

RELATED METHODS: *Awareness Raising, Appreciative Inquiry, Dilemma Games, Empathising*

Methods to raise awareness of sustainability-related issues and opportunities include a range of workshop formats, events, gamified approaches and routines designed to improve alignment between espoused values with daily practices and experiences.[60] These include large-scale events as well as small-scale techniques that can be integrated in daily meetings, such as 'moments of truth' to speak up and articulate cultural tensions.

CHALLENGE: Communicating official values as abstract statements often fails to motivate and direct innovation processes or engage diverse stakeholders because they are detached from daily practices and experiences. *How can values be filled with life to better convey their meaning and relevance?*

APPROACH: Raise awareness about values in strategies, policies and practices in experiential workshops, events and routines such as 'moments of truth'. They allow employees to experience, apply, interpret and reflect on the implications and importance of values.

EXAMPLE: A large German inspection company[61] is fostering sustainable innovation through experimentation and risk-taking. To achieve this, the company hosts events that encourage employees to learn from failure and develop a risk-bearing mindset.

24.
APPRECIATIVE INQUIRY

Appreciative Inquiry[62] focuses on amplifying existing cultural strengths. For instance, in a company where employees consistently demonstrate collaboration across departments, *Appreciative Inquiry* highlights instances where this collaboration has led to successful project outcomes, thereby encouraging such collaborative efforts. Similarly, if an organisation exhibits a dedicated customer-centric focus, *Appreciative Inquiry* brings attention to cases where prioritising customer needs resulted in increased their satisfaction and loyalty, motivating the organisation to further embrace customer centricity.

Appreciative Inquiry originates from the tradition of strengths-based management[63] and facilitation methods that 'bring the whole system into the room'. It can engage as many as a thousand or more internal and external stakeholders, building on configurations of strengths rather than on their individual merits.

CHALLENGE: Problems in complex systems like an organisation's culture have multiple, difficult-to-diagnose causes, and the potential negative effects of attempted fixes are difficult to predict. Exploring and strengthening cultural capabilities can be more impactful than focusing on problems. *How can we identify cultural strengths and create a positive outlook?*

APPROACH: Use *Appreciative Inquiry* together with problem-solving approaches to pose positive, open-ended questions and co-create a desired future culture based on the culture's existing strengths.

EXAMPLE: Dairy Management and the mining firm, Fairmount Minerals, used *Appreciative Inquiry* summits to engage a large number of employees in aligning their cultural strengths and co-creating coherent, system-wide strategies and rapid prototypes for sustainable innovation.[64]

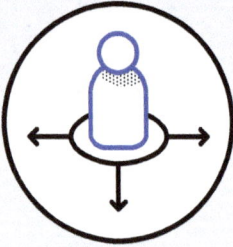

**25.
DILEMMA
GAMES**

Dilemma Games help people interpret values and their tensions, values-action gaps and trade-offs through vivid examples of specific behaviours. The dilemmas can be more generic, like those in the Global Compact Dilemma game[65] or more specific with respect to the individual organisation. Specific dilemmas are usually sourced within in the company, as in the case of the Corporate Sustainability Innovation Game developed for Deutsche Telekom.[66]

CHALLENGE: Values and the priorities they represent have to be interpreted and weighed against each other in order to guide decision-making and devise courses of action. This makes it challenging to embed organisational values into strategic and operational decision-making. *How can we turn abstract organisational values into actionable heuristics?*

APPROACH: Prompt employees to interpret and apply values through direct interaction in *Dilemma Games*. Clarify employee notions, beliefs, attitudes and intentions to align individual and organisational values, sensitising individuals to potential conflicts.

EXAMPLE: The CSI game developed for Deutsche Telekom confronts players with dilemmas in corporate sustainability and values-based challenges that the players address, turning them into seeds for innovation.

26.
EMPATHISING

Empathising[67] harnesses contradictions among stakeholder values as sources of innovation (see also section 3.1.2). For instance, Tchibo, the German coffee and retail chain launched the Worldwide Enhancement of Social Quality (WE) programme to improve working conditions throughout its supply chain.[68] This programme uses iterative, structured, trust-based stakeholder dialogues to facilitate shared inquiry and foster mutual empathy and respect. Each dialogue series focuses on unique local challenges, with, for example, workers, their representatives and management engage in roleplay to explore adverse working conditions. By highlighting relational aspects of human rights issues, rather than relying on regular audits, the programme transforms workplace dynamics, leading to meaningful and lasting improvements of working conditions.

CHALLENGE: Tensions arising from divergent stakeholder values can be sources of sustainability trade-offs, leading to win-lose outcomes or synergies fostering win-win outcomes. *How can we tap differences and conflicts between stakeholders as sources for innovation?*

APPROACH: Encourage stakeholders to see their differences not as conflicts that require a middle-ground compromise, but as something to be harnessed to ideate solutions from a more holistic perspective.

EXAMPLE: Non-profit and for-profit firms are driven by different cultures comprising different sets of values. *Empathising* was used in eight cases of corporate and non-profit organisations partnering in the UK, resulting in sustainable innovation outcomes.[69]

4.3.3 Practices and Methods: Revisiting Values and Integrating Stakeholders

The third set of practices and methods examines the ethical and normative foundations of the organisation to advance its dynamic capabilities of learning and adaptation. This set addresses the question:

> How can we review our values to better align them with changing stakeholder priorities and emerging sustainability challenges?

Several methods feed into two distinct practices, *Stakeholder Values Integration* and *Identity Development*, to iteratively revise an organisation's guiding principles and policies and its sustainable innovation efforts.

27. STAKEHOLDER VALUES INTEGRATION

28. CO-CONSTRUCTION

Sustainable innovation cultures respond to changing stakeholder values and emerging sustainability challenges through continuous and proactive *Stakeholder Values Integration*[70] (see the five maturity levels in section 3.1.3). This practice moves beyond defensive risk mitigation and negotiating interests to actively change stakeholder values with the goal of refining guiding principles and strategic decision-making. At a lower maturity level, innovation cultures integrate stakeholder values sporadically or implicitly, while at more advanced levels, organisations proactively collect feedback and mobilise stakeholder values to reprioritise its organisational values (see GLS Investments; case 18 in section 12.3.2).

CHALLENGE: Stakeholder concerns are often seen as a set of risks or conflicting interests to be managed, but a proactive approach is needed. *How can stakeholders be actively involved in transforming our organisational innovation culture?*

APPROACH: Monitor stakeholders' behaviours and viewpoints to better understand and integrate their values into the organisation's guiding principles, policies and innovation strategy.

RELATED METHODS: *Co-construction, Values Jams*

If organisations are to foster a culture of continuous learning and adaptation and remain relevant in today's fast-changing world, they must conceive sustainable innovation cultures that continuously reconceptualise their values. The *Co-construction*[71] method recognises that understandings of responsibility vary across different groups in research, innovation and society. To address these differences, *Co-construction* initiates constructive debate and negotiation among a wide range of external stakeholders to identify and apply values that guide responsible and sustainable innovation.

CHALLENGE: Values are systems of priorities that need to be continuously reflected on and refined to ensure a positive impact on values-based and sustainability-oriented objectives. *How can we facilitate constructive debate and negotiation among stakeholders to ensure our values remain relevant?*

APPROACH: Enhance reflexive processes among various stakeholders through constructive debate, negotiation and learning activities.

EXAMPLE: The European ResAGorA project involved 80 stakeholders from industry, civil society, policy-making and academia in five *Co-construction* workshops to test and refine a governance framework for responsible innovation.[72] The workshops aimed to clarify and recognise the varying perceptions of responsibility across different stakeholder groups.

29.
VALUES JAM

A *Values Jam*[73] gathers and aggregates employee values to renew or extend the organisation's official values or other guiding principles. For instance, IBM's 72-hour *Values Jam* engaged 50,000 employees in an online dialogue, redefining the three basic values that shaped had shaped IBM's innovation strategies for decades.[74] One value, 'innovation that matters for our company and the world', built on the pride employees had in the company's history of societal innovation. This event triggered a 'global innovation outlook' that identified innovation areas such as the environment, healthcare and water, initiating open conversations among hundreds of customers, academics, government agencies, NGOs and consultants.[75]

CHALLENGE: Stakeholder participation in the redefinition of values and guiding principles enhances their validity. By involving a diverse range of stakeholders in the process, organisations can tap into distributed knowledge and expertise. *How can an organisation's values for innovation be collaboratively revised and broadly communicated, even across countries and time zones?*

APPROACH: Engage employees in an open online communication format, a 'jam', to review and redefine values that guide innovation activities. A *Values Jam* involves extensive preparation and requires that top management follows up on its results.

EXAMPLE: IBM held a 72-hour values jam in 2003 with 50,000 employees participating with the goal of redefining values that would provide future direction for the company's process, service and business model innovation for the following decades.

30.
IDENTITY AND
POLICY REVIEW

Periodic reviews of an organisation's guiding principles are essential, particularly during exceptional times, such as a generational transition in a family business or a merger between two companies. An ongoing practice of *Identity and Policy Review* involves a systematic and iterative review of the organisation's ethical foundations and of the policies implementing its guiding principles. This practice supports identity development[76] by avoiding inconsistencies between guiding principles and practices (values-action gaps) that lead to inefficiency, loss of credibility and cultural erosion and rigid policies that could lead to bureaucratic processes and demotivate employees.

CHALLENGE: Development of organisational identity and policies needs to balance cultural alignment with operational flexibility. *How can we review and develop our organisational identity and policies?*

APPROACH: Have the leadership regularly review and, if necessary, revise the organisation's guiding principles in response to changing stakeholder expectations and market conditions. Regular reviews ensure that policies are both structured and adaptable – they translate guiding principles into action while staying aligned to support an evolving identity.

RELATED METHODS: *Guiding Principles Review*

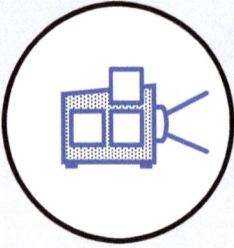

31. GUIDING PRINCIPLES REVIEW

In contrast to the bottom-up approach of a *Values Jam*, a *Guiding Principles Review*[77] takes a top-down approach. Selected members of the organisation, often the leadership team, consolidate the organisation's cultural notions and guiding principles to prioritise values of sustainability and provide guidance for the further development of organisation's identity and policies.

This *Guiding Principles Review* is exemplified by visionary leaders such as Ray Anderson of Interface (see section 3.1.4) or Dr. Venkataswamy of Aravind Eye Care System, who show how even personal initiatives can trigger a transformation towards a sustainable innovation culture. Dr. Venkataswamy made it his mission to 'eradicate needless blindness', by aligning his company's innovation culture – including its notions, practices and artefacts – around the goal of making eye care more efficient, inclusive and scalable.[78] Starting from a single 11-bed hospital Aravind has grown into a large network of hospitals, eye care facilities and educational institutions. It has performed almost ten million free or low-cost eye surgeries.[79]

CHALLENGE: Sustainability-oriented cultural change may be hindered by management objectives that are unclear or misaligned with values-based sustainable innovation. *How can we consolidate and align our guiding principles with sustainable innovation?*

APPROACH: Review collaboratively and, if needed, redefine values, purpose, mission or vision statements serve to consolidate the guiding principles and prioritise values of sustainability.

EXAMPLE: Aravind's founder articulated a mission to 'eradicate needless blindness', which aligned the entire organisation around making eye care highly efficient, inclusive and scalable. Operations are performed on a freemium basis by well-trained medical staff.

IN SUM

Conceiving the role of culture in supporting sustainable innovation is indispensable for co-creating effective interventions and approaches over the short and medium term to cultivate sustainable innovation. Business anthropology and the ethnographic approach provide the basic methodology for understanding organisational culture. By combining these approaches with the practices and methods outlined in this chapter, you can identify the core values, feasibility and viability of sustainable innovation management. This helps to reveal tensions and values-action gaps and to understand how practices and artefacts either facilitate or hinder the translation of sustainability values into novel, value-adding outcomes.

Chapter 5 /
Co-creating Targeted
Interventions

Conceiving an innovation culture is an ongoing task in any organisation, even though the magnitude of this task will be different for each company and will vary depending on the size, age and type of organisation. The task of conceiving an existing culture is key to professionalising sustainable innovation management and developing a sustainable innovation culture by understanding the existing situation and its challenges, including notions of its future outlook, its tensions and values-action gaps. This cannot be done in isolation but requires contributions and commitment from stakeholders both inside and outside the organisation. Co-creating and collaborative formats of interaction provide a privileged entry point to clarify basic notions, specify guidelines and policies, resolve tensions and close values-action gaps, and align values with practices and supporting artefacts. Our guiding question for this chapter is therefore:

> How can we use targeted interventions to address sustainable innovation challenges, introduce new practices and explore opportunities?

Before coming back to this guiding question and providing a methodological outline (section 5.2), we first describe its conceptual foundations and its benefits compared to more traditional approaches. However, regardless of the approach, its objectives depend on the results of the conceiving activities: clarification of ill-defined values and specification of basic notions or policies, resolution of tensions or values-action gaps and exploration of untapped opportunities for sustainable innovation.

5.1   Co-creating for Impact

The revision of values and related notions provides an example to illustrate the co-creating approach and its benefits compared to more traditional approaches. The definition of values, guiding principles and policies is often still seen as the sole task of top management. Especially in hierarchically organised companies, it is still a common practice for leadership teams to gather for an *Off-Site Event* every few years to review their organisation's values, purpose, mission, and/or vision and related policies. This is followed up with a communication campaign to disseminate the results and embed them on an operational level.

If *Off-Site Events* are done professionally, in addition to clarifying guidelines and strategies, they can also refresh management's views on its own organisation by providing opportunities to discuss new insights and strategies. In such events the configuration of internal and external participants (such as facilitators or area experts) is critical to achieving the desired results. However, the problem remains as to how off-site results can be translated into on-site policies and operations.

To overcome the problems related to hierarchical divisions, co-creating does not solely rely on the cooperation within a relatively small group of top managers. Instead it pursues a more inclusive approach to collaborating with stakeholders, even if *Off-Site Events* may still be part of the approach. Co-creating as a term was initially introduced in a context of innovation marketing and referred to an integration of customers as a source of competence into new product development.[1] It is used for idea generation and selection as well as interactive value creation[2] involving collaboration between supply and demand-side partners, for instance when sports shoes or shirts are custom-designed by the buyer and manufactured on demand. Today, the approach is widely adopted to drive socially grounded innovation,[3] across different disciplines and societal initiatives. In our context, we understand co-creating as a general methodology involving several practices and methods to engage stakeholders in collaborative interventions to promote a sustainable innovation culture.

> Co-creating is not just an ideation method – it is an overarching approach to address cultural challenges and explore sustainable innovation practices and methods.

For instance, methods like *Values-Based Business Modelling* or *Ecosystem Modelling* are often used to generate and evaluate ideas for strategic innovation. However, they can also be applied to address values-action gaps in business model design and ecosystem development and to explore untapped opportunities in strategic partnerships. Compared with the top-down approach, co-creating formats come with several benefits for cultural development. They can:
- leverage experience-based knowledge that is widely distributed inside and outside the organisation
- spur creativity through the mindful configuration and collaboration of diverse participants
- flexibly integrate different stakeholders in preparation for events and discussion of results through online or offline interaction formats
- ensure commitment and ownership through participation
- help to spread the word across different participant communities

The case of Pelliconi[4] demonstrates how co-creating can reinvent sustainable innovation practices and culture across a whole company.

CASE 10. Pelliconi's Co-creating Approach to Sustainable Innovation

Founded in 1939 in Bologna, Pelliconi has evolved from a small manufacturer of crown caps into a global leader in the production of metal and plastic closures for the food and beverage industry. Its founder Angelo Pelliconi had discovered an ingenious process of recycling tin containers used for military rations to produce metal caps. Ever since, their continuous commitment to innovation and sustainability has characterised the company's identity. Today, the company continues to rely on recycled materials for its production, producing over 30 billion units annually.

Co-creating is at the heart of Pelliconi's approach to sustainable innovation. Internal and external stakeholders are systematically involved at every step of its innovation process: ideation, conceptualisation, prototyping, industrialisation and commercialisation.[5] By engaging stakeholders early and continuously, it ensures that every aspect of the product development process is informed by multiple perspectives, reducing errors and enhancing the alignment of products with market needs such as design, functionality, safety, accessibility and resource traceability.[6]

At the beginning of the ideation stage, Pelliconi encourages input from a wide range of stakeholders. For instance, its Call for Ideas on the Desall crowdsourcing platform invites professional designers, design and architecture firms and freelancers to contribute their innovative concepts.[7] Additional practices for *Engaging in Open Innovation* leverage partnerships with start-up incubators, universities and companies from across the economy to explore new technologies and business models.

Pelliconi's innovation department focuses on digitalisation and the development of sustainable products, proposing an initial concept and asking stakeholders to develop it with further ideas and assessments of its feasibility. Its Champions of Innovation[8] community is instrumental for internal *Knowledge Sharing* (see also the *Employee Resource Groups* method). Silvia Salvadori, their innovation digital programme manager underlines the benefits of internal collaboration in terms of reducing development errors: 'As an innovation team, we initially work a bit like a start-up, but we continuously compare ourselves with the various corporate bodies to bring possible critical issues of the project to light as soon as possible.'[9] This approach ensures that diverse perspectives contribute to the ideation process and that potential challenges are identified early, reducing the risk of costly development errors.

In the conceptualisation and prototyping stages, Pelliconi refines its new product ideas by seeking feedback from both internal teams and external partners, such as suppliers, research institutions and end customers. This stage is crucial for estimating customer desirability, technical feasibility, economic viability and the sustainability-related benefits of new concepts and prototypes. 'In some cases, it was the end customers themselves who pointed out the benefits that we had not yet noticed,'[10] says the corporate innovation manager, Matteo Mingardi. One of the standout examples of Pelliconi's co-creating approach is the development of an eco-friendly, flower cap, designed with softer edges and 68 percent thinner than traditional crown caps. The product was developed in continuous dialogue with customers and other stakeholders, who informed its technical, user experience and resource efficiency benefits: that is, soft edges, easy opening and a thinner cap.

The industrialisation and commercialisation stages involve scaling up production while maintaining the standards established during the prototyping stage. Here, Pelliconi's engages in co-creating primarily with its suppliers and sub-suppliers, who are integrated into the production process. The company actively works with these stakeholders, sharing knowledge and best practices to help them adopt a more sustainability-oriented culture. It uses targeted initiatives to promote a sustainability-oriented mindset, encourages them to invest in environmental certifications and innovations and regularly conducts audits to ensure their compliance with Pelliconi's code of conduct. This proactive engagement helps to foster a sustainable innovation culture throughout the business ecosystem and ensures that Pelliconi's sustainability standards are met across the board.

5.2 Preparing, Conducting and Bundling Co-creative Activities

Co-creating is sometimes misunderstood as a more or less spontaneous activity without clear rules and goals. The opposite is true. Effective co-creating requires a well-defined framework, thorough preparation and clear commitment to follow-up in order to ensure productive collaboration and relevant outcomes. Each co-creating session targets a specific challenge, sets up a safe space empowering participants for the collaborative exploration of opportunities, follows a simple workflow and combines suitable facilitation methods and techniques.

5.2.1 Setting the Right Targets

Co-creating builds on the insights gained from the conceiving activities, targeting specific challenges to sustainable innovation. These challenges arise from a range of sources, including the need to revise fundamental values and notions, tensions between espoused values, and the values-action gaps between espoused values and actual daily practices. In addition, co-creating seeks to explore untapped opportunities for sustainable innovation. The main challenge and objective for an intervention is identified as the most critical hurdle to overcome in order to establish or promote a sustainable innovation culture.

Defining a suitable challenge involves consideration of a number of different factors. First, the challenge must be specified at an appropriate level of abstraction. It should be broad enough to justify a collective effort but manageable given available resources and time. An example of a challenge that proved to be too broad, which we considered addressing in our work with the technical inspection company (case 9: section 4.1.5), focused on balancing interests and achieving consensus among its business units. It was a critical challenge, but addressing it would have required extensive and ongoing efforts to mediate between the group's executive board and the business unit leaders. It was therefore considered beyond the scope of a targeted intervention.

Second, a suitable challenge should not be too narrow either, as overly specific challenges require specialised expertise that does not always benefit from a co-creating approach. In the inspection company case, we considered mainstreaming existing innovation methods like scorecards and *Innovation Impact Assessments* as challenges that were too specialised to address with co-creating.

Third, the relevance of existing initiatives must be considered. If a challenge is already being addressed effectively, it may not be necessary to duplicate efforts. In the inspection company case, we found that local employee initiatives and experiments to drive sustainable innovation did not always attract the attention, managerial support and budget resources needed to implement them. However, the company had already started addressing these issues with practices and methods such as enhanced *Facilitating Idea Management, Ideation Contests and Markets* and *Inviting for Informal Exchange*. In other cases, co-creating can help redesign or simplify ongoing efforts, making them more inclusive and effective.

As a suitable challenge in the inspection company case (chapter 7), we considered a cultural tension between two opposing approaches to sustainable innovation: an outside-in absorption of external knowledge and stakeholder engagement and an inside-out leveraging of internal knowledge and expertise in technical inspection and sustainability to business partners, political stakeholders as well as other companies and organisations. While both approaches were equally important to the company's innovation strategy, the exploration of opportunities to develop a sustainability-oriented business ecosystem, where the company would play a pivotal role in promoting the sustainable performance of other firms, had not yet been embedded in the organisation's culture through corresponding notions, practices and artefacts. Therefore, the company's leadership team prioritised the challenge of developing competences and exploring the potential for sustainable ecosystem innovation.

5.2.2 Engaging the Right Participants

Once a suitable challenge has been identified, we need to select and customise co-creating approaches and methods to address the challenge, also considering factors such as the effort required and the scope of the intervention. In the case of the inspection company, we considered techniques from Futures Search[11] and Open Space[12] conferences. However, the original formats engage up to hundreds of participants to bring the whole system into the room and establish common ground. Time and budget constraints required this approach to be downscaled, reducing the number of participants, while ensuring that all relevant organisational departments were sufficiently represented and that a wide range of cultural notions and strategic perspectives could be generated.

Unlike large-scale crowdsourcing initiatives taking place online, co-creating usually draws on direct interpersonal interaction among participants in a shared creative space. This makes it critical to engage the right stakeholders and to facilitate dynamic interactions. Employees from different hierarchical levels may be engaged and external stakeholders like experts, business partners and customers, or indeed anyone who is directly impacted by or has an interest in the cultural challenge being addressed. Co-creating operates on the premise that everyone is an expert in their own individual experience, be it professional or cultural, regardless of their formal role or level of expertise. A diversity of perspectives ensures that the process is holistic and inclusive, considering a wide range of insights and ideas. Still, one needs to prioritise the most relevant stakeholders so as to ensure meaningful contributions.

5.2.3 Setting Up a Safe Space and Empowering Participants

To ensure effective facilitation of the co-creating sessions, certain requirements must be met. First, whether participants co-create in a physical workspace or online, they need to feel that they are in a safe space. Here a 'safe space' is not merely about creating a pleasant environment. It is about fostering a climate of mutual respect where individuals can freely express their thoughts and ideas without fear of negative consequences.[13] This openness is crucial for authentic dialogue and creative thinking to flourish. Warm-ups and energisers help participants overcome communication barriers and build rapport before entering the session.

A second requirement for effective co-creating is to empower participants.[14] *Empowerment* fosters a sense of agency, providing participants with a clear understanding of their options and the potential impact of their contributions. Unlike consensus, which can be challenging to achieve in diverse groups, empowerment focuses on ensuring that all participants feel that their participation is valued. When individuals perceive their role in the process as meaningful, they are more likely to support the outcomes, even if these do not align perfectly with their personal preferences. Like empowerment, achievement of mutually beneficial outcomes fosters a shared sense of ownership and commitment. It is vital not only during the co-creating activities but also in translating their outcomes into the subsequent cultivating of notions, practices and artefacts.

The third requirement for effective co-creating is specifying the conceived challenges and objectives for the intervention. Challenges are often the result of insufficiently defined values and policies, cultural tensions, or values-action gaps, and need to be framed as opportunities for co-creative exploration and collaborative intervention. This involves engaging participants in structured dialogues to bring latent tensions to the forefront and reflect on how these tensions can contribute to the pursuit of shared goals.

For instance, in the inspection company case (case 4: section 3.1.1), we found that one of the major cultural tensions that undermined the company's sustainable innovation efforts was related to its legacy of success based on values of safety, reliability and trust. Although they play a crucial role for every inspection company, these values and related practices also limited *Experimentation* with unconventional approaches and the willingness to enter new markets in pursuit of sustainable innovation.

Entrepreneurially minded employees felt that they weren't receiving managerial support and sufficient financial resources for their endeavours, while others felt that *Experimentation* was at odds with the company's promise of outstanding reliability. Employees engaged in a co-creating session, acknowledging potential synergies between the values of reliability and control and the pursuit of sustainability-oriented technological innovation and market growth. They came up with innovative approaches to expand inspection and certification into new areas such as vehicle data management, sustainability inspections for vehicles and sensor technologies monitoring vehicle maintenance and driver performance, determining their effect on vehicle lifespan and sustainability.

5.2.4 Facilitation Using Storyboards

Dedicated facilitators play an essential role in the success of co-creating by helping define the session's boundaries and focus during the preparation phase. During the co-creating session, they introduce background information, provide clear instructions, ensure focus and engagement and moderate feedback. Post-session, they again play a crucial role in highlighting key takeaways, synthesising results, as well as triggering and tracking follow-up activities.

STORYBOARDING

Since numerous stakeholders need to be involved in a variety of interactive formats, a structured approach is needed to ensure the encounters run smoothly and bring about the desired results. Storyboarding is an ideal approach to creating compelling co-creating formats with meaningful interaction and actionable results. Storyboards (approach 6) structure the flow of activities, discussions and output.[15] They help systematically incorporate methods that cater to diverse learning styles and participation preferences, while also anticipating potential challenges. Storyboards are visualised in a table or map and serve as a reference during the workshop, especially if different moderators are involved in the workshop.

APPROACH 6. Key Elements of a Storyboard for Co-creation Workshops

A storyboard comprises the key elements of a workshop: its objectives and expected results, each step of the co-creative journey, the facilitation methods and potential challenges.

Objectives of the workshop such as ideation or the exploration of a new method should be aligned with expected output and desired outcomes. For an ideation workshop, an output could be developing innovative and actionable business ideas in collaboration with selected ecosystem partners, while an outcome could be sensitising partners for new ecosystem business opportunities in response to emerging sustainability challenges. For an assessment of a new method like *Values-Based Ecosystem Modelling*, the output could be modelling the exchange of benefits in a future ecosystem, while an outcome could be insights into the method's usefulness in enhancing ecosystem development.

The co-creative journey for the participants is usually divided into stages like an introduction, some immersion in the topic (such as a sustainable innovation or cultural challenge), collaborative activities and feedback, some synthesis to achieve the objectives and assignment of follow-up actions and responsibilities to implement the results. Each stage can be broken down into steps, each with simple instructions and techniques (like storytelling, roleplay, brainwriting). Facilitators should prepare exemplary results for each step to illustrate what kind of results are expected.

The storyboard also specifies the timeframe, materials and participants (facilitators plus plenary groups or specific individuals) needed for each step along with icebreakers, warm-up or refocusing exercises and backup activities. Some consideration should go into potential difficulties and what might go wrong. Techniques like 'parking' ideas that are interesting but beyond the scope of the session help keep participants focused and the workshop on schedule.

Reviewing the storyboard with stakeholders or co-facilitators before and after each session allows the co-creating approach outlined in the storyboard to be iteratively refined, increasing the desired impact in the next iteration.

CO-CREATIVE ENVISIONING AND THE CASE OF MICHELIN

The case of the multinational tyre and engineering materials manufacturer Michelin (case 11 below) shows a good example of the application of a co-creating workshop format. The initiative grew out of the observation that Michelin, like many other companies, had well-defined values and sustainability-related ambitions in its corporate policies, but it was unclear how they would operationalise them in a new business area, in this case the sustainable mobility business. To address this challenge and to project sustainable mobility business for the future, a co-creating session applied one of the foresight methods, *Envisioning*, not for the whole firm, but for a specific area of product, process, service, business model or ecosystem innovation that would inspire and direct sustainable innovation in targeted areas. The case description and results show that while new business was envisioned, both the method and results it generated await further cultivating before they can become integral parts of the innovation culture.

CASE 11. Envisioning New Mobility Business at Michelin

We facilitated a full-day co-creating workshop at Michelin's headquarters in Clermont-Ferrand, France[16] with the aim of sparking Michelin's sustainable innovation culture. Using *Sustainability Foresight*, we guided the integration of Michelin's core values, purpose, activities and ambitions into a new vision for sustainable mobility by 2035 and explored potential innovations to its business model to realise this new vision. A further goal was to harness the power of a more contextualised, 'local' *Envisioning*, drawing on Michelin's long-standing heritage as a symbol of its small hometown, Clermont-Ferrand.

For over 135 years Michelin has been one of the largest employers in the Clermont-Ferrand region and has established long-lasting partnerships with the local municipality and other key stakeholders in the city's mobility ecosystem. Michelin has a unique opportunity and a significant responsibility to drive sustainability mobility in Clermont-Ferrand, while also creating business advantages by leading the sustainable transformation of the local mobility ecosystem. Furthermore, Clermont-Ferrand is an ideal test market for sustainable innovations, allowing the company to pilot and refine new ideas before scaling them to global markets.

We brought together a diverse group of nine managers and employees from Michelin, representing the foresight, corporate social responsibility, business modelling, and research and development departments. Using co-creating methods and Sustainable Business Model Design Patterns,[17] we designed a comprehensive workshop format with three distinct phases: prioritisation, *Envisioning* and implications.

PHASE 1: PRIORITISATION

First, participants reviewed and prioritised future mobility scenarios as well as Michelin's values and sustainability ambitions. Each participant then presented his or her own interpretations of the company's scenarios, values and ambitions. Then, using dot voting each participant prioritised the most essential factors according to three criteria: personal desirability, relevance for sustainable future mobility and values fit for Michelin. Accessibility, circularity and public regulations were considered the most significant factors for the future of sustainable mobility, while Michelin's most important contributions were associated with the core value of 'respect for the environment' and strategic ambitions to reach net-zero, in-use carbon emissions and full circularity of tyres. These key priorities aligned participants around a set of shared values and goals, pinpointed major challenges and opportunities for sustainable innovation and provided thematic anchors for the subsequent *Envisioning* and business modelling activities.

PHASE 2: ENVISIONING

In the *Envisioning* phase, the participants worked with selected local sites in Clermont-Ferrand (e.g. the main square, the train station, the outskirts, or a parking lot) to envision the potential of sustainable mobility in 2035. Techniques like imagining 'heaven and hell' scenarios helped them to specify both hopes and risks for each location. For example, they imagined a hell scenario for grocery shopping mobility in the future city of Clermont, revolving around increased consumption and delivery journeys, no transparency, little or no social contact with buyers and no local-to-local product supplies. A heaven scenario envisioned eco-friendly grocery deliveries around the clock and hubs for local trade and business.

Next, each group combined one organisational value, one strategic ambition and one future mobility scenario to develop site-specific scenarios into business model innovation ideas. Using sustainable business model design patterns and elevator pitch templates, they specified the benefits and challenges associated with each business model idea. For example, in one scenario, Michelin's disused production facilities in Clermont-Ferrand were reimagined as on-site research and development testbeds for new mobility services and offerings. This vision included partnerships with other companies and stakeholders to explore new prototypes and services, which could then be expanded into other city areas and integrated into larger ecosystems like public transport and municipal services. The group proposed engaging test users from the local community in exchange for free mobility offerings under test conditions. The resulting data would then be sold to business clients, providing an additional revenue stream.

Each group sketched further sustainable business models for their scenarios, which included:

- a renewable and regenerative park community enabled by a Michelin mobile app
- free public transportation cross-subsidised by Michelin through service sales to public transport fleets
- integrated multiple public transport modalities in a single user-friendly, mobility-as-a-service platform
- enhanced access to medical technologies and expertise in remote areas
- a mobility-as-a-service app integrated to optimise urban rail transit
- a neighbourhood sharing platform to promote local exchanges and mobility sharing
- village grocery hubs offering automated last-mile deliveries on demand

PHASE 3: IMPLICATIONS

The final phase staged a fishbowl discussion with participants taking the roles of an EU official, a corporate social responsibility (CSR) manager and Michelin's CEO in 2035. Three participants and a facilitator led the conversation in an inner circle while the other participants sat in an outer circle, listening, taking notes and stepping into the inner circle to take over one of the roles. This dynamic setup allowed for an in-depth exploration of the proposed business models through the lens of three major approaches to sustainable innovation: legislative, socio-ecological and economical. The roleplay highlighted the diverse considerations and priorities that different internal and external stakeholders bring to the table when discussing sustainable business model innovation.

For instance, the roleplay discussion of the renewable and regenerative park community model underscored the importance of collaboration between the public and private sectors in realising this model and explored how regional economies and local partnerships could support a sustainability transition. In other discussions the participants recognised the pivotal role of regional economies of proximity and the potential for entering related markets such as health, energy and logistics. The role of legislation was seen as essential for providing reliable government regulations, economic incentives and platforms to foster collaboration among companies and stakeholders.

These insights were summarised as a fictional future press release entitled Michelin's Eco-Mobility Revolution: Clermont-Ferrand Pioneers Sustainable Change. It captured a vision of how Michelin could develop new business and lead the sustainable mobility transition, supported by new EU regulations and promoted by community partnerships.

5.2.5 Bundling and Scaling Co-creating Activities

Co-creating can advance sustainable innovation capabilities in a multi-session activity involving diverse participants to explore potential innovations. By bundling different co-creating workflows, an organisation can target overarching challenges or goals. Moreover, platforms that facilitate ongoing employee interaction and dialogue can scale up the impact of their co-creating initiatives as in the cases of Interface and Xerox. These platforms enable the incubation of new co-creating initiatives, mainstream effective approaches throughout the organisation and provide continuous support for implementing results.

CASE 12. Employee-Driven Co-creating to Foster Sustainable Innovation at Interface and Xerox

Interface's QUEST (Quality Utilising Employees' Suggestions and Teamwork) initiative[18] was launched in 1995 to engage cross-functional teams worldwide in finding pragmatic solutions to cutting waste. The teams received bonuses based on the impact of their solutions and each team was encouraged to cut waste by ten percent every year. This initiative not only strengthened Interface's sustainable innovation culture but also delivered significant cost savings, demonstrating the tangible benefits of employee-driven co-creating. For example, a 'portable creel' system was developed by one of the teams, optimising yarn usage and reducing scrap yarn by an estimated 54 percent.[19] Another example is Xerox's Earth Awards initiative. It encouraged employee-driven sustainable innovation projects that led to significant cost savings, reducing plastic waste, converting waste into electric power and optimising water use in key manufacturing processes.[20]

DECENTRALISED AUTONOMOUS ORGANISATIONS

To institutionalise co-creating as an organisational practice, decentralised autonomous organisations (DAOs) provide a framework for multi-stakeholder collaboration. DAOs enable participants to coordinate and make consensual decisions without relying on a centralised authority, reducing the likelihood of unsustainable practices driven by narrow interests. By building on blockchain technology,

DAOs maintain a transparent and unalterable record of decisions, transactions and project outcomes. Token-based incentivisation or smart contracts can be integrated to coordinate action towards common sustainability goals, making funding dependant on predefined thresholds. While risks related to uncertain regulation, technological barriers and governance capture persist, the maturation of DAOs for Impact[21] bears promising potential for sustainable innovation both within traditional organisations and across emerging, sustainability-oriented community ecosystems.

5.3   Practices and Methods: Co-creating

Like the other 3C activities of conceiving and cultivating, co-creating workflows draw on proven practices and validated methods from academic studies and practitioner white papers. Suitable practices and methods for clarifying and specifying basic notions or resolving tensions between different values or stakeholder groups have already been presented in the context of conceiving. Specifically, practices and methods for revisiting values and integrating stakeholders (chapter 4.3.3), such as practices like *Stakeholder Values Integration* or methods like the *Values Jam* or *Dilemma Games*, help an organisation understand its existing culture and collaboratively specify basic notions and values of sustainability. Additionally, co-creative interventions can be designed to tackle organisation-specific challenges such as addressing tensions or risks, including greenwashing due to new partnerships (case 6: section 3.1.3).

The following research-based practices and methods provide additional templates for targeted interventions. Again, three guiding questions help select suitable approaches to start with.

5.3.1 Practices and Methods: Co-creating with Internal Stakeholders

The hidden treasure of an intrinsically motivated workforce is key to fostering sustainable innovation. The first set of practices and methods helps tap this potential by enabling employees across all levels to actively support the sustainability transition.

How can we engage employees to collaboratively drive sustainable innovation by experimenting with new methods and artefacts?

32. VALUES-BASED IDEATION AND ASSESSMENT

The practice of *Values-Based Ideation and Assessment* leverages methods that apply values of sustainability to address latent opportunities and risks throughout the innovation process. At the ideation stage, values-based heuristics are used to identify opportunities and generate ideas in response to sustainability challenges or to champion individual employees through methods such as *Sustainable Innovation Time* and *Values-Based Intrapreneurship*. At the selection and screening stage, methods such as *Lead User Integration* and *Ideation Contests and Markets* focus managerial attention towards projects with potential impact on stakeholder values. Subsequent prototyping of innovation ideas can be supported by value-sensitive design, which fosters sustainable innovation by implementing human values across three iterative phases: conceptual (identifying potentially conflicting stakeholder values), empirical (exploring user values, needs and practices) and technical (redesigning existing or prototyping new systems embodying values identified in the conceptual and empirical phases). *Values-Based Business Modelling* uses values-based heuristics to identify potential for strategic renewal towards sustainable value creation, delivery and capture.

CHALLENGE: As societal and customer priorities change, new business opportunities as well as boundaries and risks emerge. How can we harness the potential of stakeholder values to reveal otherwise latent opportunities, boundaries and risks for sustainable innovation?

APPROACH: Apply sustainability-related values and concepts as heuristics for ideation and as criteria for the assessment of intermediary results in innovation management. This is supported via design methods that facilitate internal crowdsourcing, business modelling, or value-sensitive design.

RELATED METHODS: *Sustainable Innovation Time, Values-Based Intrapreneurship, Ideation Contests and Markets, Values-Based Business Modelling*

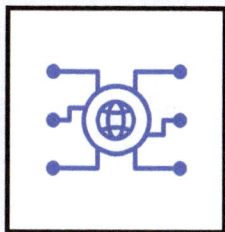

33.
FACILITATING IDEA MANAGEMENT

Several methods contribute to *Facilitating Idea Management*,[24] which establishes a consistent practice promoting collaboration and *Knowledge Sharing*. Co-creating methods such as *Sustainable Innovation Time*, *Values-Based Intrapreneurship* and *Ideation Contests and Markets* harness the collective intelligence of the entire workforce for the generation, evaluation and selection of sustainable innovation ideas.

Expert idea management is usually supported by a digital platform. Artificial intelligence (including semantic technologies, natural language processing and deep learning solutions) facilitate idea management by automating the classification and enrichment of ideas or by linking ideas to associated datasets and projections.[25] For instance, an employee may submit an idea to 'replace our 13-Inch MacBook Pro laptops with 13-Inch MacBook Air laptops to reduce the amount of GHG emissions from our operations'.[26] Using openly available life-cycle assessment data, an AI-powered idea management system can identify sources and display specific GHG emissions data for both laptop models, along with their estimated environmental impact, allowing decision-makers to gain clearer insight into the potential benefits of the proposed process innovation.

CHALLENGE: Tapping into the distributed experience of the workforce uncovers ideas for sustainable innovation that individual innovation teams might overlook. *How can we harness the collective intelligence of the entire workforce to ensure continuous improvement and an alignment of outcomes with stakeholder needs?*

APPROACH: Facilitate the exchange of ideas, feedback and knowledge by establishing communication channels, such as social networks and innovation platforms. Ideas and associated data and feedback are collected, evaluated and prioritised, often with the help of digital platforms and AI tools.

RELATED METHODS: *Sustainable Innovation Time, Values-Based Intrapreneurship, Ideation Contests and Markets*

34.
SUSTAINABLE
INNOVATION
TIME

Sustainable Innovation Time[27] fosters intrinsic motivation and creativity by allotting working time for employees to pursue their own sustainable innovation initiatives – which also benefit the employer. Among companies like 3M, Facebook and Atlassian, Google was the first one to experiment with 'innovation time-offs' that give one day per week for employees to work on personal projects of interest to the company? This led to major innovations for the Alphabet group, such as AdSense and Google News.[28] Companies like Philips have also adapted this approach to foster co-creating in the context of sustainable innovation.

CHALLENGE: New ideas need a degree of freedom from operational pressures and established routines to flourish. *How can we encourage employees to tap into their values and intrinsic motivation and develop their own sustainable innovation initiatives?*

APPROACH: Use Innovation Time to empower employees to propose their own projects and provide them time to pursue these projects during their regular working hours.

EXAMPLE: Philips[29] gives scientists in its innovation department time on Fridays to work on their own sustainable innovation projects. They can also apply for three-month research fellowships to pursue ideas of interest. Philips also eases the conditions for the evaluation of these projects.

35.
VALUES-BASED
INTRAPRENEUR-
SHIP

Values-Based Intrapreneurship fosters intrapreneurship with tools like the Values-Based Intrapreneurship Kickbox[30] and the open-source Adobe Kickbox toolkit to systematise collaborative creativity around stakeholder values. Adobe Kickbox provides employees with step-by-step guidance and resources to experiment with innovation projects. It has been used by thousands of organisations, some of which have tailored it to their specific organisational values and goals. For instance, Swisscom[31] developed its own software to run Kickbox and formulated key statements as values-based guidelines for its implementation. 'Life's a Pitch' encourages continuous communication about and validation of employee ideas. 'Better to ask for forgiveness than to ask for permission' is a slogan that demonstrates a goal-oriented mentality that disrupts the corporate rules.

CHALLENGE: The hidden potential of human resources needs to be unlocked to generate new ideas and sustainable outcomes. How can we foster intrapreneurship to explore unconventional ideas for sustainable innovation?

APPROACH: Employ intrapreneurship toolboxes like Adobe Kickbox to engage employees in a values-based innovation process, fostering sustainability literacy and inspiring sustainable innovation projects.

EXAMPLE: The Adobe Kickbox programme[32] inspired Swisscom to initiate new sustainability projects and multi-disciplinary teams. All employees' job descriptions now include proficiency in the use of the Kickbox to reinvent the telecom sector.

36. IDEATION CONTESTS AND MARKETS

Ideation Contests and Markets[33] use the potential of Gamification to engage and motivate employees and other stakeholders in contributing to the innovation process. Ideation Contests foster collaboration (e.g. through the exchange of feedback) by incentivising participants with points, badges, or real-world rewards. Ideation Markets offer participants a virtual currency to invest in ideas, determining which will be promoted to the implementation phase.

CHALLENGE: Employees possess valuable knowledge and a keen awareness that enables them to effectively evaluate opportunities and risks in sustainable innovation projects. How can we generate new ideas, encourage the collaborative assessment of innovation projects and aggregate diverse perspectives on their potential outcomes and impact?

APPROACH: Use game elements in Ideation Contests and Markets to motivate the generation, screening and promotion of sustainable innovation ideas. To qualify for funding, ideas must meet a predefined threshold of points or virtual investments.

EXAMPLE: The CEC Shoe Design Contest[34] engaged large manufacturers to 'design an innovative organic shoe based on fashion trends, authentic materials, cultural values and regional techniques.'

5.3.2 Practices and Methods: Co-creating with External Stakeholders

The second set of co-creating practices and methods focuses on integrating external stakeholders' values and sustainability priorities as pivots for ideation and strategic development.

How can we engage external stakeholders in collaborative idea generation and the exploration of sustainable innovation practices?

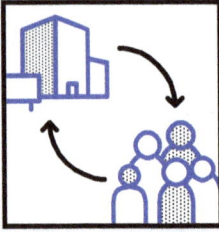

37. ENGAGING IN OPEN INNOVATION

By *Engaging in Open Innovation*[35] organisations interact with external actors to exploit knowledge outside-in or to explore knowledge inside-out. An example of outside-in open innovation is Michelin's Movin'On initiative that establishes collaboration even with competitors to address sustainable innovation challenges, such as reducing microplastics from rubber wear-off with alternative tyre materials.[36]

An example of inside-out open innovation is Tesla's decision to open its electric vehicle patents to competitors, enabling other companies to leverage Tesla's technological advancements in electric vehicles and charging infrastructure.[37] Sometimes outside-in and inside-out approaches are coupled, as in the case of Unilever's partnership with start-ups and research institutions through its Foundry platform.[38] This initiative invites external ideas and technologies (outside-in) while simultaneously sharing Unilever's expertise and resources (inside-out) to co-develop sustainable solutions, such as upcycling Unilever's factory plastic waste into emergency shelters or collaboratively exploring new alternative protein products.

CHALLENGE: Sustainable development requires collaboration across a wide range of stakeholders. *How can we exchange resources, knowledge and technologies with a wide range of stakeholders to spur sustainable innovation?*

APPROACH: Engage in outside-in, inside-out and coupled open innovation based on shared values of sustainability. Outside-in open innovation applies external knowledge, mainly from market actors such as partners and competitors. Inside-out open innovation turns knowledge and resources into external business opportunities through, for example, licensing, spin-offs, joint ventures and consulting. Coupled open innovation connects internal and external knowledge through collaborative relationships.

RELATED METHODS: *Ideation Contests and Markets, Lead User Integration*

**38.
LEAD USER
INTEGRATION**

**39.
SUSTAINABLE
MARKET
CREATION**

Lead User Integration[39] allows companies to learn from users and experts who are already addressing sustainability challenges ahead of the market. This approach has been successfully employed by several user innovation communities, who have generated and mainstreamed sustainability solutions, such as redesigned furniture (IKEA Hackers),[40] electronics for monitoring household energy consumption (OpenEnergyMonitor), local ecosystems for recycling plastic (Precious Plastic) and open maps and geodata (OpenStreetMap).[41]

CHALLENGE: Frequent and intensive experience with products, services and other offerings makes users uniquely qualified to identify entry points and support the implementation of sustainable innovation. *How can we tap users' widely distributed knowledge and ideas?*

APPROACH: Engage with lead users who face sustainability challenges ahead of the market. By working with them directly or through a dedicated online community, organisations can gain valuable insights into the challenges and potential solutions before they become mainstream.

EXAMPLE: Lead users from the IKEA Hackers community creatively repurpose furniture, providing the company with ideas for sustainable product designs that promote reuse and minimise environmental impact.

Sustainable Market Creation[42] builds on *Values-Based Business Modelling* to identify, design and implement new value propositions that drive market and societal shifts towards sustainable consumption and production. For example, companies offering plant-based foods or renewable energy solutions not only exploit new market opportunities but also encourage broader societal adoption of sustainable innovations, leading to a systemic transformation of industries and communities. This approach also addresses the needs of underserved customer groups, providing access to vital services such as healthcare and essential products like construction materials.

CHALLENGE: Sometimes new markets are still needed to serve neglected customer segments or to push the adoption of sustainable products and services. *How can we match latent demand with sustainable supply?*

APPROACH: Create new, sustainability-oriented markets that address latent needs and shape the sustainability-oriented transformation of societal behaviours and patterns of consumption and production.

RELATED METHODS: *Values-Based Business Modelling*

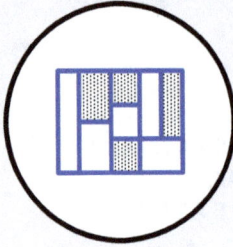

40. VALUES-BASED BUSINESS MODELLING

Values-Based Business Modelling[43] uses stakeholder values and the organisation's guiding principles to design new business models or redesign existing ones. Rather than taking up the next best idea, entrepreneurial teams need to explore the scope and depth of business design options, evaluate the strengths and weaknesses of each business model component and establish a shared understanding about its guiding principles.

Companies proceed in at least three different ways.[44] First, they can introduce new value propositions that align with customer priorities – such as health, safety, or sustainability – as exemplified by Danone's creation of nutrient-enriched products targeting undernourished populations.[45] Second, they can use their organisation's values to drive innovations in specific business model components like supply chains or cost structures, as seen in Interface's gradual eco-efficient transformation. Third, they can modify their business model to focus on addressing societal challenges and sustainability goals.[46] The Lab of Tomorrow,[47] a business development programme, has developed numerous cases of successful private sector collaboration between European companies and local stakeholders in emerging market economies.

CHALLENGE: Entrepreneurial teams need to assess their options before designing a new business based on shared values and often unspoken principles and assumptions. *How can we help teams specify their guiding principles and goals and assess their options before designing a new business?*

APPROACH: Start by creating common ground with *Values-Based Business Modelling* among different stakeholder values and the organisation's guiding principles. This provides a shared basis to generate and assess alternative sustainable business model designs. Values-based Business Modelling guardrails collaboration, providing methods for ideation and criteria for prioritising ideas or intermediary results.

EXAMPLE: The Lab of Tomorrow facilitates business model innovations grounded in the UN's Sustainable Development Goals to incubate joint ventures between German companies and stakeholders from the developing world.

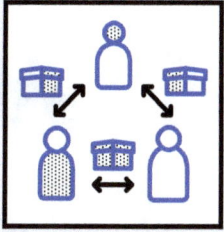

41.
ENGAGING
IN INNOVATION
ECOSYSTEMS

Ecosystems of interdependent parties can achieve a higher impact on sustainable development than individual organisations. *Engaging in Innovation Ecosystems*[48] involves a broader and longer-term interaction between organisations, individuals and resources that co-evolve to support innovation within an industry or location.

A notable example is the Danish Kalundborg industrial ecosystem, which is made up of eight private and public partners and involves approximately 50 symbiotic exchanges of by-products, surplus and waste materials on a commercial basis.[49] On a larger scale, a renewable energy ecosystem is a prime example of an innovation ecosystem, bringing together governments, manufacturers, utilities, NGOs and private households around the shared goal of a green energy transition.

CHALLENGE: Business actors and other stakeholders need to understand the benefits of engaging in long-term collaborative partnerships before making a commitment. *How can we enhance sustainable value creation by creating synergies, collaborative actions and redistributing mutual benefits among multiple stakeholders?*

APPROACH: Nurture sustainable innovation through collaborative efforts over the long term, sharing resources and aligning objectives together with market and non-market actors from governments, academia, NGOs and local communities.

RELATED METHODS: *Values-Based Ecosystem Modelling*

42.
VALUES-BASED
ECOSYSTEM
MODELLING

Values-Based Ecosystem Modelling[60] integrates stakeholder values into the design of sustainability-oriented business ecosystems (see chapter 7). In contrast to traditional business ecosystems built around shared economic interests, a values-based approach focuses on forming partnerships to pursue shared sustainability goals and sustainable value creation.

CHALLENGE: Business ecosystems transcend traditional organisational boundaries and the established notions, practices and artefacts of any single organisation. *How can we facilitate the formation of sustainable business ecosystems based on shared values and visions?*

APPROACH: Set up co-creating workshops to reflect on stakeholder values, sustainability challenges and business case drivers, leveraging shared priorities for new ecosystem development.

EXAMPLE: To envision its role in future sustainability-oriented ecosystems, an inspection company reviewed future trends, current stakeholder relations and sustainability drivers.

5.3.3 Practices and Methods: Sustainability Foresight

A third set of co-creating practices and methods derives strategic measures through the development of probable, possible and desirable future scenarios. It addresses the question:

How can we proactively explore opportunities for sustainable innovation, avoid unintended consequences and enhance resilience?

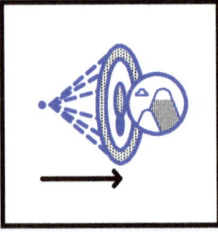

43.
SUSTAINABILITY FORESIGHT

Sustainability Foresight is 'the application of future-oriented practices and methods to facilitate sustainable development and enhance organisational preparedness for future sustainability challenges'.[51] This approach is instrumental in addressing grand challenges through innovation and leading sustainable development 'from the future'.[52] Methodologically it distinguishes between exploratory, strategic and normative approaches to future scenarios.

Exploratory approaches focus on deriving future scenarios from current trends, helping to identify future opportunities and assess the robustness of ideas and concepts for sustainable service, product and process innovations. Strategic approaches build on exploratory scenarios to shape strategic development, including issues of market positioning and opportunities for business model innovation. Both exploratory and strategic approaches can feed into normative future scenarios that are based on stakeholder values to Envision desirable futures (see section 2.1.1). Normative scenarios go beyond improving competitiveness to contribute to organisational identity. These scenarios inform the *Backcasting* or *Roadmapping* of strategies that strengthen resilience and anticipate changing regulations impacting sustainability management.

CHALLENGE: Daily pressures, short-termism and a lack of resources and focus override the mid- and long-term considerations of the holistic understanding needed to create a future-oriented perspective on sustainable development. *How can foresight methods and normative scenarios inform sustainable innovation management?*

APPROACH: Apply foresight methods and scenario management to drive transformation. Anticipate emerging business risks to improve organisational preparedness for sustainability-related challenges and to identify opportunities for sustainable innovation.

RELATED METHODS: *Envisioning, Backcasting, Roadmapping*

44.
ENVISIONING

Envisioning involves exploring desirable future scenarios that are grounded in the guiding principles of an organisation and the values of participating stakeholders. The case of Michelin (case 11: section 5.2.4) illustrates an approach to specifying location-based scenarios for new business development. On a European scale, the European Environment Agency envisioned four distinct imaginaries to illustrate desirable pathways for the sustainability transition. These scenarios were driven by national initiatives, European regulation and market-based measures, companies pursuing sustainable innovation and civil society.[53]

CHALLENGE: To guide collaboration, sustainability-related values and strategies need to be articulated with compelling visions and actionable business models. *How can we envision sustainable futures that help stakeholders identify new business opportunities?*

APPROACH: Use *Envisioning* to accommodate diverse stakeholder values and formulate normative scenarios for mutually desirable futures. These scenarios help formulate implementation strategies for sustainable innovation.

EXAMPLE: *Envisioning* was used by Michelin to collaboratively integrate the company's values, purpose and activities into location-specific visions for sustainable mobility in 2035 and develop the potential business model innovations needed to realise this goal.[54]

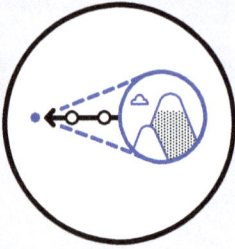

45.
BACKCASTING

Backcasting[55] supports corporate foresight by working its way backwards from a desirable future scenario to the intermediate actions needed to approximate that scenario. For example, in the 1990s, Electrolux[56] adopted the Framework for Strategic Sustainable Development (FSSD) and envisioned a future free of harmful emissions. This commitment led to the replacement of ozone-depleting chlorofluorocarbons (CFCs) in refrigerators with hydrocarbons (HCs) as an ideal alternative.

However, the available refrigeration technology at that time was not sufficiently advanced to handle the highly flammable HCs. Employing Backcasting, Electrolux opted for an intermediate step. They used hydrofluorocarbons (HFCs), which did not deplete the ozone layer but emitted greenhouse gases. This interim solution allowed time to develop safe HC-based technology, which was introduced in European products in 1995. This phased strategy balanced short-term feasibility with long-term sustainability goals, demonstrating how Backcasting can enable organisations to navigate complex transitions through intermediate steps.

Backcasting was also used to inform Electrolux's strategy to limit its use of rare-earth metals. Electrolux lobbied the Swedish government to ban the use of heavy metals in batteries.[57] Years later, CEO Leif Johansson declared in a public speech: 'It was not until ten years later that we fully realised how much money we had saved and earned from applying the FSSD to our business.'[58]

CHALLENGE: Normative scenarios and visions depict desirable futures to strive for but give no directions on how to transform cultural notions, practices and artefacts to reach those futures. How can we specify required changes and interventions needed to work towards a future vision?

APPROACH: Start by working backwards from a desired future state to discover and implement the necessary intermediate steps to approximate that future state. Backcasting helps turn far-reaching goals and values into a sequence of actionable and measurable objectives.

EXAMPLE: Backcasting informed Electrolux's[59] strategy to phase out harmful chlorofluorocarbons by first adopting emission-intensive hydrofluorocarbons as an interim solution while developing safer climate-neutral hydrocarbon technology. This phased approach allowed Electrolux to address immediate environmental concerns while progressing toward a long-term sustainable solution.

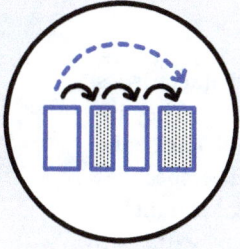

46.
ROADMAPPING

In contrast to the retrospective perspective of *Backcasting*, *Roadmapping*[60] projects ahead to determine the necessary steps to reach a desirable future, outlining the objectives, actions and resources. A notable example of *Roadmapping* is Unilever's Sustainable Living Plan[61] (concept 2: section 2.1.1), which defined over 70 time-bound targets together with measurable indicators for the company's sustainability transition.

CHALLENGE: Far-reaching goals cannot be achieved in a sprint. They are an endurance race, demanding a strategic approach that takes time and resources. *How can we specify incremental steps and metrics to track progress in the pursuit of long-term strategies?*

APPROACH: Outline the steps and milestones needed to achieve long-term strategic goals and visions with *Roadmapping*. Typically, the roadmap consists of short-term objectives, plans, actions and metrics to track progress.

EXAMPLE: Unilever's Sustainable Living Plan provided a roadmap that integrated sustainable growth into the company's long-term strategy and encouraged employees to engage in innovation projects to achieve the targets, such as the Small Actions, Big Difference Fund.[62]

IN SUM

Surveying these co-creating practices and methods, some common characteristics emerge. Essentially, they all break out of habitual ways of doing things. They integrate stakeholders (beyond the usual suspects) from both inside and outside the traditional boundaries of the organisation. Or they emphasise future perspectives rather current trends. These co-creating activities leverage empirical insights to explore novel approaches to addressing challenges and task domains within an existing innovation culture. This can yield either new ideas and starting points for sustainable innovation, emerging from collaborative ideation and community-based assessment, or the establishment of new practices of stakeholder integration and sustainability foresight, which can help cultivate sustainable innovation throughout the organisation.

Chapter 6 /
Cultivating Sustainable Innovation

Culture does not change arbitrarily, nor can it be imposed top-down, reduced to a new mindset or engineered and implemented voluntarily following a blueprint. Rather, it requires the nuanced interplay of consistent effort to understand the situation and its prospects, focused collaboration to address vital challenges and persistent dedication to build a sustainable innovation culture. We have already explored how cultural challenges can be conceived and entry points for interventions identified as well as how targeted responses can be co-created. However, simply exploring possibilities for innovation and introducing new methods is not enough. We must also cultivate sustainable innovation. This can only be done by prioritising critical task domains as part of a medium-term strategy.

These task domains and objectives will depend on the results of the previous activities of conceiving and co-creating and they will be guided by the three dimensions of notions, practices and outcomes (chapter 4: Introduction). This will involve mainstreaming values, related notions and their implications, establishing new practices and introducing suitable artefacts to support them, ultimately driving sustainable innovation across all business areas.

The concept of cultivation refers to the purposeful shaping of an innovation culture (section 6.1). Upon closer examination, we emphasise the need to mainstream not only values and guidelines, but also policies and sustainability-related criteria for innovation projects. We also highlight the need to establish guardrail practices and the role of artefacts in facilitating those practices (section 6.2). Sustainable innovation practices and methods drive transformation by promoting sustainability literacy and capacity building, facilitating collaboration and knowledge exchange and formalising the management of impact (section 6.3).

In sum, the ultimate sustainable innovation challenge for an organisation is to cultivate its values and mediated practices to bring about the desired outcomes, both amplifying their environmental impact and gaining a competitive edge in the market. This challenge yields our third guiding question:

> How can we cultivate virtuous circles that repeatedly and reliably generate sustainable innovation as an outcome and ultimately achieve the desired impact?

6.1 Cultivation

In our context of sustainable innovation cultures, the term cultivation highlights the co-evolution of organisational identity, social interactions and material culture. The use of the term in everyday language and its original use in sociology provide valuable insights on how to understand and shape cultivation in the context of organisations and innovation.

> Cultivation refers to deliberate and systematic efforts to purposefully shape, sustain and renew the innovation-related notions, practices and artefacts of an organisation – its innovation culture – in a sustainability-oriented manner.

6.1.1 Origins of the Term Cultivation

Originally, the term 'cultivation' meant preparing soil and tending plants to produce food in agriculture. In its figurative sense, 'to cultivate' means developing qualities (e.g. cultivating a sense of confidence), relationships (cultivating a friendship), skills (cultivating drawing skills) or interests (for instance in literature by reading). It involves the development of individual and group characteristics that would not come about naturally, but for which individuals have an inherent propensity.[1] The concept of cultivation puts culture into a dynamic perspective, highlighting the mutually transformative relation between one's subjectivity, social partners and mediating artefacts.

In science, the term cultivation was first used in the early 20th century by the German sociologist Georg Simmel to describe how an individual's inner imagination and its external objectivation as culture mutually transform each other. In Simmel's words 'by cultivating things, that is, increasing their value beyond what their natural mechanism provides us with, we are cultivating ourselves: it is the same process of value enhancement that starts from us and returns to us'.[2]

Psychologists picked up this concept to denote the value of cultural artefacts in their potential to further human development.[3] Accordingly, cultural development takes place not only through the interaction of individuals with social partners but also through the individual's interactions with artefacts and the meanings that they attach to them. The other way around, the specific characteristics of artefacts provide cultural media that engender subjective possibilities and objective opportunities for the formation of the self and the development of social systems.[4] The transactions between individuals, social groups and culture are thus facilitated by 'purposively created objects, settings and other components of the culturally structured environment.'[5]

6.1.2 Cultivating of Sustainable Innovation in an Organisation

Both Simmel's understanding of reciprocity and the role of artefacts in meaning-making practices yield insights into conceptualising the cultivation of sustainable innovation. First, we should not misconceive the development of an innovation culture as a one-way street where employees are expected to unquestioningly adopt the values and goals of their organisation, aligning with one another across hierarchical levels and producing innovations as an outcome. The vertical integration of values (see case 9, section 4.1.5) provides a vivid example of challenges that even a mature, sustainability-oriented company has difficulty dealing with. Here, we are considering reciprocal transactions between an organisation's members and how individuals actively interpret, negotiate and sometimes challenge cultural values, practices and artefacts.

Second, cultivating sustainable innovation requires the introduction of supportive artefacts, such as documents, templates, tools and changes to the physical environment. The repeated interaction by employees with these artefacts helps them refine their understanding and application, as well as adapt them to suit their own skills, needs and preferences. For example, using a values-based or sustainable business modelling template rather than the conventional Business Model Canvas engages users in the systematic consideration of the social and ecological dimensions of their business.[6] Advanced software tools for ESG or *Innovation Impact Assessment* enable even more comprehensive approaches to sustainable innovation management and cultural development. A recent example from Deutsche Bahn (DB) railway company underscores how this can look in practice.[7]

> **CASE 13. German Railways' Cultivation of Data-Driven Sustainability Management**
>
> The German railway Deutsche Bahn (DB) has long maintained a sustainability department with specialised teams in climate protection, noise control and nature conservation. ESG reporting is a well-established practice for DB, but the initial European Corporate Sustainability Reporting Directive demanded a far more comprehensive data-driven approach. DB chose not to purchase an off-the-shelf ESG software solution and instead had its sustainability and IT departments join forces to develop an internal ESG data management platform, building on DB's existing business intelligence infrastructure and financial reporting systems. The ESG platform was developed to enable retrospective reporting as well as strategic transition planning and scenario modelling towards the company's ambitious sustainability objectives.
>
> The success of this initiative depended on a gradual process of cultivation enabling the sustainability and IT departments to leverage their unique expertise to iteratively implement and co-develop the data management solution. Initially, DB's IT experts prepared uniform data-collection templates for the different sustainability teams, recognising that each team had its own metrics and varying degrees of data maturity. Once an initial, low-fidelity version was in use, platform development continued with iterative co-creating, enabling the continuous adaptation of the tool to the needs of the individual sustainability teams and further stakeholders. Repeated communication, workshops and retrospectives revealed insights about where the system needed adjustments – prompting the fine-tuning of workflows and reporting templates to match evolving requirements, such

as team-specific metrics, DB's internal sustainability ambitions, changes in
the regulatory landscape and the growing demand for data-driven sustainability management.

The cultivation of sustainable innovation is a mid- to long-term goal, moving beyond quarterly or annual reports and demanding a more comprehensive approach
to organisational or corporate sustainability than individual problem-solving.
Rather than treating sustainability as an add-on, cultivation takes a holistic,
transactional and transformative approach that links personal and organisational development to environmental features and acknowledges the need for shared
values to efficiently collaborate towards common goals.

6.2 Cultivating Values, Practices and Artefacts for Sustainable Innovation

How can organisations cultivate sustainable innovation to establish a supportive
culture? Following the conceiving of values, tensions, values-action gaps and task
domains and co-creative interventions to address challenges of limited scope, cultivation mainstreams clarified values, introduces new practices and artefacts and
systematically enters opportunities to drive sustainable innovation.

> Cultivating sustainable innovation requires a holistic approach that inter-
> twines the mainstreaming of values, establishing new practices and the
> mediation of artefacts.

First, mainstreaming values involves embedding shared values and related notions
and implications into daily actions and decision-making processes once they have
been clarified and major tensions have been resolved. These values provide the
foundation to consolidate organisational identity, policies and governance. They
are also the starting points for envisioning guidelines and new sustainable business models for individual business fields (see case 11: section 5.2.4) and heuristics
that inform innovation practices.

Second, new practices are established to sustain the values, implement guiding
principles and close values-action gaps. Here bottom-up and top-down approaches complement one another. The bottom-up approach elaborates on informal
practices and methods initiated by individual employees or teams, facilitated by
supportive measures such as fostering psychological safety, promoting *Experimentation*, empowering employees and decentralising rigid governance structures. In
parallel, practices can be drawn from the research literature and the repository of
practices and methods presented in this book, providing a top-down approach to
establishing new practices.

Third, artefacts support the mainstreaming of values and the establishment of
practices. Artefacts – such as guiding principles and policy documents, account-

ability frameworks, decision-making matrices and checklists, templates and digital tools – provide tangible expressions of values, ensuring that they are not only articulated but also operationalised and measured effectively. Artefacts also act as media that facilitate the implementation of desired practices and guardrail deviations from them. The 3C activities constitute a methodology for cultivation: mainstreaming values, establishing new practices involving mediating artefacts and cultivating outcomes.

6.2.1 Mainstreaming Values

The first step is to translate the values that have been clarified in the stages of conceiving and co-creating into guiding principles, actionable policies and governance structures that underpin innovation management. The next steps depend on the maturity of the organisation's values-based innovation culture and whether the values are implicitly effective, globally defined, differentiated, actively or proactively managed (see section 3.1.3).

> The objective of mainstreaming values is to embed shared values, identified and clarified in the stages of conceiving and co-creating, into everyday actions and decision-making processes.

CULTIVATING IMPLICIT VALUES

At the implicit level of maturity, many organisations, including market leaders, do not proactively manage the values that underlie their innovation strategies and practices, nor do they reflect on the tensions and values-action gaps that hinder these efforts. Cultivation starts by building on the insights generated through conceiving and co-creating to address this lack of awareness and to define shared organisational values on a global level. Even fuzzy aspirations like former Google's 'Don't be evil' provide cues for decision-making and action and mobilise employees' support for or against innovations. Besides offering broad implications for innovation management, such guiding principles formulate ethical considerations as enduring and generalisable criteria for decision-making.[8]

CULTIVATING GLOBAL VALUES

Defining guiding principles on a global level is only a first step. Organisations must reinforce values, guiding principles and policies with consistent *Policy Communication* (e.g. through a *Cultural Dictionary*). Providing accessible and detailed references on the meaning of organisational values raises awareness and increases cultural literacy and engagement throughout the organisation. Google's early 'Don't be evil' motto, for instance, was continuously refined and elaborated in a corporate code of conduct. As Google's global reach and range of services expanded, the company faced increasingly complex ethical dilemmas in the management of innovation projects, such as aligning search results with China's state censorship in the Dragonfly project or developing AI-powered surveillance in the Pentagon project Maven.[9] As the meaning of 'evil' became less self-evident, Google introduced more specific and elaborate guiding principles and policies to guide its workforce.[10]

CULTIVATING SPECIFIC VALUES

Further mainstreaming of values differentiates them with respect to organisational subcultures and innovation projects. Appropriate communication, understanding and assimilation are needed if values are to be relevant and compatible with the specific notions and practices of an individual team or project. It is helpful to illustrate verbal formulations of values with concrete role model examples of accomplished individuals and proven practices and methods. For instance, *Aspirational Narratives* along with storytelling and supportive visual representations can inspire others to pursue specific values and strategic goals. *Awareness Raising* workshops, *Tailored Communication* campaigns and *Mandatory Training* sessions help to convey these values and their practical significance to individuals and teams, taking into account their unique needs and context of work.

CULTIVATING ACTIVE MANAGEMENT OF VALUES

Mature organisations not only communicate values, but also actively manage them to drive innovation. Feedback loops and validated metrics enable them to assess adherence to their values and guiding principles. For instance, they introduce measurable key value indicators (see case 5: section 3.1.3) or translate stakeholder values into a heuristic for ideation or into evaluation criteria for innovation projects. Measurable indicators, stakeholder feedback and criteria for project evaluation allow organisations to screen and redirect innovation efforts that fail to make material contributions to sustainability. For instance, Bosch Thermotechnik introduced a CO_2 Flag in its innovation management process, requiring all projects to demonstrate how they contribute to reducing CO_2 emissions.[11]

CULTIVATING PROACTIVE MANAGEMENT OF VALUES

Organisations proactively managing values do not treat them as predefined and stable entities but as flexible and context-specific 'evaluative devices',[12] remaining open to different interpretations over time, across situations and by different stakeholders. A proactive approach takes their openness to interpretation as an opportunity to invite context-specific deliberation and collaborative prioritisation, allowing flexibility and adaptability in the face of complex dilemmas and emerging sustainability challenges. By harnessing the generative potential values to spark discussions and constructive debate, organisations can transform tensions between conflicting values into opportunities to find common ground, foster win-win synergies and embrace ambidextrous innovation approaches, as illustrated by the case of Ecosia[13] (case 14).

Ecosia is a search engine that reinvests its profits into tree planting projects around the world. Its six core values serve as guiding principles for the company's strategic and operational decisions: namely, impact, integrity, sustainability, leadership, user focus and happiness. However, the values offer guidance and direction and are not written in stone. They are continuously renegotiated and refined in response to internal and external feedback and resulting cultural tensions (as in case 6: section 3.1.3). This continuous revision of organisational values reflects critical moments in Ecosia's business development.

For instance, the core value of integrity has served to prioritise user privacy as a key value proposition for Ecosia's users. The company's founder and CEO, Christian Kroll and a former product manager, Corrie Wiren, highlight the tension between the prioritisation of privacy and the potential of collecting more user data to optimise the search engine's features or generate additional profits by selling data to advertisers.

Although privacy has always been essential for Ecosia, this commitment makes it 'difficult to tailor products for users'. In spite of this disadvantage, Ecosia continues to maintain a high standard of user privacy, upholding its core value of integrity, even if it means sacrificing improvements to the user experience (aligned with the core value of 'user focus') and the number of planted trees (linked to the core value of 'impact'). This prioritisation, however, remains open to ongoing discussion and revision as new ideas emerge to expand the company's value propositions. For instance, ideas to personalise search results with recommendations for sustainable lifestyle choices would require more extensive use of user data.

Ecosia revises and reprioritises its core values not only to guide decision making in its business development, but also as a proactive response to societal shifts. Spurred by public debates on social inclusion – such as those prompted by the Black Lives Matter movement – Ecosia's team revisited the meaning of the core values happiness and sustainability and on the role social inclusion plays in specifying those values. As a result, Ecosia reviewed the contractual agreements with its tree-planting partner organisations, ensuring that they provide fair wages and working conditions and support the communities involved in their projects. In addition, the green search engine specified the value of user focus in relation to web search accessibility, identifying new pathways for innovation.

Ecosia's proactive approach to managing organisational values and the tensions between them underscores the importance of continuous reinterpretation and renegotiation of values in the face of ethical dilemmas, societal shifts and evolving stakeholder expectations. The case shows how reordering or redefining core values does not indicate a lack of consistency in their understanding or application. Rather, ongoing reflections and reinterpretations of the values and their relative importance ensures a more deliberate and values-based approach to strategic decision making and sustainable innovation.

6.2.2 Establishing New Practices

Along with mainstreaming values, cultivation focuses on establishing, refining and sometimes formalising practices and methods that show promise during the conceiving and co-creating activities.

> Sustainable innovation practices are established as an integral element of employees' daily work. Practices and methods can be adopted from this book (see overview on page 96 ff) or developed from informal practices initiated by individual employees or teams.

In the bottom-up approach, informal practices are identified, endorsed by the organisational leadership, refined and aligned with the innovation strategy. When conceiving innovation cultures, we often find that individual employees or teams are questioning established routines and are already experimenting with sustainable innovation practices. Cultivation emphasises the importance of refining these grassroots efforts and embedding them into the organisation's policies and innovation frameworks. Supportive measures empower employees to become active agents of innovation and cultural change.

ENSURING PSYCHOLOGICAL SAFETY, EXPERIMENTATION AND DECENTRALISATION AS SUPPORTIVE MEASURES

One important condition to encourage a bottom-up search for sustainable innovation practices is to create a workplace environment that functions as a safe space. Psychological safety denotes an environment where employees feel safe to take risks, voice their opinions and learn from their mistakes.[14] This encourages employees to speak up and make suggestions for new practices or improving existing ones. Employees that feel psychologically safe are also more likely to disagree with practices and values-action gaps that appear counterproductive for the organisation's priorities.[15] To promote psychological safety, leaders need to communicate it explicitly as a priority. They need to openly discuss its benefits and specify its principles in relation to organisational values, innovation activities and cultural development.

Employees that experience a high level of psychological safety are more willing to engage in *Experimentation* with new methods. For instance, employee-led *Experimentation* with new approaches to governance and collaboration can address cultural tensions and values-action gaps, often more effectively than traditional top-down governance. This is well-illustrated in the case of the healthcare system in Alberta, Canada, where *Experimentation* played a pivotal role in reconciling tensions between healthcare managers and physicians about conflicting values of profitability versus patient care (see case 14 below). This case demonstrates how informal efforts between opposing parties are able to find a common ground and engage in joint innovation projects, which were then scaled into formal practices and structures that foster ongoing collaboration.

CASE 15. Informal Collaboration Practices to Reconcile Tensions in Alberta's Healthcare System

In 1994, the regional health authorities of Alberta, Canada introduced a new, business-like health care institutional rationale emphasising cost-effectiveness, efficiency and customer satisfaction. This challenged the existing medical professionalism rationale, which prioritised physician expertise and the physician-patient relationship. Physicians resisted these changes, leading to ongoing tension and an 'uneasy truce', where neither rationale became dominant.[16]

Despite the rivalry, the two parties began negotiating and experimenting with practices that enabled the reconciliation of both rationales. One such practice centred on separating medical decisions from administrative decisions. Although physicians were officially excluded from administrative boards, their medical actions influenced costs, prompting managers to seek their informal input when taking administrative decisions. Over time, these informal interactions evolved into formal governance structures such as Physician Liaison Councils, through which physicians obtained an official advisory role. Administrative managers usually heeded the advice of physicians when decisions influenced medical treatment but retained full control over decisions about budget and service delivery. Gradually, this division of decision-making responsibilities – medical versus administrative – became a standard practice, facilitating coexistence and collaboration between the two groups.

Further collaboration between Alberta's physicians and administrative staff was facilitated through joint innovation projects in experimental sites, such as forming interprofessional teams, redesigning homecare, reorganising medical treatments and offering chronic care services in unconventional settings like community centres and patients' homes. In these projects, physicians preserved authority over medical decisions, while administrators focused on the business-oriented priorities and the efficient use of public funds. The local experiments further supported the reconciliation of the two institutional rationales and the cultivation of a complementary relationship between medical professionals and administrators.

The overarching practices of *Empowerment* and *Decentralisation* complement *Experimentation* by mobilising employee contributions that would lack resonance in traditional hierarchies and governance structures. First, *Empowerment* provides individual employees or small teams with the authority, resources, guidance and supportive structures to establish their own initiatives as standard practices across the organisation. For instance, Interface's QUEST and Xerox's Earth Awards co-creating initiatives (case 12: section 5.2.5) underscore the substantial impact on energy and environmental efficiency that can be achieved when employees are entrusted with both the autonomy and resources to champion sustainable innovations.

Next, *Decentralisation* gives employees the opportunity to tailor practices to their specific work context. A prime example is holacracy, a decentralised management approach that allows individuals and teams to redefine organisational practices and decision-making structures in line with their own needs and competences.[17] In a holacracy, employees form circles of expertise, each operating under a 'no-objections' principle giving them the freedom to define how they contribute to organisational goals, describe their tasks and responsibilities and share progress updates. For example, in the case of bol.com, a benefit corporation (B Corp) certified online marketplace, holacracy is used to form cross-functional teams with the autonomy to choose how they reach organisational objectives.[18]

ASSESSMENT AND REFINEMENT

To further systematise the cultivation of established practices, organisations need to assess their results and validate how they lead to the desired outcomes and impacts. Once a new innovation practice is established, it is necessary to assess its outcomes and impact on innovation performance and positive cultural change.

Theory of Change is an approach to plan and explain how a change effort – like introducing new sustainable innovation practices – can lead to long-term impact. Like the *Results Chain* method, it outlines the steps needed to reach a goal by connecting stakeholder actions, results and outcomes in a logical sequence. These steps are shown in a visual map that highlights how each part leads to the next, what is needed to make progress and when each step should happen. This approach helps track progress, evaluate success and make informed changes as needed.

SCALING AND SUSTAINING

Successful pilots for new sustainable innovation practices by individual employees or teams – for example as a result of co-creation, *Experimentation*, *Empowerment* or *Decentralisation* – can be scaled across an organisation. Engaging a diverse range of stakeholders to provide feedback during this phase ensures that the practices are adaptable to various contexts within the organisation. Iterative adjustments based on their feedback helps to scale new practices in a way that can accommodate the unique cultural, operational and strategic needs of different teams. For instance, a practice initially designed for product development will require modifications before it can be used in other contexts, such as marketing or supply chain management.

Scaling practices requires allocating and developing the necessary resources. *Mandatory Training* and *Human Resource Development* programmes equip employees with the skills and knowledge needed to adopt the new practices effectively. Support systems and artefacts such as mentoring, dedicated tools or platforms for collaboration can help embed these practices into daily routines. Without adequate resources, even promising initiatives will not gain traction.

After new practices become widely established, organisations must ensure that they can be sustained over the long term. This involves integrating new employ-

ees into the cultural fabric through routines or rituals that make the practices habitual. For example, *Inviting for Informal Exchanges*, *Off-Site Events* and *Employee
Resource Groups* dedicated to sustainable innovation fosters reflection and improvement on the newly established sustainable innovation practices. By sharing
stories of positive impact or failure, employees are encouraged to make new practices an integral part of their individual and organisational identity.

6.2.3 Mediating Artefacts

Following self-reflection and the specification of values, tensions and values-
action gaps and building on intensive social collaboration, the material side of
culture comes into focus: the tools and artefacts that mediate and streamline its
development.

> Artefacts such as tools, materials and frameworks play a pivotal role in
> cultivating sustainable innovation. They facilitate the mainstreaming of
> organisational values and policies, and they provide stability, guidance and
> structure to establish and streamline desired behaviours and sustainable
> innovation practices.

ARTEFACTS FOR GOVERNANCE

Artefacts serving governance purposes – such as policy documents, accountability frameworks or decision-making matrices – establish clear guardrails to prevent
deviations from desired practices. These artefacts clarify roles, responsibilities and
procedures, promoting transparency and reducing ambiguity in decision-making.
For instance, accountability frameworks create a culture of ownership and trust
by specifying who is responsible for which tasks. Decision-making matrices, on
the other hand, ensure that decisions and practices are grounded in sustainability values by providing structured ways to evaluate options, prioritise actions and
resolve conflicts.[19]

ARTEFACTS FOR OPERATIONAL PURPOSES

Artefacts such as checklists, templates, data management tools and visual aids
streamline regular operations, reduce complexity and provide guidance, for example, when onboarding new members. Furthermore, they standardise tasks,
making them easier to replicate and adapt across teams. For example, templates
for project proposals or progress reports ensure consistency in documentation,
while data management tools facilitate communication and collaboration, break-
ing down silos within the organisation.

   User-friendly, flexible and easily scalable software solutions are indispensable
operational artefacts. As seen in the German Railway case (case 13: section 6.1.2),
systems for collecting and analysing sustainability-related data and systems for forward-looking action and transition planning should be integrated with financial
reporting systems in use. Following the system value approach (section 2.1.1), they

do not just calculate with financial data but also with environmental and social data points measured, for example, in kilowatt hours or in social metrics from surveys. Apart from business intelligence solutions from major vendors, specialised ESG applications are available to support data-driven sustainability management.

Operational artefacts – including indicators, software tools and data-collection methods – are instrumental for introducing *Context-Based Reporting* methods and aiding related practices and communication strategies. For instance, a sustainability dashboard on the corporate website can track metrics such as community impact, carbon emissions and resource consumption in relation to thresholds and allocations, communicating transparently the company's sustainability performance to its stakeholders. AI-powered tools can support *Context-Based Reporting* by providing insights on critical areas for improvement, taking into account changing thresholds and allocations (see section 3.3.2).

UPDATES AND FLEXIBLE WORKFLOWS

As business challenges and practices continue to evolve, artefacts should follow, allowing flexible workflows and updates. For example, the inspection company from our field study on values-based innovation cultures (section 4.1.5) sought to foster sustainable innovation across its subsidiaries by introducing an *Innovation Impact Assessment* process. Using criteria derived from United Nations' SDGs framework, the assessment was focused on all of the company's innovation projects and service offerings. It helped to make the progress on projects more visible and promoted accountability without openly discrediting teams that lag behind.[20] However, the initial implementation of the assessment was time-intensive, requiring up to three hours to assess each of the company's some 2000 innovation projects and service offerings. To streamline the process, the company adjusted the supporting artefacts and refined the procedures for using them.

6.2.4 Cultivating Outcomes

Two criteria must be fulfilled for an organisation to move beyond mere declarations of goodwill or strategic intent and achieve success for sustainable innovations: real-world implementation (e.g. market presence) and positive impact on sustainable development. Sustainability strategies must be translated into decision-making processes and practices that iteratively approximate the desired outcomes, giving the organisation a competitive edge and impact. Artefacts play a pivotal role in this endeavour, demonstrating that sustainability values and goals are not only aspirational but also actionable and measurable. By simultaneously cultivating values, practices and artefacts, organisations build the cultural foundation to turn values of sustainability into economically, socially and environmentally valuable outcomes.

However, this cultural alignment between values, practices and artefacts is a necessary, but not yet sufficient condition to establishing sustainable innovation cultures. Innovation must be understood as an outcome and sustainable innovation as an outcome that creates or redistributes environmental, social and economic value (section 2.1.3). Several practices and methods ensure that these outcomes are achieved and that values of sustainability are efficiently transferred into sustainable processes, products, services, business models or other types of innovation. Sustainability-oriented *Management Systems* can be used to professionalise innovation management and *Sustainable Finance and Investment* to plan, monitor and adapt investments under conditions of uncertainty. *Context-Based Reporting, Result Chains* and *Innovation Impact Assessment* are indispensable methods to achieve the desired impact, while ensuring that the organisation operates within boundaries of local thresholds and allocations. They continuously review intermediate results so that processes and activities can be iteratively finetuned.

The path of this learning journey can be smoothed by the experiences of other companies and experts, as documented throughout this book. In addition to proven practices and methods, we highlight valuable outcomes – from a simple online tool provided by Interface to calculate harm costs (section 12.4) to new sustainable business models and ecosystems (chapter 7). This book points the way for companies and other organisations to establish their own unique sustainable innovation culture by introducing impactful practices and methods.

6.3 Practices and Methods: Cultivating Sustainable Innovation

Advanced practices and methods cultivate sustainable innovation literacy, enhancing skills and competencies as well as frameworks and tools that facilitate sustainable innovation across the organisation and even across its ecosystems. Practices and methods from the 3C activities of conceiving and co-creating play an important role in cultivating sustainable innovation. This section reviews additional practices and methods to mainstream values of sustainability and related notions, introduce new practices and mediating artefacts and systematically tap into opportunities for innovation and ensure desired outcomes.

6.3.1 Practices and Methods: Promoting Sustainability Literacy and Capacity Building

The first set of practices and methods supports the mainstreaming of sustainability-related values and policies and putting them into practice. It addresses the unique needs, skills, competencies and awareness levels of individual employees or teams and asks the question:

How can we mainstream values and related notions to promote sustainable innovation literacy and develop human resources to turn strategies into practice?

NEWS

47.
POLICY
COMMUNICATION

Policy Communication[21] moves beyond the general fostering of sustainability-oriented innovation efforts. In order to perpetuate a virtuous cycle of continuous conceiving, co-creating and cultivating of guiding principles and organisational policies, *Policy Communication* draws on stakeholder input and management guidance. Input for specifying the policies aligned with organisational values and guiding principles can be gathered from employees and other stakeholders through conceiving practices and methods such as *Contextual Inquiry*, *Cultural Surveys* and *Sensemaking*. Desired actions and behaviours can then be modelled to facilitate understanding and interpretation of values as well as guiding principles and policies in diverse situations, teams, functions or projects. Engaging employees, *Policy Communication* ensures that the values of sustainability and related policies are not only understood but also effectively integrated into a variety of organisational contexts.

CHALLENGE: Guiding principles and statements need to be clear, consistent and sufficiently well-defined to direct situated action. *How can we ensure that values, guiding principles and policies will be well understood by different stakeholders in different situations?*

APPROACH: Communicate guiding principles and related policies, embedding values in practice and demonstrating how they are applied in day-to-day decisions and activities.

RELATED METHODS: *Cultural Dictionary, Tailored Communication*

**48.
CULTURAL
DICTIONARY**

Cultural Dictionaries[22] raise awareness and foster sustainability literacy through clear and direct communication. Basic concepts can be defined using the European Sustainability Reporting Standard or the Climate Dictionary of the United Nations Development Programme.[23] A dictionary serves as a reference for preparing sustainability-related statements and ambitions. Backing up definitions with illustrations of desirable (or unacceptable) behaviour contextualises a term and helps convey its meaning. Social media campaigns can provide further clarification and facilitate dissemination.

CHALLENGE: Employee collaboration and commitment can be hampered when basic notions and priorities are poorly understood or differently interpreted. *How can we enhance sustainability literacy and create a common ground of understanding?*

APPROACH: Disambiguate and effectively communicate cultural concepts and how to enact them with a *Cultural Dictionary*. It provides a common language and promotes awareness, literacy and engagement around sustainability and related values.

EXAMPLE: An energy technology company introduced a *Cultural Dictionary* featuring interviews where employees from different backgrounds shared how they understood and applied newly introduced sustainability values.

49.
TAILORED
COMMUNICATION

Instead of targeting the entire organisation, *Tailored Communication*[24] aligns messages with individual or subcultural notions and priorities. To address the needs and preferences of different target groups, it typically follows insights generated through the conceiving practices of *Contextual Inquiry* and related methods.

Tailored Communication is more effective in promoting stakeholder engagement and behavioural change than traditional one-size-fits-all communication, because it recognises the diverse backgrounds, beliefs and behaviours of individuals.[25] Several strategies help to tailor messages to the preferences and needs of individuals or small groups.[26] For instance, peripheral strategies involve modifying the visual presentation of messages, such as formatting, colours, images and headings. Evidential strategies provide data about how an issue impacts a particular group, which can be used to sensitise the group to the issue. Linguistic strategies ensure that messages are delivered in the target audience's preferred language and communication style. Constituent-involving strategies draw input directly from the cultural members for the co-creating of messages. Finally, sociocultural strategies design messages that resonate with deeply held values and beliefs, acknowledging how these underpin group identity and experiences.

An example of sociocultural tailoring can be found in the case of the Dutch coffee company Jacobs Douwe Egberts and its transition to a sustainability culture. In this case, *Memetics*

research into employee perspectives on sustainability and cultural change enabled the company to send them tailored messages about cultural change.[27] For example, employees who equated sustainability with environmental conservation received messages emphasising the prevention of harms, while those concerned about the need to reduce the use of plastics in packaging received content aligned with their concerns. Employees perceived tailored messages as more attractive, intelligible and motivating than generic messages.

CHALLENGE: One-size-fits-all messaging loses its relevance for specific audiences. *How can we adequately address individual communication needs and preferences?*

APPROACH: Tailor messages to each individual and subculture's sustainability literacy knowledge and ambitions. Understand your stakeholders to effectively use communication methods to target media and shape messages.

EXAMPLE: Employees of the Dutch coffee company Jacobs Douwe Egberts shaped messages about cultural change that were tailored to their employee's individual notions of sustainability and cultural change, making them more attractive, intelligible and motivating than non-tailored messages.[28]

50.
INCENTIVISATION

Incentivisation[29] is an ongoing organisation-wide practice that rewards all employees who contribute to the organisation's sustainable development goals. Several guidelines suggest how to devise sustainability-oriented incentives.[30] First, the criteria must be measurable, relevant, challenging and transparent. Second, incentives must be supported by shareholders and aligned with the organisation's strategy, values and aspirations for long-term development. Third, organisations must have a flexible compensation structure that allows for the seamless integration of sustainability criteria. And fourth, *Incentivisation* must balance and not outweigh an employee's existing intrinsic motivation with extrinsic rewards.

CHALLENGE: Many employees do not receive motivating recognition for their value-creating contributions. *How can we keep up the motivation of all employees to actively contribute to sustainable innovation initiatives?*

APPROACH: Continuously align performance measurement, award systems and positive recognition with employee contributions to sustainable value creation and the achievement of sustainability-related objectives.

RELATED METHODS: *Incentivisation Schemes*

51.
INCENTIVISATION SCHEMES

Incentivisation Schemes[31] are a first step to promoting desirable behaviours and results of targeted employee groups (e.g. innovation managers) or sustainability projects. The Dutch paint and chemicals company, AkzoNobel, was among the first to introduce a sustainability-oriented Incentivisation Scheme in 2009, rewarding its board of directors based on the company's three-year average position in the Dow Jones Sustainability Index.[32]

The company had faced criticism that the external sustainability index was an unreliable benchmark because it used untransparent metrics, overemphasised policy commitments over measurable performance and depended heavily on self-reported data. Suspicions also arose that the new Incentivisation Scheme aimed to replace regular bonuses, which had become untenable following the 2008 financial crisis. In response to this controversy, AkzoNobel introduced a new Incentivisation Scheme that rewarded senior managers based on measurable indicators of sustainability performance, rather than on subjective evaluations made by a committee.

CHALLENGE: Employees might lack the motivation to collaborate in sustainable innovation projects if only individual contributions and short-term financial achievements are incentivised. How can we motivate contributions to sustainable innovation projects?

APPROACH: Use indicators to assess employees and incentivise desirable behaviours or valuable results of a sustainable innovation project. Awards and bonuses are balanced with non-financial benefits such as access to professional development.

EXAMPLE: The Dutch paint and chemicals company, AkzoNobel, introduced a bonus system to reward senior managers for meeting long-term sustainability targets.[33] The system ties 30 percent of the managers' long-term incentive bonus to the company's sustainable innovation performance.

52.
ATTRACTING THE
RIGHT TALENT

For *Attracting the Right Talent*,[34] companies need to screen candidates based on technical competencies and sustainability-related notions and priorities. In addition to educational and job-specific requirements, competencies should include an understanding of or experience with sustainability reporting as part of the selection criteria. Screening candidates with personal values of sustainability contributes to unearthing the 'hidden treasure' of an intrinsically motivated workforce. *Aspirational Narratives* play an important role in attracting and retaining candidates who are drawn to purpose-driven work. Moreover, organisations should seek to hire underrepresented groups including diverse ethnicity, gender, age, religion and ability. Attracting a diversified workforce is not only an essential element of social sustainability but also an asset for gaining new and rich perspectives on sustainable innovation (see case 1: section 2.3.3).

CHALLENGE: Sustainable innovation cultures are formed by organisational members who bring a wide range of expertise and a profound commitment to sustainability values. *How can we discover and engage highly motivated, skilled and knowledgeable talent to drive sustainable innovation?*

APPROACH: Implement 'a recruitment and selection process that takes into account both competencies and sustainability-oriented values'.[35]

RELATED METHODS: *Aspirational Narratives*

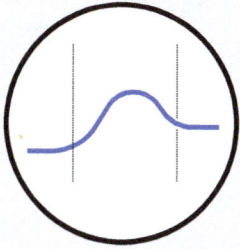

53.
ASPIRATIONAL NARRATIVES

We communicate about events, but also about values and goals within the framework of stories and narratives. *Aspirational Narratives*[36] frame sustainable innovation as an organisational goal that is intrinsically motivated and ambitious. This type of narrative contrasts with ambiguous and accountable narratives of sustainability. Ambiguous narratives are found in organisations that present notions of sustainability as an add-on, without articulating clear definitions, drivers, motivations and responsibilities for sustainability management. Accountable narratives highlight performance metrics, reporting, compliance, incremental improvements and the responsibilities of a specialised sustainability department.

Aspirational Narratives, by contrast, specify notions of sustainability in terms of ambitious objectives for sustainable innovation. They are more likely to support the mainstreaming of innovation-supportive values, such as risk-taking, experimentation and adaptability along with the establishment of corresponding innovation practices.

CHALLENGE: Convincing and coherent stories and narratives promote commitment, a willingness to innovate and a shared identification with forward-looking strategies. *How can we craft narratives that inspire proactive and purpose-driven engagement for sustainable innovation?*

APPROACH: Frame the pursuit of sustainability-related values as an organisational purpose with *Aspirational Narratives* and formulate hopeful and ambitious objectives for sustainable innovation.

EXAMPLE: A comparative multi-case study demonstrated that the *Aspirational Narratives*[37] in an American textiles company and a Belgian household goods company were related with more innovation-supportive values (i.e. flexibility, freedom, risk-taking, experimentation, continuous learning and change) compared to other companies with ambiguous and accountable (focused on compliance and metrics) narratives of sustainability.

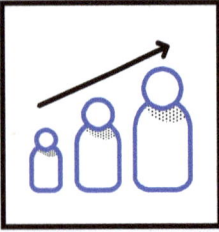

54. HUMAN RESOURCE DEVELOPMENT

55. MANDATORY TRAINING

Human Resource Development[38] is not just a practice, but a discipline of its own. It includes several subordinate practices such as onboarding, employee training, career development and succession planning. From a cultivation perspective, Human Resource Development seeks to align employee skills and competencies on the one side and task demands and challenges on the other.[39] Clear goals for success and constructive feedback are key for individuals to experience a sense of flow, maintain intrinsic motivation and further develop capabilities for sustainable innovation. Mandatory Training ensure that employee skills grow with the size and complexity of sustainable innovation challenges.

CHALLENGE: Sustainable innovation cultures rely on human resources and personal competencies. How can we empower employees with the skills and competences needed to drive sustainable innovation?

APPROACH: Foster personal growth, motivation and a sense of flow through 'onboarding and clear communication of values to new employees',[40] employee training, career development and succession planning.

RELATED METHODS: Mandatory Training

Mandatory Training[41] ensures that all employees, regardless of their role, department or experience, receive the same foundational knowledge and competencies and develop a shared understanding of organisational values and practices. Large companies invest in their own corporate universities to foster custom learning and deliver their own training programs.

CHALLENGE: Alignment with the organisation's values, strategic goals and operational standards empowers employee performance. How can we mainstream a shared understanding of the organisational values and convey the competences needed to turn them into practice?

APPROACH: Further sustainability literacy and the acquisition of knowledge across teams with Mandatory Training. It imparts essential sustainable innovation skills and competencies.

EXAMPLE: Interface provides mandatory sustainability training to all new employees to inform them of ongoing activities and encourage them to engage in sustainable innovation.[42] Optional advanced training is also offered to develop societal problem-solving skills.

6.3.2 Practices and Methods: Promoting Social Interactions

The next set of practices and methods focuses on cultivating social interactions. These are a significant factor in both hindering and facilitating the mainstreaming of values and the establishment of new practices. They range from the daily informal exchanges that take place between employees to more deliberate forms of collaboration and knowledge exchange, together with interactions with stakeholders outside of the organisation.

> How can we promote sustainability-oriented collaboration, knowledge exchange and stakeholder engagement?

56. INVITING FOR INFORMAL EXCHANGE

Interpersonal relationships and informal inter- actions often reveal notions and perspectives that may remain hidden in formal meetings due to hierarchical pressures or group dynamics. For instance, a CSR manager (case 9: section 4.1.5) recalls a canteen discussion where a previously sceptical colleague expressed newfound support for sustainability efforts, despite opposing them in formal meetings. The canteen conversation bridged the gap between formal opposition and personal reflection, demonstrating the potential of informal settings to shift personal perceptions about the official organisational values and strat- egies. *Inviting for Informal Exchange*[43] on a reg- ular basis through methods like *Off-Site Events* and *Employee Resource Groups* can help build trust among employees and overcome resistance to newly introduced values and practices that they might otherwise conceal.

CHALLENGE: Informal interactions in an atmos- phere of trust and openness consolidate rela- tionships and motivate engagement for cultural transformation. *How can we facilitate the sharing of sentiments and ideas employees might other- wise conceal?*

APPROACH: Create opportunities for informal ver- bal or non-verbal interpersonal communication. Facilitate the flow of ideas, knowledge and emo- tions in everyday activities that are not focused on problem-solving.

RELATED METHODS: *Off-Site Events, Employee Resource Groups*

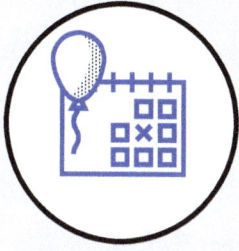

57.
OFF-SITE EVENTS

Routine activities and daily meetings can lead to monotony and disengagement, limiting the potential of dynamic knowledge exchange and collaboration. *Off-Site Events*[44] refresh interactions among employees in a new, engaging context.

CHALLENGE: Changing places allows employees to take new perspectives and the time spent together consolidates relationships. *How can we use special spaces and times to promote interpersonal experiences and facilitate deliberation?*

APPROACH: Bring employees away from their usual workplace to detach them from their daily routines with *Off-Site Events*. Have them work together on unfamiliar yet important tasks and participate in team-building activities.

EXAMPLE: In 2020, the green search engine, Ecosia, responded to the heated debates stirred by the Black Lives Matter movement by engaging its employees in an *Off-Site Event* with the goal of establishing accessibility and inclusivity as guiding values for product development.[45]

58. EMPLOYEE RESOURCE GROUPS

Employee Resource Groups[46] are employee-led groups formed around shared interests. Typically, they focus on advocacy for the rights of underrepresented employee groups, but in recent years they are also being formed to promote corporate contributions to sustainability. *Employee Resource Groups* invite staff members to in-person networking events, regular meetings or online platforms for information sharing. They offer several key benefits, including opportunities to collaborate and network informally with colleagues from different departments, fostering a sense of belonging that extends beyond one's team or department. They facilitate knowledge exchange and joint engagement in intrapreneurial projects. Support from higher management encourages the formation and development of *Employee Resource Groups* to leverage these benefits.

CHALLENGE: Sustainability-minded employees may not be aware of one another and lack opportunities for collaboration. *How can we encourage ongoing cross-functional collaboration among motivated employees?*

APPROACH: Form sustainability-oriented resource groups by identifying (e.g. via surveys) and bringing together employees with strong commitment to sustainability. They can be supported as intrapreneurial teams or promotors of sustainability literacy.

EXAMPLE: A project manager in a large science-based manufacturer started a resource group to inspire sustainable innovation efforts (see section 10.3.3). By promoting the group at company events, she mainstreamed the initiative in other departments.

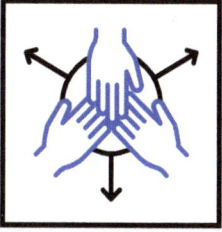

59.
PARTICIPATIVE
DECISION
MAKING

Traditional stakeholder engagement limits participation to deliberation and advisory inputs without giving stakeholders influence over decision-making. Such limited engagement risks perpetuating the status quo and alienating participants who feel their contributions lack meaningful impact.[47] To avoid the pitfalls of superficial engagement, *Participative Decision Making*[48] ensures that stakeholders have a tangible role in shaping organisational outcomes.

Business models of cooperative ownership[49] as well as decentralised, autonomous organisations (section 5.2.5) institutionalise participative decision-making by diffusing governance and ownership among members, ensuring that key decisions are made collectively through democratic voting or algorithmic consensus mechanisms.

CHALLENGE: Typical stakeholder engagement restricts participation to deliberation and advisory inputs, perpetuating existing power structures and making stakeholders feel their input is ignored. *How can we translate stakeholder contributions into actionable strategies and policies for sustainable innovation?*

APPROACH: Actively involve stakeholders in decision-making processes concerning sustainable development to ensure that innovation development is aligned with values of equity.

RELATED METHODS: *Stakeholder Advisory Board*

60.
STAKEHOLDER
ADVISORY BOARD

Interactions with external stakeholders can provide a wide range of insights on and potential solutions to sustainable innovation challenges. Overarching practices of *Inclusive Deliberation* offer one way to engage a broad range of stakeholders and source such insights. However, effectively addressing issues of sustainability often requires expertise in topics such as environmental management, technologies, economics and social sciences. To ensure this expertise is available, *Stakeholder Advisory Boards*[50] engage a number of thought leaders to provide advice on broad issues of sustainability and specific business opportunities. Examples are the Ecomagination advisory board,[51] which supports the business development of sustainability-oriented technologies at General Electric and the Sustainability Advisory Board at Siemens[52] (see case 18: section 12.3.2). Engagement in advisory boards can be complemented by open channels of communication to facilitate stakeholder feedback and requests. The EU offers a stakeholder request platform to address suggestions regarding the EU Taxonomy.[53]

CHALLENGE: Sustainability management requires advanced expertise in diverse topics and an impartial perspective on the current level of corporate unsustainability. *How can we assimilate impartial, expert contributions that question internal assumptions and ensure that sustainable innovation projects meet standards and thresholds?*

APPROACH: Establish advisory boards to receive constructive critique on issues of integrity and sustainable development from a competent external perspective.

EXAMPLE: Siemens maintains an external perspective on its sustainability-related performance and challenges by regularly consulting with its Sustainability Advisory Board. It is made up of eight leading experts from academia and industry from a range of disciplines and regions around the world.[54]

6.3.3 Practices and Methods: Ensuring Positive Impact

The final set of cultivating practices and methods ensures that sustainable innovation efforts lead to desirable outcomes and have a substantial positive impact. They promote accountability, transparency and the alignment of innovation practices and material artefacts with respect to sustainability values.

> How can we professionalise practices and introduce artefacts
> that ensure the positive impact of innovation efforts?

61. MANAGEMENT SYSTEMS

Companies that seek to translate their values of sustainability into organisational practice often measure their progress in terms of individual performance indicators instead of applying systemic approaches. A management system is a 'set of interrelated or interacting elements of an organisation to establish policies and objectives and processes to achieve those objectives'.[55] Sustainability-oriented *Management Systems*[56] 'help organisations achieve their environmental, social and economic goals while minimising their negative impacts'.[57]

The International Organisation for Standardisation (ISO) has defined management systems for different areas of organisational development, such as quality assurance (ISO 9001),[58] environmental management (ISO 14000),[59] occupational health and safety, corporate social responsibility and innovation. The innovation management system clarifies fundamental notions and terms, requirements for certification and provides guidelines for professional innovation management (ISO 56000-56002).[60]

Management systems are combined into an integrative system[61] to meet the diverse requirements of sustainable innovation management, which realises sustainable value from innovation investment in the face of uncertainty. For example, a company adopts an innovation management system to professionalise its efforts in this area, incorporating values of sustainability into its innovation culture. The Managing by Sustainable Innovational Values model[62] is specifically designed to act as an innovation management

system that aligns economic, social and emotional values of sustainability with innovation management efforts. In parallel, environmental management systems track these innovations, minimising their harm to the environment. Last but not least, quality assurance systems help maintain and continuously improve output consistency, ensuring that products and services meet both regulatory standards and evolving stakeholder expectations.

CHALLENGE: Best practices and codified knowledge allow companies to benefit from investments in sustainable innovation. *How can we establish transparent, systematic and reliable processes to ensure sustainable innovation projects are successful?*

APPROACH: Introduce standardised management systems for innovation management, environmental management and quality management to consolidate good management practices. They can be introduced and certified to establish policies, processes and criteria for sustainable innovation management, professionalising the integration of sustainability values in innovation projects and the screening and redirecting of innovation projects that fail to make material contributions to sustainable development.

RELATED METHODS: *Materiality Assessment, Context-Based Reporting, Results Chain, Innovation Impact Assessment*

62.
MATERIALITY
ASSESSMENT

Materiality Assessment[63] identifies and prioritises the most important aspects (their 'materiality') of sustainability performance and the challenges an organisation faces based on their relevance to the organisation and its stakeholders. There are two main perspectives on materiality: the business case perspective, which relates materiality to the potential risk of sustainability issues for the company's financial performance and the societal impact perspective, which relates materiality to the company's environmental, social and economic impacts. The EU Commission requires companies to adopt a double materiality approach, integrating both perspectives (see section 2.1.1).

Since the business case and the societal impact perspectives often conflict, organisations may attempt to alleviate the tension between them by focusing on win-win scenarios that serve both perspectives. However, this can leave important sustainability challenges unaddressed. A more effective alternative acknowledges the paradox and encourages transparent dialogue about the tensions between perspectives, opening the door for internal and external discussions about these challenges and innovative solutions to address them.[64] One way to facilitate transparent communication about a company's double materiality is to account for the role of different business model configurations and how they give rise to specific risks, opportunities and impacts, as exemplified in the case of Port Esbjerg.

CHALLENGE: Companies need to focus their innovation efforts on sustainability challenges with high impact on the company, society and the environment. *How can we prioritise and focus our efforts on sustainability challenges that matter most to our business and its stakeholders?*

APPROACH: Identify and prioritise key issues that affect an organisation's ability to create long-term value with *Materiality Assessments*. They help organisations to optimise resource allocation and improve risk management in sustainable innovation projects.

EXAMPLE: A case study of Port Esbjerg, Denmark's leading port for shipping offshore wind turbines, combined a double materiality assessment with business model analysis, linking business model configurations to both financial materiality and material impacts on sustainable development. This integrated approach informed the identification and prioritisation of ten material impacts and related KPIs, such as energy and water efficiency on the port premises, green energy investments and stewardship of oil and gas regulations.[65]

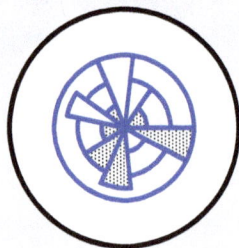

63.
CONTEXT-BASED REPORTING

Conventional ESG progress reporting builds on relative benchmarks but ignores the natural limits of the Earth's carrying capacities and regional resource availability, which can lead to a misconception of the design space for sustainable innovation efforts. *Context-Based Reporting*[66] moves beyond double *Materiality Assessment* and grounds sustainability ambitions and practices within science-based limits, regional thresholds and allocations (see section 2.1.1). It provides reliable guardrails for safe and just development, prioritising task areas for sustainable innovation activities. Sustainable development performance indicators (SDPI) support such *Context-Based Reporting*.[67] Several companies have participated in pilot testing and use of the indicators,[68] including the South Korean semiconductor manufacturer SK Hynix, the Spanish Mondragon and the German producer of beauty products and naturopathic medicines Weleda.[69]

CHALLENGE: Organisations need an authentic perspective on their value creation and harm creation to understand and prioritise their sustainable innovation challenges. *How can we reliably assess our sustainability performance and define the design space for sustainable innovation efforts?*

APPROACH: Ground sustainable innovation ambitions and practices on scientific insights and fair allocation of resources using *Context-Based Reporting*. It addresses evidence-based limits, regional sustainability thresholds and the allocation of usable resources to provide a reliable structure not just for reporting a relative progress, but for 'authentic sustainability assessment'.

EXAMPLE: The companies SK Hynix, Mondragon and Weleda, among others, have adopted sustainable development performance indicators in their reporting strategies, reflecting global sustainability norms and local resource boundaries.[70]

64.
RESULTS
CHAIN

Results Chains[71] can be used to estimate the sustainability impact of business activities in the future. The OECD Development and Assistance Committee defines Results Chains as causal sequences that 'stipulate the necessary sequence to achieve desired objectives beginning with inputs, moving through activities and outputs and culminating in outcomes, impacts and feedback'.[72]

Differences between stakeholder outcomes, impacts and feedback need to be identified, taking into account their value as perceived by the stakeholders.[73] Outcomes reflect a positive or negative, intended or unintended change in the situation of a stakeholder that results from innovation activities, regardless of whether a stakeholder recognises and appreciates this change or considers it appropriate. Impacts reflect a broader systematic change as a result of business activities, irrespective of the subjective perceptions of stakeholders. Value, on the other hand, is 'an outcome or impact that an affected or unaffected stakeholder recognises, appreciates, considers appropriate and desires for him or herself or a different stakeholder'.[74]

CHALLENGE: Many organisations struggle to justify their sustainable innovation efforts or to demonstrate that their outcomes contribute to sustainable development. How can we estimate and communicate the long-term results and positive impact of sustainable innovation projects?

APPROACH: Establish a structure with Results Chains to assess, manage and demonstrate how business activities trigger different levels of change, from outputs to outcomes and ultimately development impact and perceived value.

EXAMPLE: The GIZ development agency uses Results Chains to help business environment reform projects to identify their expected results, test whether the intervention rationale is sound, identify critical success factors and effectively communicate the expected project results with stakeholders.[75]

65. INNOVATION IMPACT ASSESSMENT

66. SUSTAINABLE FINANCE AND INVESTMENT

Innovation Impact Assessments[76] engage stakeholders and employ data-based evidence to establish indicators and prioritise thresholds at which innovation projects should be implemented, rejected or entered into a risk management process. An intuitive approach to indicator selection prioritising the most tangible or familiar indicators is ill-advised as it may lead to omitting key areas of analysis.[77] The definition of indicators for advanced *Innovation Impact Assessments* should be informed by methods such as *Materiality Assessments, Context-Based Reporting* and *Results Chains*.

CHALLENGE: Organisations that lack a standardised framework to compare the potential impacts of innovation projects will struggle to make stage-gate decisions. *How can we systematically assess sustainable innovation projects against criteria that measure their potential impact?*

APPROACH: Translate sustainability values into indicators, heuristics and criteria that inform decision-making at different innovation stages with *Innovation Impact Assessments*. They are co-developed to ensure alignment with organisational and departmental goals and values.

EXAMPLE: A German inspection company[78] has customised ten indicators derived from the SDGs to inform innovation stage-gate decisions. Peer-to-peer assessments are introduced to break silos and inspire heterogeneous subsidiaries (e.g. IT and mobility) to learn from each another.

Sustainable Finance and Investment[79] transforms financial planning and management accounting to align with sustainability-related values, goals and transition plans (see chapter 12 for more on financial planning). As an ongoing practice, *Sustainable Finance and Investment* reviews the allocation of resources, uncovers new revenues (e.g. from *Values-Based Business Modelling* or *Values-Based Ecosystem Modelling*) and refines sustainability-oriented financial metrics and accounting methods, such as *Life Cycle Cost Analysis* and *Sustainable Innovation Financing*.

CHALLENGE: Just like other priorities such as safety or human resource development, sustainable innovation needs financial planning, management accounting and transformation. *How can we manage financial resources and investments in innovation projects that lead to long-lasting, positive and measurable social and environmental impacts?*

APPROACH: Integrate sustainable transformation and financial planning for sustainable innovation to provide employees with the necessary funding and resources for putting sustainable innovation strategies into practice.

RELATED METHODS: *Life Cycle Cost Analysis, Sustainable Innovation Financing*

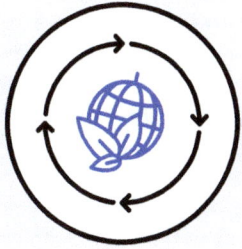

67.
LIFE CYCLE COST ANALYSIS

Many sustainable innovation – such as energy-efficient buildings, electric vehicle fleets and circular economy manufacturing processes – often yield long-term financial benefits, including lower energy costs, reduced waste management expenses and increased operational efficiency. However, they require significant initial investment. *Life Cycle Cost Analysis*[80] estimates the total cost of owning or using an asset throughout its entire life cycle, helping decision-makers evaluate the trade-offs between short-term expenses and long-term economic performance and account for their environmental responsibilities.

CHALLENGE: Sustainable innovations often involve high initial costs but lead to long-term benefits like reduced waste and operational savings. *How can we assess the long-term advantages of innovative sustainable solutions and ensure that they outweigh costs of a major investment?*

APPROACH: *Life Cycle Cost Analysis* helps project teams assess the true value of sustainable innovations over time, ensuring that short-term expenses do not detract from long-term gains.

EXAMPLE: A *Life Cycle Cost Analysis* of a construction project in the US Pacific Northwest found that, while initial costs for mass timber building are higher than those for concrete, it reduces emissions and offers long-term economic benefits, including energy efficiency and lower maintenance expenses.[81] This validated the advantages of a higher initial investment in mass timber construction.

68.
SUSTAINABLE INNOVATION FINANCING

Despite preliminary evidence for superior performance in risk management, innovation and resilience, the business case for sustainability is difficult to prove due to its longer time horizon, complexities in measurement, attribution of tangible and intangible benefits as well as trade-offs. To address these challenges, novel instruments and business models for *Sustainable Innovation Financing*[62] have been developed to fund sustainable innovation projects. For example, green bonds raise funds for environmentally beneficial innovation projects, such as improving resource or energy efficiency. Sustainability-linked loans offer improved terms and reduced interest rates, depending on the borrower's achievement of predetermined sustainability targets.

Reduced capital costs can be reinvested in sustainable innovation projects. Achievement of sustainability-related outcomes is also key to client-provider relations in the success-based contracting model, often used in the public sector, as well as in the pay-for-success business model.[83] Financing business models can also trigger sustainable innovation in the supply chain, as seen in the collaboration between Walmart and the Hongkong and Shanghai Banking Corporation (HSBC), where suppliers are incentivised to improve their environmental performance in order to benefit from preferential financing rates and early invoice payments.

CHALLENGE: Investments in sustainable innovation can be difficult to justify if they do not immediately pay off. *How can we secure funding for sustainable innovation projects, despite uncertain short-term returns?*

APPROACH: Employ sustainability-related financing instruments to create financial flexibility, enabling investment in sustainable innovation at reduced costs of capital.

EXAMPLE: Walmart supports its suppliers in reducing their emissions and improving energy efficiency through a collaboration with HSBC.[84] The bank provides early invoice payments to eligible suppliers as well as financing rates linked to their carbon emissions, science-based sustainability targets and impact reporting.

IN SUM

Rather than facilitating individual sustainable innovation projects, these practices and methods promote sustainable innovation literacy, collaboration and human resource development, while ensuring that innovation efforts lead to a positive impact on sustainable development.

> Cultivating practices and related methods helps to align organisational notions, practices and artefacts in order to establish a sustainable innovation culture.

In doing so, they close the cycle of conceiving, co-creating and cultivating, preparing the ground for spinning a new virtuous cycle that perpetuates cultural development.

In the third part of this book, we will explore how the practices and methods presented in this second part are applied in different European countries and industries. As you read these insightful cases, observe how the 3C framework activities of conceiving, co-creating and cultivating have empowered companies to identify and effectively address their most pressing sustainable innovation challenges.

PART III

CASES /

European Companies on their Journeys to Establish Sustainable Innovation Cultures

Part III is dedicated to all the companies and organisations around the world that are struggling to put their sustainability strategies into action. We worked with eleven of them in Germany, Italy, Spain and Poland to understand their strategies and practices together with the persistent challenges they are facing. And we engaged in co-creating with them to devise targeted responses to the challenges they prioritised. Each of the following chapters 7–10 presents one of these cases. Each case shows how unique efforts to establish a sustainable innovation culture unfold in a real-life context and in a different market and national environment. Each case shows how selected practices and methods (from part II) are adapted and introduced in a particular company.

In Germany (Chapter 7), we look into the case of an inspection company that has introduced sustainability as a core value for innovation, cultivated advanced methods such as *Innovation Impact Assessment* and already earned high recognition for its dedicated efforts. We address the challenge of taking a sustainable innovation culture to the ecosystem level, showcasing an exemplary workflow and results using *Values-Based Ecosystem Modelling*.

In Italy (Chapter 8), our colleagues from Firenze University studied the case of an energy technology company. Challenges for co-creating were prioritising sustainability in its innovation strategy and developing the operative aspects of the cultural transformation. Practices and methods such as a company-wide Ideation Contest and *Innovation Impact Assessments* were initiated to further develop sustainability orientation in an industry still struggling to fully embrace values of sustainability.

In Poland (chapter 9), our colleagues from Cracow University of Technology studied the case of a robotics company to understood how investments in people and technology combined with management by values are critical conditions for sustainable innovation. We see practices and methods such as *Empowerment, Failure to Success, Incentivisation* and *Human Resource Development* as well as methods like *Sustainable Innovation Financing* at work to support a sustainable innovation culture in a challenging market environment.

In Spain (Chapter 10), our colleagues from Completense University of Madrid looked into the sustainable innovation management challenges of science-based companies, which are grounded in scientific rigour and knowledge. Their sustainable innovation challenges persist in cross-functional alignment, the need for function-specific *Innovation Impact Assessment* and *Empowerment* of employees engaged in bottom-up innovation initiatives. Moreover, a cohesive communication strategy around sustainable innovation achievements and efforts was missing. Co-creative *Envisioning* supported one of these companies to develop actionable initiatives involving training, new collaborations and creating a dedicated team to foster *Tailored Communication*.

The insights from these case studies can, of course, only be transferred to other cases subject to the same theoretical premises. One of the few similarities between them is that they are all commercial companies based in Europe with global operations. Otherwise, the four case studies cover a range of different maturity levels, market environments and challenges for developing sustainable innovation cultures. The German inspection company is ready to carry its own successful transformation into its business ecosystem. In contrast, the technology company is still struggling to prioritise sustainability issues internally and with business customers from the traditional energy industry. In Poland, a robotics company operates in a market environment where suppliers and customers often need to be convinced of the benefits of sustainable business practices and values-based management. For the expert-driven culture of science-based companies, on the other hand, the main challenge is to adequately communicate their own efforts and achievements in sustainable innovation. The lessons learned from these cases are, however, also relevant for other companies and stakeholders facing questions of communication, market development or the development of their business ecosystems in the context of sustainable development.

Chapter 7 /
From Safety to Sustainability – The Case of an Inspection Company in Germany

by Henning Breuer, Kiril Ivanov, Roman Meier-Andrae

Founded on the premise of ensuring safety for diverse clients and business partners, inspection companies are equally values-based organisations and natural ecosystem players. Establishing sustainability as a core value alongside safety empowers them to act as role models for business partners and mainstream sustainable innovation culture across the ecosystems they are engaged in.

7.1 From the Adoption of New Values to the Formation of New Ecosystems

Companies that already spearhead the sustainability transition can also empower strategic partners to put values of sustainability into daily practice. A technical inspection company from Germany is such a company, with strong foundations and capabilities to contribute to sustainable development. Like other inspection companies, it was founded 150 years ago in order to increase the safety of industrial steam boilers and other technical equipment. Based on values of safety, it facilitated the rise of whole industrial ecosystems, such as mobility, training, IT, engineering and mining and aerospace, among others. Continuing its history of protecting human life, the adoption of sustainability as core value is a natural move.

> **CONCEPT 6. Technical Inspection as a Values-Based Business**
>
> One hundred fifty years ago, an industrial steam boiler exploded in the Großer Mayerhof brewery in Mannheim. Numerous workers were injured, one stoker died immediately. The crack in the boiler's casing could have been easily recognised, but the operating personnel did not detect the defect, nor would they have seen the risks involved. Accidents of this kind have become more frequent since the beginning of industrialisation in Europe and overlaid its benefits with images of destruction. In January 1866, 22 entrepreneurs from Baden therefore founded the first Society for the Supervision and Insurance of Steam Boilers.[1]
>
> Within just a few years, the steam boiler inspection associations that emerged shortly afterwards not only managed to recognise hundreds of defects and prevent explosions, but also contributed to the development of safety standards and norms for technical monitoring. After foreign associations joined, the German organisation was renamed the International Association of Steam Boiler Inspection Associations in 1888. Soon, motor vehicles, lifts, roller coasters and other technical instalments were also tested – including, already in 1921, the height of chimneys in the interests of emission protection.[2] Ensuring the safety of technical installations remains the main concern of the technical inspection organisations to this day. In this sense they were founded as values-based organisations dedicated to ensuring safety, and they empowered the rise of safety culture for themselves as well as for their business partners and industries.

> Parallel to the regular involvement of independent experts, companies
> themselves are also paying more attention to the safety of systems and
> processes. Especially in technology companies, safety culture – that is, the
> behavioural patterns in dealing with safety issues – is an important topic. Can
> we hope for similar developments when it comes to sustainability?

The technical inspection company (which we will call TIC) made this development explicit in the year 2018 when sustainability was officially established as one of six core values and as a key component of its strategy. Numerous initiatives promote environmental responsibility, such as energy-efficient projects and waste reduction programs, some of them leading to significant improvements. In 2023, TIC further demonstrated its commitment by publishing detailed progress reports highlighting advancements in their Corporate Responsibility Roadmap and achieving key sustainability goals. These efforts were widely acknowledged when the inspection company scored among the top five, respectively one percent, of companies that participated in an annual independent quality assessment of its sustainability management system. This highlights the company's consistent commitment to corporate responsibility and environmental stewardship.

TIC also offers a range of customer-facing services aimed at promoting sustainability. These include testing, inspection, certification, engineering and training services that help clients align their operations with environmental standards. They support the energy transition with expertise in hydrogen and carbon management, provide ecological construction supervision, identify energy-saving potential and promote sustainable resource management. TIC also assists with the sustainable digitisation of IT systems and ensures the safety of future energy carriers like hydrogen through rigorous testing and certification processes.

In spite of the company's deeply engrained dedication to values of safety and sustainability, some challenges persist in establishing a sustainable innovation culture. They illustrate challenges and opportunities for forerunners in corporate sustainability. We will zoom in on one of these challenges: namely, the challenge of trying to establish a sustainable innovation culture not only within the limits of a single company, but across the ecosystem partners that the company draws on and contributes to. We outline a co-creating format to address this ecosystem challenge and provide illustrative results.

7.2   Good Practices and Persisting Challenges of an Inspection Company

TIC provides a revealing case of how an organisational culture that has always been dedicated to values of safety adopts sustainability-related values as new priorities integral to its culture, innovation strategy and operations. Values of safety and impartiality[3] have guided its expansion into other domains of testing, inspection and certification beyond industry, such as mobility, training, IT, engineering, mining and aerospace, among others. Its values-based history and maturity in managing these values professionally provides the organisation with a head start in the current transition to establishing sustainable innovation cultures. It also provides other companies with many good practices and methods to learn from. However, it also creates challenges in trying to leverage the potential that is already in place.

To gain a broad understanding of the company's transition towards a sustainable innovation culture we conducted field interviews with employees dealing with innovation and sustainability as part of their job profile. They came from various hierarchical levels, business divisions, innovation-related functions and locations. We followed a rigorous process of framing, accessing, investigating and interpreting (see chapter 4.2) and found six key insights: 1) sustainable innovation culture, 2) vertical integration, 3) horizontal collaboration, 4) ecosystem capabilities, 5) practices and methods, and 6) hidden treasures. They reveal challenges and entry points for managerial interventions to further advance TIC's sustainable innovation culture (see table 3). We will discuss one of them and show how it was addressed.

Insights	Illustrative Statements We want (desire) ... so that (values) ... but (tension) ...
1. Sustainable innovation culture	'We want to establish a sustainable innovation culture so that we can act on our values like sustainability, safety and trust, but in some cases, our history and engineering mindset prevent us from fully embracing a failure-tolerant, stakeholder-inclusive and sustainable innovation culture.'
2. Vertical integration	'We want to collaborate across hierarchical levels based on shared values so that we can achieve a higher impact with our joint efforts, but our strategy and values are not consistently adopted and backed up with supporting measures.'
3. Horizontal collaboration	'We need to collaborate across divisions so that we can learn from one another and leverage distributed knowledge for sustainable value creation, but the division of efforts and returns often remains uncertain and breeds conflicts.'
4. Ecosystem capabilities	'We want to keep absorbing external knowledge, collaborate and exchange perspectives with business partners as well as universities, legislators and civil society so that we can capture opportunities that ensure positive impact, but driving sustainability on an ecosystem level while developing our established business is challenging.'
5. Practices and methods	'We have successfully experimented with new practices and methods so that we can establish a sustainable innovation culture, but some of them face resistance while others are not yet adequately managed due to increased complexity and perceived disconnection from our familiar corporate values and ways of working.'
6. Hidden treasures	'All employees expect to align their personal (idealistic) values with the TIC organisational values so that they can fully engage and make the world a better place, but many struggle to keep the spirit alive as company culture changes.'

TABLE 3. Ethnographic insights on tensions and values-action gaps in an inspection company

7.3   Insight into Ecosystem Capabilities

Before showing how we addressed this insight, we will first present our empirical findings on ecosystem capabilities. Due to its historical development and its sustainability strategy, we initially assumed that the inspection company might already be a respected facilitator of the corporate and institutional ecosystems now driving the sustainability transition (figure 6). Results from our field interviews showed some evidence for such a move from safety-related to sustainability-related ecosystem development. For instance, respondents mentioned lively exchanges with academics at public conferences with the potential to form collaborative research projects or even joint spin-off ventures. Some mentioned ongoing discussions with ministries and legislators. Some highlighted the important challenge to adequately identify customer needs for sustainable innovation.

However, the field study also pointed to the untapped potential for joint value creation and the exchange of benefits building on partner relations. For instance, employees reported on their personal engagement in local initiatives to foster the sustainability transition in their region. These initiatives were praised for their intangible benefits of networking, building informal relations and enabling a free flow of ideas and perspectives. However, they were not considered as potential sources of any financial or other tangible strategic benefits for the company.

Other respondents stressed that digitalisation and networked systems require the collaboration of diverse experts beyond conventional (e.g. automobile) engineering. Moreover, as digitalisation creates demand for third-party inspection in new areas like generative AI application and data marketplaces, TIC's transformation into a sustainable innovation culture can benefit from capturing these emerging opportunities. However, a potential expansion into new business areas stood against current strategic priorities to advance sustainable value propositions in regulated markets, such as vehicle and industrial inspection.

In sum, we see sustainability-related activities involving external partners, but they do not reinforce each other or even fit together. They do not make up a strategy as an integrated set of choices to achieve an outcome.[4] An illustrative statement sums up the insight: 'We want to keep absorbing external knowledge, collaborate and exchange perspectives with business partners as well as universities, legislators and civil society so that we can capture opportunities that ensure positive impact, but driving sustainability on an ecosystem level while developing our established business is challenging.'

We differentiated this insight into the three key aspects of reputation, outside-in and inside-out innovation, and we initiated more coordinated action on this last aspect to prepare new, collaborative and sustainability-oriented business activities.

Reputation is an essential asset of the organisation and a driver of new business cases for sustainability. Safety is a fundamental value for technical inspection agencies. Their reputation in impartially ensuring safety was maintained in spite of the liberalisation of the inspection market in Germany in the 1990s, which created new trade-offs between short-term economic interests and the promise of ensuring the safety of everything that bears its quality seal.[5] In navigating between these tensions, TIC kept its commitment to safety and impartiality.

However, while much has been achieved in the area of safety, the same level of commitment and achievement needs to be demonstrated in sustainability. Participation in industry benchmarks like the Green Button, awarded to sustainably manufactured textile products, acknowledgements like the EcoVadis medals, values-based partnerships to pursue common sustainability goals, and external sustainability communication strengthened TIC's legitimacy and reputation, positioning the company as a recognised leader and enabler of sustainability. A more systematic communication of achievements and participation in certifications can further enhance their reputation for improving sustainability performance, which is regarded as a 'door opener for further developments' (as one of the respondents put it).

Outside-in absorption of external knowledge and stakeholder participation nourishes sustainability-related competences that further enhance the company's reputation. Employees learn from regular informal and formal interactions with external stakeholders such as regulators, NGOs, academic partners, suppliers, business actors from other industries, customers and even competitors. Employees regularly participate in academic conferences and projects or personally engage in local sustainability initiatives, allowing for exploration and an exchange of perspectives and networking regardless of whether they promise short-term financial returns. However, it is not always easy to appreciate the positive contribution of these informal exchange formats. Key knowledge, skills and methods are also taught in through professional development programmes and an internal academy. Some third parties are directly involved in procuring success-critical competencies or in assessing whether innovation proposals are aligned with corporate and stakeholder values or might harm TIC's reputation.

Untapped potential is especially seen as moving inside-out, leveraging internal knowledge and expertise in technical inspection and sustainability to inspire business partners, advise political stakeholders and offer new specialised services fostering sustainability for other companies and institutions. Participating in certification committees and advising regulators represent powerful levers for generating and scaling sustainability impact outside the company's boundaries. TIC's auditing services are offering companies protection from scandals and disasters, which are major sustainability risks. An open challenge for the near future is how TIC can offer specialised services to design, assess and verify sustainability in business operations, diffusing sustainable innovation to other companies and in new markets.

7.4   Lessons Learned from the Insight

Backed by its dedication to the values of safety and impartiality, TIC mediates between its business partners, private customers, political actors and regulatory boards, creating unique value for each of them. Now it strives to extend this heritage through *Engaging in Innovation Ecosystems*, where it provides specialised sustainability-oriented services and enables sustainable value creation for multiple associated actors. However, initiating, maintaining and renewing innovation ecosystems is challenging for any mid-sized or larger company because the ecosystem perspective exceeds the boundaries of the company and its current competences.

Ecosystems also require high levels of trust between participants and conviction about their reputation and expertise. Moreover, the many relations and interactions require continuous sensitivity and prioritisation, when a comprehensive overview of potential ecosystem developments is lacking. A *Values-Based Ecosystem Modelling* workshop facilitates first steps in this direction.

7.5   Co-creating with Values-Based Ecosystem Modelling

One important challenge that sustainability-oriented companies are facing is how to strengthen its own innovation culture through collaboration and how to leverage their ecosystem to foster sustainable innovation beyond the boundaries of the company.

For an inspection company its daily business involves advancing inspection standards, participating in regulatory bodies, engaging in legislative processes on the national and international level, advising standardisation organisations (such as ISO or DIN) and working in industry initiatives (such as GAIA-X based Data Spaces) and working groups for testing, inspection and certification. These activities also have the potential to contribute to the sustainable development of clients and business partners.

New sustainability-related problems and ideas for solutions emerge from daily contact with different kinds of clients (e.g. car workshops, fleet and individual car owners) and the challenges they are facing as well as from participation in industry initiatives and governmental bodies. Its good reputation as a trusted and impartial service provider with great technical expertise puts the company into an excellent position to turn open issues into new business opportunities. However, this potential has not yet been tapped systematically and even knowing where to start was an unresolved question.

Values-Based Ecosystem Modelling is the method we specified and applied to address the challenge: How can external interfaces be professionalised to share and absorb sustainability-related expertise and inform decision-making on the basis of high reputation and topic leadership? A co-creating format[6] helps envision sustainability-oriented ecosystems based on a review of trends, desirable stakeholder relations and sustainability drivers. The flow of activities is depicted in figure 6 below, proceeding in five steps, each addressing one question:

1. What affects the future of our ecosystem?
2. How can we build on our stakeholder relations?
3. How can sustainability drivers enhance our future ecosystem?
4. What are we doing in the future? How did we make it there?
5. What should our future sustainable business ecosystem look like?

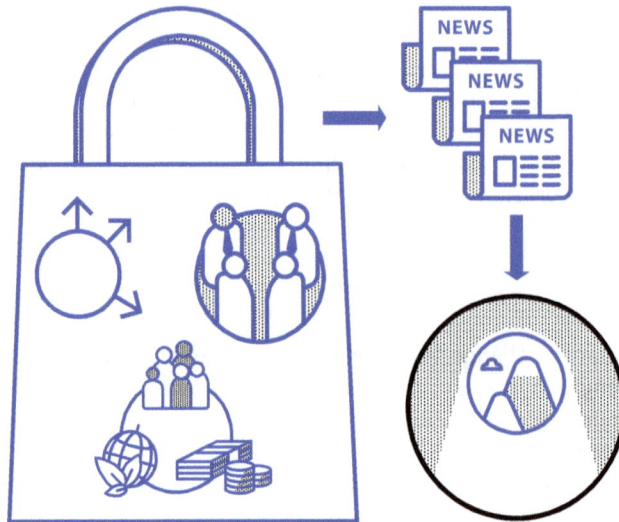

FIGURE 6. Workflow for workshops on *Values-Based Ecosystem Modelling*

APPROACH 7. Co-creative Exploration of Sustainable Ecosystem Innovation

The leadership team chose three focal points for exploring sustainable ecosystem innovation: the core inspection business, type approval and certification.[7] The central challenge was formulated: *How can we leverage external interfaces to drive sustainability-oriented innovation?* To address this challenge, we created a long list of relevant stakeholders, identified their roles and mapped how each stakeholder benefits from the inspection com-pany – and vice versa – using a matrix. For example, business clients (such as workshops and car dealerships) expand their service portfolios by offering on-site inspection, gain financial benefits by resolving the technical defects that they find and bolster their reputation under the inspection company's trusted seal. In return, they help the inspection company acquire customers and provide suitable environments for inspections. This exercise highlighted those exchanges of benefits among stakeholders that were clearly defined

228

and those that were uncertain, helping us prioritise the following key stake-holder groups: private and business clients, original equipment manufacturers (OEMs), supervisory authorities and the company's employees.

Five workshop tasks were designed and performed by a small group of internal experts. Additional stakeholder representatives were to be included in follow-up activities. Some exemplary results from the five tasks of the workshop:

1. MAPPING FUTURE TRENDS: Participants first mapped current trends to address the question: *What affects the future of inspection/ type of approval/ certi-fication?* They identified emerging developments such as sensor technology, connected cars, electromobility, data ecosystems, autonomous driving, pre-dictive services, urbanisation and car sharing. These trends highlight poten-tial opportunities to enhance existing services, such as using digital twins or artificial intelligence to offer remote or predictive inspections or cross-selling sustainability-oriented consultancy services to business clients.

2. EVALUATING STAKEHOLDER RELATIONSHIPS: In a second step we reviewed relationships to the five stakeholder groups, asking 'prouds' *What do we feel proud of concerning the present-day relations with this stakeholder group?*, asking 'sorries' *What do we feel sorry about?* and asking about untapped potentials *What potentials remain untapped?* We also asked for a fictious outlook on 'hell' *How could this relationship worsen? How could we make it worse?* and on heaven *What would improve this relationship beyond belief? What might a radical, ideal solution to any persistent problem look like?* Participants considered that advanced stakeholder relations can be built on managing the data of multiple stakeholders, providing customers with virtual reality access to inspection to increase transparency and customer satisfaction, introducing contactless and automated PTI (periodical technical inspection) and engaging all employees in innovation projects. Equipped with a range of responses to these questions, participants sketched headlines onto newspaper templates illustrating ideal stakeholder relationships in the future, for instance: 'Inspection company manages data from manufacturers and service providers'.

3. ELABORATING SUSTAINABILITY DRIVERS: We handed out sustainability-related business case drivers[8] and asked: *How can sustainability drivers help ad-vance the sustainability of a future business ecosystem?* For instance, when looking at revenue models, the group explored new cash flow opportunities, such as from monitoring environmental impact across a vehicle's life cycle and selling the data to OEMs, private customers, insurers and governments.

4. ENVISIONING NEW BUSINESS OPPORTUNITIES: Participants gathered outputs from the previous tasks and combined them into building blocks for a future ecosystem. Four building blocks, each representing a potential new business opportunity, were found: proof-on-demand inspection, technical sustainability inspection, data platform to prolong vehicle component lifespan and vehicle sensors for improving sustainable driver behaviour. Each building block was described in a hypothetical press release looking ahead to 2030 and stating:

What are we doing in the future? What is a barrier we had to overcome? How we did we do it? And which one of our core values is supported? One news article, for instance, showed how the inspection company was tracking component performance throughout a vehicle's life cycle and selling the data on durability, safety and sustainability to OEMs and service providers.

5. ECOSYSTEM MODELLING: In the final step, we addressed the question: *How can actors exchange benefits in a sustainable business ecosystem in 2030?* The four building blocks and the initial stakeholder groups were depicted in a system image showing the exchange of benefits from new services, revenues and valuable assets such as data between the ecosystem actors. In this data-driven sustainable ecosystem, all innovations should enable collecting, enriching, processing and/or selling data. TIC Mobility should create the conditions for such projects, for example, in terms of technical feasibility, employee competencies, eliminating legal constraints and ensuring business viability.

These results suggested initial ideas for policy, strategy and new business development. However, there are several gaps to be filled through in-depth assessment of the four business opportunities, and follow-up activities should be undertaken to envision not just these initial components, but the big picture of the future ecosystem.

TIC Mobility is also experimenting with solutions that go beyond traditional inspections, such as assessing the carbon footprint of electric vehicles. These experiments help them develop the necessary standards together with customers, ensuring safety and sustainability as well as strengthening trust in TIC's mobility services. These experiments and new business opportunities are being explored in an ecosystem of start-ups, universities, partners and customers. This collaborative approach aims to foster innovation and can potentially lead to the creation of future business ventures.[9]

7.6   Lessons Learned from the Project

The ecosystem challenge goes beyond the boundaries of a focal company and takes the mission to establish sustainable innovation cultures to a higher level. As illustrated by the inspection company case, innovation and sustainability orientation can be enhanced outside-in and inside-out. Outside-in, companies can draw on the capabilities and resources of partners to strengthen their sustainable innovation culture. Inside-out, they can leverage their own experiences and expertise to foster the sustainable development of the ecosystems they are engaged in. Doing so they build on strengths like their own experience-based expertise and reputation while addressing their weaknesses and the persistent challenges they face, like the ones described in this chapter.

A forward-looking workshop approach that explores future trends, selected stakeholder relations, and sustainability-oriented business case drivers allows *Envisioning* a company's *Engagement in Open Innovation* and in *Innovation Ecosystems*. However, further co-creating sessions with stakeholder representatives is needed to specify the mutual exchange of benefits, model new collaborative business and outline roadmaps for its development in order to achieve a higher impact through sustainable innovation.[10] Values-based companies and ecosystem players like inspection companies can serve as role models and pioneers, showing how sustainable innovation culture can be taken to the ecosystem level.

7.7   Key Takeaways

For the inspection company, the ethnographic study provided important insights into the company's innovation culture. Some insights challenged initial assumptions and pointed to overlooked task areas for sustainable innovation, while others highlighted good practices and strengths that had already been established. The company assumed responsibility for protecting human life as a core value, not just in terms of safety but also through contributions to sustainable development. Follow-up co-creating activities should build on already established good practices and strengths as well as on integrating stakeholders to drive sustainable innovation to the ecosystem level.

Chapter 8 /
Cultural Transformation in the Italian Oil Industry

by Raffaella Montera (Pegaso University), Chiara Guiggiani (Foundation for Research and Innovation, University of Florence), Alessandro Monti (Foundation for Research and Innovation, University of Florence), Mario Rapaccini (University of Florence)

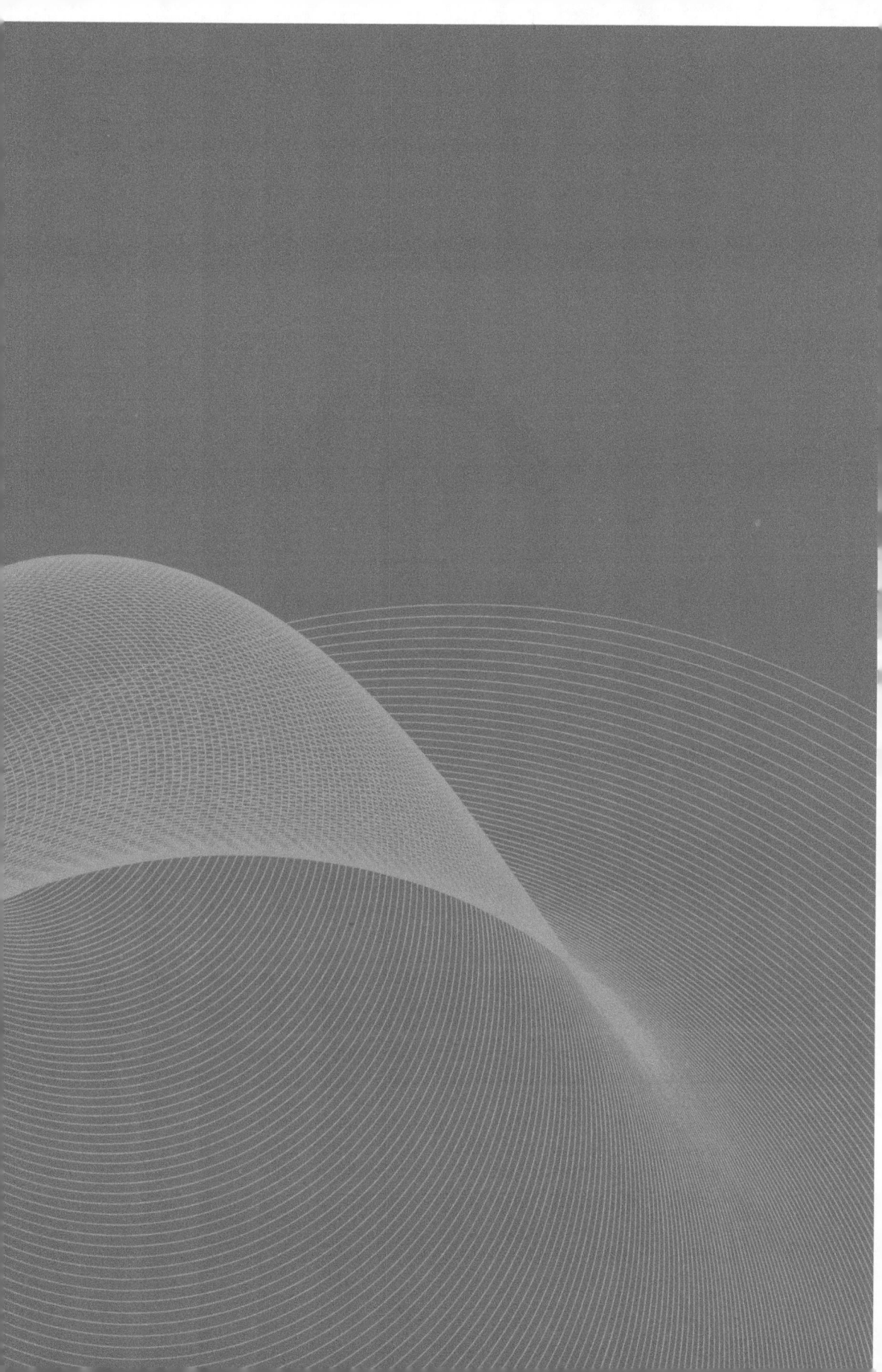

This chapter explains how an energy technology company, particularly its IT division, faces significant cultural challenges to sustainable innovation, requiring a fundamental shift to mainstream values and establish new practices.

> The case outlines how the company implemented co-creating and cultivating methods to address key challenges and lead the way towards the sustainability transition in its industry.

FIGURE 7. Cultivating of sustainable innovation evolving around the metaphorical illustration of a tree

8.1 Sustainable Innovation Challenges

The energy technology sector has had a massive impact on climate change. Most greenhouse gas emissions in the atmosphere are attributed to emissions generated by products and processes in the energy sector.[1] In particular, carbon emissions from the combustion of fossil fuels are a major driver of global warming.[2] In addition, the extraction and transportation of natural gas, a significant component of the energy industry, contribute to methane emissions. Methane is a potent greenhouse gas that intensifies the greenhouse effect and accelerates global warming.[3] Oil and gas exploration often lead to deforestation and changes in land use, contributing to the release of stored carbon into the atmosphere. The impact of these activities on ecosystems exacerbates the effects of climate change.[4] Despite this devastating impact on the climate, the major oil companies have exerted pressure on governments against emission regulation and even denied anthropogenic climate change. These behaviours have discredited an entire industry and have caused serious harm to humanity and the planet.

There is now an increasing global emphasis on transitioning away from fossil fuels and towards renewable energy sources to mitigate climate change. Energy technology companies need comprehensive sustainable strategies to mitigate their environmental impact. While efforts are underway within the industry, a holistic transition towards renewable energy and environmentally conscious practices is imperative for a more sustainable development.

To establish and drive values-based and sustainable innovation, energy technology companies must cultivate environmental awareness and responsibility. This involves acknowledging the industry's responsibility for the environment and taking proactive measures to minimise its negative impact.[5] A key step in this transformation is the cultivation of sustainable innovation cultures based on *Participatory Decision Making* and *Stakeholder Values Integration*. Inclusivity fosters creativity within innovation cultures and validates the impact of innovation by ensuring a variety of stakeholder perspectives.[6] Energy technology companies should invest in *Human Resource Development* programmes that promote values of sustainability and build a dynamic and adaptive workforce.[7] A culture of continuous learning is also essential to fostering sustainable innovation. Only by contributing to sustainable development can energy companies maintain their commercial role in the global energy landscape.

Many energy technology companies are willing to diversify their business models and invest in regenerative energy, positioning themselves as responsible stewards of the planet.[8] This shift is not solely driven by the need to comply with stringent European regulations or to evade the taxation of carbon emissions, but also by a growing recognition of the importance of sustainability for both people and the planet. In particular, European regulations, such as the European Green Deal and the EU Emissions Trading System, have set ambitious targets for reducing greenhouse gas emissions.[9] These policies incentivise energy technology industries to innovate and adopt greener technologies to meet the new more rigorous standards. Non-compliance can result in significant financial penalties, thus acting as a strong motivator for change.

Beyond regulatory compliance, there is a notable shift in corporate ethos towards values of sustainability. This transformation is partly driven by consumer demand for environmentally friendly products and services, influencing companies to align their operations with these expectations. Companies that fail to adapt, risk losing their competitive edge in the market. Moreover, the financial community is increasingly prioritising environmental, social and governance (ESG) criteria in their investment decisions. Investors are now more likely to support businesses that demonstrate a commitment to sustainable practices. This trend further incentivises energy technology companies to invest in green technologies and sustainable operations.

Efforts are being made in the industry to take advantage of these developments, including investments in cleaner technologies, carbon capture and storage, and diversification into renewable energy. However, the overall impact of the sector on climate change remains detrimental and requires continued attention and concerted efforts to further a transition towards more sustainable practices.

What is more, energy technology companies are increasingly prioritising values of sustainability, integrating them into both their internal operations and their external market strategies. Understanding the difference between internal and external development is crucial for appreciating the breadth of sustainable innovation efforts.[10]

Internally, companies initiate a variety of process and normative innovations to enhance their environmental and social impacts. For instance, process innovations include reducing greenhouse gas emissions, improving energy efficiency and minimising waste in their operations. Normative innovations include the introduction of values, policies and codes of conduct that promote, for example, diversity, equity and inclusion.

With regard to their external development, companies focus on sustainable product and service innovations as outcomes. While internal efforts focus on operational efficiencies and fostering social outcomes for employees, external efforts are geared towards creating market solutions that drive broader environmental and social benefits. Both dimensions are crucial, with internal actions laying the groundwork for responsible operations and external strategies pushing forward the global sustainability agenda through innovative products and services.

The energy technology company of this case study (hereafter named Alpha) is no exception. It is undergoing a process of radical and fast-paced organisational change. Internally, it has implemented programmes to optimise facilities and reduce energy consumption, such as installing energy-efficient lighting and upgrading heating, ventilation and air conditioning systems. Additionally, the company promotes employee well-being and diversity through policies and initiatives for *Human Resource Development* and *Attracting the Right Talent*. Externally, it makes significant investments in technology innovations that support the energy transition.

A notable example is an investment in hydrogen projects. Collaborating with selected clients, the company is developing advanced solutions for hydrogen production, storage and distribution. These technologies are aimed at reducing carbon emissions and promoting the use of cleaner energy sources. Moreover, the company's product portfolio includes solutions for carbon capture and storage, which help industries manage their emissions more effectively. Across the energy technology industry, other energy companies can, must and want to play a positive role in the sustainability transition. In this context, more and more energy companies are investing in clean energy and undertaking a profound organisational shift for establishing sustainable innovation cultures.

Now let us focus on how Alpha – specifically, its Italian IT branch – is facing cultural challenges that require a significant shift of values and practices. This case demonstrates how the company has adopted two targeted approaches to tackle sustainable innovation challenges, both of which have a high potential for replication in the same or in other industries.

8.2 Ethnography to Conceive Sustainable Innovation Culture

The ongoing cultural shifts in the energy technology industry offer valuable insights on how to advance sustainable innovation cultures globally. Alpha, one of the world's leading energy technology companies, is a case in point. With over a century-long tradition in providing solutions to energy and industrial customers and with operations in more than 120 countries, this company shows how values of sustainability shape corporate identity and drive innovation management in the energy sector.

The company's official values and strategy are centred on advancing energy solutions that are cleaner, safer and more efficient. Its strategic priorities are shaped by a commitment to ESG principles, aiming to create value for stakeholders while addressing global energy challenges. The set of official values that drive the company's operations and strategic decisions include:

- INTEGRITY: maintaining the highest ethical standards in all business dealings
- TEAMWORK: collaborating across geographies and functions to deliver superior results
- PERFORMANCE: achieving excellence through continuous improvement and innovation
- SAFETY: ensuring the health and safety of employees, customers and communities
- SUSTAINABILITY: committing to sustainable practices to minimise environmental impact and support the transition to cleaner energy

Alpha's strategic focus is on technology innovation, digital transformation and sustainable development. Regarding technology innovation, the company makes significant investments in research and development to drive technological advancements in energy production. This includes developing cutting-edge solutions in oilfield services, gas technology and energy transition technologies such as hydrogen solutions and carbon capture, utilisation and storage. When it comes to digital transformation, a key component of the company's strategy is leveraging digital technologies to optimise operations and improve efficiency. Advanced analytics, AI and machine learning are employed to enhance predictive maintenance, optimise production and reduce downtime. With reference to sustainable development, the company is deeply committed to supporting the global energy transition with a set of ambitious targets to reduce carbon footprint and actively develop technologies that support cleaner energy production.

Using *Rapid Ethnography* we conceived Alpha's sustainable innovation culture, identifying seven key insights: 1) sustainability literacy, 2) vertical integration, 3) reductionist approach, 4) authentic communication, 5) orchestrating stakeholder relationships, 6) establishing practices from the bottom-up, 7) balancing diversity (see table 4). Each insight is described in more detail in the table below.

Insights	Illustrative Statements We want (desire) ... so that (values) ... but (tension) ...
1. Sustainability literacy	'We want to mainstream a shared sustainability literacy so that each employee understands and fulfils their role in driving clean energy innovations, but communication barriers between higher-level staff and operational employees remain a significant obstacle.'
2. Vertical integration	'We want to leverage collaboration across hierarchical levels so that that top management's sustainability goals translate into coordinated actions at the base, but middle managers remain unaware of their decisive role to bridge communication gaps.'
3. Reductionist approach	'We want a more sustainability-oriented innovation process so that our company leads the energy transition, but we continue to put more trust in the conventional market rationale and emphasise economic concerns.'
4. Authentic communication	'We want to gain a green corporate image so that we communicate our identity with pride, but balancing between authenticity and ambition is challenging.'
5. Orchestrating stakeholder relationships	'We want to orchestrate stakeholder relationships through open innovation and ecosystem engagement so that our leadership in sustainability spurs genuine commitments across suppliers and customers, but we cannot guarantee their continued dedication once they have purchased our green products and services.'
6. Establishing practices from the bottom–up	'We want to leverage the potential of bottom-up and informal initiatives for sustainable innovation so that we can make a big leap in our cultural transformation, but we still lack advanced methods and practices to harness this potential.'
7. Balancing diversity	'We want to hire young talent so that we can leverage their creativity and expertise, but we should also ensure a balanced integration with the expertise of senior employees.'

TABLE 4. Ethnographic insights on tensions and values-action gaps in an energy technology company

SUSTAINABILITY LITERACY: Alpha's corporate culture and the meaning of its espoused values evolve in response to new external pressures (i.e. the Kyoto Protocol) and internal challenges. Internally, the company has undertaken a cultural transformation with the goal of promoting clean technology adoption in the energy technology industry. This involves an evolution of its organisational values from being technical and narrowly defined towards becoming subject to interpretation. This means that the company's sustainable innovation culture changes in relation to how the company's values are redefined and mainstreamed. This requires the concurrent development of two types of literacy: first, a semantic literacy that creates a common basis for *Knowledge Sharing* regarding sustainability. And, second, an organisational literacy that defines the functional roles that are responsible for specific sustainability issues.

Alpha develops semantic literacy about sustainability-related values through a series of workshops and training sessions that educate employees on, for example, the carbon footprint, the circular economy and renewable energy. These sessions ensure that everyone – from factory workers to top executives – has a shared understanding of these terms and their relevance, giving them a shared language and knowledge base to communicate about sustainability. For example, when discussing product design, engineers and marketers are able to communicate effectively about how to minimise environmental impact, leading to more innovative and sustainable product solutions. However, one respondent reported that while higher-level 'employees are engaged in defining and communicating new values in accordance with the language specificities in different departments', workers at the bottom of the organisational pyramid face a linguistic barrier, as the values are communicated in English.

VERTICAL INTEGRATION: Top managers have a clear understanding of the cultural transformation undertaken by Alpha, in terms of both revised values and sustainability strategy. However, there is misalignment with the lower-level managers who autonomously interpret the changes imposed from above. For example, the top management has introduced a new policy to significantly reduce greenhouse gas emissions by 30% within two years across all operations. However, the interpretations of this policy by lower-level managers vary widely, leading to inconsistent implementations across the organisation.

An operational manager focuses primarily on reducing emissions through quick fixes, such as upgrading heating, ventilation and air conditioning systems as well as installing energy-efficient lighting. He does not, however, consider more comprehensive changes to operational processes or equipment that could lead to long-term emission reductions. A procurement manager interprets the directive as a mandate to source materials from suppliers who have certifications for environmental standards. A research and development manager views the directive as an opportunity to innovate and develop new products that use renewable energy sources.

However, all these employees are not coordinating with other departments, resulting in innovative solutions that are not necessarily aligned with current manufacturing capabilities or market demand. This misalignment leads to an inconsistent implementation of sustainability-related values to drive innovation, reducing the transformational impact of the cultural change across the organisation. The role of middle management becomes crucial to allow a smooth exchange of guidelines from top managers to lower managers, but they are lacking awareness about their decisive role.

REDUCTIONIST APPROACH: Despite its increasing awareness of the importance of sustainable innovation for competing in the current economic scenario, the company seems to have adopted a reductionist approach to sustainable innovation. By 'reductionist approach', we mean that the company treats sustainability as a secondary or incidental aspect of its innovation strategy rather than integrating it as a core principle. This could be due to the company still being in the early stages of its cultural transformation and global energy transition. Key characteristics of the reductionist approach are the following:

- SUSTAINABILITY CONCERNS ARE NOT A DRIVER OF INNOVATION: In Alpha, sustainability concerns are not always the primary driver of innovation. Instead, it is often considered after the innovation process is complete, if at all.
- POST-INNOVATION CONSIDERATIONS: Sustainability considerations are incorporated only after the main innovation decisions have been made, rather than being a foundational part of the process.
- MARKET-DRIVEN INNOVATION: There is no proactive effort towards sustainable innovation that is independent of market demand. Economic variables – such as cost, marketability and profitability – are driving the company's innovation choices.
- LACK OF HOLISTIC INTEGRATION: Alpha has yet to achieve a holistic integration of sustainability concerns into its organisational culture and innovation strategies.

For instance, when the company's research and development department is tasked with developing a new product, its primary focus is on improving performance and reducing costs. The team designs and tests several prototypes without considering their environmental impact or potential sustainability benefits. After finalising the design, Alpha collects feedback from the market indicating a growing preference for sustainable products. In response, the company retrofits the innovation project's output with a few eco-friendly features, such as using recycled materials and improving energy efficiency. These sustainability-related features are added primarily because of market demand and potential economic benefits, such as better market positioning and compliance with emerging environmental regulations, rather than a genuine commitment to sustainability.

Thus, while the company does eventually incorporate some sustainable features into the product, they are not integral to the initial product development process. The focus remains on traditional economic drivers, confirming a reductionist approach. The company's innovation strategy is still far from being holistic, with sustainability considerations only addressed incidentally and in response to external pressures rather than as a proactive, integral components of innovation.

AUTHENTIC COMMUNICATION: The key challenge for communication in the context of sustainable innovation lies in balancing authenticity with ambition, effectively managing communication flows inside and outside the company.

The primary challenge for internal communication lies in mainstreaming values of sustainability across all levels and functions of the organisation. Not all employees are informed about sustainability-related initiatives, as only few of them have read the latest corporate sustainability report. This indicates a lack of awareness of and engagement with sustainability-related topics and the company's ongoing cultural transformation.

Externally, Alpha faces the challenge of crafting a green corporate image that promotes the reputation and legitimacy it needs to operate in the global energy technology market. A respondent highlighted the risk of reputational damage if ESG data are not communicated accurately and transparently, as this could lead to accusations of greenwashing. Additionally, with high CO_2-emitting products still in its portfolio, Alpha must ensure that it clearly communicates its efforts to improve its product mix, so that both employees and external stakeholders can register the progress being made. As the company strives to project its sustainable development efforts, it must carefully balance its current situation with its ambitious goals, ensuring that public statements are credible and backed by daily practice.

ORCHESTRATING STAKEHOLDER RELATIONSHIPS: Transforming both strategy and culture towards sustainable innovation requires fostering stakeholder relationships within the business ecosystem, particularly by *Engaging in Open Innovation* and *Engaging in Innovation Ecosystems*. In this context, Alpha is well integrated with major suppliers and energy customers, who have altered their business priorities in light of its ongoing energy transition and its disruptive impact on the energy market. By adopting sustainability as a core corporate value, the company has positioned itself as a leader of the energy transition and a role model for its suppliers and customers. Still, rather than resting on its achievements as an early mover in integrating values of sustainability into corporate management, it continues to learn from other more advanced incumbents.

For example, it benchmarks top players in the fashion and food industries as references for the depth of the cultural transformation they have achieved. However, even though the company is an inspiration for its partners, it cannot know whether their commitment to sustainability is genuine. Even though Alpha provides green products and services, it remains the clients' responsibility to determine how they utilise these offerings – and whether they choose to mainstream sustainable energy consumption in their own operations.

Establishing Practices from the Bottom-up: Alpha's operational transformation towards sustainable innovation is still a new and widely unexplored territory for the company. This becomes evident from the absence of sustainability-oriented *Management Systems* and associated methods to guide the implementation and evaluation of sustainable innovation. As a result, a wide variety of informal practices have emerged at the bottom level of the company, driven by individual employees' experiences and their trial-and-error approach to implementing the value of sustainability.

Despite their informal nature, these practices can be leveraged as foundations to establish new evidence-based practices throughout the organisation. For example, an employee, who was passionate about energy conservation, started an informal campaign to reduce energy consumption in his office building. The campaign, which focused on optimising thermostat settings, reducing unnecessary lighting and unplugging equipment after hours, led to significant savings and was successfully replicated across other locations. However, Alpha still needs to recognise the potential of other similar bottom-up initiatives and establish them across the entire organisation.

BALANCING DIVERSITY: Alpha's diverse workforce is a unique and vital asset for the cultivation of sustainable innovation. The resourcefulness, sustainability focus and digital expertise of younger employees have accelerated the adoption of new manufacturing techniques and the integration of clean, smart technologies into production processes. Meanwhile, the deep industry knowledge and confidence of experienced employees have ensured smooth transitions from prototype to production, meeting all regulatory standards. The innovations introduced by younger employees, when validated and refined by the experienced team, have led to successful project outcomes.

However, when investigating the company, we found that the potential of intergenerational cooperation to foster sustainable innovation is still largely underutilised. The speed, creativity and sustainability mindset of younger employees has not yet been fully synergised with the experience and confidence of employees with long tenure. For example, recent engineering graduates and seasoned project managers with a track record of leading large, complex projects rarely work together on the same team.

8.3   Co-creating to Enhance Alpha's Innovation Strategy and Cultural Transformation

To address these challenges with co-creating, we worked closely with Alpha's IT branch and its senior managers. We selected a number of insights based on criteria such as current corporate interests and strategic alignment and specified the following two challenges to address:

- PUSHING SUSTAINABILITY IN THE INNOVATION STRATEGY: Despite growing awareness of the importance of sustainable innovation for the company's competitiveness, Alpha continues to adopt a reductionist approach to sustainable innovation. Sustainability criteria and KPIs are only used to evaluate innovation projects ex-post rather than from their outset. This means that sustainability is treated as a secondary or incidental factor, rather than being integrated as a core principle.
- DEVELOPING THE OPERATIVE ASPECTS OF THE CULTURAL TRANSFORMATION: The company's cultural shift towards sustainable innovation is still in its early stages, lacking the support of *Management Systems* and associated methods for implementing and evaluating sustainability initiatives. In response, a variety of informal practices have emerged at the grassroots level, driven by individual employee efforts and a trial-and-error approach. While these practices are informal, they represent an untapped potential for building evidence-based, formal sustainability practices across the organisation.

To address these two challenges to sustainable innovation, we devised two co-creating formats for targeted interventions: an ideation contest and an innovation impact assessment.

IDEATION CONTEST FOR NEW SUSTAINABLE INNOVATION PROJECTS

We started by launching a company-wide *Ideation Contest* to gather a wide range of sustainability-oriented ideas related to both products and processes, ensuring cross-functional participation and relevance for all corporate operations. This *Ideation Contest* addressed a noticeable lack of concrete actions from the bottom-up level in the field of sustainable innovation, beyond a few occasional initiatives where employees gathered to discuss the topic but did not follow up on their ideas. The contest aimed to foster a mindset shift and empower employees, especially from younger generations, to contribute freely to sustainable innovation, unbound by existing barriers, change resistance and the conventional business rationale.

To facilitate the process of collecting ideas from all employees interested in developing sustainable innovation projects and to enable out-of-the-box thinking, we defined an innovation funnel process, which was then taken up by a group of young talents. They initiated a platform for collecting ideas that addressed environmental challenges, such as water conservation, waste reduction and CO_2 emission minimisation. After the submission stage, a selection process determined the best ideas and granted the owners with a budget for the feasibility study, after which the idea could be sponsored.

The *Ideation Contest* provided an opportunity for employees to participate in sustainable innovation efforts without needing to be concerned by economic or decision-making limitations. The process encouraged collaboration between idea providers and managers in charge of the development of their idea, allowing employees to work on their ideas from conception to implementation. The first call for ideas collected almost 250 ideas, demonstrating a successful effort to integrate sustainability into the innovation process and reduce the reductionist approach to sustainable innovation.

The *Ideation Contest* enabled the evaluation, selection and sponsorship of bottom-up initiatives. It also positioned sustainability in technical and vertical projects at the very beginning of the process, countering the reductionist approach to sustainable innovation. Such a call for ideas is an informal way to stimulate a grassroots cultural transformation and sustainable innovation in a controlled environment, starting with the employees of a single company or a single branch, as in this case.

CO-CREATING AN INNOVATION IMPACT ASSESSMENT

The second co-creating measure focused on developing sustainability KPIs for *Innovation Impact Assessment*. Typically, when the technology readiness level of an idea or project is quite high, very specific KPIs can be applied during structured processes such as the technological and/or product development phases (TD/PD), where it would be possible to numerically quantify specific information (e.g. materials, production process, etc.). However, at the early stages of innovation, before the TD/PD phases, there is only a rough conceptual idea and quantification is not possible.

The reasoning on new customised KPIs considered that if sustainable innovation is to be introduced in the equation, for example, in the IT branch, the set of KPIs should be adapted over time with more elaborate indicators and thresholds. Following this approach, the *Ideation Contest* generated a first set of KPIs, applying them to other processes and divisions in order to set up general sustainability criteria as a minimum sustainability standard for the early stages of Alpha's innovation process.

The newly introduced *Innovation Impact Assessment* follows a dynamic iterative process. In a typical scenario, a project would begin a first round of evaluation, with sustainable KPIs with a low threshold level. The purpose of starting like this is to ensure that most initial ideas will meet the basic criteria, pass the first decision gate and gradually improve over time. In further evaluations, the KPI thresholds are set higher or with additional technical requirements, allowing the project to evolve. For example, in the first generation of sustainable projects, a KPI reassessment of ongoing projects is performed to increase thresholds and technical requirements. In the second generation of sustainable projects, higher KPIs arising from the experience of the previous generation of projects is set. This mechanism is then reiterated for the third, fourth and further generations of this type of projects.

As sustainable projects evolve, the KPIs for them are reassessed and adjusted, leading to higher thresholds and more stringent requirements in subsequent project development. This iterative approach ensures that sustainability criteria are incorporated throughout all innovation stages and with respect to all three sustainability dimensions: economic, environmental and social.

The introduction of the *Innovation Impact Assessment* is an iterative process, which requires parameters to be adjusted. KPIs are dynamic and adaptable, and they can be evaluated differently according to the project type. For instance, a project with high impact on social sustainability might have lower environmental or economic impact, but if social sustainability is a company priority, the social indicators will take precedence in the selection processes. Nonetheless, the *Innovation Impact Assessment* ensures that project evaluations are better informed and values-based, highlighting the crucial importance of implementing sustainability KPIs from the outset of innovation projects.

The co-creating process has spawned a methodology with a high degree of replicability that can be exploited in many enterprise typologies. A set of cards was developed to simplify the implementation of such methodology, exploiting a gamified approach to trigger cultural change toward sustainable innovation.[11] For instance, one card set, Formalising Sustainable Informal Practices, facilitates workshops to integrate informal sustainability initiatives into formal practices through an iterative, reflective process.

The co-creating measures in this case produced KPI guidelines for low-level managers to contribute to sustainable innovation and for middle and high-level managers to ensure that innovation efforts have a sustainable business impact. It became clear that establishing sustainability-related KPIs and embedding cultural changes is a gradual process, especially for companies just beginning their transition to corporate sustainability. Moreover, the case showed that sustainable innovation is constantly evolving in the energy technology industry, both as a concept and as a process. Regular reflection and re-evaluation of priorities is needed at least every six to twelve months, in order to align with the company's values and shifting market trends, while maintaining a focus on business outcomes.

One key lesson learned from collaboration with the company is how bundling different measures, such as the *Ideation Contest* and the *Innovation Impact Assessment*, can help synergise parallel efforts for greater impact. For example, the *Ideation Contest* needs indicators to evaluate the potential projects, which could then be used to become KPIs in an *Innovation Impact Assessment* of ongoing projects. The latter will enable optimisation of the KPIs, which will then feed back into new indicators for future contests, creating a cycle of continuous fine-tuning, customisation and learning.

Through the bundling of the two co-creating measures, the company was able to follow up on the sustainable innovation projects emerging from the bottom-up, opening the call to literally everyone in the company and making the process democratic, open and inclusive. This also marks a significant step towards cultural transformation, as sustainability is now not only part of the company's values but also enacted in practice, through its ongoing co-creating activities and the funds allocated to develop the most feasible and interesting ideas.

8.4   Key Takeaways

The sustainability transition is finally making its first significant steps globally, at different stages and in different forms. This is also true for energy technology companies, and the example in this chapter speaks for itself. These types of companies are a fertile ground for cultivating sustainable innovation. But for new values to take root, it is important to remember that ideas come from the ground up, a ground that first has to be fertilised, for example, by harnessing the expertise of lower-level managers.

The case study presented here demonstrates that the cultural transformation towards sustainable innovation is a complex and ongoing journey that requires concerted effort and collaboration across all organisational levels. Moreover, this transformation requires a re-evaluation of existing values and practices, which may have been contributing to unsustainable patterns of production and consumption, and the adoption of new mindsets that embrace innovation as a means to create positive environmental and social impact.

The process put in place by Alpha is highly replicable. The KPIs used in the *Innovation Impact Assessment* can be adjusted to any company's needs, the thresholds are variable and meant to be highly flexible in the first steps and become more binding later on. Likewise, *Ideation Contests & Markets* can be easily adjusted by any company and in any industry.

A key takeaway is that the cultivation of sustainable innovation is not only an opportunity for every energy technology company and its value chain, but also a necessity. In the case of Alpha, a big and initially hesitant energy technology company embraced the pathway of sustainability-oriented transformation. However, for this shift to have a lasting impact across industrial, economic and societal levels, the corporate value chains will need to overcome their hesitancies too and follow in the steps of the big player. While the journey will be challenging, value chain players can benefit from the leadership and guidance of the Alpha company, which has already taken the first steps towards a more sustainable future.

Chapter 9 /
Investments in People and Technology along with Management by Values in Poland

by Katarzyna Matras-Postołek, Piotr Beńko, Małgorzata Ciesielska, Jacek Kasz (Cracow University of Technology) & Irena Śliwińska (Kraków University of Economics)[1]

Without investments to engage a highly qualified workforce, it is not possible to develop cutting-edge innovations. Neither is it possible without systematic investments in the company's technology development. Beyond these financial prerequisites, sustainable innovations require that all actions are based on values that are understood and shared by all stakeholders (figure 8).

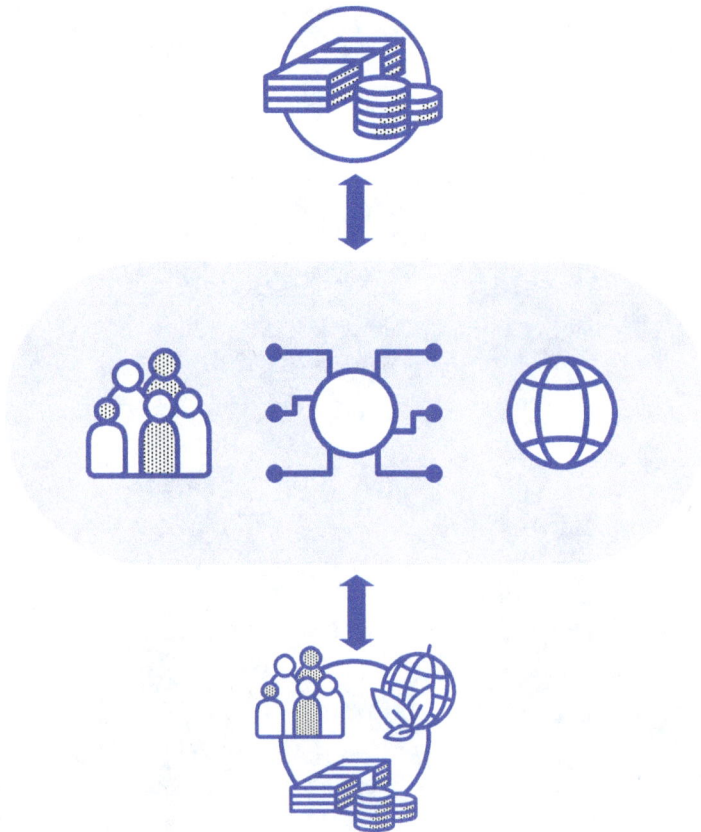

FIGURE 8. Investments in people and technology along with management by values as prerequisites for sustainable innovation

Innovation development in companies requires long-term investments in people and technology along with management by values to generate sustainable outcomes and financial returns in the future.

9.1 Sustainable Innovation Challenges

The last 35 years have witnessed extensive and dynamic political, social and economic changes in Poland and other countries of the former Eastern bloc. The transformation of the economy from a model based on state ownership and central planning to a free-market system has been a difficult and costly process.

Thanks to the dynamic growth of the private sector in Poland, intense international exchange and, ultimately, joining the European Union, Polish companies have gained access to the European Economic Community's financial and political tools, especially the EU framework programmes that support innovation. However, the low equity of Polish companies and lack of extensive experience and capabilities have hindered their development and the possibility of competing with companies from other countries. Despite multiple successes and an increasing understanding of sustainable innovation and entrepreneurship, the growth of Polish companies is held back by limitations imposed by regulations, technology and human resource management challenges.

In this context, we used *Rapid Ethnography* to conceive the innovation cultures of seven Polish engineering companies that are leading the sustainability transition across the sectors of transportation infrastructure, healthcare, renewable energy, robotics, technical services, and water and sewage. This allowed us to determine the key barriers that make it difficult for Polish companies to succeed in sustainable innovation as well as to identify the practices that allowed these companies, operating in difficult socio-political conditions, to gain a competitive edge in Poland and the international market.

In this chapter, we will discuss the challenges and tasks for creating sustainable innovation cultures in the Polish market. We found these through ethnographic field interviews with nine respondents from seven organisations. Then we focus on the case of one robotics company whose history and market position illustrate a unique and unorthodox approach to develop best practices and succeed with sustainable innovation.

9.2 Ethnographic Insights

Our investigation of sustainable innovation cultures in Poland includes seven organisations, including design companies, manufacturing companies and even municipal organisations. Apart from the Polish-owned and operated organisations we worked with, we also cooperated with the Polish division of an international corporation which is particularly active in the Polish market. Some of the companies were members of a cleantech cluster, others were partners of the Cracow University of Technology.

Our ethnographic field interviews with nine respondents from these companies revealed four insights explaining intentions, values and tensions in sustainable innovation and related practices: 1) values-based innovation management, 2) sustainable innovation methods and practices, 3) market and regulatory response and 4) resource restrictions and conflicting values (table 5).

Insights	Illustrative Statements We want (desire) ... so that (values) ... but (tension) ...
1. Values-based innovation management	'We want to integrate the priorities of our company leaders as well as external stakeholders into our innovation management processes so that we can run our business in a stakeholder-inclusive way, but we end up defining organisational values detached from our core business.'
2. Sustainable innovation methods and practices	'We want to engage in sustainable innovation so that that we can improve our sustainability performance, but we are still searching for suitable methods and practices that can adapt sustainable innovations to the needs of the market.'
3. Market and regulatory response	'We want to introduce high-quality sustainable solutions to the market so that we can exploit the growing market niche, but legislative and customer adoption barriers prevent us from doing so.'
4. Resource restrictions and conflicting values	'We want to develop sustainable innovations so that we realise our corporate values and goals, but we struggle in a challenging business environment of meagre resources, conflicting stakeholder values and political unrest.'

TABLE 5. Overview of the insights from the field research conducted in Poland

We used inductive content analysis[2] to identify patterned challenges emerging from the interviews and participant observations without applying preconceived categories and theories. These recurring challenges we translated into task domains for intervention (see section 4.2), which were crucial for several of our partner companies.

IDENTIFYING MARKET NICHES: Some companies focus their innovation efforts on uncontested market niches. For instance, a crane manufacturing company became aware of the lack of specially designed cranes for recovering derailed trains. Recognising a promising market niche, it entered the railway industry. By developing an extended, safe system of railway hydraulic cranes, the company became a market leader, first in Poland and then throughout Europe. However, the company avoids sustainable innovation projects that address saturated markets, deeming them as difficult, expensive and requiring excessive effort.

EMPLOYEE COMPETENCIES: All respondents emphasised that sustainable innovation management requires an adequately educated and competent workforce. Employees should be capable of forming cohesive and cooperative teams, where each member understands and fulfils their role. For example, a departmental head of a water and sewage company explained that he often has to take on tasks originally assigned to external companies or project leaders. This situation leads to reduced engagement from these collaborators and delays in the seamless execution of projects. He attributes the challenge of poorly qualified workforce to high staff turnover, often due to hiring people only for specific projects.

EMPLOYEE RESISTANCE TO CHANGE AND MANAGERIAL SUPPORT: In this category, a strong obstacle is noted when employees do not receive support from the management and board members. The employees feel ignored and, as a result, do not identify with the company's values and activities. If tasks are adequately allocated, biases can be overcome and, consequently, difficult tasks can be performed that deliver innovative results. An important issue is to build staff awareness of new sustainable innovation methods, technologies and products.

For example, older employees in the wastewater company, who were used to a different project management style, have problems adapting to the workplace of today with its new technologies, management strategies and communication styles. The respondents point to the need for a smooth and harmonious generational change at all levels – among specialists, but also managerial staff. Good practice is handing over the management of the company to a younger generation – as the former president of ASTOR did – so that a younger generation of managers can gradually take over new functions and responsibilities while preparing for the sustainable innovation challenges ahead.

DIFFERENT VALUES AND PRIORITIES: When a company and its stakeholders have different values and priorities, it is difficult for them to cooperate and achieve common goals. If the stakeholders have completely different values, cooperation in general and sustainable innovation efforts in particular become extremely difficult. For instance, in water management projects, the successful implementation of innovations often relies on the active involvement of subcontractors. However, these subcontractors frequently prioritise efficiency and profitability over values of sustainability. A key challenge for the water and sewage company in our study was managing relationships with subcontractors who try to complete projects quickly and cheaply at the expense of quality and long-term sustainability goals.

TECHNOLOGY-RELATED BARRIERS: Major challenges result from client companies lacking the technological base to adequately adopt and implement innovations. Some hesitate to adopt advanced technologies due to the technical and economic risks involved. For example, downtime on railroads or construction sites caused by the charging times of electric batteries in new eco-efficient vehicles, such as cranes, makes these solutions less attractive to customers. It is only due to EU's Green Deal legislation that customers consider more ecological solutions. To address such technological barriers to implementation, companies must adapt their sustainable innovation efforts to customer needs. This includes investing in research and development for more efficient and user-friendly solutions, engaging in stakeholder education to reduce perceived risks and promoting collaborative innovation to align sustainability goals with practical, cost-effective implementation.

POLITICAL, ECONOMIC AND FINANCIAL UNCERTAINTY: Other frequently emphasised challenges are administrative barriers, limited investment budgets, low engagement in innovation efforts due to high costs, unpredictable market trends, high uncertainty about future legislation, and economic instability due to stock market and currency fluctuations. These challenges were largely attributed to the Covid-19 pandemic and the war in Ukraine, which created a highly uncertain business environment in Poland.

9.3   Conceiving Innovation Culture

One of the seven engineering companies we closely worked with is ASTOR, a leading European company delivering state-of-the-art technology for manufacturing automation, process robotics and IT systems for production management and monitoring. ASTOR's distinctive values-based approach to management has been conducive to its success. We review the company's history, core values and organisational practices that it has developed over the years.

ASTOR was established during the transformative period following the abolition of socialism in Poland, which marked the beginning of a new economic era. It was founded in 1987 by a student at the Cracow University of Technology and started as a family business run by two brothers. At first, it supplied control parts for small production lines to other companies. In time, the company specialised in assembling industrial robots and successfully competed in the Polish market. After 2004, when Poland entered the European Union, ASTOR successfully expanded into the international market.

ASTOR has defined a set of core values and principles, such as reliability, freedom, responsibility and a win-win approach to cooperation. These values support its mission to modernise the industry through employee development and the vision to 'responsibly and humanistically lead the way to the industry of the future'.[3] ASTOR has also adopted UN's SDG framework to specify guiding principles for sustainability management and reporting.[4]

In the field interview, the chairman of the strategic council explains the company's values-based approach: *'We have been true to our ideals and to the people who put their trust in us. ASTOR's management policy is to follow the values that form the company's mission and the vision for its growth. 'Our claim is "Technology meets people". For ASTOR, people and technology are essential. An important part of the company's operation is to support the growth of the people we work with. As part of the ASTOR Academy and ASTOR Consulting, we share our technological and business knowledge with engineers and managers.'*

The robotics solutions offered by ASTOR promote eco-efficient operational processes and optimise the consumption of resources such as energy, costs, production times and materials. The focus on eco-efficiency provides the basis for the company's long-term strategy, while considering the environment and stakeholder values.[5] The company drives innovation through initiatives like the ASTOR Innovation Room and the ASTOR Robotics Centre, which showcase Industry 4.0 technologies and support robotics and automation projects, such as research and development, technology testing and professional training.

However, the most important and valued sustainable innovation project at ASTOR is the educational robot Astorino, distributed by Kawasaki Robotics. Astorino was designed to make industrial robotics education more accessible. Unlike traditional industrial robots, which are expensive, potentially dangerous and difficult to repair, Astorino is a reprogrammable robot made using cost-effective 3D printing technology that is safe to use and easy to repair. Students first assemble the robot, learning its mechanics and then programme and operate it. With one robot per two to three students, compared to the usual 10-16, Astorino transforms robotics education into an engaging practical experience.[6] Comprehensive teaching materials further support educators in leveraging the potential of Astorino to mainstream robotics education in high schools and universities.

Through the field interviews we conducted to conceive the company's culture, we identified several sustainable innovation practices of ASTOR, including a values-based approach to managing stakeholder relationships and sustainable budget planning using a technology index. A short review of these practices demonstrates how to successfully implement sustainable innovations in a context of economic instability and a competitive business environment.

A VALUES-BASED APPROACH TO MANAGING STAKEHOLDER RELATIONSHIPS

ASTOR uses a values-based approach to manage its relationships with internal and external stakeholders. With respect to its internal stakeholders, it recognises the role of a highly qualified and motivated workforce as a key corporate asset. A major challenge is to retain, upskill and motivate its workforce. The company addresses this challenge through practices rooted in its core values of freedom and responsibility, such as *Empowerment*, *Failure to Success*, *Incentivisation* and *Human Resource Development*.

It empowers employees to voice their opinions, including critical ones, without fear of reproach. Employees can propose innovation projects and challenge counterproductive practices, knowing their perspectives are valued and considered in decision-making processes. They are also encouraged to learn from, rather than avoid, mistakes. *Human Resource Development* is driven by a training programme paid by the company and adjusted to the employees' professional needs, while *Incentivisation* uses a profit-sharing system to foster the employees' sense of ownership, responsibility and long-term engagement in innovation projects.

Based on its core value of engaging in win-win cooperation, ASTOR manages its relationships with clients and partners by seeking common ground based on shared values. This approach demands flexibility and open communication to align with stakeholder expectations. However, while ASTOR prioritises meeting client expectations, it steadfastly refuses to compromise on its non-negotiable core values and principles, such as reliability and quality, even at the risk of losing clients. In one instance, the company agreed to a lower price for a solution by excluding some of its minor features. However, it did not agree to compromise reliability and exclude any of the system's major functions. Afterwards, the client trusted the company's product range and no longer sought to limit the functionality of its orders. This demonstrated the advantages of ASTOR's values-based approach for building trust and fostering long-term relationships.

ASTOR has introduced a pioneering tool to drive sustainable and technological development: the ASTOR Technology Index (ITA).[78] This innovative tool enables manufacturing companies to assess their technological capital, which ASTOR defines as the machinery and production lines integral to modern manufacturing. It then supports a continuous reinvestment strategy to enhance technological capital, enabling companies to increase their efficiency, profitability and sustainability.

The ITA addresses one of the key challenges in Poland's industrial sector – the ageing technological infrastructure. While technological goods are typically depreciated over five years, many enterprises continue to use outdated equipment, effectively eroding their technological capital instead of expanding it. This stagnation is compounded by traditional business models that fail to adequately balance investment between technological upgrades and labour. As a result, many companies struggle to sustain competitiveness and transition towards Industry 4.0. By measuring the ratio of expenditure on technological capital to expenditure on labour in production capital, the ITA provides a clear benchmark for evaluating technological progress. The scale ranges from 0–100 in practical application, with '0' representing a factory without machinery and '10' representing the average Polish company. A score of '20' represents a leading Polish plant that continually invests in its technological capital, while '100' reflects a world-class enterprise. The theoretical upper limit is 1000 points, representing complete manufacturing automation.

Importantly, the ITA establishes a framework for reinvestment: profits generated through technological improvements are reinvested to further enhance production capabilities, creating a virtuous cycle of innovation and growth. A decrease in the ITA signals declining competitiveness, prompting immediate corrective actions such as increasing investment in advanced technologies. Higher ITA values correlate with greater production efficiency, enabling companies to increase wages, reduce resource consumption and improve overall sustainability. The ITA not only measures a company's current technological standing but also serves as a strategic tool for promoting sustainable development in the long term. By aligning business practices with the principles of Industry 4.0, the ITA helps organisations to iteratively optimise their technological and eco-efficiency potential.

In the field interview, ASTOR's co-owner explains: '*Strictly speaking, the ITA is the capability for effectiveness. It is important to remember that the index should be calculated for a company as a secondary measure. First, we should invest and run the business following our plans and then we calculate the ITA. It is also important to compare the current value with the result from the last year, the year before that, what the result should be the next year and what value we want to achieve. The ITA helps the management to create the development strategy, define the revenue potential and assess if the company is becoming more modern.*'

9.4 Co-creative Assessment of Challenges, Practices and Foundations

After conceiving the corporate cultures of the seven companies, we proceeded with identifying and addressing their most relevant challenges with co-creating (see chapter 5). We started with two questions: How should a sustainable business be run in a challenging environment? and How can communication and cooperation with stakeholders be improved to achieve sustainability goals? To address these challenges and identify possible responses, we reviewed all sustainable innovation challenges and good practices that were conceived through ethnographic inquiry. The co-creating format focused on discussing these challenges and practices and translating them into three types of actionable statements: What should we start doing? Which practices should we stop doing? And which practices should we continue doing? Results included the following statements:

- Start a public discussion on sustainable innovation. Foundations, associations and industry events are good platforms for shaping views and tools for lobbying regulatory institutions.
- Start communicating the benefits of sustainable innovation to your clients. The long-term economic benefits of SOI must be highlighted.
- Start thinking about employees. Introduce, for example, a company bond for employees, offering higher interest rates than available bank deposits.
- Stop policies that hinder investment.
- Stop outsourcing crucial tasks. Key technical competencies must be within the company; not everything can be outsourced.
- Stop being afraid of making outside-the-box decisions. Innovation is a risk.
- Continue budget planning that accounts for upcoming changes, in particular increases in employee costs.
- Continue proactively increasing salaries against inflation to retain key employees.
- Continue to treat changes as opportunities for company development.

We summed up these statements in three foundational pillars to reinforce a sustainable innovation culture at engineering companies such as ASTOR:

1. PEOPLE: People are key for sustainable innovation management. The cost of losing even one highly specialised employee is enormous. To minimise turnover, the company needs to increase the motivation and competences of its employees through practices such as *Incentivisation* and *Human Resource Development*.

2. VALUES-BASED MANAGEMENT: A values-based approach to managing stakeholder relationships demonstrates the importance of flexibility in meeting stakeholder expectations while upholding core values that are integral to the company's identity – such as sustainability, reliability and quality – as in the case of ASTOR. Such an approach provides the means for building trust and fostering long-term relationships based on common values.

3. TECHNOLOGY: The challenge of ageing technological infrastructure can be ad-

dressed by encouraging companies to assess and reinvest in their technological capital. Budget planning should take into account the ratio of technological to labour expenditure to contribute to gaining a competitive edge and transitioning to Industry 4.0 and a sustainable economy.

9.5 Key Takeaways

In this case of an engineering company, strengthening a sustainable innovation culture involves three key elements: people, management by values and technology. First, people are crucial to introducing sustainable innovation and that is why companies should focus on *Human Resource Development* practices to retain skilled employees and foster continuous learning, keeping employees engaged and motivated. Second, a strategic approach of values-based management provides the direction for these efforts. Leaders must clearly communicate the corporate sustainability vision, mission and associated values, aligning stakeholders and inspiring win-win collaboration. Third, sustainable innovation requires systematic investments in technology to optimise the use of resources (e.g. money, time, materials) and ensure long-term efficiency, including eco-efficiency.

Chapter 10 / Sustainable Innovation Challenges in Science-Based Companies in Spain

by Carmen Abril, Complutense University Madrid

Science-based companies, grounded in scientific rigour and knowledge, face unique challenges when managing sustainable innovation. Their distinct cultural characteristics add complexity to the process. Through field research into the innovation practices of two leading science-based companies, we identified the most common challenges these firms encounter on their journey towards sustainability (figure 9).

Effective communication strategies, the dismantling of organisational silos and cross-functional coordination are critical to overcoming the sustainable innovation challenges that science-based companies are facing. By fostering clear, consistent communication and ensuring that the various departments work seamlessly together, these companies can more effectively integrate sustainable practices into their operations and innovation processes.

FIGURE 9. Investigation into the sustainable innovation challenges faced by science-based companies and recommended solutions

10.1 The Case of Two Science-Based Companies

In this chapter, we report of a study of two science-based companies in Spain. Company A is a global leader in general science and industrial products. Company B is a European frontrunner in the aerospace industry. Despite competing in different fields, both companies share a core scientific orientation that shapes not only their operations but also their approach to sustainability. Each has declared sustainability as a core value and strategic priority, embedding sustainability-related values into their missions. Yet when it comes to developing their sustainable innovation cultures, some persistent challenges still require attention. Why is it that even companies strongly committed to sustainability encounter persistent challenges in creating a transformative sustainable innovation culture?

In general, science-based companies are distinguished by their deep commitment to rigorous scientific knowledge, high specialisation and expertise and a focus on technical innovation to satisfy highly demanding customers. They face particular challenges to developing sustainable innovation cultures, such as a sometimes conservative mindset, reduced willingness to embrace rapid changes, language barriers, secrecy in research and development and customer tyranny.[1] Recommendations from our research to address these challenges include bridging silos, expanding knowledge across the life cycle of their products, broadcasting sustainability-related achievements, promoting *Employee Resource Groups*, setting measurement systems to signal actions and building a long-term strategic communication plan to engage stakeholders.

In the following pages, we explore the specific challenges these science-based companies face in cultivating sustainable innovation. We reveal how regulatory demands, customer-driven pressures and organisational silos underpin a narrow and reactive approach to sustainable innovation in these two companies. Both companies tend to see sustainable innovation as a response to customer and regulatory demands rather than as an internally driven pursuit of long-term impact.

Furthermore, communication challenges – such as top-down sustainability messaging that lacks relevance across specialised functions – compromises cultural alignment, leaving some employees perceiving that sustainable innovation is not an organisation-wide priority but rather a concern limited to the environmental and manufacturing departments.

We examine these challenges through the perspectives of various managers, highlighting how function-specific perspectives and departmental key performance indicators (KPIs) can contribute to more focused sustainability efforts. In doing so, we uncover a range of informal grassroots initiatives led by employees with a strong personal commitment to sustainability, efforts that illustrate the potential of bottom-up contributions to shaping a more authentic and impactful culture.

This chapter not only outlines the primary challenges facing science-based companies but also offers a co-creating approach for addressing these issues. We propose a framework that emphasises cross-functional alignment, *Tailored Communication* and the *Empowerment* of grassroots efforts to foster a genuinely integrated sustainable innovation culture. Ultimately, this exploration invites leaders in science-based industries to consider how a comprehensive, proactive approach can help their organisations embed sustainability at the core of their innovation strategies.

10.2 Unique Cultures for Sustainable Innovation

Science-based companies, particularly in sectors like chemicals and aerospace, face a unique set of hurdles in adopting sustainable innovation stemming from the complexities of their core technologies, the stringent regulatory landscape and the need to protect intellectual property while pursuing open innovation.[2] These companies are often structured around specialised technological expertise, driving both incremental and radical innovations that are foundational to their market positions. However, this specialised focus comes with high technological complexity, making internal innovation both resource-intensive and complex. This complexity extends beyond product development into areas such as sales and marketing, demanding substantial effort and coordination across teams.

The substantial initial investment in sustainability-oriented research and development poses a significant challenge, especially when outcomes are uncertain and the payoff may not be immediate. For science-based companies, these financial uncertainties create internal delays. Stakeholders are often reluctant to fund projects with intangible or long-term returns, preferring those with clearer paths to profit. This aversion is heightened in industries where innovation cycles are inherently long and significant lead times are required to bring new products to market. Balancing resources for these projects against short-term, revenue-generating initiatives remains a persistent struggle. Moreover, the need to align innovation timelines with evolving sustainability standards creates further strain, as goals may shift faster than a product can be developed and commercialised.

Adding to these financial and resource constraints is a regulatory environment that requires careful navigation. Science-based industries must comply with an array of regulations that vary by region, especially given the potential environmental and health risks associated with their technologies. Ensuring compliance with these diverse standards often adds complexity and cost, slowing the path to market for sustainable products and further complicating sustainable innovation initiatives. As sustainability standards become more stringent, these companies are challenged to adopt values of sustainability without compromising the compliance that their reputation and market access depend on.

Another layer of complexity arises from the power dynamics with their large and influential customer base. Many science-based companies depend on a few powerful customers who exercise considerable influence over their product development choices. These customers, who often prioritise reliability and cost-effectiveness, may be hesitant to adopt more sustainable products if such changes involve increased costs or operational adjustments. This reluctance can create a barrier to the adoption of sustainable innovations, as companies may find themselves constrained by the demand to keep costs competitive, even when more sustainable options are available.

Even though major customers may be interested in products that enhance their own sustainability KPIs, they are often reluctant to pay a premium price for these solutions. The influence of these customers can limit a company's willingness to invest in sustainable alternatives, as it must balance environmental objectives with the need to retain key business relationships and avoid the risk of customers switching to more cost-effective suppliers.

Protecting intellectual property (IP) while *Engaging in Open Innovation* poses another barrier. The proprietary nature of many scientific innovations in these fields can make firms hesitant to collaborate with external partners, despite the fact that complex sustainability challenges often demand such cooperation. In industries where competitive advantages rely on closely guarded technologies, the risk of losing IP through partnerships can deter firms from the open exchanges that might otherwise accelerate sustainability efforts across the sector.

Furthermore, science-based companies frequently encounter challenges in bridging diverse scientific disciplines within their own structures. The interdisciplinary nature of sustainability requires expertise from various domains to work cohesively – a formidable task in firms where departments often operate independently, focusing on highly specialised objectives. In aerospace, for example, achieving sustainability goals may involve aligning expertise from materials science, engineering and environmental science, each with different technical priorities and operating standards. This internal disconnect can slow down progress and lead to inefficiencies that are difficult to overcome.

Beyond these internal challenges, market conditions play a considerable role in shaping the commitment to sustainability. Despite the increasing emphasis on environmental responsibility, market demand for sustainable products can be inconsistent, particularly if these alternatives come at a higher cost. Customers and investors may pressure firms to prioritise projects that deliver immediate financial returns, which often conflicts with the long-term view required for sustainability. This short-term market focus makes it difficult for companies to justify investments in sustainable innovation, which may promise significant impact over the long run but cannot deliver the immediate profitability that many stakeholders seek.

These difficulties extend across the supply chain as well. Many science-based companies rely on complex global supply chains to source materials that are challenging to replace with sustainable alternatives. For instance, sourcing environmentally friendly materials that meet the strict performance standards of aerospace applications or chemical products can be prohibitively complex and costly. This dependency on conventional materials not only impacts the company's ability to innovate sustainably but also complicates logistics, with the added burden of mitigating the carbon footprint associated with extensive global supply chains.

Cultural and organisational inertia also affects the ability to adopt a sustainable innovation culture. Organisational inertia is defined as the inability of an organisation to keep up with a rapidly changing environment. This inertia stems from a natural tendency for organisations to resist change and cling to established beliefs, attitudes and routines.[3] In firms with long-established practices focused on technical achievement, a shift to prioritise sustainability requires significant changes in company culture and incentives. Employees and leadership accustomed to traditional innovation models may be slow to adopt a sustainability-oriented approach, particularly if this shift involves modifying performance metrics or retraining employees in new sustainable practices. Without aligning the organisation's values and objectives towards sustainable innovation, efforts can remain fragmented or even counterproductive.

Together these challenges highlight why science-based companies can be perceived as slower to respond to society's demands for sustainable practices. Given the technical and regulatory complexities, companies in sectors like chemicals and aerospace cannot risk overstating their contributions to sustainability. The threat of greenwashing accusations is real, and these firms often adopt a cautious approach in promoting their sustainable innovation achievements to avoid misrepresentations that could jeopardise their reputation.

10.3 Four Insights

To conceive the transition of science-based companies towards a sustainable innovation culture, we conducted desk research on each firm and *Rapid Ethnography* interviews with respondents across various functions (as outlined in chapter 4). Interviewees represented a range of hierarchical levels, business divisions, innovation-related roles and geographical locations, including Spain, Germany, France, the Middle East and the United States.

The *Rapid Ethnography* approach was designed to provide an in-depth view of the daily operations, attitudes and behaviours that shape sustainability efforts. In the two companies in our sample, we identified four main insights into the challenges of embedding a sustainable innovation culture in these science-based companies (see table 6).

Insights	Illustrative Statements We want (desire) ... so that (values) ... but (tension) ...
1. Narrow scope of sustainable innovation	'We want to have a better shared understanding of what sustainability means for our company, so that we can have a higher sustainability impact in individual functions and divisions, but we have divergent perspectives and KPIs on what sustainability is across functions, business units and backgrounds.'
2. Reactive sustainable innovation	'We want to sell more sustainability-oriented products and services as they are demanded so that we can more proactively lead the sustainable transformation, but we are more reactive to current customers' problems and often disregard the opportunities that sustainability offers to add value to the customer.'
3. Communication and engagement for sustainable innovation	'We want to be informed about sustainability achievements and initiatives so that we can be more engaged in them, but the communication is scarce, unclear and silo-dependent.'
4. Misaligned metrics for Embedding Sustainability Values	'I want to track my individual efforts and impact on the overall corporate sustainability, so that I can improve and be motivated to continue doing so, but I do not have any guidelines or KPIs to measure my performance.'

TABLE 6. Ethnographic insights on tensions and values-action gaps in two science-based companies

In our research, we observed that science-based companies tend to limit the scope of their sustainable innovation efforts, often focusing exclusively on the environmental dimension of sustainability. This focus aligns with the perspective that sustainable innovation generates new products and processes that benefit the natural environment in addition to delivering economic performance.[4] However, an exclusive emphasis on environmental concerns (related to waste, water, chemicals), often leads to overlooking the social dimension of sustainability and its potential to broaden the overall impact of innovation.

Furthermore, the specialisation that is intrinsic to science-based companies, creates challenges in cross-functional communication and mutual understanding, which are critical in advancing a holistic sustainable innovation agenda. The compartmentalised nature of these organisations means that different functions – each responsible for part of the development process – often have differing interpretations and goals regarding sustainability. This disconnect hinders the ability to collaboratively define and pursue unified sustainability objectives across functions.

While companies have a general desire to enhance their sustainability impact, they have a compartmentalised and narrow perspective on sustainable innovation due to the perspectives, metrics and goals that vary across departments. Several factors contribute to this narrowed scope. First, there is a lack of sustainability literacy. That is, there is a lack of shared understanding regarding what sustainability truly entails for each product or process, particularly in areas like research and development, marketing and manufacturing. Each function often possesses only a partial view of the product's full life cycle, resulting in fragmented assessments that fail to capture the holistic impact of products from inception through end-of-life. For instance, a marketing and industrial business development manager noted differing perspectives on sustainability. While marketing teams consider the full product life cycle, the research and development and manufacturing teams often focus solely on technical aspects.

Second, the multinational nature of these companies introduces further complexities. Operating across diverse regions, science-based companies must navigate different regulatory landscapes and cultural attitudes towards sustainability. These geographical differences can make it challenging to foster a consistent and unified sustainable innovation culture in the organisation, as the dialogue around sustainability goals is continually influenced by local regulatory pressures and societal expectations.

Ultimately, these dynamics reveal a need for a more comprehensive approach to sustainable innovation in science-based companies – one that emphasises cross-functional alignment, shared sustainability literacy and a balanced view that includes social, economic and environmental impacts. Addressing these gaps will be essential for science-based companies to broaden their sustainability scope and deliver more impactful and inclusive innovations.

Our research revealed a persistent tension between embracing a proactive sustainable innovation strategy that could deliver broad, longer-term value and meeting the immediate needs of customers. As a result of this tension, science-based companies often follow a reactive approach to sustainable innovation, driven primarily by regulatory requirements and the demands of a few influential customers who shape the specifications of tenders. This reactive stance reflects a constrained ability to lead the sustainable transformation, as the innovation agenda is often shaped by compliance and customer expectations rather than by internally driven sustainability goals.

This reactive approach to sustainability is characterised by additional organisational challenges. Differences in decision-making speed and agility between headquarters and subsidiaries complicate efforts to align on sustainable innovation initiatives. Effective communication is essential for aligning sustainability goals and organisational values among internal stakeholders, yet this alignment remains difficult to achieve given the diversity of stakeholder perspectives and objectives.

For instance, an innovation department head from a subsidiary highlighted headquarters' risk-averse approach to innovation, contrasting it with the subsidiary where *Experimentation* and learning from failure are encouraged. The respondent suggested that to alleviate the tension the headquarters needed to develop more flexibility and trust and allow some degree of failure, providing it ultimately leads to an overall positive result. This example underscores how divergent attitudes towards risk and adaptability among stakeholders hinder a proactive approach, as the values of both parties impact the scope and ambition of sustainability initiatives.

Furthermore, the coordination of interdisciplinary teams as well as the integration of sustainability practices throughout the supply chain can be seen as burdensome, especially when the customer does not explicitly require more sustainable solutions (as one respondent from sales remarked). Without a strong demand signal from key customers, there is often a reluctance to invest resources and effort to push sustainability-driven projects forward.

Overall, these findings reveal a need for science-based companies to foster a more proactive approach to sustainable innovation management. This shift would involve embracing a longer-term perspective towards the value of sustainability and building internal alignment and stakeholder collaboration mechanisms to advance sustainable innovation projects beyond regulatory and customer-driven demands. Achieving this will require overcoming existing organisational and cultural challenges, including risk perceptions and operational inertia.

Managing communication regarding sustainable innovation presents a significant challenge in science-based companies. The technical requirements of business units and functions in these companies complicate the establishment of a cohesive, global communication strategy. In both companies, we observed that sustainability objectives are typically communicated through top-down state-ments. This centralised approach to communication often fails to address the specific needs and priorities of different departments, functions and regions, re-sulting in a disparity between the overarching corporate goals and their practical application.

Another dimension of the communication challenge is the conservative com-munication style inherent in science-based industries, where companies exercise caution in publicising their sustainability achievements. Unlike other organisa-tions that often take an assertive stance in promoting their environmental con-tributions, science-based companies tend to communicate sustainability progress in a measured, modest manner. The rigour and thoroughness required for testing and validation in these firms slow down the process of sharing achievements, as considerable time and resources are invested to ensure that the claims made are accurate and reliable. This cautious approach is also rooted in a desire to prevent accusations of greenwashing, which could severely impact a science-based com-pany's reputation – a critical asset in sectors where credibility and technical accu-racy are paramount.

Many employees feel frustration due to the lack of clear, accessible communi-cation about sustainability efforts. The top-down communication model typically lacks mechanisms for employee involvement and accountability, leaving employ-ees feeling disconnected from the company's sustainability goals and unable to actively contribute to them. For instance, one respondent shared his concern that 'at the corporate level, there are a lot of decisions that are hard to understand, not because they are not adequate (they are more intelligent than me), but because people do not understand them'.

Despite this communication gap, we observed that some employees, driven by personal commitment to sustainability, take the initiative to experiment with small-scale, informal sustainable innovation practices in their functions. These grassroots efforts, while modest, play a significant role in advancing sustainability goals. Employees experiment with sustainable practices through a trial-and-error approach, developing informal initiatives that despite their localised nature lay the groundwork for more sophisticated practices.

For example, one employee in the US Chemical Business Unit created a survey to get colleagues interested in developing a sustainable approach to their jobs. She collected a database of colleagues personally engaged in sustainability efforts and started to organise informal online meetings to share ideas and explore areas of collaboration. The colleagues created a Resource Group that grew with time. They led several conferences on corporate sustainability and organised a 'sustainability week', inviting guest speakers to contribute to sustainability literacy throughout the organisation. These bottom-up efforts were approved by top management, be-coming a source of inspiration for future grassroot initiatives in the organisation.

Still, the presence of functional silos, complex hierarchies and bureaucratic hurdles make it difficult for intrinsically motivated individuals to connect with like-minded colleagues or form communities around shared values of sustainabil-ity. Remote work arrangements and a lack of structured channels for interaction further limit the formation of networks that could amplify bottom-up initiatives, as those are triggered by informal and personal channels more difficult to create in this context.

The *Empowerment* of individuals and *Employee Resource Groups* are promising approaches to advance sustainable innovation cultures in science-based companies. These approaches hold the potential to work across different functions and business units, enabling motivated employees to drive sustainable innovation and, in turn, spread enthusiasm and commitment throughout the organisation. For employees who feel constrained by the lack of formal sustainable innovation channels, bottom-up initiatives offer an outlet for their passion and contribute to building a community of practice around sustainability. Grassroots efforts serve as an essential element for establishing sustainable innovation practices and developing a more cohesive and transformative approach to sustainable innovation in science-based companies.

MISALIGNED METRICS FOR EMBEDDING SUSTAINABILITY VALUES

Embedding Sustainability Values through a robust measurement system is essential for organisations that want to emphasise the strategic importance of sustainability-related issues, learn from their sustainable innovation initiatives and improve over time. However, in the companies we studied, key performance indicators (KPIs) for sustainable innovation are primarily aggregated at the overall corporate level and designed for high-level reports that are communicated only on an annual basis. This approach to *Innovation Impact Assessment*, while useful for external reporting, introduces two major challenges in the organisations we studied.

First, the lack of detailed, function-specific KPIs limits individual accountability. With sustainable innovation results presented as aggregated metrics, employees across various departments are not given ownership of these goals, which can lead to disengagement. Without relevant, accessible KPIs for each function, employees struggle to see how their individual contributions align with and impact the overall corporate sustainability objectives. Second, the reported KPIs typically focus on environmental metrics associated with manufacturing processes, such as water usage, carbon footprint, waste reduction and energy consumption. While these indicators are critical, they inadvertently frame sustainable innovation as an issue solely relevant to the production and environmental departments.

As a result of such values-action gaps, many employees perceive sustainability as a limited, function-specific responsibility rather than an integrated, organisation-wide commitment. This perception undermines the holistic nature of sustainability, which ideally should permeate all aspects of the company, including departments like sales, marketing and HR, which could also contribute meaningfully to sustainable innovation if equipped with relevant guidelines and indicators.

Several respondents highlighted a gap between their desire to engage in sustainable innovation practices and the tools provided by the organisation to facilitate such engagement. Without individualised metrics, employees do not have the feedback they need to evaluate their contributions or make informed improvements, reducing their motivation to actively support the company's sustainability objectives.

10.4 Co-creating to Address Communication Challenges

After presenting the four key challenges to the boards of directors of the two companies, we reached a consensus to focus on one central issue that appeared to have a spill-over effect on the others: communication and engagement for sustainable innovation. Following an intensive discussion, the boards recognised that improving communication around sustainable innovation would not only address persistent cultural tensions and values-action gaps but could also indirectly support the resolution of related challenges.

With this focus established, we proceeded to delve deeper into the communication challenges and explore potential interventions to overcome the main hurdles. To ensure a comprehensive approach, we involved employees across the organisation, following the principle of 'bringing the whole system in the room' (see section 5.2). We designed a co-creating workshop format and structured it to be participatory and dynamic, engaging a cross-functional group of employees from both science-based firms. Participants from diverse functions – including innovation, sales, communication, human resources, research and development, and product development – were invited to contribute their perspectives and expertise.

The workshop methodology guided participants through a series of activities to envision an ideal future state, assess the current situation and collectively create actionable initiatives to bridge the gap between the two. We brought together employees from various departments to collaboratively envision the future of sustainability-oriented innovation in their companies. It was a dynamic session, filled with lively discussions and creativity. Borrowing from the Futures Search[5] approach to *Envisioning*, the workshop started by recognising how organisations are perceived both positively, as 'prouds', and negatively, as 'sorries', in terms of sustainability and from the perspectives of their key stakeholders (employees, customers, collaborators, influencers and regulators).[6]

After a discussion of innovation opportunities driven by the 'prouds' and 'sorries' that had been identified, the group proceeded to envision a desirable future, reflecting on possible risks and challenges. Following this *Envisioning*, participants elicited and prioritised several initiatives for implementation. These initiatives aimed at building a stronger, more cohesive approach to sustainable innovation communication, ultimately helping to align the organisation's strategic vision with practical, cross-functional implementation.

The elicited and prioritised initiatives in the co-creating workshop addressed the need for a more structured and authentic internal communication strategy, greater focus on *Tailored Communication* and training for customer-facing teams, proactive collaboration with regulators and the appointment of a dedicated sustainable innovation communication team. Together these measures aim to promote transparency, foster employee and stakeholder involvement and ensure that values of sustainability and strategic goals are well integrated in the organisation's communication strategy.

	Identified challenges	Recommended actions
Internal communication strategy	Centralised, ad hoc communication managed by a single individual, lacking consistency and cohesion across sustainable innovation topics	Appoint a dedicated sustainable innovation communication team responsible for consistent, clear and aligned sustainable innovation messaging
	No dedicated communication strategy for sustainable innovation, with sustainable innovation messaging diluted among other corporate news	Develop a comprehensive, multi-channel and tailored communication strategy that integrates sustainable innovation goals across all functions and levels, ensuring that sustainability messaging is prominent and clearly linked to the company's core mission and goals
Employee engagement in sustainable innovation	Communication perceived as non-systematic and overly formal	Develop a structured *Tailored Communication* plan that resonates with employees through authentic and relatable messaging
	Messages focused narrowly on aspects like CO_2 emissions and monetary savings, limiting relevance	Expand the focus of messages to include diverse sustainability achievements, such as energy initiatives and waste reduction, to demonstrate company-wide commitment
	Many employees unaware of key sustainable innovation initiatives, such as 100 % green energy use	Create regular, interactive channels (e.g. workshops, intranet updates) for *Awareness Raising* about ongoing sustainable innovation projects
Customer and stakeholder engagement	Lack of a systematic approach to external communication on sustainability efforts	Develop a *Tailored Communication* strategy for customers, suppliers and academic partners
	Sales teams lack training and resources to position sustainability as a value-added proposition	Provide sales training on sustainability value propositions and integrate sustainable innovation into the customer interaction process
	Technical achievements (e.g. waste management in aerospace) remain siloed in internal departments	Simplify technical sustainable innovation achievements for broader audiences, equipping sales and customer-facing teams with accessible, impactful messages to share
Engagement with regulators	Lack of a proactive approach to influencing regulatory sustainability agendas	Establish dedicated communication channels with regulatory bodies to advocate for sustainability standards and share industry insights
	Absence of strategic initiatives to incorporate sustainability criteria into industry tenders	Develop a strategic plan for influencing tender criteria, emphasising the inclusion of sustainability metrics and benefits as core evaluation elements

TABLE 7. Lessons learned through co-creating in science-based companies

10.5 Bridging Theory and Practice

We find significant intersections and tensions between the theoretical conceptu-
alisations of sustainable innovation in science-based companies and the realities
they face. In theory, sustainable innovation emphasises a holistic integration of
environmental, social and economic values across all organisational functions.
However, the cases demonstrate that science-based companies often adopt a nar-
rower, more environmentally focused approach, driven largely by regulatory compliance and the demands of powerful customers. This reactive stance contrasts
with the proactive, transformative sustainable innovation models suggested in
the literature, where internal motivation and a shared organisational vision for
sustainability are paramount.[7]

One key challenge is aligning the notions and practices of sustainable innovation in highly specialised, functionally siloed science-based companies. Theoretical frameworks foster cross-functional collaboration and shared sustainability objectives, yet in practice science-based companies struggle with fragmented
understanding and alignment. Differences in departmental priorities and performance indicators contribute to a perception that sustainable innovation is a manufacturing or environmental concern, rather than a shared, organisation-wide
commitment.

This dissonance underscores the need for tailored, function-specific KPIs
that promote accountability and clarify each department's role in sustainability. Such tailored KPIs and *Innovation Impact Assessments* would empower employees across functions to participate in sustainability initiatives meaningfully, reinforcing sustainable innovation as a shared, integrated goal rather than a
production-focused directive. Creating clear guidelines and relevant metrics for
diverse departments could foster a stronger, company-wide sustainable innovation culture and support employees who wish to make a measurable impact on
sustainability.

Another area where theory and practice diverge is in the communication and
dissemination of sustainable innovation achievements. While theoretical models encourage transparent and engaging communication as a means to foster a
sustainable innovation culture, science-based companies often adopt a cautious
approach, constrained by rigorous validation processes and a strong aversion to
greenwashing. They do so to guard their reputation in view of its critical role in
determining corporate performance.[8] This risk-averse stance may safeguard reputation, but it also disengages employees who seek a clearer idea of their company's
sustainability progress and their own role in it.

Our findings also highlight the potential of informal grassroots initiatives in
establishing the values and practices needed to drive a sustainable innovation culture. Theoretical concepts frequently emphasise top-down change as a driver of
sustainable innovation, yet in practice, bottom-up contributions – driven by the
personal commitment of employees to sustainability – emerged as valuable, albeit
underrecognised, forces for change. These initiatives illustrate that the *Empowerment* of employee-driven action can act as a powerful complement to formal sus-

tainable innovation programmes, supporting a strategic transformation towards sustainability while increasing the necessary social capital.[9]

Our empirical study advances our understanding in several ways. First, we disclose how the practical implementation of sustainable innovation in science-based companies often diverges from theoretical models. Second, we highlight the challenge of cross-functional alignment in science-based companies, where function-specific silos and the lack of tailored sustainable innovation metrics contribute to a fragmented approach. Third, looking at science-based companies, we provide an answer to fill a gap in knowledge[10] regarding drivers of green product innovation practices from a sectorial perspective. Fourth, we contribute to the open debate on the role of informal, bottom-up initiatives in driving sustainable innovation culture development in structurally and hierarchically complex organisations.

In this regard, our study sheds new light on the wider topic of doing well by doing good under specific organisational settings,[11] suggesting that practices such as *Experimentation*, *Decentralisation* and *Empowerment* of grassroots initiatives alongside formal sustainable innovation programmes enhance engagement and broaden the reach of sustainability efforts in science-based sectors.

10.6 Key Takeaways

Our findings suggest that for science-based companies, embedding sustainable innovation requires going beyond current approaches. The focus on environmental goals may lead companies to overlook the social dimensions of sustainability. To cultivate a holistic sustainable innovation culture, firms need to encourage cross-functional alignment and foster a shared understanding of sustainability across all departments (for sustainable innovation literacy, see case 9 in section 4.1). This broadened approach would help integrate sustainable innovation more fully into the organisation, moving beyond traditional environmental perspectives.

Currently, sustainability efforts in science-based companies are largely reactive, shaped by regulatory requirements and customer demands rather than proactive, forward-looking strategies. To lead in sustainable transformation, companies would benefit from developing internally motivated sustainable innovation cultures that anticipate rather than simply respond to external pressures.

Tailored Communication around sustainable innovation remains a challenge, with companies often using top-down messaging and adopting an overly modest stance when communicating achievements. This cautious approach stems from rigorous validation processes but can hinder employee engagement. Creating a more open, transparent communication style that involves input from employees at all levels can foster a sense of ownership and deepen awareness of sustainability objectives across organisations.

Another barrier to the cultivation of sustainable innovation lies in how sustainability performance is measured. Sustainable innovation metrics tend to focus on corporate-level indicators, such as water usage or energy consumption, but often overlook function-specific KPIs that could make sustainability feel relevant to every department. By developing metrics for *Innovation Impact Assessment* that resonate with specific functions, companies can promote individual accountability and encourage all employees to view sustainability as a shared responsibility.

While formal sustainable innovation communication and coordination may sometimes fall short, informal initiatives are emerging from employees who are personally committed to sustainability. These grassroots efforts, though modest, play an important role in advancing sustainable innovation and establishing a foundation for broader cultural change. Recognising and supporting these bottom-up initiatives could build a culture of sustainability from the ground up, sparking greater engagement and innovation across the company.

In sum, establishing an advanced sustainable innovation culture in science-based companies requires a proactive, inclusive approach that unites diverse functions, emphasises transparent communication, and values contributions from both top-down and grassroots levels. By addressing these areas, companies can enhance their positive impact and drive innovation across all aspects of their company.

PART IV

CROSS-CUTTING ISSUES /

Mergers, Financing and Forward-Looking Cultures

The final part of the book is dedicated to two cross-cutting issues in establishing a sustainable innovation culture and an outlook into the future.

In chapter 11 we look into a merger and acquisition case from Slovenia. A traditional brewery with two rival beer brands is confronted with sustainable innovation challenges when a global incumbent acquires both brands and prioritizes values of sustainability over heritage. Through participative engagement, knowledge transfer and supply chain collaboration, the brewery successfully adopts the new values, transforming itself from a legacy-driven business into a future-oriented, environmentally responsible industry leader. The author helps facilitate this transformation as a consultant and derives some recommendations for consultants or mentors in a similar position.

Chapter 12 is dedicated to the financing of sustainable innovation cultures, countering the assumption that organisational culture is solely about 'soft' factors. It shows established ways of financing sustainable transformation and how sustainable innovation can be integrated into financial planning. This has implications for the accounting and financing functions in organisations. Of the numerous illustrative examples in this chapter, a case study on a sustainability-oriented investment management company stands out.

An Outlook shows how forward-thinking companies can achieve competitive advantages and create sustainable value and advance their own transformation despite changing environmental conditions by bundling collaborative forces in sustainable innovation ecosystems. In the future, intelligent systems will further expand our human abilities in shaping sustainable innovation cultures.

Chapter 11 /
Developing Sustainable Innovation Cultures during Mergers and Acquisitions: The Case of Two Breweries in Slovenia

by Ladeja Godina Košir, Founder & Executive Director Circular Change / Co-chair ECESP

Mergers and acquisitions often present an array of challenges: clashing organisational values and identities, uncertainty among employees and pressures to streamline operations swiftly. For many companies, especially in traditional industries, these transitions become an unsurmountable obstacle to achieving long-term goals such as creating positive impact through sustainable innovation. To overcome this challenge, companies need to review their organisational cultures and find new ways to support sustainable innovation across locations, functions and hierarchical levels through consistently aligned notions, practices and artefacts.

> This chapter explores how two rival Slovenian breweries navigated a merger and subsequent acquisition by a global brewing group, transforming their legacy cultures and strategies into shared commitment to sustainable innovation.

Their journey reveals how organisations can embrace collaboration, reimagine partnerships and embed systemic thinking into their operations, even under the pressure of restructuring and integrating divergent notions and operational practices. By following up on the step-by-step integration of two initially divergent cultures, this case illustrates how to maintain local heritage while meeting the demands of global sustainability agendas.

FIGURE 10. Facilitating mergers and acquisitions by establishing a clear new sense of direction towards sustainable development

11.1 A Tale of Two Local Rivals

This story of two local rivals, their merger and subsequent acquisition by an international brewing brand unfolds in ten scenes.

SCENE 1: THE MERGE OF TWO TRADITIONAL BREWERIES

Imagine this: Two iconic national beer brands, each deeply rooted in tradition, have been fierce rivals for years. In a small country of just two million people, beer preference is more than just a casual choice, it's a statement of identity. *'Tell me which brand you prefer, and I'll tell you who you are.'*

For decades, these two beers were produced by two independent breweries, each located in a different region of the country. The rivalry wasn't just about taste. It was about heritage, loyalty and even a touch of friendly animosity. People took pride in 'their' beer, often defining themselves by their choice. Then came the unexpected: a merger.

When the two breweries united under one company, the first shockwave hit the nation. What would happen to their beloved brands? Would their distinct flavours remain untouched? Was one brand about to disappear? Conversations at bars, family gatherings and sports games revolved around the same question: Was this the end of an era?

But the real challenge was just beginning to unfold. How do you unite two historically opposing identities under one corporate strategy without alienating loyal consumers? And, more importantly, what happens when business rationale collides with deep-rooted cultural traditions?

Bang! Just like in all good fairy tales, a greater power appears and causes an even greater challenge. Just as the nation is coming to terms with the merger, a global brewing giant with a clear agenda – and different priorities – enters the stage. It acquires both national brands, and people fear the worst. Will their beloved beers lose their authenticity? Will local traditions be swallowed by corporate efficiency?

Now, imagine stepping into the role of CEO of this newly merged brewery. It might sound like a dream job – except for one catch. Your primary mission is not just to preserve brand heritage or soothe emotional anxieties about beer identity. Instead, the new owners have to mainstream a new priority: sustainable development.

Why? Because in today's market, future competitiveness and regulatory compliance depend on corporate sustainability. The international group acquiring the brewery sees this as a 'must have', not a 'nice to have'. Their strategy focuses on reducing carbon emissions, embracing principles of a circular economy, conserving water, promoting responsible consumption and supporting local communities. These are not just seen as marketing efforts but as fundamental drivers of long-term growth, resilience and value creation.

The challenge? Until now, the local brewery that merged with its rival focused on values such as tradition, local impact and community support. The portfolio of the two rival brands under one roof consisted of non-alcoholic beverages. The merged company sponsored cultural and sporting events and released sustainability reports, although sustainability was never at the core of its business model.

Key performance indicators (KPIs) focused on market share, consumer loyalty and sponsorship visibility, while sustainability reporting remained a separate supplementary section rather than a core part of its business strategy. As a result, sustainability factors were not embedded in KPIs or integrated into the main annual report but treated as an appendix, lacking real influence on decision-making and performance evaluation.

After the acquisition by a global market leader, everything had to change. The question is: *Can you transform a business deeply rooted in its heritage into a future-proof, sustainability-oriented market leader, without losing what made it special in the first place?*

SCENE 2: THE INTERNATIONAL TAKEOVER

The new international owner is a large global brewing brand with corporate sustainability at the core of its business strategy. It prioritises corporate sustainability by setting stringent targets for carbon reduction, water conservation and waste management, aligning with global initiatives that drive long-term environmental and social impact. Sustainable development is a core value shaping all their business decisions and operations.

This creates a shift in perspective. While local values have traditionally linked issues of sustainability to sponsorship and community-based benefits, the international brand brings a more profound approach, emphasising the implementation of circular economy principles as well as long-term environmental and social impact.

SCENE 3: UNITING FOR A SUSTAINABLE FUTURE

Managers who previously led the local brands initiated a special task force to bridge the gap between the distinct business cultures of the large international brewing brand and the two merged local breweries. Their existing cultures are deeply rooted in tradition and local branding. The newly formed culture is driven by sustainability and innovation.

The task force conceives these differences and designs a roadmap for embedding sustainability into operational processes – while respecting the identity and heritage that had made the two formerly rival brands national favourites. The road ahead is clear. Engage employees, address scepticism and integrate sustainable innovation efforts throughout the value chain, while establishing sustainability practices and tracking sustainability performance across business operations.

Practices of *Inclusive Deliberation* (e.g. open dialogue, co-creating workshops and *Values-Based Ideation and Assessment*) engage employees to generate new ideas and propose solutions, ranging from renewable energy use and waste reduction to sustainable sourcing practices. These practices ensure that sustainability is not just a top-down directive, but a shared priority shaped by those directly involved in the company's operations. Representatives from all departments – including research and development, marketing, sales, logistics and maintenance – are invited to take part in defining how values of sustainability will be integrated into daily business practices. This inclusive approach fosters ownership, innovation and a shared commitment to the company's future.

Yet despite this inclusive approach, scepticism remains. Many employees still question the need for change. Why fix something that has worked well for nearly a century? To shift this mindset, leadership must go beyond explaining sustainability goals. They need to showcase real benefits, provide clear incentives and empower employees to be active contributors in shaping the transformation.

SCENE 4: AWARENESS RAISING WORKSHOPS

A series of *Awareness Raising* workshops are launched to ensure that sustainability becomes a practically relevant and relatable concept for all employees. Representatives from each department attend the introductory session, which focuses on the meaning of the essential notions of sustainability and the circular economy. The guiding question is simple. *What's in it for me?* Clear language and concrete examples are used to illustrate benefits such as reducing energy costs through more efficient equipment, optimising resources and minimising waste.

Furthermore, the task force managers raise awareness of what the long-term benefits of a sustainability-oriented approach to innovation are and why sustainability is embedded in the KPIs of the global brand. A special guest from the multinational parent company's headquarters joins the session, offering a broader perspective on sustainability. This presentation connects global environmental challenges to everyday business operations, explaining how corporate sustainability is not just a responsibility but a strategic advantage. The company's commitment to the UN's Sustainable Development Goals is outlined, explaining how these goals shape decision-making, investments and long-term planning.

The discussion highlights real-world initiatives that have already delivered results, including the company's shift towards zero-waste breweries and its transition from a linear to a circular economy. Employees learn about the structured approach to maximising circularity, focusing on reducing waste, increasing the use of recycled materials and designing products for reuse. Packaging is another key area of innovation, building on global best practices to ensure materials are recyclable, sourced sustainably and part of a closed-loop system.

Through these insights, local employees begin to see sustainable development not only as an abstract goal but as a clear pathway to efficiency, resilience and future-proofing the business. The workshop concludes with an interactive session where participants map out opportunities for sustainable transformation within their own departments, ensuring that change starts from within.

SCENE 5: ENGAGING IN OPEN INNOVATION

To expand the impact of internal cultural development, local employees are encouraged to Engage in Open Innovation with partners across the value chain, collaborating with packaging suppliers, logistics providers and the HORECA, the hotel, restaurant and catering network to identify and implement sustainable solutions. This stakeholder involvement turns sustainability from a corporate goal confined to a single organisation into a series of sustainable innovation endeavours that spread throughout the entire value chain.

Beyond relations with immediate partners, open innovation engagement also extends to the wider community. NGOs are invited to a meeting where they share their concerns, ambitions and solutions. What emerges is not just consultation but an engaging and respectful dialogue with both local and global C-level executives, fostering a deeper understanding of sustainability as a driver of innovation and long-term success.

SCENE 6: ENGAGING IN INNOVATION ECOSYSTEMS

Workshops continue, shifting the focus from internal transformation to collaboration across the entire value chain. For the first time, suppliers are actively challenged to propose innovative sustainable solutions, particularly in reducing plastic use. What unfolds is surprising. Many suppliers already have circular solutions but have not been invited to present them. Now, with sustainability becoming a strategic priority, they seize the opportunity.

The discussions go beyond plastic packaging. One supplier presents a new type of bottle label – easier to remove, requiring fewer chemicals in the recycling process and using minimal printing with non-toxic inks to improve recyclability. Another introduces a redesigned multipack solution for cans, eliminating the need for plastic rings in favour of fibre-based carriers made from renewable materials. The enthusiasm is contagious, and soon suppliers, logistics partners and distribution networks are collaborating on broader innovations, such as returnable packaging models and optimised transport routes to cut emissions. This shift highlights a key lesson:

> The difficulties in shaping sustainable developments were not due to a lack of solutions but to a lack of dialogue and systems thinking.

By actively inviting partners into the conversation, the brewery transforms its supply chain from a linear process into a dynamic, collaborative business ecosystem where sustainability drives both innovation and competitiveness.

SCENE 7: KNOWLEDGE SHARING

With no internal sustainability leader in place, a local employee previously responsible for quality control is appointed as the new sustainability manager. While experienced in operational excellence, he lacks in-depth knowledge of sustainability principles. To bridge this gap, headquarters assigns an international sustainability expert for a six-month engagement, ensuring hands-on support and daily knowledge exchange.

This collaboration goes beyond theoretical training. Together, they tackle concrete challenges, from integrating new KPIs into daily business operations to embedding a more systemic approach to sustainability. Discussions focus on circular economy principles, resource efficiency and long-term value creation. Step by step, sustainability shifts from being a separate reporting requirement to a core business driver.

One of the first internal changes – a simple switch from bottled water to tap water – causes an unexpected cultural shock. Employees, long accustomed to the convenience of single-use plastics, find it hard to adjust. The irony is evident. The brewery's most recognised non-alcoholic product has always been packaged in plastic bottles. Yet, this small shift results in significant plastic savings and becomes a symbolic step towards deeper transformation.

What starts as structured *Knowledge Sharing* evolves into something far greater. Through daily collaboration, shared problem-solving and mutual respect, the sustainability expert and the local manager develop not just a professional partnership but a true friendship, reinforcing that change is ultimately about people, trust and collective growth.

SCENE 8: ESTABLISHING SUSTAINABILITY-ORIENTED MANAGEMENT SYSTEMS

Corporate sustainability has become a pillar of the local subsidiary's strategy. At a decisive board meeting, the leadership team introduced new KPIs and a real-time monitoring tool to track sustainability performance across business operations. Unlike previous years, where sustainability reporting was relegated to a separate appendix, it is now fully integrated into financial and operational reporting, reflecting its role in economic, environmental and social impact.

The new KPIs cover key areas such as carbon footprint (tracking reductions across production, transport and supply chain activities), energy efficiency (measuring improvements in renewable energy use and operational energy savings), water stewardship (setting targets for water reduction and wastewater treatment efficiency), circular packaging (ensuring higher recycled content, recyclability and reusable packaging options) and waste reduction (monitoring landfill diversion rates and closed-loop material recovery). Each department is accountable for specific sustainability targets, aligning sustainability efforts with business performance.

As the final transition unfolds, the international sustainability expert steps back, transferring full responsibility to the local sustainability manager. No longer just an observer or learner, he is now leading the sustainability-oriented transformation of the company. His journey from quality control to sustainability leadership symbolises the broader shift within the company. A move from traditional business thinking to a future-oriented, systemic approach where sustainability is not a constraint but a catalyst for efficiency, innovation and growth.

SCENE 9: ONGOING TASK FORCE ACTIVITIES

The task force continues its activities across various levels, including production processes, packaging, logistics and partnerships with hotels, restaurants, cafés and catering services. The company's core values – a passion for quality, enjoyment of life, respect for people and the planet and a commitment to innovation – are deeply embedded in its operations. Sustainability is understood not merely as an environmental concern but as a holistic approach that encompasses social responsibility, economic viability and environmental stewardship. Employees actively contribute ideas and solutions to support the transformative process towards a more sustainable circular production and consumption of products.

With a strong emphasis on communicating its sustainability initiatives as a case study, the local company gains visibility within the multinational corporation. It is now committed to investing a substantial amount in order to become one of the largest breweries in the group by 2030. This investment is directed towards sustainable development, with the ambition to achieve carbon neutrality in production by 2030. The company recognises that producing the best beer involves not only taste and quality but also responsible practices towards people, the environment and the economy, embodying a comprehensive approach to sustainability management and innovation.

The sustainability strategy focuses on three key areas: environmental preservation, social sustainability and responsible consumption, contributing to a more responsible, fair and healthy society. In addition to the goal of carbon neutrality, the local company is committed to raising awareness about responsible alcohol consumption and developing options like alcohol-free beverages. Furthermore, the company remains a significant supporter of local sports, reflecting its dedication to community engagement and well-being.

This strategic focus on sustainability not only enhances the company's reputation within the multinational group but also sets a benchmark on how to navigate the intricate challenges of mergers and acquisitions. By aligning with sustainability values and goals while establishing them in operational practices, the local company bolsters its credibility in both local and international markets.

11.2   Effective Actions for Sustainable Transformation

Over the course of a year, I had the privilege of serving as an external adviser to this local subsidiary company undergoing a significant sustainability transformation. My role was to guide the organisation through this journey, focusing on fostering internal collaboration, establishing a dedicated task force and ensuring a shared understanding of sustainability principles.

A pivotal aspect of this transformation was the creation of a specialised task force. This group comprising representatives from key departments was instrumental in aligning the organisation's sustainability goals with its core values. By bringing together diverse perspectives, we ensured that sustainability became an integral part of the company's culture, driving meaningful and lasting change.

Securing the trust and support of the CEO and the leadership team was crucial. Their endorsement provided the necessary resources and authority to drive change effectively. Through Practices of *Inclusive Deliberation* and *Awareness Raising* workshops, we engaged employees at all levels, encouraging them to contribute ideas and solutions. This participative approach not only enhanced the quality of our sustainability initiatives but also fostered a culture of innovation and shared responsibility.

By integrating these elements – employee engagement, collaboration, shared understanding and leadership support – we laid a strong foundation for a successful sustainability transformation against the odds of ongoing and turbulent merger and acquisition processes. Our holistic approach ensured that sustainability became an integral part of the organisation's culture, driving meaningful and lasting change.

11.3 Systemic Change in Mergers and Acquisitions

Some practices and methods proved particularly effective in navigating through the stages of conceiving, co-creating and cultivating during this transformative journey. The lessons learned here provide guidelines for facilitation in similar cases of mergers and acquisitions.

CONCEIVING

1. FOSTER OPEN DIALOGUE: Encourage open dialogues and be receptive to ideas from all levels. For instance, during our workshops, we implemented 'idea boards' where employees could anonymously submit suggestions. This approach not only produced innovative ideas but also made employees feel heard and valued. (*Inclusive Deliberation*)

2. CELEBRATE SMALL WINS: Recognise and celebrate small victories to build momentum and maintain morale. After successfully reducing plastic usage in the office, we held a small celebration to acknowledge the team's efforts, reinforcing the positive impact of their actions. (*From Failure to Success*)

3. DEMONSTRATE POSITIVE IMPACTS: Showcase the tangible benefits of sustainable practices for both the company and the community. By sharing case studies of companies that successfully integrated sustainability, we inspired confidence and commitment among employees. (*From Failure to Success*)

4. LEVERAGE LEADERSHIP: Demonstrate commitment to values of sustainability through your actions. By actively participating in the conceiving activities, engaging in environmental stewardship and leading by example, leadership can inspire the entire organisation. (*Symbolic Ethical Leadership*)

CO-CREATING

5. FACILITATE THE EXCHANGE OF IDEAS: Encourage employees to share their ideas and suggestions through methods such as suggestion boxes or brainwriting sessions. For example, during our transformation, we introduced a monthly Innovation Hour where employees from all departments could present their sustainability ideas, leading to several successful initiatives. (*Ideation Contests and Markets, Sustainable Innovation Time*)

6. ENCOURAGE EXPERIMENTATION AND RISK-TAKING: Workshops and collaborative projects can spark creativity and uncover new solutions. During our sustainability journey, we piloted a zero-waste initiative in one department. Despite initial challenges, the pilot provided valuable insights that informed a company-wide rollout, demonstrating the importance of viewing failures as learning opportunities. (*Experimentation*)

7. ENGAGE WITH THE LOCAL COMMUNITY: Help organisations to integrate local values and traditions with their corporate and the global sustainability goals. Finding a balance can drive smoother transitions. (*Engage in Open Innovation*)

8. DEVELOP INNOVATION ECOSYSTEMS: Guide the organisation in building strong networks with suppliers and other value chain partners based on sustainability values. Collaborative problem-solving with the broader ecosystem can yield innovative solutions and reinforce internal relationships. (*Engage in Innovation Ecosystems*)

CULTIVATING

9. STREAMLINE COMMUNICATION: Establish transparent communication channels to keep everyone informed and engaged. We set up a dedicated sustainability newsletter to share progress, challenges and upcoming initiatives, ensuring that all employees are aligned and informed. We ensured that notions of sustainability are explained in simple language with concrete examples. We addressed different employee groups to ensure understanding and buy-in. (*Policy Communication* and *Tailored Communication*)

10. INCENTIVISE CONTRIBUTIONS: Positively reinforce and reward those who contribute significantly to sustainability initiatives. We proposed a Sustainability Champion nomination, recognising employees who demonstrated exceptional commitment to sustainable practices, motivating others to engage. (*Incentivise*)

11. PROMOTE CONTINUOUS EMPLOYEE DEVELOPMENT: Invest in continuous learning opportunities to equip employees with the necessary skills and knowledge. We organised monthly sustainability workshops, covering topics from waste management to energy efficiency, empowering employees to contribute effectively. (*Human Resource Development*)

12. PROVIDE EMPLOYEE TRAINING: Offer ongoing education on sustainability topics to build competencies. We implemented a quarterly sustainability training programme, covering areas like energy efficiency and waste reduction, which equipped employees with the knowledge to contribute effectively to our initiatives. (*Mandatory Training*)

13. EMPOWER EMPLOYEES: Apply a participative approach, engaging all employees to play a part in the sustainability journey. Use participative approaches to engage them in defining and implementing sustainability practices. (*Participative Decision-Making*)

14. PRIORITISE SUSTAINABILITY: Work with the leadership to embed sustainability in the core business strategy and KPIs. Support the establishment of regular reporting systems on sustainability metrics to maintain focus and accountability. (*Management Systems*)

15. LEVERAGE KNOWLEDGE SHARING: Promote the company-wide utilisation of expertise and benchmarking of best practices from international actors as well as the building of local capacities. Coaching and mentorship can also be effective drivers. (*Knowledge Sharing*)

Sustainable transformation is a journey, not a destination. It requires ongoing commitment, adaptability and the collective effort of the entire organisation. In cases of mergers and acquisition, it also requires dedicated efforts to align the merging partners or to onboard subsidiaries. By implementing these practices and methods, you can create a resilient and sustainable future development for your growing organisation.

11.4   The Power of Mentorship

In the organisational transformation presented in this chapter, bringing in a sustainability expert from another country for six months proved instrumental to its success. The external expert provided on-the-ground support, facilitating knowledge sharing and closely monitoring the process. His presence was invaluable and encouraging for the local sustainability manager, who was assuming a completely new role. This mentorship not only facilitated skill transfer but also provided the local manager with the confidence and guidance needed to lead the sustainability initiatives effectively. It underscored the importance of hands-on training and continuous support in embedding sustainability into the core of the company's operations.

In today's rapidly evolving landscape, fostering a culture of co-creating and community is essential for organisations striving to remain agile and innovative despite the challenges of rapid growth and constant change. Drawing on my year-long experience as an external adviser, I observed that mentorship and peer-to-peer exchange are pivotal in this endeavour. They encourage *Knowledge Sharing* and collective problem-solving and enhance a sense of community and mutual support. When employees feel valued and heard, they are more likely to engage and contribute to the organisation's goals.

In conclusion, mentorship and peer-to-peer exchange are not merely supportive elements but are integral to the success of sustainable transformation. By fostering trust, encouraging co-creating and celebrating the joy of sharing knowledge, organisations can cultivate a resilient and sustainable future. We may not have all the answers, but we do have each other.

Chapter 12 /
Sustainable Finance and Investments for Sustainable Innovation Cultures

by Gregor Erkel & Henning Breuer

In response to growing demand for sustainable products and services, processes and business models, many organisations are seeking to establish a sustainable innovation culture – a commitment to innovation management that addresses environmental and social challenges alongside traditional economic goals. Sustainable innovation cultures turn values of sustainability into novel regenerative outcomes that are economically, socially and environmentally beneficial (see chapter 3).

Creating such a culture demands a substantial commitment of time, energy and capital, as well as an organisational shift towards values of sustainability and goals that transcend immediate profit. It requires significant financial resources to initiate, develop and maintain such a culture, as well as adaptive financing strategies and a transformation in the finance functions. Financial resources are essential to funding innovation projects and initiatives in research and development, workforce training and sustainable technology investments. Beyond initial funding, ongoing investment is necessary to maintain momentum, scale sustainability-oriented practices and build resilience in the innovation ecosystem. Financial planning and accounting play central roles in managing these complexities, ensuring sustainable innovation aligns with long-term growth and financial viability.

> This chapter explores the interconnected roles of financial planning, financing and organisational transformation in the finance functions of sustainable innovation cultures. It shows how to effectively allocate financial resources, how to finance the transformation and how to cultivate sustainable innovation without compromising financial stability or other strategic objectives.

12.1 Financing Sustainable Transformation

Traditional financing approaches, which often prioritise quick returns and low-risk projects, may struggle to support long-term transformative innovations. Creating a sustainable innovation culture presents specific financial challenges.

Since there are always many factors that influence financial results, measuring the direct financial impact of specific sustainability initiatives is difficult. Nevertheless, one of the most prominent examples in financing sustainable transformation in business is the American outdoor apparel and equipment retailer Patagonia and its commitment to 'Save Our Home Planet' (case 15).

CASE 16. Patagonia's Approach to Financing Sustainable Transformation

Patagonia, an outdoor clothing and gear company, is a prominent example of a company that prioritises long-term sustainability over short-term profits. Already in the 1970s its founder Yvon Chouinard demonstrated that sustainability can be a successful business strategy. Until this day, Patagonia makes

sustainable development a core priority for its business strategy and operations, enhancing its brand reputation, attracting loyal customers and improving employee engagement. While initial investments appear costly, long-term
benefits include reduced environmental risks, improved resource efficiency
and access to new markets for Patagonia.

Financial planning and accounting systems have to be adapted to measure
and track the long-term value of sustainability initiatives. In pursuit of its core
values of quality, integrity, environmentalism and justice, the company takes
pride in not being bound by convention but rather 'developing new ways to do
things'.[1] Patagonia invests with a long-term perspective and is still financially
successful.

In order to measure and track the long-term value creation of sustainability
initiatives, financial planning and accounting systems must be adapted. In
line with its core values , the company invests with a long-term perspective
and is still financially successful. The most important principles of corporate governance are derived from Patagonia's core values revolving around
environmental protection and social responsibility. These include minimising environmental impact by reducing the carbon footprint as well as using
recycled materials and advocating for environmental protection. Fair labour
practices are ensured by paying fair wages and creating safe working conditions for employees and suppliers. The company donates a significant portion
of its profits to environmental organisations.

The company's financial approach includes long-term investment in sustainable initiatives. For example, the development of innovative environmentally friendly materials, such as investments in research and development for
recycled polyester, organic cotton and other sustainable materials. Promoting
supply chain transparency and sustainability by working with suppliers to
improve working conditions and reduce their environmental impact is also
an important component. The company supports environmental activism
by funding environmental organisations and campaigns. Another important
initiative is the Earth Tax, where Patagonia donates one percent of its sales
to environmental organisations. The company also promotes conscious
consumption by encouraging customers to repair and reuse their products
instead of buying new ones.

Despite these long-term investments in sustainability, Patagonia has
achieved significant financial success due to continuous sales growth over
the years. The company benefits from strong brand loyalty as its commitment
to sustainability has built a strong and loyal customer base. The company's
strong environmental and social image has enhanced its brand image and
attracted top talent.[2]

Patagonia, a Certified B Corporation, is a spearhead in sustainable business
transformation with its purpose of 'We're in business to save our home planet'.
However, more conventional companies and organisations have also successful-

ly explored financing options to align with goals of sustainable development. By securing diverse financing sources, organisations can support sustainable innovation without destabilising existing operations or compromising their other strategic priorities.

> Proven practices to finance sustainable transformation include the reallocation of resources, the use of sustainability-linked financing options and a sustainable business model design.

INTERNAL REALLOCATION OF RESOURCES

Finance teams can prioritise sustainable projects within existing budgets by, for example, redirecting funds from non-essential projects or even reallocating CSR budgets towards sustainable innovation practices and initiatives. A consumer goods company can reallocate significant budget resources from traditional advertising channels like television commercials and print ads to sustainable product development and marketing communication. First, they develop and promote a new line of eco-friendly products, which involves funding research and development for sustainable materials, investing in eco-friendly packaging and launching targeted marketing campaigns that highlight the environmental benefits of the new products.

Second, they support environmental initiatives and partner with environmental organisations to launch educational campaigns to raise awareness about related environmental issues. By reallocating budget resources towards these initiatives, the company can increase its brand value and attract environmentally conscious consumers. Clearly communicating this decision to reallocate part of its marketing budget towards sustainability initiatives can improve relationships with stakeholders such as employees, investors and key market partners. Improving their environmental impact by investments in eco-friendly products and supporting environmental initiatives creates both positive impact and a competitive edge in the market.

Complementary practices and methods like *Results Chain Matrix, Innovation Impact Assessment* and *Adopting Sustainable Management Systems* are crucial to ensure positive outcomes and impact of these reallocated funds. Tracking key performance indicators (KPIs) such as sales of eco-friendly products, customer engagement with sustainability campaigns and brand perception among target audiences is essential to understanding the effects of such decisions and adapting and optimising them in future periods.

GREEN BONDS AND SUSTAINABILITY-LINKED LOANS AND CONTRACTS

External financing options – such as green bonds, sustainability-linked loans and impact investment funds – can provide dedicated capital for sustainable innovation initiatives. These financing tools are often offered at competitive rates and designed to lower financial barriers for sustainable innovation. As the funding is tied to sustainability outcomes, they encourage adherence to sustainability goals, aligning financial with ethical objectives. For instance, Danish renewable energy company Ørsted issued green bonds to develop offshore wind farms in the Netherlands.[3]

These wind farms now generate renewable energy for hundreds of thousands of homes, significantly reducing carbon emissions and advancing the global transition to clean energy. Contracting that applies the pay-for-success business model pattern makes payment dependant on predefined outcomes to stimulate adoption of more sustainable solutions. For instance, Washington DC hedged its performance risks and the associated costs of stormwater runoff infrastructure with success-based payment thresholds.[4]

SUSTAINABLE BUSINESS MODEL DESIGN AND STRATEGIC PARTNERSHIPS

Sustainable business model design patterns describe further financing options such as crowdfunding, profit reinvestment or customer financing.[5] For instance, sustainability-oriented companies such as Ecosia and Enpal were not only able to reinvest part of their profits, but they could also leverage their customer base to crowdfund innovation projects to deal with unresolved challenges such as re-manufacturing solar panels. Collaboration with industry partners and using government grants and public funding initiatives can alleviate some of the financial burdens, particularly for high-impact, long-term sustainability projects. Strategic partnerships also introduce shared expertise and resources, enhancing project feasibility. For instance, in northern Germany, the Renewable Energies in the Northern Region project brings together companies and municipalities to develop virtual powerplants.[6]

As for strategic planning it is important not just to create individual funding options, but to configure financial resources so that they contribute to the joint goal of sustainable innovation and cultural development.

12.2 Financial Planning for Sustainable Innovation

Effective financial planning for sustainable innovation involves not only allocating resources but also adapting budget forecasts and timelines to account for the unique aspects of sustainable innovation projects. Traditional project timelines, often optimised for rapid return on investments, may not be suitable for initiatives that require longer time periods to realise both financial and environmental returns.

A range of practices allows financial planners to support the development of a sustainable innovation culture in their organisation. They include establishing dedicated funds, flexible budget allocation, multi-year planning and evaluating return on investments in a comprehensive manner.

Allocating specific funds for sustainable innovation initiatives allows for focused investment and enables clear reporting on the performance and impact of sustainable innovation projects. For instance, funds for research and development can be dedicated to experiment with sustainable materials, processes and product designs. Some funds do not just provide capital but also offer platforms for collaborating and scaling solutions. For example, the German multinational chemical and consumer goods company Henkel invests in start-ups working on innovations in materials and technologies that can help the company to achieve its sustainability goals with new packaging and materials.[7] Likewise, IKEA has invested in initiatives like the IKEA Foundation and IKEA GreenTech that support companies developing renewable energy solutions, sustainable forestry practices and innovative materials.[8]

FLEXIBLE BUDGET ALLOCATION

Financial planning should allow for the allocation of funds towards emerging sustainable innovation projects. Flexibility in budget allocation supports adaptability, allowing organisations to invest in new sustainable technologies or practices as they appear in the market. This flexibility allows for faster decision-making as opposed to budgets which are fully allocated across the company for the next period. Key criteria to invest flexible budgets are strategic alignment of the investment with core values and long-term goals. They need to consider the financial risk a company is willing to take, the targeted return on investments, as well as the opportunity cost of an alternative. The potential impact and scalability of technologies have to be taken into consideration, as well as an organisational assessment concerning the level of the company's expertise and, last but not least, the cultural effect on the company and its stakeholders.

One example is establishing a dedicated 'green innovation fund' with predefined criteria for flexible budget allocation. These criteria can include alignment with the company's carbon reduction targets, the potential to achieve a minimum return on investments within a specified timeframe, the technology readiness level exceeding a certain threshold, and achieving a positive impact on the local community and environment. By establishing clear and transparent criteria, companies can ensure that their flexible budget allocation process is aligned with their sustainability goals and supports informed decision-making.

INCORPORATING MULTI-YEAR PLANNING

Sustainability efforts typically span multiple years. Multi-year planning provides the needed financial perspective to support long-term sustainable innovation efforts and ensures these initiatives remain financially viable over extended periods. Besides, these efforts often require significant upfront investment which may not be completely funded in one period and may take years to develop and implement before they yield substantial returns. Multi-year planning provides a roadmap for these long-term initiatives, ensuring consistent support and preventing short-term pressures from derailing critical projects.

This goes hand in hand with four advantages: planning security, risk reduction, financial adaptability and investor confidence. First, by outlining the financial needs of sustainable innovation projects over several years, organisations can secure in advance the necessary resources (budget, personnel, etc.). This avoids sudden funding cuts that could halt progress or compromise the project's success. Second, long-term planning allows for the identification and mitigation of potential risks associated with sustainable innovation. This could include unforeseen technological challenges, changing market conditions or evolving regulatory requirements. Third, multi-year financial visibility enables better-informed decision-making. Organisations can assess the long-term financial viability of sustainable innovation projects, compare them to other investment opportunities and adjust their strategies as needed. Fourth, demonstrating a long-term commitment to sustainability through multi-year plans can enhance investor confidence. It signals a responsible and forward-looking approach that aligns with growing investor interest in environmental, social and governance (ESG) factors.

Metrics to assess long-term return on investment account for the longer payback periods of investments in sustainable innovation (approach 8).

APPROACH 8. Metrics for Financial Planning

Financial planning should incorporate metrics that account for long-term returns, including indirect benefits such as enhanced reputation, brand loyalty and regulatory compliance.

Various metrics are used to assess environmental performance, for example, the reduction of greenhouse gas emissions, tracking both absolute and relative reductions across the value chain. Likewise, resource consumption is monitored, in particular the reduction in consumption of water, energy and raw materials. Another important aspect is waste reduction, as measured by the amount of waste generated and the amount diverted from landfills. The impact on biodiversity is also assessed, for example, by the success of measures to protect local ecosystems and species diversity. Finally, compliance with environmental regulations and industry standards is tracked.

Financial performance is assessed using various metrics. These include monitoring long-term revenue growth driven by sustainable products and services. Likewise, long-term cost savings associated with resource efficiency and waste reduction are tracked. Another important aspect is evaluating the reduction of financial risks associated with environmental and social impacts. Additionally, brand equity is monitored, particularly brand reputation and customer loyalty associated with sustainability initiatives. Finally, investor confidence is tracked, with a focus on investor sentiment and ESG ratings.

Long-term financial performance is assessed through various metrics. These include calculating the net present value (NPV) of long-term investments in sustainable innovations, taking into account both tangible and intangible benefits. Furthermore, the long-term return on investments of sustainability initiatives is tracked over a period of several years. Finally, the growth of market share in sustainable product categories is monitored.

EVALUATING OVERALL RETURN ON INVESTMENTS

Sustainable innovation projects facilitate the generation of new business cases by reducing operational costs and compliance, by generating new revenues – for example, through sustainable value-adding services – by increasing efficiency, reputation as well as workforce commitment and attractiveness.[9] They also have the potential to benefit from innovation and ecosystem development with key stakeholders. Accordingly, long-term returns should be considered, not just the low-hanging fruits of cost savings from energy efficiency or reduced waste, but also intangible benefits like brand loyalty, market differentiation and regulatory advantages. Calculating the overall return on investments of sustainable projects is crucial for validating ongoing investment in innovation, for example, by calculating the total costs and financial returns, but also quantifying environmental and assessing social benefits to come up with an aggregated return on investments.

APPROACH 9. Calculating Overall Return on Investments

Let us consider the example of installing solar panels for a manufacturing facility. This investment brings both tangible and intangible benefits. Tangible benefits include cost savings from reduced electricity bills due to solar energy production, potential government subsidies or tax incentives for renewable energy plants, and reduced maintenance costs for traditional energy sources. In addition, financial returns come from potential revenue from selling excess energy to the grid and an increase in the value of the property due to the solar panels. Intangible benefits include brand loyalty from positive public perception and increased customer loyalty due to the company's commitment to sustainability. Likewise, market differentiation comes from a competitive advantage by positioning the company as an environmentally conscious leader. Additionally, regulatory benefits come from compliance with future environmental regulations and potential access to government grants and incentives.

To calculate an overall return on investments, the following four steps are required:

1. QUANTIFICATION OF TANGIBLE BENEFITS: Annual cost savings from reduced electricity bills are calculated, the value of government subsidies and tax incentives is estimated, the potential revenue from the sale of excess energy is determined and the increase in the value of the property due to the solar panels is assessed.

2. MONETARY VALUE OF INTANGIBLE BENEFITS: Increase in customer retention rate and revenue due to improved brand perception is estimated, the potential

premium that can be charged for products or services due to the company's sustainable image is assessed and the potential value of avoiding future fines or penalties for non-compliance with environmental regulations is estimated.

3. CALCULATION OF TOTAL COST: The initial investment cost of installing the solar panels as well as ongoing maintenance and operating costs are taken into account.

4. CALCULATION OF NET PRESENT VALUE (NPV): The future cash flows (cost savings, revenue and intangible benefits) are discounted to their present value using an appropriate discount rate.

12.3 Financial Accounting and Transformation Within the Finance Function

While financial planning focuses on allocating resources, financial accounting monitors the use of these resources to ensure they yield desired results and align with organisational objectives. Financial accounting in the context of sustainable innovation requires specific practices, methods and metrics to accurately assess the success of sustainable projects.

> Key practices for financial accounting include using customised KPIs, and methods of life cycle costing and risk management. Together they contribute to a profound transformation of the finance function.

CUSTOMISED KPIS, LIFE CYCLE COSTING AND RISK MANAGEMENT

Customised KPIs are required since traditional KPIs may not accurately capture the success of sustainable innovation initiatives (see case 5 on key value indicators in section 3.1.3). Financial accountants should move beyond traditional KPIs and implement metrics that capture ESG impact, such as carbon reduction, resource efficiency or social value. These metrics provide a more holistic view of sustainable innovation success.

Life Cycle Cost Analysis (see section 6.3) addresses the challenge that innovative processes or products contributing to sustainable development may incur higher upfront costs but offer long-term benefits and savings over time, such as reduced waste, energy and operational costs. In the context of innovation project assessment, life cycle costing assesses total costs over the entire lifespan of a project, helping accountants to evaluate the true financial viability of sustainable innovations and to ensure that short-term expenses do not detract from long-term gains.

Carpet tile manufacturer Interface (case 7, section 3.1.4) conducted life cycle cost analyses for its production processes and offered its customers an online cost calculator, which included initial product costs as well as maintenance and equipment costs for alternative flooring choices. This showed that while using more sustainable materials and production methods initially incurs higher expenses, significant long-term cost savings could be achieved through reduced waste, lower energy consumption and lower maintenance costs. Taking this holistic view allowed Interface to demonstrate to its customers the true costs and benefits of its sustainable innovations.[10]

Risk management is critical to any investments in innovation, since outcomes and timelines are uncertain. Financial accounting must include risk assessments tailored to each project. This involves setting tolerance levels for budget overruns and delays as well as contingency plans for potential obstacles. An illustrative example of effective risk management in innovation investments is the development of new drugs in the pharmaceutical industry. A pharmaceutical company investing in the research and development of a revolutionary cancer drug faces considerable uncertainties regarding efficacy, approval and timing.

To manage these risks, the company integrates detailed risk assessments into its financial accounting. Tolerance values for budget overruns and delays are defined for each project stage. In addition, detailed contingency plans are developed, for example, in the event of negative clinical trial results, unexpected regulatory hurdles or problems in the supply chain. Through this proactive risk assessment and the development of contingency strategies, the company can minimise the potential financial impact of uncertainties and increase the likelihood of successful project completion.[11]

TRANSFORMATION WITHIN THE FINANCE FUNCTION

Mainstreaming values of sustainability and an accompanying mindset are key to cultural development in general and to transforming the finance function in particular. Accountants should be encouraged to consider the strategic benefits of sustainable projects and work collaboratively with other departments, such as research and development and operations, to ensure alignment between financial and sustainability goals. Taken together these measures help to transform the finance function in a sustainability-oriented manner (see concept 2), as the case of Unilever illustrates (case 17).

CASE 17. Green Bonds in Unilever's Sustainable Living Plan

Unilever, a global consumer goods company, has made significant strides in integrating sustainability into its core business strategy. Its 2010 Sustainable Living Plan set ambitious targets to reduce its environmental footprint and increase its positive social impact while growing its business. The company embedded sustainability concerns in new product development. Unilever redesigned product formulations and packaging to reduce environmental impact, investing in sustainable sourcing of raw materials and promoting products with positive social and environmental benefits. In addition, the company linked sustainability to financial performance by establishing clear metrics to track progress against its sustainability goals and linked those metrics to executive compensation.

They also issued green bonds to finance sustainable projects and integrated ESG factors into their investment decisions. And last but not least, by fostering a culture of sustainability, Unilever invested in *Awareness Raising* training and education programmes encouraging employees to adopt sustainability-oriented practices. It also engaged with suppliers, customers and other stakeholders to promote sustainable consumption and production. By embedding sustainability values and practices throughout the organisation, Unilever has demonstrated that it is possible to achieve both environmental and social goals while delivering strong financial performance. This approach has helped Unilever build a resilient and sustainable business that is well-positioned for the future.[12]

This transformation allows finance functions to not only monitor expenditures, but also to play an active role in cultivating sustainable innovation by balancing cost control with an understanding of sustainable value creation.

The relationship between cultural development, financial planning and accounting is one of dynamic interdependence. Financial resources, strategic financing and an adaptive finance function are conducive to establishing and maintaining a sustainable innovation culture. By integrating these elements, organisations can create a feedback loop where sustainable projects are funded, monitored and refined, with finance teams providing real-time insights into the achievement of both financial and sustainability outcomes and impact.

However, a sustainable innovation culture requires a symbiotic relationship between the values-driven innovation culture, financially disciplined structures and empirical insights. Without financial planning, sustainable innovations lack the resources to come to fruition. Without financial accounting, they may exceed budget limits or veer from strategic objectives. The interplay between these elements is crucial for ensuring that sustainable innovation efforts are financially viable and aligned with organisational policy and goals. The case of GLS Investments illustrates how values-based cultural transformation and sustainable innovation feed into one another (case 18).

CASE 18. **Cultural Transformation and Financing Sustainable Transformation at GLS Investment**[13]

GLS Investment Management is a full subsidiary of the GLS bank. The bank was founded 50 years ago as the first sustainable bank in Germany, investing in social and environmental projects in the business fields of renewable energies, education and culture, social and health, nutrition, housing and a sustainable economy. On its website, GLS Investments claims to be one of the most stringent developers of sustainable fund concepts, managing funds on a long-term basis from a social, environmental and economic perspective.

Notions of sustainability are key to the mission of the company as well as its values: 'respect for life and concern for the peaceful coexistence of all cultures based on individual freedom and responsibility'. The bank's actions are guided by a commitment to preserve the life chances of present and future generations and promote their further development. We talked to the two managing directors, Marvin Mechelse and Karsten Kührlings, to understand their approach to sustainable finance and to learn from their experiences in establishing a sustainable innovation culture.

Both have been engaged in organisational development for some years, understanding it as a long-term process that requires cultivating four closely related dimensions of change: culture, structure, behaviour and attitude. Within this basic framework, GLS Investments applies its own formats of several practices and methods described in this book, including practices such as Stakeholder Integration and *Inviting for Informal Exchange* and methods such as *Empathising, Policy Reviews, Dedicated Training, Values-Based Ecosystem Modelling, Employee Resource Groups, Stakeholder Advisory Board* and *Result Chain Matrix*.

A challenge in the structural dimension, a 'main element to drive innovation', lies in leveraging multiple perspectives and distributed decision-making, transforming a hierarchical organisation based on management directives to decentralised organisation cultivating a perception of opportunities and risks. Sustainable investment is a 'people business', with human capabilities seen as an essential resource and values of diversity playing an important role in promoting gender diversity, gender equity as well as diversity of origin and age groups. Several formats have been established to practise an open, transparent and appreciative interaction among the 47 employees.

However, both directors noticed a 'harmony trap', a need for harmony, which can be particularly pronounced in people with high normative standards in a values-based culture and which can stand in the way of open debate. 'If conflicts cannot be expressed or resolved, no innovation can emerge.' To counter this tendency, the company offers open spaces for resonance and reflection (*Inviting for Informal Exchange*), such as 'circles of colleagues' (*Employee Resource Group*) reflect on attitudes and behaviours and empower self-organisation with the support of a professional coach. The coach facilitates formats such as retrospectives or case reviews, which help employees address the uncertainties resulting from the new, decentralised structure. Employees also have the opportunity to reflect on their own behaviour, both their own attempts to avoid uncertainty and their perceptions of 'new solution spaces' that they can proactively use. Co-creating and experimentation with such formats are seen as essential to developing a learning organisation, 'and we certainly have not tapped into all of them yet, we are at the beginning of this continuous active learning process that we envision'.

Externally, in relation to bank customers and investment objects, structural elements facilitate routines (rather than standards) in strategic decision-making and innovation development. Guiding principles, such as 'making sense comes before making profit' and 'the economic aspect is the result of entrepreneurial action, not the goal or purpose', prioritise social and environmental value creation. Investment and financing principles and criteria have been formulated to structure the bank's own sustainability research projects, profile investments based on facts and assessments and guide their review and decision-making in a sustainability advisory board.

This board is composed of mainly external stakeholders and experts, including technical environmental protection specialists and representatives from specialised NGOs (see *Stakeholder Advisory Board* in chapter 6). Another specialised advisory board evaluates projects with the Global South, where higher ethical standards are applied to particularly complex challenges. Sometimes external studies from specialised institutes and research on new technological trends inform the assessment, such as whether to enter or how to approach certain markets with controversially discussed microfinance.

In the end it is always a single case decision, not an automated procedure based on quantitative ESG or similar ratings. Following a multi-stage review process, an independent body of sustainability experts takes case-by-case decisions which equity or bond titles enter the company's 'investment universe', from which internal portfolio experts select and compose their funds. Likewise, the overarching investment and financing principles are also iteratively reviewed internally and discussed in the advisory board, as 'the world keeps turning, and because it is a normative discourse, attitudes sometimes shift'.

For Marvin Mechelse and Karsten Kührlings, innovation involves questioning their own products and business model. 'Innovation is where our business model comes in. And that's how to create investment vehicles that give money a positive impact.' An impact concept, such as the *Result Chain Matrix* (see chapter 6) helps to identify the most important levers for the intermediary between investors and investees, considering their business model, investment volume and the specific output of different instruments such as securities versus microfinance funds.

Competencies in networking and partnering with NGOs, federations like SOS Children's Villages, other financial service providers, or entering into joint ventures enable the company to explore and invest in a range of company or projects (see *Values-Based Ecosystem Modelling* in chapter 5). GLS invests in green bonds via its investment vehicles (funds) to facilitate transformation in companies. However, its innovation challenge is not just to repurpose standardised investment products such as securities funds, but to change the instruments and mechanisms that translate financial means into desired impact. Alternative investment funds or evergreen investing into promising social ventures, which take off pressure for rapid investor return or profitable exit, provide relevant, though narrow paths in the highly regulated financial market.

Direct interaction with European sustainable finance regulators is one option to facilitate the formation of new investment ecosystems. 'Our strategy is to promote sustainability in the product and in the business model', explains Mechelse as head of accounting. He adds that budgets do not always help in

putting this strategy into practice but might rather prevent impactful investments or trigger unjustified investments in order to stay in the annual budget
plan. While multi-annual plans still play an important role, each idea and each
potential innovation is evaluated as a single case with help of agile management methods. Financial flexibility is ensured with buffers for unforeseen
expenses, risk-bearing capacity and dividends to GLS bank as the owner.

Both managing directors highlight the importance of a sense of timing and
maturation in innovation, acknowledging that everything and every innovation has its own time. For instance, a performance measurement system that
might have been too advanced and ambitious two years ago might become
necessary to implement soon. 'Part of innovation is also questioning the status quo, your own offerings, your own business model. We are now at an early
stage, but we are having this discussion.'

12.4 Building Financially Resilient Sustainable Innovation Cultures

Sustainable innovation culture, supported by robust financial planning and an
adaptive finance function, is increasingly essential in today's sustainability-driv-
en competition. However, creating and maintaining this culture requires strategic
financing options, a rethinking of traditional budgeting approaches and a trans-
formed finance function capable of balancing financial rigour with sustainability
goals. By addressing these elements, organisations can integrate sustainable innovation into their core strategy, positioning themselves for long-term resilience
and market leadership.

From a more traditional standpoint, an organisation's ability to foster a sustainable innovation culture hinges on its financial planning and accounting practices. By implementing robust financial systems tailored to the unique demands
of sustainable innovation, organisations can pursue meaningful change without
compromising financial stability. Sustainable innovation culture, supported by
strategic financial planning and accounting, enables organisations to be agile,
resilient and impactful, as the following examples of Interface (also see section
3.1.4), Patagonia and Novozymes illustrate.

The flooring company Interface has demonstrated agility through its Mission
Zero initiative, aiming to eliminate all negative environmental impact. They have
adapted by developing innovative recycling processes, using bio-based materials
and collaborating with suppliers to minimise their carbon footprint. Interface has
received numerous awards for its sustainability leadership, including the Index
Award and the World Environment Center Gold Medal.

Patagonia's commitment to environmental protection has built strong brand
loyalty and customer trust. This strong brand equity has made them more resilient
to economic downturns and competitive pressures. Their focus on product durability and repair services further strengthens their resilience by reducing reliance

on constant consumption. Patagonia's continued growth and strong brand reputation despite economic fluctuations demonstrate its resilience.

The biotechnology company Novozymes develops enzymes and microbes for use in various industries, including food, agriculture and bioenergy. Their innovations have enabled more sustainable agriculture practices, reduced reliance on fossil fuels and improved resource efficiency. Novozymes has consistently demonstrated positive environmental and social impact by constantly reducing greenhouse gas emissions, improving water usage efficiency and increasing agricultural yields.

To thrive in a world increasingly focused on sustainability, organisations must align innovation with long-term financial foresight, positioning themselves as leaders in economic, social and environmental value creation. The integration of financial planning and accounting to create sustainable innovation cultures is not just becoming increasingly necessary, it is becoming an indispensable pathway to resilience and a basic requirement for future success.

Chapter 13 /
Outlook: Forward-Looking Cultures

by Henning Breuer

Three emerging global challenges face those seeking to establish sustainable innovation cultures: a crisis of supportive institutions, the ecosystem challenge and new technological frontiers in innovation development. A decisive role in meeting these challenges is played by practices and methods such as *Context-Based Reporting*, *Sustainable Finance* and *Sustainability Foresight*, *Employee Resource Groups*, *Empathising* and *Sensemaking*. Together they contribute to mastering the higher art of developing a sustainable innovation culture.

STAYING ON TRACK IN A CRISIS OF INSTITUTIONS

We are currently facing a temporary 'sustainability recession' on a global scale as well as a weakening of democratically elected institutions in certain countries. These institutions are crucial for fostering innovation and sustainable development. As 2024 Nobel Prize winners Daron Acemoglu and James A. Robinson showed, inclusive economic institutions are essential for upholding the rule of law, protecting private property rights, striking a balance between freedom and regulation in markets, and promoting open access to education and equity in life opportunities. When paired with inclusive political institutions, they foster participation, competition and innovation, laying the foundation for liberal democracies.[1]

Moreover, these institutions encourage sustainable innovation with a long-term focus on the common good. They formulate binding standards for transparency on the environmental, social and governmental (ESG) performance of business enterprises. A weakening of these institutions leads to the cursory or selective enforcement of regulations, increasing compliance risks and uncertainty for companies. The pressure on independent media and non-governmental institutions also challenges stakeholder engagement and erodes trust, casting doubt on the value of participation, which had been taken for granted.

How should companies and other organisations respond in such an environment? Many are overwhelmed, fire-fighting those external threats that appear most severe. Others, however, are taking a longer-term approach, translating sustainability-related challenges into new business opportunities by innovating their processes, offerings and business models. After our journey through the basic concepts, practices and exemplary cases of sustainable innovation, it is no surprise that we are encouraging companies to take an engaged stand for democratic participation and sustainability values. This is the key to transforming the economy towards long-term resilience and sustainable development.

> In spite of global uncertainties and regional rollbacks, forward-looking companies are taking the lead by embarking on their own sustainability-oriented transformation, positioning themselves to outperform their competitors.

Their managers are trying to meet the public's expectations for ethical leadership.[2] Their guiding principles, strategies and practices to gain competitive advantage and to create impact may vary, but their values of sustainability paired with professional innovation practices create sustainable innovation cultures that will out-perform more short-sighted competitors.

Economic activity can serve societal goals, and the UN's Sustainable Development Goals provide a global framework for preserving the minimal conditions for both human well-being and economic prosperity while remaining within the planetary boundaries of the Earth's carrying capacity. Since global institutions and regulatory bodies do not yet require companies to meet minimum environmental and social standards, companies are relatively free to choose whether they prioritise values of sustainability or exploit short-term opportunities, even at the expense of other people and future generations. However, such short-sighted strategies exacerbate rather than mitigate uncertainties. They lead directly to difficulties in remedying the negative effects of one's own actions and in adapting to foreseeable changes in the requirements of customers and regulatory institutions. Forward-looking companies, in contrast, not only gain a sense of directional certainty by basing their actions on values, but also create a competitive advantage by delivering long-term system value.

Global development goals have been translated into thresholds and fair shares of usable resources, enabling each company to recognise the scope of its own development and, with help of tools such as *Context-Based Reporting*,[3] plan its own business activities. These boundaries delineate what sort of development path is safe and just for a company to pursue, while opening up a spectrum of possibilities in which creativity, innovation and competition can thrive. *Sustainability Foresight* practices empower forward-looking companies to systematically explore this future design space and reap the many benefits it holds. These include engaging a motivated and qualified workforce, creating new business cases for sustainability, reducing costs and risks while gaining in efficiency and reputation, tapping new revenue streams and enhancing innovation and ecosystem collaboration, safeguarding their supply chains and staying ahead of regulation.[4] They use *Sustainable Innovation Financing* to access financial incentives from governments and impact investors (see section 6.3.3). The main benefit, however, is that these companies are building up resilience by proactively coping with uncertainty and preparing their own operations against a multitude of risks.

Whether a company practices *Sustainability Foresight* or chases short-term and fast-fading benefits, even in unsustainable industries the value of these benefits is being recognised. Many companies are now diversifying their business models, while others are introducing their own strategies to drive innovation and get ahead of the competition, not just in economic terms, but also in the creation of social and environmental value. One of the first lessons they learn is that single measures or innovations in products, services and business models are not enough to meet the challenges they are facing. It takes a whole culture, a fundamental overhaul of the company's values, practices and mediating artefacts, to create sustainable value and comply with fast-changing demands from the marketplace and from global environmental threats to resilience.

But how to turn one's existing culture into a sustainable innovation culture? Values have long been acknowledged as 'the bedrock of any corporate culture',[5] providing common ground for aligning current priorities, but also crystallising debates about a company's future path towards development. Values can be turned into systemic value through the 3C framework activities of conceiving a particular culture, co-creating interventions and cultivating sustainable innovation. The 68 practices and methods described in this book are drawn from scientific research and support these activities, offering a rich variety of cases and examples to learn from the experiences of others.

MEETING THE ECOSYSTEM CHALLENGE

As a company progresses on its sustainable innovation journey, it becomes increasingly clear that this transformation cannot be undertaken alone. Instead, companies are collaborating in ecosystems where they use digital platforms to share data and capabilities, exchange benefits and develop new offerings. A new ecosystem economy of collaboration has emerged. In some cases, proven practices of sustainability-minded companies can inspire entire ecosystems to cultivate sustainable innovation (see chapter 7), but to date the emerging ecosystem economy has not been systematically aligned with the requirements of sustainable development.

> Ecosystems can leverage the impact of sustainable innovation and promote business transformation. They also bring new challenges as they go beyond organisational boundaries, established management frameworks and the cultural practices and competences of the workforce.

A number of challenges to creating a sustainability-oriented business ecosystem have been documented in empirical studies[6] and related research.[7] Collaborators need to establish trust and manage risks stemming from new rules and interdependencies. Shared values and visions, cultural notions and governance mechanisms are needed to coordinate interests and efforts into novel outcomes. Experiences with methods such as *Values-Based Ecosystem Modelling* are just a starting point to identifying shared values, managing collaborative practices and refining mediating artefacts that allow a company to create and run a sustainability-oriented business ecosystem.

NEW FRONTIERS OF THE ALIGNMENT PROBLEM

The exponential development of systems that imitate human intelligence offer great opportunities as well as challenges for innovation cultures. We use the term 'intelligent systems' to refer to the technologies of artificial intelligence, machine learning, natural language processing and robotics. We have already discussed some tools, media and collaboration platforms that advance sustainable innovation (sections 3.3.2 and 6.2). Still, these systems do not take the fundamental task off our hands that sustainable added value needs to be created in a repeated and reliable manner. On the one side, how can organisational values and long-term goals be aligned with the design of intelligent systems? On the other side, how can innovation and sustainability professionals keep track of or even stay ahead of rapidly evolving technological systems.

From the viewpoint of organisational innovation culture, this 'alignment problem'[8] consists of a mismatch between organisational values and 'intelligent' artefacts that mediate innovation practices, leading to values-action gaps and unsustainable practices. The opaque processes of intelligent systems require human supervision. However, the human supervisors themselves are often fed with biased information from these systems and the data they draw on. Unless the data an intelligent system is trained on stems from validated sources, it is inherently biased, just like the evaluation criteria in ESG scoring systems can be flawed. Sustainable development goals are not yet embedded in the design and objectives that intelligent systems optimise for, which can lead to opacity in decision-making and hedge responsibility for potentially harmful results. Furthermore, there are growing concerns about the waste and consumption of resources and energy caused by these systems.

> Next generation Management Systems and value-aligned intelligent systems[9] are being developed to incorporate organisational values, guiding principles, sustainability objectives and changing regulations into their learning and decision-making processes.

New systems are being developed with explicit sustainability constraints and human feedback as well as auditable systems and interpretation features that improve the tracking and adjustment of sustainability-related decisions. International bodies like the UN, OECD, WEF and the EU, with its AI Act,[10] are providing guidelines and policies on how to incorporate values of sustainability into the future development of artificial intelligence and related systems.[11] However, it should be noted that the benefits of these systems for sustainable innovation have yet to be proven and individual organisations that try to align these systems in pursuit of their values, strategies and operations are likely to face significant challenges.

Currently the only practical way out for innovation managers is to observe, test and evaluate technological developments and to seek a lively exchange with stakeholders and peers. In sum, the goal is for innovation managers to develop their own human competencies and abilities. Freely organised *Innovation Time*, but also tailored interventions and projects allow time for employees to explore and give them the resources they need to seize opportunities. Organisational continuity is provided by *Employee Resource Groups*, exchanging up-to-date knowledge and experiences and steering transformation with intelligent systems.

Deliberately creating a culture is, first of all, a human endeavour. Empathy is a precondition of any culture, enabling understanding, sharing and coordinating in social groups. Sustainable innovation challenges are often ambiguous and require human sensemaking to frame problems, navigate uncertainty and innovate beyond algorithmic capabilities.[12] *Empathising* and *Sensemaking* are indispensable to navigating ethical dilemmas, contextualising decisions and engaging stakeholders at emotional and strategic levels. Likewise, aligning organisational values, practices and material artefacts, including artificially generated content, depend on human judgement, collaboration and adaptive learning.

Transformation has always been crucial to survival in business, but today developing sustainable innovation cultures can be considered a higher form of the art of doing business. As an undertaking that is fundamentally characterised by uncertainty, the concept of innovation implies the unlikely success of this undertaking. After all, innovation is not just about generating promising new ideas and creating working prototypes, but also about their adoption in the real world, whether in a market or a company. Sustainable innovation doesn't stop there, as it also requires the creation of economic, social and environmental value as well as the promotion of sustainable development. Finally, the idea of a generative culture implies that contributions to sustainable development are not only made in individual cases but repeatedly and reliably, and not only in isolation but also in ecosystems of interdependent partners.

This could seem close to impossible, if we did not already have outstanding examples from firms like Ecosia, Interface, Patagonia, Unilever and TÜV NORD – along with the many others portrayed in this book – who demonstrate how it can be done. They show us which practices and methods are conducive to sustainable innovation cultures and how to cope with the tensions and challenges that remain, even for role models in their industry. It takes a whole culture to bring about sustainable innovation on a reliable basis. In this book, we showed how such cultures can be developed. It's now up to you to begin creating your own sustainable innovation culture.

APPENDICES

Glossary of Key Terms

The glossary gives an overview of essential terminology used throughout the book. Each entry comes with a reference to the section where each term is introduced more comprehensively.

ARTEFACTS: Human-made objects bearing cultural significance. They include tools designed to perform a specific task or function, also software and data (section 2.3.4).

3C ACTIVITIES: The three basic activities of the 3C framework are 1) conceiving values and related notions, practices and artefacts to address cultural challenges; 2) co-creating interventions to address these challenges; and 3) cultivating sustainable innovation by mainstreaming values and related notions, establishing new practices and introducing new artefacts.

CO-CREATING: A methodology involving several practices and methods to engage stakeholders in collaborative interventions to promote a sustainable innovation culture. A 3C framework activity, co-creating follows up on conceiving and serves to clarify and specify basic notions, resolve tensions, close values-action gaps and explore forward-looking opportunities for sustainable innovation (section 5.1).

COMMONS: Social, environmental, and economic resources accessible to all members of society (section 2.1.1).

COMPETENCES: Areas of expertise that are directly associated with work results required to achieve team or organisational goals and are typically linked to specific tasks, roles or professional domains.

COMPETENCIES: Specific combinations of critical skills, knowledge, behaviours and attitudes that are required to achieve competences and to be successful in a role.

CONCEPTION: The second 3C framework activity involves, with respect to notions and values, the review of guiding principles and policies in order to identify implicit tensions within the organisation's systems of priorities, between the values of different stakeholders and how values are managed for innovation. With respect to practices, conceiving means identifying values-action gaps and understanding the role of mediating artefacts that can facilitate or hinder attempts to align practices with organisational values (section 4.1).

CULTIVATING: The third 3C framework activity involves deliberate and systematic efforts to shape, sustain and renew culture. In our context the system of notions, practices and artefacts make up an organisational innovation culture (section 6.1).

ORGANISATIONAL CULTURE: A generative system of notions, practices and artefacts that distinguishes one organisation from another, translating organisational values into new forms of value creation.

GUIDING PRINCIPLES: Values that are codified by the organisation as value, purpose, mission, and/or vision statements. Guiding principles are reinforced through management measures (section 3.1.2).

IMPACT: A positive or negative, intended or unintended, actual or desirable change on natural, human, social, intellectual, constructed or financial capitals[1] resulting from the aggregated outcomes of an implemented innovation.

INNOVATION: A 'new or changed entity, realizing or redistributing value'. These entities can be a product, service, process, model or method (section 2.1.2).[2]

MANAGEMENT: 'Coordinated activities to direct and control an organization', here 'with regard to innovation'.[3] Normative management deals with establishing principles, policies and values that define an organisation's identity and aspirations to generate a specific impact. Strategic management deals with business design and development to achieve differentiation and competitive advantage based on the principles, policies and values defined by normative management. Operational management deals with translating an organisation's normative and strategic agendas into daily operations (section 3.1.3).

MATERIALITY: In the context of auditing, accounting and reporting, materiality refers to the significance of information for the user's decision-making. In the context of sustainability management, materiality defines the sustainability issues that matter most to an organisation and its stakeholders. Materiality Assessments typically identify and prioritise environmental, social and governance (ESG) factors based on their impact on a company's financial performance (outside-in) and the company's impact on society and the environment (inside-out). In Context-Based Reporting, materiality is grounded in science, human needs and local social and environmental thresholds that constrain sustainable development (sections 2.1.1 and 6.3.3).

METHOD: In our case, purposeful and replicable approach or intervention addressing a particular challenge to cultural development. When methods are systematically applied over time and adapted to the needs of the organisation, they turn into practices (section 2.3.4).

NARRATIVE: A coherent framework of meaning through which an organisation interprets its identity, purpose, values and direction over time. It contains but differs from stories, i.e., textual passages relating a course of events arranged in a timeline.[4]

NOTION: An understanding of a term in ordinary language, shaped by its use in practice and context. Values as notions of the desirable as well as notions of what is considered feasible and viable are critical to sustainable innovation culture (section 2.3.4).

OUTCOME: a positive or negative, intended or unintended change in the current situation or the future potential to meet the needs of any stakeholder, resulting from the aggregated outputs of innovation activities, practices and projects. [5]

OUTPUT: tangible and measurable results that are directly produced by completing (innovation) project tasks and activities.[6]

PARTICIPATORY OBSERVATION: An immersive research method where a researcher actively participates in the day-to-day activities of the cultural group he or she is studying, while simultaneously observing and recording their experiences (chapter 4).

PRACTICE: Actions, behaviours and rituals that employees perform on a more or less regular basis (section 2.3.4).

SKILLS: Specific, learned abilities to perform tasks or activities effectively.

STAKEHOLDER: Any person or group of people affected by or contributing to the success or failure of an organisation's activities (section 2.1.1).

STRATEGY: A deliberate and integrated set of choices that position the organisation to achieve its aspirations. They do this by providing guardrails for operational management and everyday practice (section 3.1.1).

SUSTAINABLE INNOVATION LITERACY: Integration of shared sustainability values and a common understanding of key concepts and skills across the organisation, complemented by role-specific competences in individual departments (section 4.1.5).

SUSTAINABILITY: 'A form of intergenerational ethics in which the environmental and economic actions taken by present persons do not diminish the opportunities of future persons to enjoy similar levels of wealth, utility, or welfare'[7] (section 2.1.1).

SUSTAINABLE DEVELOPMENT: Development that 'meets the needs of the present without compromising the ability of future generations to meet their own needs'; 'a process of change in which the exploitation of resources, the direction of investments, the orientation of technological development; and institutional change are all in harmony and enhance both current and future potential to meet human needs and aspirations.'[8] (section 2.1.1).

SUSTAINABILITY MANAGEMENT: An organisation's concerted efforts to contribute to sustainable development (section 2.1.1).

SUSTAINABLE INNOVATION: The systematic integration of sustainability-related values and considerations into innovation activities to create or redistribute economic, social and environmental value through new or changed entities – such as products, services, business models or ecosystems – or processes for an organisation and its stakeholders (section 2.1.3, also for sustainability innovation and sustainability-oriented innovation).

SUSTAINABLE INNOVATION CULTURES: Generative systems made up of shared notions, practices and artefacts that turn values of sustainability into novel regenerative outcomes that are economically, socially and environmentally beneficial.

SYSTEM VALUE: 'Value that accrues in dynamic balance across all capitals and the systems associated with them.' The various types of capital include natural, human, social, intellectual, constructed and financial.[9]

3C FRAMEWORK: A structured approach for steering iterative development of sustainable innovation cultures in a virtuous cycle of three interconnected activities: 1) conceiving values and related notions, practices and artefacts to address cultural challenges; 2) co-creating interventions to address these challenges; and 3) cultivating sustainable innovation by mainstreaming values and related notions, establishing new practices and introducing new artefacts.

VALUE CREATION: The process by which organisations generate benefits for stakeholders. In standard economic theory, this refers to benefits for customers, economic returns for shareholders and investors and broader economic activity that benefits society. An extended concept of value creation includes not only financial outcomes but also the maintenance, unlocking and sharing of social, environmental and other non-monetary benefits for a wide range of stakeholders.[10] In contrast, value damage refers to the harmful social and environmental impacts of organisations (section 2.1.1).

VALUES-BASED INNOVATION MANAGEMENT: A management framework that integrates the values of different stakeholders into managing innovation processes and activities in order to ensure long-term positive impact.[11]

VALUES OF SUSTAINABILITY: Notions of the desirable in an organisation related to sustainable development, regularly expressed by the intended outcomes and positive impact that an organisation pursues. Besides values of intergenerational and intragenerational justice and equity of opportunities as core values of sustainable development,[12] values of environmental stewardship and social responsibility are also relevant (section 3.1.1).

UNINTENDED CONSEQUENCES: Outcomes or impacts of innovation activities that are not intended or foreseen (sections 2.1.3 and 3.1.3).

VALUES: Subjective notions of the desirable[13] and ordered systems of priorities that act as criteria for decisions and evaluations (section 2.2.4).

About the Authors

HENNING BREUER

Henning Breuer researches, teaches and consults in the fields of innovation management and business psychology. He is a Professor of Business and Media Psychology at the Media University Berlin, founder of UXBerlin – Innovation Consulting, and has worked in executive education and consulting with universities and companies in Europe and the United States.

Since 2001, Henning has worked with multinational corporations, SMEs, public organisations and start-ups, providing consultancy services in the areas of sustainable innovation culture and business models, future scenarios and ethnographic stakeholder research. Henning has co-authored publications for journals, conferences and textbooks on values-based innovation management, sustainable business model design, gamification for innovators and entrepreneurs, and sustainable innovation cultures. As a visiting researcher and professor, he has worked at the University of Chile (Santiago) and Waseda University (Tokyo). He studied psychology, philosophy and law in Berlin and Tübingen, and received his PhD in psychology from the University of Magdeburg.

KIRIL IVANOV

Kiril Ivanov has completed a doctorate at the Centre for Sustainability Management at the Leuphana University Lüneburg, with a dissertation focused on values-based and sustainable innovation. As a researcher at the Media University of Applied Sciences, he has contributed to EU-funded research projects on gamification, values-based innovation cultures and strategic foresight for sustainability. He teaches courses in innovation and entrepreneurship, business anthropology and gamification for organisations, while also collaborating with UXBerlin – Innovation Consulting on projects involving ethnography and values-based business development.

Acknowledgements

The insights presented in this book build on results from the European IMPACT project, which leveraged the knowledge from extensive literature reviews, first-hand ethnographic research, co-creating and professional development work-shops with leading European firms, more than 20 expert interviews, together with 120 survey responses from other experts.

IMPACT stands for 'Creating values-based innovation cultures for sustainable business impact'. The three-year project was based on the observation that while many companies in Europe had adopted sustainability goals as part of their mission and strategies, few had established practices in their organisational culture and managed innovation centred on values of corporate sustainability. Through the project we identified good practices as well as barriers for values-based and sustainable innovation, and we experimented with suitable methods to overcome the barriers and establish sustainability-oriented innovation cultures.

Numerous voices and hands have contributed to this book and the ideas it presents. First and foremost, we thank the academic partners who joined us for research, design and facilitation throughout the IMPACT project: Dr. Sandra Dijk and Timo Brunner from HHL Leipzig coordinated the project and contributed with their ideas and feedback to the content creation throughout the project. At Media University of Applied Sciences Berlin, Prof. Dr. Klaus-Dieter Schulz and Prof. Dr. Roland Freytag enabled the implementation of the IMPACT project, Atreyee Chakraborty supported our literature review as student assistant. The Florence team was composed of Prof. Dr. Mario Rapaccini of the University of Florence, Dr. Alessandro Monti and Dr. Chiara Guiggiani from the Foundation for Research and Innovation of the University of Florence, Dr. Raffaella Montera, now with Sapienza University, and Francesco Bellosi from Laika. The Krakow team at the Cracow University of Technology included Prof. Dr. Katarzyna Matras-Postołek, Dr. Jacek Kasz, Dr. Piotr Beńko, Małgorzata Ciesielska and Dr. Irena Śliwińska now at the Krakow University of Economics. Carmen Abril of Complutense University Madrid worked very closely with us throughout the project as part of the core academic team, together with Dr. Mercedes Rubio Andrés, and focused on the literature review and expert interviews. Lucija Barisic, Steffen Conn and the whole growing community of the International Society for Professional Innovation Management (ISPIM) helped us get further experts on board, discuss intermediary results and spread the word about our efforts – a great thank you to you all for your valuable support!

Paul Lauer did outstanding job in editing the manuscript and the concise descriptions of practices and methods. He substantially helped us to ensure a consistent style and flow across the chapters from different authors. Elmar Birk and Vincent Beck took on the design challenges to create the layout and cover design and to render our visual vocabulary and the combinations of its elements to represent practices and methods in a consistent style.

We thank Stefan Giesen, Maximilian Gessl and André Horn of De Gruyter for their support in production and distribution, online and in-person at conferences around the world. We thank the contributors of the IMPACT project who worked on the industry cases in the different countries and shared their knowledge and expertise on sustainability challenges, innovation practices and cultural issues in their organisations.

GERMANY: Our colleagues from the TÜV NORD Group, especially Roman Meier-Andrae (former Head of IT and Digitalisation), Dr. Dietmar Schlößer (Director Digitalisation & Innovation) and Dr. Irina Fiegenbaum (Senior Manager Digitalisation & Innovation) provided invaluable insights into how sustainability values and sustainable innovation practices transform the traditional safety cultures of technical inspection companies.

ITALY: We thank Marco Buzzo, Martina Conti, Saverio Gradassi, Andrea Masi, Sultan Sevilay Murat, Teresa Pucci, Marco Ruggiero, Angela Serra and all the Baker Hughes employees and managers who made themselves available for the project activities.

POLAND: We thank Janusz Kahl of the South Poland Cleantech Cluster, who actively participated in the research activities and helped us to engage several companies that are leading the sustainability transition in Poland. We also thank Stefan Życzkowski from ASTOR for inspiring discussions that helped to deepen the analysis of the topic. Deep appreciation to all Polish respondents who generously shared their insights on sustainability-oriented innovation in their companies.

SPAIN: We extend our thanks to Teresa Gallo of 3M Spain and Emilia Santiago of Alter Technologies for generously sharing their insights. Their thoughtful contributions and inspiring perspectives encouraged us to look beyond conventional approaches and enriched the depth of our research.

Co-funded by the
Erasmus+ Programme
of the European Union

IMPACT Project Number: 621672-EPP-1-2020-1-DE-EPPKA2-KA
Project Duration: January 2021 – December 2023

The IMPACT project has been funded with support from the European Commission. This publication reflects the views only of the authors, and the Commission cannot be held responsible for any use which may be made of the information contained therein.

STATEMENT ABOUT THE USE OF GENERATIVE AI

The entire text was originally written by the authors and chapter co-authors. We employed AI tools in individual places for language enhancement, editorial refinement and exploration of related literature. Final editing and professional copyediting were conducted by the authors with Paul Lauer.

To streamline the writing process and enhance text clarity and comprehensibility, we made selective use of DeepL and Open AI's ChatGPT-4o. To ensure transparent and accountable use of these tools we used them consistently in three distinct ways:

1. To reduce redundancy by condensing paragraphs without compromising meaning.
2. To enhance the writing style and comprehension by restructuring sentences and sourcing synonyms for improved clarity and coherence.
3. To explore arguments and debates related to the theses from our initial literature reviews.

Endnotes

Preface

[1] Elkington, J. 2024. After the Sustainability Recession: It's time to expand our focus from responsible business to regenerative markets. https://www.sustainabilityprofessionals.org/after-the-sustainability-recession. Accessed: 1 June 2025.

PART I

Chapter 1

[1] The first chapter is based on the podcast by Henning Breuer 2024. Sustainable Innovation Cultures. How can organisations turn sustainability strategies into daily practices? https://www.uxberlin.com/podcast-sustainable-innovation-cultures/. Accessed 1 June 2025

PART II

Chapter 2

[1] Freeman, R. 2010. *Strategic management: A stakeholder approach*. Cambridge University Press.

[2] Ripple, W.J. et al. 2024. The 2024 state of the climate report: Perilous times on planet Earth. BioScience, biae087, https://doi.org/10.1093/biosci/biae087

[3] McManus, P. 1999. *Histories of Forestry: Ideas, Networks and Silences*. The White Horse Press.

[4] James, S. 1998. *Seeing like a State: How Certain Schemes to Improve the Human Condition Have Failed*. Yale University Press.

[5] Meadowcroft, J. 2025. Sustainability. *Encyclopedia Britannica*. https://www.britannica.com/science/sustainability. Accessed 1 June 2025.

[6] Brundtland, G. 1987. The Brundtland report: 'Our common future'. *Report of the World Commission on Environment and Development 4* (1).

[7] Brundtland, G. 1987.

[8] Brundtland, G. 1987.

[9] Hahn, R. 2022. *Sustainability management. Global perspectives on concepts, instruments, and stakeholders*. Fellbach, Germany: Published by Hahn Rüdiger.

[10] Starik, M. and Kanashiro, P. 2013. Toward a Theory of Sustainability Management. *Organization & Environment* 26 (1): 7–30. doi: 10.1177/1086026612474958.

[11] David Green, head of a lens manufacturer that partners with Aravind in India to eliminate needless blindness, claims to be free of fear of competition: 'I am waiting for companies to compete with me or to put me out of business for the benefit of the poor' Seelos, C. 2014 Theorizing and strategizing with models: Generative models of social enterprises. *International Journal of Entrepreneurial Venturing*, Vol. 6, No. 1, (pp. 6–21).

[12] Bansal, P. and Roth, K. 2000. Why Companies Go Green: A Model of Ecological Responsiveness. *Academy of Management Journal* 43 (4): 717–736. doi: 10.5465/1556363.

[13] Hahn, R. 2022.

[14] Schaltegger, S., Hörisch, J., and Freeman, R. 2019. Business Cases for Sustainability: A Stakeholder Theory Perspective. *Organization & Environment* 32 (3): 191–212. doi: 10.1177/1086026617722882.

[15] In contrast, for an anthropological perspective, see Graeber, D. 2013. It is value that brings universes into being. *HAU: Journal of Ethnographic Theory* 3 (2): 219–43.

[16] Breuer, H., Fichter, K., Freund, F., and Tiemann, I. 2018. Sustainability-oriented business model development: principles, criteria and tools. *International Journal of Entrepreneurial Venturing* 10 (2): 256. doi: 10.1504/IJEV.2018.092715.

[17] Lüdeke-Freund, F., Froese, T., Dembek, K., Rosati, F., and Massa, L. 2024. What Makes a Business Model Sustainable? Activities, Design Themes, and Value Functions. *Organization & Environment* 37 (2): 194–220. doi: 10.1177/10860266241235212.

[18] Lawrence, J., Rasche, A., and Kenny, K. 2019. Sustainability as Opportunity: Unilever's Sustainable Living Plan: 435–455. doi: 10.1007/978-94-024-1144-7_21.

[19] Lüdeke-Freund, F., Froese, T., Dembek, K., Rosati, F., and Massa, L. 2024.

[20] Lawrence, J., Rasche, A., and Kenny, K. 2019.

[21] Unilever. 2025. Livelihoods. https://www.unilever.com/sustainability/livelihoods/. Accessed: 1 June 2025.

[22] Lawrence, J., Rasche, A., and Kenny, K. 2019.

[23] Bill Baue follows the International Integrated Reporting Council's proposition of six essential capitals that are involved in system value creation: natural, human, social and relationship, intellectual, manufactured and financial; see system value in the glossary of key terms and Baue, B. 2020. From Monocapitalism to Multicapitalism: 21st Century System Value Creation. r3.0 White Paper No.1.

[24] The Corporate Sustainability Reporting Directive and the EU taxonomy require even mid-sized companies not just to professionalise their sustainability reporting, but to innovate their business models, e.g. in order to contribute to one of six environmental goals (circular economy, climate protection, adaptation to climate change, water/marine protection, environmental pollution and biodiversity/ ecosystems). New European supply chain laws (especially the Corporate Sustainability Due Diligence Directive/ CSDDD) require larger companies of more than 1000 employees to review and report on human rights and environmental risks in their corporate supply chains, to take preventive and remedial measures and to align their sustainability strategy to the goals of the 2015 Paris Agreement (limiting global warming to 1.5 degrees Celsius). Even associations like the Business Roundtable of more than 200 CEOs of major US companies are moving beyond the conventional view on value creation and claim that companies should serve all their stakeholders.

[25] The population problem has no technical solution; it requires a fundamental extension in morality. Hardin, G. 1968. The trage-

dy of the commons. *Science, 162*(3859), 1243-1248.

[26] In environmental terms, companies monitor and reduce their ecological footprint and greenhouse gas emissions, improve resource efficiency and waste management and try to preserve biodiversity. In social terms, they engage with stakeholders, review labour practices, value distribution and community relations and adhere to human rights. Governance pertains to robust corporate oversight, transparency, ethical conduct, accountability and compliance with regulatory frameworks. ESG integration requires the adoption of comprehensive reporting standards, such as the Global Reporting Initiative (GRI) or the Sustainability Accounting Standards Board (SASB), facilitating transparency and comparability of sustainability performance. Furthermore, it leverages sustainable finance mechanisms, including green bonds and impact investing, to align capital allocation with sustainability objectives. ESG-driven strategies assess and mitigate risks and seek to enhance corporate resilience, to foster innovation and to contribute to sustainable development.

[27] Rockström, J., Gupta, J., Qin, D., Lade, S., and Abrams, J. 2023. Safe and just Earth system boundaries. *Nature* 619 (7968): 102–111. doi: 10.1038/s41586-023-06083-8.

[28] Rockström, J., Gupta, J., Qin, D., Lade, S., and Abrams, J. 2023.

[29] Science-based tools like the Earth System Impact score (ESI) clarify a company's local environmental impact into global effects on climate and nature. Crona, B., E. Wassénius, G. Parlato, S. Kashyap. 2024. Doing Business Within Planetary Boundaries. Research brief. Stockholm Resilience Centre (Stockholm University) and the Beijer Institute of Ecological Economics (Royal Swedish Academy of Sciences).

[30] Breuer, H. 2023. Sustainability Foresight – Practices and Methods for Future-Oriented Innovation Management. Proceedings of ISPIM Innovation Conference 2023, Ljubljana. https://www.uxberlin.com/wp-content/uploads/2024/04/2023_Sustainability_Foresight_ISPIM.pdf. Accessed: 1 June 2025.

[31] European Environment Agency. 2022. Scenarios for a sustainable Europe in 2050. https://www.eea.europa.eu/publications/scenarios-for-a-sustainable-europe-2050/the-scenarios. Accessed: 1 June 2025. Using key-factor and consistency analysis, the project developed four distinct imaginaries. Each highlights one major protagonist: In 'technocracy for the common good' sustainability is ensured through monitoring and state control of social and ecological systems. In 'unity in adversity', the EU is empowered to enforce boundaries for economic activity through regulatory and market-based measures. In 'the great decoupling', innovative companies drive technological innovation, decoupling GDP growth from environmental harm. In 'ecotopia', civil society drives changes and technology is used sparingly to enable sustainable community lifestyles.

[32] Berkun, S. 2013.

[33] Breuer, H. and Freund, F. 2017b. Values-Based Network and Business Model Innovation. *International Journal of Innovation Management* 21 (03). doi: 10.1142/S1363919617500281.

[34] ISO. 2025. ISO 56000:2025. Innovation management — Fundamentals and vocabulary. https://www.iso.org/standard/84436.html. Accessed: 1 June 2025. First published 2018, the ISO 56000 family of standards provides a reference for practitioners and theorists dealing with implementation,

maintenance and improvement of innovation management systems. It distinguishes between different types of innovation in products, services, processes, models and methods, ranging from incremental to radical innovation. ISO 56002 also refers to supportive culture and work environments that – among others – encourage risk-taking and learning, build on shared values and balance 'assumption-based and evidence-based analysis and decision-making' ISO. 2019. ISO 56002:2019 Innovation management — Innovation management system — Guidance. https://www.iso.org/standard/68221.html. Accessed: 1 June 2025. Related standards are still being discussed that cover the basic terminology and conceptual foundations to facilitate consistent communication, but also requirements, guidelines, tools and methods for managing innovation.

[35] Jaruzelski, B., Loehr, J. & Holman, R. 2011. Why Culture is Key. *strategy+business magazine*, issue 65 https://www.strategy-business.com/article/11404. Accessed: 1 June 2025.

[36] OECD. 2005. *Oslo manual: Guidelines for collecting and interpreting innovation data*, third edition. Paris: OECD Publishing.

[37] Hippel, E. 2006. *Democratizing Innovation*. Cambridge, MA, London: MIT Press.

[38] Chesbrough, H. 2003. *Open innovation: The new imperative for creating and profiting from technology*. Harvard Business Press.

[39] Christensen, C., Michael E., and McDonald, R. 2013. *Disruptive innovation*. Brighton, MA, USA: Harvard Business Review.

[40] Mauborgne, R. and Kim, W. 2017. *Blue Ocean Strategy*. Macat Library. doi: 10.4324/9781912281015.

[41] Osterwalder, A. and Pigneur, Y. 2010. *Business model generation: a handbook for visionaries, game changers, and challengers*. John Wiley & Sons.

[42] Ries, E. 2017. *The lean startup. How today's entrepreneurs use continuous innovation to create radically successful businesses*. New York: Currency.

[43] Breuer, H. and Freund, F. 2017a. *Values-based innovation management*. London: Macmillan Publishers Limited.

[44] Breuer, H., Freund, F., and Bessant, J. 2022. Editorial — Special Issue: Managing Values for Innovation. *International Journal of Innovation Management* 26 (05). doi: 10.1142/S1363919622010010.

[45] See e.g. Stähler, P. 2021: *Das Richtige gründen. Werkzeugkasten für Unternehmer*. 5th edition. Murmann.

[46] Breuer, H., Freund, F., and Bessant, J. 2022. Breuer & Lüdeke-Freund 2017 .
Boonstra, J., and Brillo, J. 2021. Shaping Sustainable Innovation Based on Cultural Values. In: Voinea, C. et al.: Sustainable innovation. Routledge.

[47] Albert, M. 2019. Sustainable frugal innovation - The connection between frugal innovation and sustainability. *Journal of Cleaner Production* 237: 117747. doi: 10.1016/j.jclepro.2019.117747.

[48] Adams, R., Jeanrenaud, S., Bessant, J., Denyer, D., and Overy, P. 2016. Sustainability-oriented Innovation: A Systematic Review. *International Journal of Management Reviews* 18 (2): 180–205. doi: 10.1111/ijmr.12068.

[49] Hansen E. and Große-Dunker, F. 2013. Encyclopedia of corporate social responsibility: Sustainability-oriented innovation, 2408

[50] Charter, M. and Clark, T. 2007. Sustainable Innovation: Key conclusions from sustainable innovation conferences 2003-2006 organised by The Centre for Sustainable Design, Farnham. https://research.uca.ac.uk/694/1/Sustainable_Innovation_report.pdf. Accessed: 1 June 2025.
See also Coad, N., and Pritchard, P. 2017. Leading Sustainable Innovation. Routledge.

[51] Hahn, R. 2022.

[52] Horbach, J., Rammer, C., and Rennings, K. 2012. Determinants of eco-innovations by type of environmental impact — The role of regulatory push/pull, technology push and market pull. *Ecological Economics* 78: 112–122. doi: 10.1016/j.ecolecon.2012.04.005.

[53] Hahn, R. 2022.

[54] As Edward Freeman commented on our 2017 textbook, Breuer, H. and Freund, F. 2017b.

[55] Freeman, R. and McVea, J. 2005. A Stakeholder Approach to Strategic Management: 183–201. doi: 10.1111/b.9780631218616.2006.00007.x.

[56] Hörisch, J., Freeman, E., Schaltegger, S. 2014. Applying Stakeholder Theory in Sustainability Management: Links, Similarities, Dissimilarities, and a Conceptual Framework. *Organization & Environment* 27 (4): 328–346. SAGE Publications Inc. doi: 10.1177/1086026614535786.

[57] The case of Tata Nano illustrates how safety-oriented innovation failed its promise; see Breuer, H. & Upadrasta, V. 2017. Values-Based Product Innovation – The Case of Tata Nano. In: Huizingh, K., Conn, S. et al. (Eds.): The Proceedings of XXVIII ISPIM Conference. Vienna.

[58] Stubbs, W. and Cocklin, C. 2008. Conceptualizing a 'Sustainability Business Model'. *Organization & Environment* 21 (2): 103–127. doi: 10.1177/1086026608318042.

[59] ISO 56000. 2020. Innovation management — Fundamentals and vocabulary. https://www.iso.org/obp/ui/es/#iso:std:iso:56000:ed-1:v1:en. Accessed: 1 June 2025

[60] Breuer, H. and Freund, F. 2017a.

[61] Bocken, N.., Rana, P. and Short, S. 2015. Value mapping for sustainable business thinking, *Journal of Industrial and Production Engineering*, 32:1, 67-81, DOI: 10.1080/21681015.2014.1000399

[62] Adams et al. 2016. differentiate between operational optimization, organisational transformation and systems building as approaches to sustainable business development.

[63] Lüdeke-Freund, F., Breuer, H., Massa, L. 2022. *Sustainable Business Model Design – 45 Patterns*. Berlin: Self-Published.

[64] Zaoual, A. and Lecocq, X. 2018. Orchestrating Circularity within Industrial Ecosystems: Lessons from iconic cases in three different countries. *California Management Review* 60 (3): 133–156. doi: 10.1177/0008125617752693.

[65] Paech, N. 2007. Directional certainty in sustainability-oriented innovation management. In: *Innovations towards sustainability: Conditions and consequences:* 121–139. Heidelberg, Physica-Verlag HD.

[66] Paech, N. 2007.

[67] Stilgoe, J., Owen, R., and Macnaghten, P. 2013. Developing a framework for responsible innovation. *Research Policy* 42 (9): 1568–1580. doi: 10.1016/j.respol.2013.05.008.

[68] Lubberink, R., Blok, V., van Ophem, J., and Omta, O. 2017. A Framework for Responsible Innovation in the Business Context: Lessons from Responsible, Social and Sustainable Innovation. In: *Responsible Innovation* 3: 181–207. doi: 10.1007/978-3-319-64834-7_11.

[69] Owen, R., Bessant, J., and Heintz, M. 2013. *Responsible Innovation.* Wiley. doi: 10.1002/9781118551424.

[70] Owen, R., Bessant, J., and Heintz, M. 2013.

[71] Lubberink, R., Blok, V., van Ophem, J., and Omta, O. 2017. Lessons for Responsible Innovation in the Business Context: A Systematic Literature Review of Responsible, Social and Sustainable Innovation Practices. *Sustainability* 9 (5): 721. doi: 10.3390/su9050721.

[72] Owen, R., Bessant, J., and Heintz, M. 2013.

[73] Lubberink, R., Blok, V., van Ophem, J., and Omta, O. 2017.

[74] Strand, R. 2019. Striving for Reflexive Science: 56–61. doi: 10.22163/fteval.2019.368.

[75] Christian, B. 2020. *The alignment problem. Machine learning and human values.* New York, NY: W.W. Norton & Company.

[76] Wickson, F. and Carew, A. 2014. Quality criteria and indicators for responsible research and innovation: learning from transdisciplinarity. *Journal of Responsible Innovation* 1 (3): 254–273. doi: 10.1080/23299460.2014.963004.

[77] Owen, R., Bessant, J., and Heintz, M. 2013.. Lubberink, R., Blok, V., van Ophem, J., and Omta, O. 2017

[78] Bright, D. and Parkin, B. 1997. *Human Resource Management – Concepts and Practices.* Business Education Publishers Ltd., 1997, 13.

[79] Marcus, G. 1998. 'That Damn Book': ten years after *Writing Culture. Etnografica* (vol. 2 (1)): 5–14. doi: 10.4000/etnografica.4414. Clifford Geertz refers to culture as webs of significance: 'Man is an animal suspended in webs of significance he himself has spun, I take culture to be those webs, and the analysis of it to be therefore not an experimental science in search of law but an interpretive one in search of meaning'; see Clifford, G. 1973. 'Thick Description: Toward an Interpretive Theory of Culture'. In: *The Interpretation of Cultures: Selected Essays.* New York: Basic Books, 3–30 (pg. 5).

[80] Jordan, A. 2013. Business *anthropology.* Long Grove, Ill.: Waveland Press.

[81] Bennett, J. 1954. Interdisciplinary Research and the Concept of Culture. *American Anthropologist* 56 (2): 169–179. doi: 10.1525/aa.1954.56.2.02a00030.

[82] Baker, L. 1995. Racism in Professional Settings: Forms of Address as Clues to Power Relations. *The Journal of Applied Behavioral Science* 31 (2): 186–201. doi: 10.1177/0021886395312006.

[83] Cited by Jordan (2013, 55) who follows Hiebert (1995) with her definition of culture 'as an integrated system of shared ideas (thoughts, ideals, attitudes), behaviors (actions), and material artifacts (objects) that characterise a group' Hiebert, P. 1995. *Cultural Anthropology.* Grand Rapids, Michigan: Baker Book House.

[84] Cherrington, D. 1989. *Organizational behavior: The management of individual and organizational performance.* Boston: Allyn and Bacon.

[85] Example from Gebauer, A. 2017. *Kollektive Achtsamkeit organisieren. Strategien und Werkzeuge für eine proaktive Risikokultur* [Organizing collective attentiveness: Strategies and tools for a proactive risk culture]. Stuttgart: Schäffer Poeschel.

[86] Janicijevic, N. 2011. Methodological approaches in the research of organizational culture. *Economic Annals* 56 (189): 69–99. doi: 10.2298/EKA1189069J.

[87] Gorton, G. and Zentefis, A. 2024. Corporate culture as a theory of the firm. *Economica.* doi: 10.1111/ecca.12537. They illustrate this by reviewing make-or-buy decisions as well as mergers and acquisitions. In make-or-buy decisions, they argue, managers take team characteristics, coordination costs and closeness to core technologies into account when deciding between the corporate culture providing a certain input or buying the same input on the market though contractual agreements. They also attribute high failure rates of mergers and acquisitions to unresolved cultural conflicts.

[88] Gerstner, L. 2004. *Who says elephants cannot dance? Leading a great enterprise through dramatic change.* New York: Harper-Business.

[89] Researchers working within an objectivistic and more specifically functionalist paradigm of cultural analysis gather organisational data to help elites, with managers typically exerting more control over employees. From this perspective, the meanings embedded in organisational cultures are seen as something the organisation has rather than what the organization is. This view shifts the focus from seeing culture as a social fact to viewing it as an ongoing process of social construction. Theaanna Kiaos. 2023. An interpretative framework for analysing managerial ideology, ethical control, organizational culture and the self, *Cogent Business & Management,* 10:1, 2163795.

[90] Cameron and Quinn, claim that no single type of culture is inherently superior. Companies should determine which type to promote based on their strategic goals and business environment. Cameron, K. and Quinn, R. 2011. *Diagnosing and Changing Organizational Culture. Based on the Competing Values Framework.* Somerset: Wiley.

[91] Denison extends Cameron and Quinn's framework by highlighting four key factors that determine a culture's impact on organisational performance: involvement, consistency, adaptability and mission. Involvement refers to the active participation and engagement of employees across all organisational levels, such as when individual employees are encouraged to initiate their own sustainability projects. Consistency involves aligning the employee's practices with the organisation's goals by establishing shared values and coordinated systems. *Innovation Impact Assessment* is one method to reinforce consistency with sustainability-related values. Adaptability refers to the company's ability to respond to external changes and market demands, such as new sustainability challenges or consumer trends. And Mission relates to the company's clear sense of purpose and long-term direction. Fondas, N. and Denison, D. 1991. Corporate Culture and Organizational Effectiveness. *The Academy of Management Review* 16 (1): 203. doi: 10.2307/258613.

[92] Globocnik, D., Rauter., R., and Baumgartner, R. 2020. Synergy Or Conflict? The Relationships Among Organisational Culture, Sustainability-Related Innovation Performance, And Economic Innovation Performance. *International Journal of Innovation Management* 24 (01): 2050004. doi: 10.1142/S1363919620500048. Linnenluecke, M. and Griffiths, A. 2010. Corporate sustainability and organizational culture. https://www.sciencedirect.com/science/article/pii/S1090951609000431. *Journal of World Business* 45 (4): 357–366. doi: 10.1016/j.jwb.2009.08.006 Reyes-Santiago, M., Sánchez-Medina, P., and Díaz-Pichardo, R. 2017. Eco-innovation and organizational culture in the hotel industry. *International Journal of Hospitality Management* 65: 71–80. doi: 10.1016/j.ijhm.2017.06.001 Rubio-Andrés, M. and Abril, C. 2024b. Sustainability oriented innovation and organizational values: a cluster analysis. *The Journal of Technology Transfer* 49 (1): 1–18. doi: 10.1007/s10961-022-09979-1

[93] For example, both clan and hierarchical cultures have been associated with either positive or negative effects on sustainable innovation performance. Abril, C., Rubio-Andrés, M., and Breuer, H., Ivanov, K. 2025 (forthcoming). Systems of Values to Build a Sustainability-Oriented Culture for Sustainability-Oriented Innovation. *International Journal of Innovation and Sustainable Development.*

[94] Boenink, M. and Kudina, O. 2020. Values in responsible research and innovation: from entities to practices. *Journal of Responsible Innovation* 7 (3): 450–470. doi: 10.1080/23299460.2020.1806451. Ivanov, K. 2022. Values-Based Business Model Innovation–The Case of Ecosia and Its Business Model. *International Journal of Innovation Management* 26 (05). doi: 10.1142/S1363919622400023

[95] Globocnik, D., Rauter., R., and Baumgartner, R. 2020.; Reyes-Santiago, M., Sánchez-Medina, P., and Díaz-Pichardo, R. 2017.; Rubio-Andrés, M. and Abril, C. 2024a. Sustainability oriented innovation and organizational values: a cluster analysis. *The Journal of Technology Transfer* 49 (1): 1–18. doi: 10.1007/s10961-022-09979-1

[96] Handy, C. 1995. *Gods of management. The changing work of organizations.* London, New York: Oxford University Press.

[97] Hofstede, G. 2011. Dimensionalizing Cultures: The Hofstede Model in Context. *Online readings in psychology and culture* 2 (8). Although organisational cultures are embedded in the context of national cultures, Hofstede stresses that they are fundamentally different. Whereas national cultures are rooted in implicit and stable values that individuals acquire from childhood, organisational cultures are rooted in practices that are conscious, visible and susceptible to change and development. Hofstede identifies a different set of dimensions to analyse organisational cultures based on their practices: process-oriented versus results-oriented, job-oriented versus employee-oriented, professional versus parochial, open systems versus closed systems, tight versus lose control, and pragmatic versus normative. He emphasises that organisations can learn or unlearn practices

across these six dimensions to deliberately transform their cultures over time.

[98] Researchers have applied Hofstede's cross-national dimensions to analyse the impact of national cultures on organisational cultures and corporate sustainability. For example: Shareholders in collectivistic cultures are shown to be more supportive of sustainability initiatives than the shareholders in individualistic cultures. Shi, W. and Veenstra, K. 2021. The Moderating Effect of Cultural Values on the Relationship Between Corporate Social Performance and Firm Performance. *Journal of Business Ethics* 174 (1): 89–107. doi: 10.1007/s10551-020-04555-9.
Firms in cultures with low motivation towards achievement and success show more positive impact on sustainability performance, whereas firms with high motivation cultures focus on growth over caring for unprivileged social groups and the environment. Tehrani, M., Rathgeber, A., Fulton, L., and Schmutz, B. 2021. Sustainability & CSR: The Relationship with Hofstede Cultural Dimensions. *Sustainability* 13 (21). doi: 10.3390/su132112052.
Power distance can influence an organisation's cultural transformation towards sustainability and be addressed with practices such as practices of *Inclusive Deliberation, Participative Decision Making or Decentralisation*. Tear, M., Reader, T., Shorrock, S., and Kirwan, B. 2020. Safety culture and power: Interactions between perceptions of safety culture, organisational hierarchy, and national culture. Safety Science 121: 550–561. doi: 10.1016/j.ssci.2018.10.014.

[99] Westrum, R. 2004. A typology of organisational cultures. *Quality and Safety in Health Care* 13 (suppl_2): ii22–ii27. doi: 10.1136/qshc.2003.009522.

[100] Schein, E. 2004. *Organizational culture and leadership*. San Francisco: Jossey-Bass.

[101] 'The culture of a group can be defined as the accumulated shared learning of that group as it solves its problems of external adaptation and internal integration, which has worked well enough to be considered valid and, therefore, to be taught to new members as the correct way to perceive, think, feel, and behave in relation to those problems. This accumulated learning is a pattern or system of beliefs, values, and behavioral norms that come to be taken for granted as basic assumptions and eventually drop out of awareness' (Schein, E. 2017 (p. 6). *Organizational culture and leadership*. San Francisco: Jossey-Bass.).

[102] Schein, E. 1996. Kurt Lewin's change theory in the field and in the classroom: Notes toward a model of managed learning. *Systems Practice* 9 (1): 27–47. doi: 10.1007/BF02173417.

[103] Schein, E. 2013. *Humble Inquiry. The Gentle Art of Asking Instead of Telling*. Oakland, CA: Berrett-Koehler.

[104] Artefacts as material cultural elements are the subject of study in a pragmatic approach to cultural analysis, in particular, Georg Simmel's concept of cultivation, which we outline in chapter 6.

[105] Todnem By, R. 2005. Organisational change management: A critical review. *Journal of Change Management* 5 (4): 369–380. Routledge. doi: 10.1080/14697010500359250.

[106] Appelbaum, S., Habashy, S., Malo, J.-L., and Shafiq, H. 2012. Back to the future: revisiting Kotter's 1996 change model. *Journal of Management Development* 31 (8): 764–782. Emerald Group Publishing Limited. doi: 10.1108/02621711211253231.

[107] Stouten, Rousseau, and Cremer synthesise elements from seven established change models, including Hiatt's ADKAR Model, Lewin's Three-Phase Process, Beer's Six-Step Change Management Model, Appreciative Inquiry, Judson's Five Steps, Kanter, Stein, and Jick's Ten Commandments, and Kotter's Eight-Step Model. However, they do not account for the transformation of organisational practices in line with the more profound levels of cultural development: namely, the ongoing readjustment of basic notions, values and assumptions. Stouten, J, Rousseau, M. and Cremer, D. 2018. Successful organizational change: Integrating the management practice and scholarly literatures. *The Academy of Management Annals* 12 (2): 752–788.

[108] Sancak, I. 2023. Change management in sustainability transformation: A model for business organizations. *Journal of Environmental Management* 330: 117165. doi: 10.1016/j.jenvman.2022.117165.

[109] Schwartz, S. 2006. A Theory of Cultural Value Orientations: Explication and Applications. *Comparative Sociology* 5 (2–3): 137–182. doi: 10.1163/156913306778667357.

[110] Rokeach, M. 1979. *Understanding human values. Individual and societal*. New York, London: Free Press; Collier Macmillan.

[111] Breuer, H. and Freund, F. 2017a.
Rindova, V. and Martins, L. 2017. From Values to Value: Value Rationality and the Creation of Great Strategies. *Strategy Science* 3 (1): 323–334. INFORMS. doi: 10.1287/stsc.2017.0038

[112] Schein, E. 2015. Organizational Psychology Then and Now: Some Observations. https://www.annualreviews.org/content/journals/10.1146/annurev-orgpsych-032414-111449. *Annual Review of Organizational Psychology and Organizational Behavior* 2 (Volume 2, 2015): 1–19. Annual Reviews. doi: 10.1146/annurev-orgpsych-032414-111449.

[113] Hogan, S. and Coote, L. 2014. Organizational culture, innovation, and performance: A test of Schein's model. https://www.sciencedirect.com/science/article/pii/S0148296313003342. *Journal of Business Research* 67 (8): 1609–1621. doi: 10.1016/j.jbusres.2013.09.007.

[114] Bourdieu, P. 2019. *Outline of a theory of practice*. Cambridge: Cambridge University Press.

[115] Bourdieu emphasises that the relationship between habitus and practice is reciprocal rather than unidirectional. In *Outline of a Theory of Practice*, he observes that habitus is 'determined by the past conditions which have produced the principle of their production, that is, by the actual outcome of identical or interchangeable past practices' (Bourdieu, 2019, 72–73). This means that while habitus influences practices, the past engagement of social actors with practices also plays a role in shaping and refining their habitus over time. Rowlands, J. and Gale, T. 2016. Shaping and being shaped: extending the relationship between habitus and practice: 91–107. Routledge. doi: 10.4324/9781315640532.

[116] Maller, C. 2023. Turning things around: A discussion of values, practices, and action in the context of social-ecological change. *People and Nature*, 5(2), 258-270.

[117] Akpa, V., Asikhia, O., Nneji, N. 2021. Organizational culture and organizational performance: A review of literature. *International Journal of Advances in Engineering and Management* 3 (1): 361–372.

[118] It also requires companies to disclose how they establish, develop, promote and evaluate their corporate culture, see European Comission. 2023. Supplementing Directive 2013/34/EU of the European Parliament and of the Council as regards sustainability reporting standards. https://eur-lex.europa.eu/legal-content/en/TXT/?uri=CELEX:32023R2772. Accessed: 1 June 2025.

[119] Schein, E. 2004.

[120] Jiang, X., Kim, S., & Lu, S. 2025. Limited accountability and awareness of corporate emissions target outcomes. *Nature Climate Change*, 1–8.

[121] Mura, M., Longo, M., Boccali, F., Visani, F., & Zanni, S. 2024. From outcomes to practices: Measuring the commitment to sustainability of organisations. *Environmental Science & Policy*, 160, 103868.

[122] Janicijevic, N. 2011.

[123] Sustainability transformations are considered wicked problems of organisational change because of the complex interplay of actors, interests, and institutional forces that they involve. Markard, J., Raven, R., and Truffer, B. 2012. Sustainability transitions: An emerging field of research and its prospects. *Research Policy* 41 (6): 955–967. doi: 10.1016/j.respol.2012.02.013. Matos, J. de and Clegg, S. 2013. Sustainability and Organizational Change. *Journal of Change Management* 13 (4): 382–386. doi: 10.1080/14697017.2013.851912.

[124] Howard-Grenville, J. 2006. Inside the 'Black Box'. How Organizational Culture and Subcultures Inform Interpretations and Actions on Environmental Issues. *Organization & Environment* 19 (1): 46–73. doi: 10.1177/1086026605285739. Isensee, C., Teuteberg, F., Griese, K.-M., and Topi, C. 2020. The relationship between organizational culture, sustainability, and digitalization in SMEs: A systematic review. *Journal of Cleaner Production* 275: 122944. doi: 10.1016/j.jclepro.2020.122944

[125] Assoratgoon, W. and Kantabutra, S. 2023. Toward a sustainability organizational culture model. *Journal of Cleaner Production* 400: 1–18. doi: 10.1016/j.jclepro.2023.136666. Baumgartner, R. 2014. Managing Corporate Sustainability and CSR: A Conceptual Framework Combining Values, Strategies and Instruments Contributing to Sustainable Development. Corporate *Social Responsibility and Environmental Management* 21 (5): 258–271. doi: 10.1002/csr.1336.

[126] Boonstra, J., and Brillo, J. 2021. Shaping Sustainable Innovation Based on Cultural Values. In: Voinea, C. et al.: Sustainable innovation. *Routledge.*

[127] Gadomska-Lila, K. 2024. Changing organisational culture for sustainability: 206–230. doi: 10.4337/9781035314225.00020.

[128] Lozano, R. 2007. Orchestrating Organisational Changes for Corporate Sustainability. Greener *Management International* 2007 (57): 43–64. doi: 10.9774/gleaf.3062.2007.sp.00005 Lozano, R. 2008. Developing collaborative and sustainable organisations. *Journal of Cleaner Production* 16 (4): 499–509. doi: 10.1016/j.jclepro.2007.01.002 Lozano, R. 2022. Organizational Change Management for Sustainability: 75–88. doi: 10.1007/978-3-030-99676-5_5.

[129] Assoratgoon, W. and Kantabutra, S. 2023.

[130] Duygulu, E., Ozeren, E., Bagiran, D., Appolloni, A., & Mavisu, M. 2015. Gaining insight into innovation culture within the context of R&D centres in Turkey. *International Journal of Entrepreneurship and Innovation Management* 19 (1–2): 117–146. Gedvilaitè, D., & Padurariu, C. 2014. Shanmuganathan, A. 2018. Product innovation: Impact of organizational culture in product innovation. *International Journal of Advancements in Research and Technology* 7: 83–89

[131] Meyer, J.-U. 2014. Strengthening innovation capacity through different types of innovation cultures. *2014 ISPIM Americas Innovation Forum*, Montreal, Canada, 5–8 October.

[132] Dombrowski, C., Kim, J., Desouza, K., Braganza, A., Papagari, S., Baloh, P., and Jha, S. 2007. Elements of innovative cultures. *Knowledge and Process Management* 14 (3): 190–202. doi: 10.1002/kpm.279.

[133] Dombrowski, C., Kim, J., Desouza, K., Braganza, A., Papagari, S., Baloh, P., and Jha, S. 2007.

[134] Asmawi, Arnifa, and Avvari V. Mohan. 2011. Unveiling dimensions of organizational culture: an exploratory study in Malaysian R & D organizations. *R&D Management* 41 (5): 509–523. Tidd, J., & Bessant, J. R. 2022. Managing innovation: integrating technological, market and organizational change. Wiley.

[135] Jucevičius, G. 2010. Culture vs. cultures of innovation: conceptual framework and parameters for assessment. In: *Proceedings of the International Conference on Intellectual Capital, Knowledge Management & Organizational Learning*: 236–244.

[136] Gedvilaitè, D., & Padurariu, C. 2014.

[137] These reviews analysed publications from the Web of Science database, sourcing articles from a range of sub-databases including SCIE, SSCI, AHCI, ESCI, and CPCI. Each review had a specific focus. The first two reviews addressed the question 'What is the current state of knowledge about sustainable innovation cultures?' The first, focused on the terms 'sustainable innovation,' 'sustainability-oriented innovation,' and 'sustainability innovation,' combined with 'culture.' Covering publications from 2010 to April 2024, it identified 67 relevant studies for in-depth analysis. The second review concentrated specifically on the term 'sustainable innovation culture' and recent publications mentioning it, published from January 2019 to February 2024. Out of 603 search results, 27 articles were deemed relevant to the development of sustainable innovation cultures and selected for in-depth review. The third review used an iteratively refined search strategy to identify literature on values-based and sustainable innovation cultures, analysing publications from 1987 to December 2023. It addressed the questions 'What is the role of values in sustainable innovation?'; 'What are the barriers to sustainable innovation?'; and 'What are good practises and methods that lead to positive sustainable outcomes?' and identified 317 papers based on three keyword categories: 1) values AND 2) (sustainable innovation OR sustainability-oriented innovation) AND 3) seventeen additional terms (e.g. culture OR barriers OR practices OR methods OR challenges OR development OR circular economy OR entrepreneurship). Of the 317 identified publications 67 were selected for in-depth analysis based on criteria such as business context applicability, relevance to sustainable innovation management, and relevance to cultural values as opposed to e.g. economic value or statistical values.

[138] Breuer, H. and Freund, F. 2017a.

[139] Ivanov, K. 2024. Values-Based Barriers and Good Practices in Sustainability-Oriented Innovation Management. https://doi.org/10.1002/csr.3016. *Corporate Social Responsibility and Environmental Management* 1 (19).

[140] See cases 6 (section 3.1.3) and 14 (section 6.2.1) on Ecosia.

[141] Siebenhüner, B. and Arnold, M. 2007. Organizational learning to manage sustainable development. *Business Strategy and the Environment* 16 (5): 339–353. doi: 10.1002/bse.579.

[142] Hörisch, J., Freeman, E., Schaltegger, S. 2014.

[143] Geradts, T. & Bocken, N. 2019. Driving sustainability-oriented innovation: a sustainable corporate entrepreneurship approach. *MIT Sloan Review* (Winter 2019).

[144] Geradts, T. & Bocken, N. 2019.

[145] Kneipp, J., Gomes, C., Bichueti, R., Frizzo, K., and Perlin, A. 2019. Sustainable innovation practices and their relationship with the performance of industrial companies. *Revista de Gestão* 26 (2): 94–111. doi: 10.1108/REGE-01-2018-0005.

[146] Chowdhury, S., Dey, P., Rodríguez-Espíndola, O., Parkes, G., Tuyet, N., Long, D., and Ha, T. 2022. Impact of Organisational Factors on the Circular Economy Practices and Sustainable Performance of Small and Medium-sized Enterprises in Vietnam. *Journal of Business Research* 147: 362–378. doi: 10.1016/j.jbusres.2022.03.077.

[147] Besides drawing on our in-depth literature analyses, we gained insights from a comparative European study of sustainable innovation cultures, involving 36 ethnographic interviews and four co-creation activities conducted across eleven sustainability-oriented companies in Germany, Italy, Poland and Spain. Another major source of insights and inspiration was a broad community of experts that we engaged through panel discussions at the European Academy of Management (EURAM) and the International Society for Professional Innovation Management (ISPIM) conferences.

[148] Trying to change mindsets by setting sustainability goals only verbally articulates a promise. Keeping the promise requires appropriate skills and expertise as well as tools or artefacts (such as IT infrastructure or physical innovation spaces). Trying to fix just one of these sets without the other can lead to detrimental effects. Rusinek, H. (2023). *Work-Survive-Balance: Warum die Zukunft der Arbeit die Zukunft unserer Erde ist* [Work-Survive-Balance. Why the Future of Work is the Future of Our Planet]. Herder.

[149] Gadomska-Lila, K. 2024.
Ketprapakorn, N. and Kantabutra, S. 2022. Toward an organizational theory of sustainability culture. *Sustainable Production and Consumption* 32: 638–654. doi: 10.1016/j.spc.2022.05.020

Chapter 3

[1] Complex adaptive systems stress the adaptive rather than generative aspects, e.g. Carlisle, Y. and McMillan, E. 2006. Innovation in organizations from a complex adaptive systems perspective. *Emergence: Complexity and Organization*, 8(1) 2–9.

[2] Weick and Sutcliff show how cultures evolve through continual learning and responsiveness to unexpected events. Weick, K. E., & Sutcliffe, K. M. 2001. *Managing the Unexpected: Assuring High Performance in an Age of Complexity*. San Francisco: Jossey-Bass.

[3] Donaldson, T. 2023. Value creation and CSR. *Journal of Business Economics:* 1–21. doi: 10.1007/s11573-022-01131-7.

[4] World Health Organization. 2017. Environmentally sustainable health systems: a strategic document. https://apps.who.int/iris/bitstream/handle/10665/340375/WHO-EURO-2017-2241-4199657723-eng.pdf?sequence=3. Regional Office for Europe. Accessed: 1 June 2025.

[5] Merck. 2025. Access to Health. https://www.merckgroup.com/en/sustainability/health-for-all/access-to-health.html. Accessed: 1 June 2025.

[6] GSK. 2013. Corporate Responsibility Report. https://www.gsk.com/media/2745/our-behaviour-factsheet.pdf. Accessed: 1 June 2025.

[7] Donaldson, T. 2023.

[8] Binder, C., Hinkel, J., Bots, P., and Pahl-Wostl, C. 2013. Comparison of Frameworks for Analyzing Social-ecological Systems. *Ecology and Society* 18 (4). doi: 10.5751/ES-05551-180426.

[9] Baue, B. 2021. From Impact Management to System Value Creation: 73–83. doi: 10.1108/978-1-78973-929-920200007.

[10] Elkington, J. 2004. Enter the triple bottom line. *The triple bottom line: Does it all add up?* 1–12. London: Earthscan.

[11] Herbertson, J. and Tipler, C. 2007. *The Natural Step Framework: From Sustainability Fundamentals to Innovation.* doi: 10.4337/9781847203052.00022.

[12] Stilgoe, J., Owen, R., and Macnaghten, P. 2013. Developing a framework for responsible innovation. *Research Policy* 42 (9): 1568–1580. doi: 10.1016/j.respol.2013.05.008.

[13] Some innovation management frameworks like values-based innovation management, disruptive innovation or open innovation, although not prescriptive with regard to specific sustainability values, have a proven record as beneficial for the translation of sustainability values and goals into successful innovation practice. Kivimaa, P., S. Laakso, A. Lonkila, and M. Kaljonen. 2021. Moving beyond disruptive innovation: A review of disruption in sustainability transitions. *Environmental Innovation and Societal Transitions* 38: 110–126. doi: 10.1016/j.eist.2020.12.001. Rauter, R., D. Globocnik, E. Perl-Vorbach, and R. Baumgartner. 2019. Open innovation and its effects on economic and sustainability innovation performance. *Journal of Innovation & Knowledge* 4 (4): 226–233. doi: 10.1016/j.jik.2018.03.004.

[14] Hyland, J., Karlsson, M. et al. 2022. *Changing the Dynamics and Impact of Innovation Management: A Systems Approach and the ISO Standard.* World Scientific Publishing Company.

[15] Dembek, K., Lüdeke-Freund, F, Rosati, F. & Froese. 2022. Untangling business model outcomes and impacts and value. *Business Strategy and the Environment.* 2023; 32:2296–2311

[16] Martin, R. 2023. Strategy In 1000 Words. A conversation between Roger Martin and ReD partners Iago Storgaard and Filip Lau. ReD Associates (https://www.redassociates.com/strategy-with-roger-martin).

[17] Breuer, H. and Ivanov, K. 2022. Case of Inspection Company in ethnographic study for the IMPACT Erasmus+ project.

[18] Schein, E. 2004. *Organizational culture and leadership.* San Francisco: Jossey-Bass.

[19] Baron, J., Hannan, M., and Burton, M. 1999. Building the Iron Cage: Determinants of Managerial Intensity in the Early Years of Organizations. *American Sociological Review* 64 (4): 527–547. doi: 10.1177/000312249906400404.

[20] British Standards Institution. 2022. PAS 808 - Purpose-Driven Organizations for Delivering Sustainability. https://www.bsigroup.com/en-GB/insights-and-media/insights/brochures/pas-808-purpose-driven-organizations-for-delivering-sustainability/. Accessed: 1 June 2025.

[21] Reficco, E., Gutiérrez, R., Jaén, M., and Auletta, N. 2018. Collaboration mechanisms for sustainable innovation. *Journal of Cleaner Production* 203: 1170–1186. doi: 10.1016/j.jclepro.2018.08.043.

[22] Epstein, M., Buhovac, A., and Yuthas, K. 2015. Managing Social, Environmental and Financial Performance Simultaneously. *Long Range Planning* 48 (1): 35–45. doi: 10.1016/j.lrp.2012.11.001.

[23] Haffar, M. and Searcy, C. 2017. Classification of Trade-offs Encountered in the Practice of Corporate Sustainability. *Journal of Business Ethics* 140 (3): 495–522. doi: 10.1007/s10551-015-2678-1.

[24] van Bommel, K. 2018. Managing tensions in sustainable business models: Exploring instrumental and integrative strategies. *Journal of Cleaner Production* 196: 829–841. doi: 10.1016/j.jclepro.2018.06.063.
Wannags, L. and Gold, S. 2020. Assessing tensions in corporate sustainability transition: From a review of the literature towards an actor-oriented management approach. *Journal of Cleaner Production* 264: 121662. doi: 10.1016/j.jclepro.2020.121662.

[25] Freeman, R. E., Parmar, B. L., & Martin, K. 2019. *The power of and: Responsible business without trade-offs.* Columbia University Press.
Freeman, R.E., Dmytriyev, S., and Phillips, R. 2021. Stakeholder Theory and the Resource-Based View of the Firm. *Journal of Management* 47 (7): 1757–1770. doi: 10.1177/0149206321993576.

[26] Watson, R., Wilson, H., Smart, P., and Macdonald, E. 2018. Harnessing Difference: A Capability-Based Framework for Stakeholder Engagement in Environmental Innovation. *Journal of Product Innovation Management* 35 (2): 254–279. doi: 10.1111/jpim.12394.

[27] Holmes, S. and Smart, P. 2009. Exploring open innovation practice in firm-nonprofit engagements: a corporate social responsibility perspective. *R&D Management* 39 (4): 394–409. doi: 10.1111/j.1467-9310.2009.00569.x.

[28] Breuer, H. and Ivanov, K. 2024. Cultural Tensions and Values-Action Gaps in Sustainability-Oriented Innovation: An Ethnographic Inquiry. *International Journal of Innovation Management* 28 (01n02). doi: 10.1142/S1363919624500051.

[29] Lewin, K. 1951. Field Theory of Social Science: Selected Theoretical Papers. *The ANNALS of the American Academy of Political and Social Science* 276 (1): 146–147. Harper & Brothers. doi: 10.1177/000271625127600135.

[30] Wansink, B. 2002. Changing Eating Habits on the Home Front: Lost Lessons from World War II Research. *Journal of Public Policy & Marketing* 21 (1): 90–99. doi: 10.1509/jppm.21.1.90.17614.

[31] Dent, E. and Goldberg, S. 1999. Challenging "Resistance to Change". *The Journal of Applied Behavioral Science* 35 (1): 25–41. doi: 10.1177/0021886399351003.

[32] Cable, M. and Bartunek, J. 2024. Revisiting "Resistance to Change": Recognizing the Tenuous Nature of a Taken-for-Granted Construct. *Journal of Management Inquiry.* doi: 10.1177/10564926241261889.

[33] Cable, M. and Bartunek, J. 2024.
Bartunek, J. and Moch, M. 1987. First-Order, Second-Order, and Third-Order Change and Organization Development Interventions: A Cognitive Approach. *The Journal of Applied Behavioral Science* 23 (4): 483–500. doi: 10.1177/002188638702300404.

[34] The Volkswagen diesel emissions scandal (also known as Dieselgate) occurred in 2015 when it was revealed that the company had intentionally programmed millions of its diesel vehicles to activate their emissions controls only during the vehicles' regular emission control inspections. This deception violated environmental regulations, leading to billions in fines, legal action and severe damage to Volkswagen's reputation. Aurand, Timothy W., Wayne Finley, Vijaykumar Krishnan, Ursula Y. Sullivan, Jackson Abresch, Jordyn Bowen, Michael Rackauskas, Rage Thomas, and Jakob Willkomm. 2018. The VW Diesel Scandal: A Case of Corporate Commissioned Greenwashing. *Journal of Organizational Psychology* 18 (1). doi: 10.33423/jop.v18i1.1313.

[35] The Apple Batterygate scandal involved the company intentionally slowing down older iPhone models through software updates, without informing users about how the updates affected device performance. When this practice was exposed in 2017, Apple faced backlash, lawsuits and accusations of planned obsolescence, forcing the company to offer reimbursements to customers and more transparency about device performance. Rodríguez-Vidal, J., Carrillo-de-Albornoz, J., Gonzalo, J., and Plaza, L. 2021. Authority and priority signals in automatic summary generation for online reputation management. *Journal of the Association for Information Science and Technology* 72 (5): 583–594. doi: 10.1002/asi.24425.

[36] An attitude 'represents a summary evaluation of a psychological object captured in such attribute dimensions as good–bad, harmful–beneficial, pleasant–unpleasant, and likable–dislikable' Ajzen, I. 2001. *Nature and operation of attitudes: Annual Review of Psychology.* psych, 52(1), 28. This characterises attitudes as more situational and object-specific than values, which are viewed as general and abstract as well as enduring and stable. Furthermore, while norms 'prescribe generally expected and required behaviours in particular situations', values are 'considered to be trans-situational criteria or beliefs used by subjects to select the desirable' Breuer, H. and F. Freund. 2017, 25.

[37] Wikström, G., Bledow, N., Matinmikko-Blue, M., Breuer, H., Costa, C., Darzanos, G., ... & Wunderer, S. 2024. Key value indicators: A framework for values-driven next-generation ICT solutions. *Telecommunication Policy*, vol. 48, no. 6, Jul. 2024, Art. no. 102778.

[38] Ivanov, K. 2024. Values-Based Barriers and Good Practices in Sustainability-Oriented Innovation Management. https://doi.org/10.1002/csr.3016. *Corporate Social Responsibility and Environmental Management* 1 (19).

[39] Based on Breuer, H., Ivanov, K., Abril, C., Dijk, S., Monti, A., Rappaccini, M., & Kasz, J. 2021. Building Values-based Innovation Cultures for Sustainable Business Impact. Proceedings of ISPIM Innovation Conference 2021, Berlin.

[40] Adams, R., Jeanrenaud, S., Bessant, J., Denyer, D., and Overy, P. 2016. Sustainability-oriented Innovation: A Systematic Review. *International Journal of Management Reviews* 18 (2): 180–205. doi: 10.1111/ijmr.12068.

[41] Feather, Norman T., C. Seligman, J. M. Olson, and M. P. Zanna. 1996. Values, deservingness, and attitudes towards high achievers: Research on tall poppies. In: *The Psychology of Values: the Ontario symposium*. NJ: Lawrence Erlbaum.

[42] Ivanov, K. 2022. Values-Based Business Model Innovation–The Case of Ecosia and Its Business Model. *International Journal of Innovation Management* 26 (05). doi: 10.1142/S1363919622400023.

[43] Ivanov, K. 2022.

[44] Reinert, H. and Reinert, E. 2006. Creative Destruction in Economics: Nietzsche, Sombart, Schumpeter: 55–85. doi: 10.1007/978-0-387-32980-2_4.

[45] Druckman, A., Chitnis, M., Sorrell, S., and Jackson, T. 2011. Missing carbon reductions? Exploring rebound and backfire effects in UK households. *Energy Policy* 39 (6): 3572–3581. doi: 10.1016/j.enpol.2011.03.058.

[46] Bohnsack, R., Bidmon, C., and Pinkse, J. 2022. Sustainability in the digital age: Intended and unintended consequences of digital technologies for sustainable development. *Business Strategy and the Environment* 31 (2): 599–602. doi: 10.1002/bse.2938.

[47] Merton, R. 1936. The Unanticipated Consequences of Purposive Social Action. *American Sociological Review* 1 (6): 894. doi: 10.2307/2084615.

[48] DeBiase, R. 2024. The Unintended Consequences of Clean Fuel Policies. College of Agricultural and Environmental Sciences. https://caes.ucdavis.edu/news/unintended-consequences-clean-fuel-policies?. Accessed 1 June 2025.

[49] Sveiby, K., Gripenberg, P., and Segercrantz, B. 2012. *Challenging the innovation paradigm*. New York: Routledge.

[50] Hoffmann, A. 2022. Interface: The Journey Towards Carbon Negative. WDI Publishing. https://store.hbr.org/product/interface-the-journey-towards-carbon-negative/W10C83. Accessed: 1 June 2025.

[51] Ray C. Anderson Foundation. 2025. Ray's Life. https://www.raycandersonfoundation.org/rays-life. Accessed: 1 June 2025.

[52] Hawken, P. 2010. The Ecology of Commerce Revised Edition: A Declaration of Sustainability. Collins Business Essentials.

[53] Anderson, R. 1994. Global Resource Conservation Kick-Off. Keynote Remarks 8/31/94. https://www.raycandersonfoundation.org/assets/pdfs/rayslife/original083194SpearinChest.pdf. Accessed: 1 June 2025.

[54] Interface. 2019a. Lessons for the Future. The Interface guide to changing your business to change the world. https://www.interface.com/content/dam/interfaceinc/interface/sustainability/emea/25th-anniversary-report/Interface_MissionZeroCel_Booklet_EN.pdf Accessed: 1 June 2025.

[55] Lovins, A. B., Lovins, L. H., & Hawken P. 1999. A road map for natural capitalism. *Harvard Business Review*, 77(3), 145-158.

[56] Interface. 2019b. The Future of Design is Biomimicry. https://blog.interface.com/future-of-design-biomimicry. Accessed: 1 June 2025.

[57] George, S. 2018. Interface goes carbon neutral for entire product range. https://www.edie.net/interface-goes-carbon-neutral-for-entire-product-range/ Accessed: 1 June 2025.

[58] Interface. 2019a. Lessons for the Future.

[59] Hoffmann, A. 2022.

[60] Makower, J. 2016. Inside Interface's bold new mission to achieve 'Climate Take Back'. https://trellis.net/article/inside-interfaces-bold-new-mission-achieve-climate-take-back. Accessed: 1 June 2025.

[61] Anderson, R. 2023. Sustainability Innovation Leaders – Planet. https://www.e-education.psu.edu/ba850/node/640). Accessed: 1 June 2025.

[62] Kajosaari, E. 2023. Community conflict and vague predictions: The five biggest reasons carbon offsetting schemes fail. https://www.euronews.com/green/2023/01/10/the-five-biggest-reasons-carbon-offsetting-schemes-can-fail. Accessed: 1 June 2025.

[63] Hoffmann, A. 2022.

[64] Interface. 2024. Sustainability is in our DNA. https://www.interface.com/GB/en-GB/sustainability/sustainability-overview.html. Accessed: 1 June 2025.

[65] Hill, K. 2015. Changing the World – One Carpet Tile at a Time. My Green Pod. https://www.mygreenpod.com/articles/interface/. https://www.mygreenpod.com/articles/interface/

[66] Ivanov, K. 2024.
Breuer, H., Ivanov, K., Abril, C., Dijk, S., Monti, A., Rapaccini, M., & Kasz, J. 2021. Building values-based innovation cultures for sustainable business impact. *ISPIM Conference Proceedings*: 1–31. The International Society for Professional Innovation Management (ISPIM).

[67] Our 3C framework for sustainable innovation culture should not be confused with the 3C framework for business environment analysis proposed in Ohmae, K. 1982. The Mind of The Strategist: The Art of Japanese Business. McGraw-Hill Inc.

[68] Geertz, C. 2008. "Thick description: Towards an interpretive theory of culture." In: *The cultural geography reader*. Routledge.

[69] Sampaio, R. 1998. The Hermeneutic Conceiving of Culture: 83–90. doi: 10.5840/wcp20-paideia199827455.

[70] As the Futures Search approach suggest, see Weisbord, M. and Janoff, S. 2010. *Future Search. An Action Guide to Finding Common Ground in Organizations and Communities*. Berrett-Koehler Publishers.

[71] Rill, B. and Hämäläinen, M. 2018. The Art of Co-creating.

Singapore: Springer Singapore. doi: 10.1007/978-981-10-8500-0.

[72] Warren, D., Gaspar, J., and Laufer, W. 2014. Is Formal Ethics Training Merely Cosmetic? A Study of Ethics Training and Ethical Organizational Culture. *Business Ethics Quarterly* 24 (1): 85–117. doi: 10.5840/beq2014233.

[73] Csikszentmihalyi, M. and Rochberg-Halton, E. 2012. *The Meaning of Things*. Cambridge University Press. doi: 10.1017/cbo9781139167611.

[74] Csikszentmihalyi, M. and Rochberg-Halton, E. 2012.

[75] Bocken, N. and Geradts, T. 2020. Barriers and drivers to sustainable business model innovation: Organization design and dynamic capabilities. *Long Range Planning* 53 (4): 101950. doi: 10.1016/j.lrp.2019.101950.

[76] Ketprapakorn, N. and Kantabutra, S. 2022. Towards an organizational theory of sustainability culture. *Sustainable Production and Consumption* 32: 638–654. doi: 10.1016/j.spc.2022.05.020.

[77] Stilgoe, J., Owen, R., and Macnaghten, P. 2013. Developing a framework for responsible innovation. *Research Policy* 42 (9): 1568–1580. doi: 10.1016/j.respol.2013.05.008.

[78] Lubberink, R., Blok, V., van Ophem, J., and Omta, O. 2017. Lessons for Responsible Innovation in the Business Context: A Systematic Literature Review of Responsible, Social and Sustainable Innovation Practices. *Sustainability* 9 (5): 721. doi: 10.3390/su9050721.

[79] Larson, A. 2000. Sustainable innovation through an entrepreneurship lens. *Business Strategy and the Environment* 9 (5): 304–317. doi: 10.1002/1099-0836(200009/10)9:5%3C304::AID-BSE255%3E3.0.CO;2-O.

[80] See also Geosocial Development in Ketprapakorn, N. and Kantabutra, S. 2022

[81] Lubberink et al. 2017, 12.

[82] Stilgoe et al. 2013, 1572.

[83] Gadomska-Lila, Katarzyna. 2024. Changing organizational culture for sustainability. In: The *Human Dimension of the Circular Economy*, Eds. Aldona Glińska-Neweś, and Pauliina Ulkuniemi, 206–230. Edward Elgar Publishing.

[84] Gadomska-Lila. 2024.

[85] Preuss, L., Walker, H. 2011. Psychological Barriers in The Road to Sustainable Development: Evidence from Public Sector Procurement. *Public Administration* 89 (2): 493–521. doi: 10.1111/j.1467-9299.2010.01893.x

[86] Inderberg, Tor Håkon Jackson, Iris Leikanger, and Hege Westskog. 2023. Institutional context, innovations, and energy transitions: Exploring solar photovoltaics with hydrogen storage at a secondary school in Norway. *Energy Research & Social Science* 101: 103147. doi: 10.1016/j.erss.2023.103147. (Thomke 2020)

[87] Deterding, S., Dixon, D., Khaled, R., & Nacke, L. 2011. From game design elements to gamefulness: defining 'gamification'. *In Proceedings of the 15th international academic MindTrek conference: Envisioning future media environment*. (p. 9).

[88] Gadomska-Lila, K. 2024.; Breuer, H., Bessant, J., Gudiksen, S. 2022. *Gamification for Innovators and Entrepreneurs*. De Gruyter. and Breuer, H., K. Ivanov, and C. Abril. 2023. Management guidelines to address cultural challenges and facilitate values-based innovation through gamification. *International Journal of Entrepreneurship and Innovation Management* 27 (3/4): 208–236. doi: 10.1504/IJEIM.2023.133383.

[89] Breuer, H., and Ivanov, K. 2022. Corporate Sustainability Innovation (CSI) Game. https://www.uxberlin.com/gamification-and-new-methods. Accessed: 1 June 2025.

[90] Hansen, E., Bullinger, A., and Reichwald, R. 2011. Sustainability innovation contests: evaluating contributions with an eco impact-innovativeness typology. *International Journal of Innovation and Sustainable Development* 5 (2/3): 221. doi: 10.1504/IJISD.2011.043074.

[91] Cool Choices. 2019. https://coolchoices.com/our-game-platform/. Accessed: 1 June 2025.

[92] IBM. 2023. The power of AI: Sustainability. https://www.ibm.com/thought-leadership/institute-business-value/en-us/report/ai-data-sustainability. Accessed: 1 June 2025.

[93] We treat these here as mediating artefacts rather than overarching practices, considering them an integral and soon to be ubiquitous part of many practices and methods. In the outlook chapter 13 we will come back to associated challenges.

[94] Jackson, A. 2024. IBM watsonx: New Technology Powers Sustainability Progress. In: Technology Magazine. https://technologymagazine.com/data-and-data-analytics/ibm-watsonx-new-technology-powers-sustainability-progress. Accessed: 1 June 2025.

[95] Breuer, H., Bessant, J., and Gudiksen, S. 2022. Gamification for innovators and entrepreneurs: Using games to drive innovation and facilitate learning. In *Gamification for innovators and entrepreneurs*. De Gruyter.

[96] EduBites. 2025. Our Suites. https://edubites.com/. Accessed: 1 June 2025.

[97] Schirmer-Kaegebein and Reinheimer. 2021. Künstliche Intelligenz zur Abbildung und Sicherung von Wissen – Nachhaltigkeit für das wichtigste Unternehmens-Asset. *HMD Praxis der Wirtschaftsinformatik* 58 (1): 116–133. doi: 10.1365/s40702-020-00699-4.

[98] Potter, B. 2024. Microsoft Cloud for Sustainability: Drive specific reduction and reporting targets with AI: https://www.microsoft.com/en-us/industry/blog/sustainability/2024/10/09/microsoft-cloud-for-sustainability-drive-specific-reduction-and-reporting-targets-with-ai/. Accessed: 1 June 2025.

[99] Andreotti, V., and Aiden Cinnamon Tea. 2025. Burnout from Humans. https://burnoutfromhumans.net. Accessed: 1 June 2025.

PART II

Chapter 4

[1] *Guiding Principles Review* for instance, takes a look into the normative foundations of the organisation, but should not be

detached from what is going on in the organisation. On the contrary, engaging employees from different hierarchical levels and functions and their experiences with different stakeholders are indispensable for gaining insights and raising commitment. Alternatively, *Awareness Raising* can be embedded through small scale reflexive techniques such as 'moments of truth' to speak up and articulate cultural tensions in daily meetings. This way, stimulating observations are situated into the contexts where they matter.

[2] Comprehensibility can be enhanced through documentation of the research process, interpretations in groups, and use of codified procedures. Empirical grounding develops insights close to the data using codified theories. Attention limitations reflect upon contextual conditions and the limits of transferability. For these and further criteria see Steinke, I. 2004. Quality criteria in qualitative research. *A companion to qualitative research* 21: 184–190.

[3] Patton, M. 2009. *Qualitative research & evaluation methods.* Thousand Oaks: Sage. Yin, R. 2017. Case study research and applications : design and methods. London: Sage

[4] Boenink, M. and Kudina, O. 2020. Values in responsible research and innovation: from entities to practices. *Journal of Responsible Innovation* 7 (3): 450–470. doi: 10.1080/23299460.2020.1806451.

[5] For the substantive approach see Schomberg, R. von. 2011 *Towards responsible research and innovation in the Information and communication technologies and security technologies fields.* Luxembourg: EUR-OP.; for the procedural approach see Stilgoe, J., Owen, R., and Macnaghten, P. 2013. Developing a framework for responsible innovation. *Research Policy* 42 (9): 1568–1580. doi: 10.1016/j.respol.2013.05.008; for the practice-based approach see Boenink, M.and O. Kudina. 2020.

[6] Willian, M. 2022. Facial Recognition Technology in the Commercial Sector. https://jtip.law.northwestern.edu/2022/09/09/facial-recognition-technology-in-the-commercial-sector/. Accessed: 1 June 2025.

[7] Boenink, M. and Kudina, O. 2020. p. 454.

[8] Boenink, M. and Kudina, O. 2020.

[9] Creswell, J. 2009. *Research design. Qualitative, quantative and mixed methods approaches.* Thousand Oaks, CA: Sage.

[10] Miller, D. 1997. *Capitalism. An ethnographic approach.* Oxford, Washington, DC: Berg.

[11] Brewer, J. and Hunter, A. 2006. Foundations of Multimethod Research. 2455 Teller Road, Thousand Oaks California 91320 United States of America: SAGE Publications, Inc. doi: 10.4135/9781412984294.

[12] Brewer, J. and Hunter, A. 2006.

[13] Malinowski, B. 2014. *Argonauts of the Western Pacific.* Routledge; Revised edition.

[14] Whyte, W. 1947. *Street corner society: The social structure of an Italian slum.* Chicago: University of Chicago Press.

[15] Parker, M. 2003. *Organisational culture and identity. Unity and division at work.* London: Sage.

[16] Parker, M. 2003.

[17] Madsbjerg, C. 2017. *Sensemaking: The Power of the Humanities in the Age of the Algorithm.* Hachette UK.

[18] Nightingale, D. and Cromby, J. 1999. *Social constructionist psychology: A critical analysis of theory and practice.* McGraw-Hill Education (UK).

[19] Cooper, R. and Edgett, S. 2008. Maximizing Productivity in Product Innovation. *Research-Technology Management* 51 (2): 47–58. doi: 10.1080/08956308.2008.11657495.

[20] *Rapid Ethnography* should be differentiated from another related approach to streamlining ethnographic inquiry, namely focused ethnography. Unlike the broader application scope of *Rapid Ethnography*, focused ethnography examines specific phenomena within sub-cultures or small groups. Knoblauch, H. 2005. Focused ethnography. In *Forum Qualitative Sozialforschung*/Forum: Qualitative Social Research (Vol. 6, No. 3).

[21] Breuer, H. 2022. Eliciting stakeholder values for strategic and values-based innovation management. In: The Proceedings of XXXIII ISPIM Conference: Copenhagen.

[22] Following Collins, J. 2001. "Good to Great: why some companies make the leap… and others do not." Harper Business; Repr.

[23] Organisational legitimacy is demonstrated by appropriate actions within a set of specific rules, norms, values, and beliefs; Suchman, M. 1995. Managing Legitimacy: Strategic and Institutional Approaches. *The Academy of Management Review* 20 (3): 571–610. doi: 10.5465/amr.1995.9508080331.

[24] Nicholls-Lee, D. 2023. The 'climate quitters' ditching corporate roles. https://www.bbc.com/worklife/article/20231016-the-climate-quitters-ditching-corporate-roles. Accessed: 1 June 2025.

[25] See UXBerlin. 2025. Sustainable Innovation Toolkits. https://www.uxberlin.com/sustainable-innovation-toolkits/. Accessed: 1 June 2025.

[26] Punch, K. 2012. *Introduction to social research. Quantitative and qualitative approaches.* Los Angeles, CA: Sage Publications.

[27] Madsbjerg, C. and Rasmussen, M. 2014. *Moment of Clarity. Using the Human Sciences to Solve Your Toughest Business Problems.* Boston, MA: Harvard Business Review Press.

[28] Fiske, S. 2007. Improving the Effectiveness of Corporate Culture. *Anthropology News* 48 (5): 44–45. doi: 10.1525/an.2007.48.5.44.

[29] Parker, Charlie, Sam Scott, and Alistair Geddes. 2020. Snowball Sampling. doi: 10.4135/9781526421036831710. Our primary contacts introduced us to potential participants at different hierarchical levels who could provide information on sustainability and innovation issues. The respondents were sent a standardised information sheet and consent form prior to the interview.

[30] Madsbjerg, C. and Rasmussen, M. 2014.

[31] Pink, S. 2007. *Doing Visual Ethnography.* London: SAGE Publications. doi: 10.4135/9780857025029.

[32] Madsbjerg, C. and Rasmussen, M. 2014. (pp. 92ff). illustrate the

importance of changing locations with the example of an informant who was reluctant to share any revealing statements in the course of several field interviews. Only after an interview could take place in the reassuring settings of his private home was the informant ready to share his personal values and concerns.

[33] Accordingly, Geertz writes: 'Doing ethnography is like trying to read (in the sense of "construct a reading of") a manuscript – foreign, faded, full of ellipses, incoherencies, suspicious emendations, and tendentious commentaries, but written not in conventionalised graphs of sound but in transient examples of shaped behaviour'; Geertz, C. 1973. *The Interpretation of Cultures*. New York: Basic Books, p.10).

[34] On mini-tour, grand tour and other types of tours see Spradley, J. 1979. *The ethnographic interview*. Long Grove, Illinois: Waveland Press.

[35] In our study comparative ethnographic study, participants shared highlights such as completing a corporate training for innovation experts, winning a sustainability award from an independent provider of sustainability ratings or launching a new innovation strategy. Examples of lowlights included several consecutive innovation project failures, lack of management support or not being able to find a good work-life balance.

[36] Dilts and Robert. 2017. *Strategies of Genius: Volume I*. Dilts Strategy Group.

[37] Saldaña and Johnny. 2023. The Coding Manual for Qualitative Researchers. https://study.sagepub.com/node/31740/student-resources/chapter-1. Sage Publications. Accessed: 1 June 2025.

[38] Madsbjerg, C. and Rasmussen, M. 2014.

[39] Joas, H. 2000. *The genesis of values*. Chicago: University of Chicago Press.

[40] Frankfurt, H. 1988. *The Importance of What We Care About: Philosophical Essays*. Cambridge: Cambridge University Press, p.16.

[41] Geertz, C. 2008. "Thick description: Toward an interpretive theory of culture." In: *The cultural geography reader*. Routledge.

[42] Holloway, I. 1997. *Basic concepts in qualitative research*. Oxford: Blackwell Scientific.

[43] Daae, J. and Boks, C. 2015. A classification of user research methods for design for sustainable behaviour. *Journal of Cleaner Production* 106: 680–689. doi: 10.1016/j.jclepro.2014.04.056. Holzblatt, K. 2016. Contextual Design: Design for Life. Morgan Kaufmann.

[44] Reiman, T. and Oedewald, P. 2002. The assessment of organisational culture. A methodological study 2140. Espoo: Technical Research Centre of Finland.

[45] Globocnik, D., Rauter., R., and Baumgartner, R. 2020. Synergy Or Conflict? The Relationships Among Organisational Culture, Sustainability-Related Innovation Performance, And Economic Innovation Performance. *International Journal of Innovation Management* 24 (01): 2050004. doi: 10.1142/S1363919620500048.

[46] Santoriello, A. 2000. Assessing Unique Core Values with the Competing Values Framework: The CCVI Technique for Guiding

Organisational Culture Change. doi: 10.15760/etd.2312.

[47] Breuer, H. and Ivanov, K. 2022. Case of Inspection Company in ethnographic study for the IMPACT Erasmus+ project.

[48] Andersen, R. 2017. Stabilizing sustainability in the textile and fashion industry 05.2017. PhD School of Economics and Management.
Breuer, H. and Freund, F. 2017. Values-based Network and Business Model Innovation. *International Journal of Innovation Management* 21 (03). doi: 10.1142/S1363919617500281
Langendahl, P.-A., Cook, M., and Potter, S. 2016. Sustainable innovation journeys: exploring the dynamics of firm practices as part of transitions to more sustainable food and farming. *Local Environment* 21 (1): 105–123. doi: 10.1080/13549839.2014.926869

[49] Madsbjerg, C. and Rasmussen, M. 2014.

[50] Breuer, H. 2022. Eliciting stakeholder values for strategic and values-based innovation management. *Proc. XXXIII ISPIM Conference*: 1–12.

[51] Andersen, R. 2017.

[52] Ye, K. 2024. Using a memetics lens to better understand tailored messages for organisational change toward sustainability. Master's thesis.

[53] Ye, K. 2024.

[54] Gutiérrez, J. and Macken-Walsh, Á. 2022. Ecosystems of Collaboration for Sustainability-Oriented Innovation: The Importance of Values in the Agri-Food Value-Chain. *Sustainability* 14 (18): 11205. doi: 10.3390/su141811205.

[55] Onkila, T., Mäkelä, M., and Järvenpää, M. 2018. Employee Sensemaking on the Importance of Sustainability Reporting in Sustainability Identity Change. *Sustainable Development* 26 (3): 217–228. doi: 10.1002/sd.1696.

[56] Weick, K., Sutcliffe, K., and Obstfeld, D. 2005. Organizing and the Process of Sensemaking. *Organisation Science* 16 (4): 409–421. doi: 10.1287/orsc.1050.0133.

[57] Weick, K., Sutcliffe, K., and Obstfeld, D. 2005. Whereas Weick takes a psychological approach to the retrospective construction of meaning after critical event, Madsbjerg takes a phenomenological approach to understand the foundations of human practices and culture.

[58] A Danish print company, New Zealand dairy farmers, and a German university have also used sensemaking to foster shared narratives and adapt sustainable practices. Strömland, J. and Acht, R. 2019. Sensemaking During a Strategic Change Process Towards Circularity: A Case Study of a Danish Print House. https://research.cbs.dk/da/studentProjects/sensemaking-during-a-strategic-change-process-towards-circularity Accessed: 1 June 2025.; Tisch, D. and Galbreath J. 2018. Building organisational resilience through sensemaking: The case of climate change and extreme weather events. *Business Strategy and the Environment*. 2018; 27: 1197–1208. https://doi.org/10.1002/bse.2062; Bien, C. and Sassen, R. 2020. Sensemaking of a sustainability transition by higher education institution leaders. *Journal of Cleaner Production*, Volume 256, 2020, 120299, https://doi.org/10.1016/j.jclepro.2020.120299.

[59] Geradts, T. & Bocken, N. 2019. Driving sustainability-oriented

innovation: a sustainable corporate entrepreneurship approach. *MIT Sloan Review* (Winter 2019).

[60] Breuer, H., Bessant, J., Gudiksen, S. 2022. Gamification for Innovators and Entrepreneurs. De Gruyter. doi: 10.1515/9783110725582.

[61] Breuer, H. and Ivanov, K. 2022.

[62] Cooperrider, D. and McQuaid, M. 2012. The Positive Arc of Systemic Strengths: How Appreciative Inquiry and Sustainable Designing Can Bring Out the Best in Human Systems. *Journal of Corporate Citizenship* 2012 (46): 71–102. doi: 10.9774/GLEAF.4700.2012.su.00006.

[63] Cooperrider, D. 2012. The concentration effect of strengths. *Organisational Dynamics* 41 (2): 106–117. doi: 10.1016/j.orgdyn.2012.01.004.

[64] Cooperrider, D. and McQuaid, M. 2012.

[65] Google Arts & Culture. 2011. UN Global Compact Dilemma Game. https://artsandculture.google.com/asset/un-global-compact-dilemma-game/LgGUttjCn-Hsbg?hl=en. Accessed: 1 June 2025.

[66] Breuer, H., Bessant, J., Gudiksen, S. 2022.

[67] Watson, R., Wilson, H., Smart, P., and Macdonald, E. 2018. Harnessing Difference: A Capability-Based Framework for Stakeholder Engagement in Environmental Innovation. *Journal of Product Innovation Management* 35 (2): 254–279. doi: 10.1111/jpim.12394.

[68] Watson, R., Wilson, H., Smart, P., and Macdonald, E. 2018.

[69] Holmes, S. and Smart, P. 2009. Exploring open innovation practice in firm-nonprofit engagements: a corporate social responsibility perspective. *R&D Management* 39 (4): 394–409. doi: 10.1111/j.1467-9310.2009.00569.x.

[70] Barile, S., Grimaldi, M., Loia, F., and Sirianni, C. 2020. Technology, Value Co-Creation and Innovation in Service Ecosystems: Toward Sustainable Co-Innovation. *Sustainability* 12 (7): 2759. doi: 10.3390/su12072759. Breuer, H. & Lüdeke-Freund, F. 2019. Values-Based Stakeholder Management – Concepts and Methods. In: Wunder, T. (Ed.): *Rethinking Strategic Management. Competing Through a Sustainability Mindset.* Berlin: Springer.

[71] Lindner, R., Kuhlmann, S., Randles, S., Bedsted, B., Gorgoni, G., Griessler, E., Loconto, A., and Mejlgaard, N. 2016. *Navigating towards shared responsibility in research and innovation. Approach, process and results of the Res-AGorA Project.* https://hal.science/hal-01298406. Germany: Fraunhofer Institute for Systems and Innovation Research (ISI).

[72] Lindner, R., Kuhlmann, S., Randles, S., Bedsted, B., Gorgoni, G., Griessler, E., Loconto, A., and Mejlgaard, N. 2016.

[73] Breuer, H. and Freund, F. 2017. *Values-based innovation management.* London: Macmillan Publishers Limited.

[74] Breuer, H. and Freund, F. 2017.

[75] IBM. 2005. Global Innovation Outlook 2.0. https://www.ibm.com/ibm/files/C685131J48569G91/GIO_2005_for-printing.pdf. Accessed: 1 June 2025.

[76] See Leadership Review in Visser, W. 2018. Creating Integrated Value Through Sustainable Innovation: A Conceptual Framework: 129–150. doi: 10.1007/978-3-319-73503-0_7.

[77] Breuer, H. and Freund, F. 2017.

[78] Breuer, H. and Freund, F. 2017.

[79] Aravind Eye Care System. 2025. Our Story. https://aravind.org/our-story/. Accessed: 1 June 2025.

Chapter 5

[1] Prahalad, C. & Venkatram R. 2000. Co-opting customer competence: 79–90. Harvard Business Review.

[2] Reichwald, R. & Piller, P. 2006. *Interaktive Wertschöpfung.* Wiesbaden: Gabler. doi: 10.1007/978-3-8349-9230-7.

[3] Voorberg, W., Bekkers, V., and Tummers, L. 2015. A Systematic Review of Co-Creation and Co-Production: Embarking on the social innovation journey. *Public Management Review* 17 (9): 1333–1357. doi: 10.1080/14719037.2014.930505.

[4] Giacomarra, M., Crescimanno, M., Sakka, G., and Galati, A. 2020. Stakeholder engagement toward value co-creation in the F&B packaging industry. *EuroMed Journal of Business* 15 (3): 315–331. Emerald Publishing Limited. doi: 10.1108/EMJB-06-2019-0077.

[5] Bentivegna, E. & D'Angelo, S. 2020. La co-creazione al centro dell'innovazione di Pelliconi (food & beverage). https://www.economyup.it/innovazione/la-co-creazione-al-centro-dellinnovazione-di-pelliconi-food-beverage/. Accessed: 1 June 2025.

[6] Pelliconi. 2025. Innovation, Life. https://www.pelliconi.com/innovation/. Accessed: 1 June 2025.

[7] Desall. 2019. Future Cap Challenge. https://desall.com/Contest/Future-Cap-Challenge/Brief. Accessed: 1 June 2025.

[8] Pelliconi. 2019.

[9] Bentivegna, E. & D'Angelo, S. 2020.

[10] Bentivegna, E. & D'Angelo, S. 2020.

[11] Weisbord, M. and Janoff, S. 2010. *Future Search: An Action Guide to Finding Common Ground in Organizations and Communities.* Berrett-Koehler Publishers.

[12] Owen, H. 2008. *Open Space Technology: A User's Guide.* Berrett-Koehler.

[13] Rill, B. and Hämäläinen, M. 2018. Understanding Co-creation: 17–38. doi: 10.1007/978-981-10-8500-0_2.

[14] Rill, B. and Hämäläinen, M. 2018.

[15] A storyboard template is available at www.uxberlin.com.

[16] The workshop was part of the Erasmus+ Partnership for Innovation Alliance on SF4S (Strategic Foresight for Sustainability), see www.sf4s-project.com. A video summary of the workshop is

available online: https://youtu.be/EFY6RpA9c2Q

[17] Lüdeke-Freund, F., Breuer, H., and Massa, L. 2022. *Sustainable Business Model Design - 45 Patterns*. Berlin: Lüdeke-Freund, Breuer & Massa.

[18] Delbard, O. 2021. How to create sustainable value? Some learnings from Interface Inc.'s 25-year journey. ESCP Impact Paper No 2021-01-EN. https://academ.escpeurope.eu/pub/IP%202021-01-EN.pdf. Accessed: 1 June 2025.

[19] Change Oracle. 2011. Ray Anderson's Sustainable Legacy: Interface, Inc. Part Two. https://changeoracle.com/2011/08/19/ray-andersons-sustainable-legacy_19/. Accessed: 1 June 2025.

[20] Deckert, A. 2009. Xerox lauds employees with Earth Awards. https://rbj.net/2009/07/15/xerox-lauds-employees-with-earth-awards/. Rochester Business Journa. Accessed: 1 June 2025. Projects were evaluated based on their innovativeness, direct benefits to Xerox, project duration, and documented, measurable results. Running for over 15 years, this programme saved over $10 million in 2010 alone. Kaye, L. 2010. Xerox employees' green ideas save company $10.2 million. The Guardian. https://www.theguardian.com/sustainable-business/xerox-employees-green-ideas-save. Accessed: 1 June 2025.

[21] WEF 2023. DAOs for Impact. White paper. https://www3.weforum.org/docs/WEF_DAOs_for_Impact_2023.pdf. Accessed: 1 June 2025

[22] Related practices from the literature: Balanced Use of Ecological, Social, and Economic Values as Ideation Heuristics in Stock, T., Obenaus, M., Slaymaker, A., and Seliger, G. 2017. A Model for the Development of Sustainable Innovations for the Early Phase of the Innovation Process. *Procedia Manufacturing* 8: 215–222. doi: 10.1016/j.promfg.2017.02.027
Environmental Championing in Eikelboom, M., Gelderman, C., and Semeijn, J. 2018. Sustainable innovation in public procurement: the decisive role of the individual. *Journal of Public Procurement* 18 (3): 190–201. doi: 10.1108/JOPP-09-2018-012.
Directed Search Patterns Based on Sustainability Values in Chen, Q., Magnusson, M., and Björk, J. 2023. Selection bias of ideas for sustainability-oriented innovation in internal crowdsourcing. *Technovation* 124: 102761. doi: 10.1016/j.technovation.2023.102761
Value-sensitive Design in Stilgoe, J., Owen, R., and Macnaghten, P. 2013. Developing a framework for responsible innovation. *Research Policy* 42 (9): 1568–1580. doi: 10.1016/j.respol.2013.05.008.
Values-Based Business Modelling in Breuer, H. and Freund, F. 2017. Values-based Network and Business Model Innovation. *International Journal of Innovation Management* 21 (03). doi: 10.1142/S1363919617500281.

[23] Friedman, B. and Hendry, D. 2019. *Value Sensitive Design*. The MIT Press. doi: 10.7551/mitpress/7585.001.0001.

[24] Related practices from the literature: Sustainability Idea Management in Perez, A., Larrinaga, F., and Curry, E. 2014.. The Role of Linked Data and Semantic-Technologies for Sustainability Idea Management. In *Software Engineering and Formal Methods*, Eds. Steve Counsell, and Manuel Núñez, 306–312Cham: Springer International Publishing.
Communication Links in Gadomska-Lila, K. 2024.

[25] Leka, S. 2024. The Role of Artificial Intelligence in Idea Management Systems and Innovation Processes: An Integrative Review: 160–164. doi: 10.1145/3660853.3660890.

[26] Related practices from the literature: Sustainability Idea Management in Perez, A., Larrinaga, F., and Curry, E. 2014 The Role of Linked Data and Semantic-Technologies for Sustainability Idea Management. In *Software Engineering and Formal Methods*, Eds. Steve Counsell, and Manuel Núñez, 306–312Cham: Springer International Publishing.
Communication Links in Gadomska-Lila, K. 2024.

[27] Geradts, T. & Bocken, N. 2019. Driving sustainability-oriented innovation: a sustainable corporate entrepreneurship approach. *MIT Sloan Review* (Winter 2019).

[28] Clark, D. 2022. Google's '20% rule' shows exactly how much time you should spend learning new skills—and why it works. https://www.cnbc.com/2021/12/16/google-20-percent-rule-shows-exactly-how-much-time-you-should-spend-learning-new-skills.html. CNBC. Accessed: 1 June 2025.

[29] Geradts, T. & Bocken, N. 2019.

[30] Kruszelnicki, J. and Breuer, H. 2021. Challenges, Lessons and Methods for Developing Values-Based Intrapreneurial Culture: 381–395. doi: 10.1007/978-3-030-69380-0_22.

[31] Kruszelnicki, J. and Breuer, H. 2021.

[32] Kruszelnicki, J. and Breuer, H. 2021.

[33] Breuer, H., Bessant, J., Gudiksen, S. 2022. *Gamification for Innovators and Entrepreneurs*. De Gruyter. doi: 10.1515/9783110725582.

[34] Hansen, E., Bullinger, A., and Reichwald, R. 2011. Sustainability innovation contests: evaluating contributions with an eco impact-innovativeness typology. *International Journal of Innovation and Sustainable Development* 5 (2/3): 221. doi: 10.1504/IJISD.2011.043074.

[35] Related practices found in Chakrabarti, R., Henneberg, S., and Ivens, B. 2020. Open sustainability: Conceptualization and considerations. *Industrial Marketing Management* 89: 528–534. doi: 10.1016/j.indmarman.2020.04.024.
Networking with Actors with Compatible and Opposing Values in Lubberink, R., Blok, V., van Ophem, J., and Omta, O. 2017. Lessons for Responsible Innovation in the Business Context: A Systematic Literature Review of Responsible, Social and Sustainable Innovation Practices. *Sustainability* 9 (5): 721. doi: 10.3390/su9050721.

[36] Sorel, P.-E. 2024. Circular economy - Materials and components. https://www.movinonconnect.com/en/coi/economie-circulaire-materiaux-composants/#. Accessed: 1 June 2025.

[37] Bessen, J. 2014. History Backs Up Tesla's Patent Sharing. https://hbr.org/2014/06/history-backs-up-teslas-patent-sharing. *Harvard Business Review*. Accessed: 1 June 2025.

[38] Unilever Foundry. 2025. Inspiring innovation through collaboration. https://www.theunileverfoundry.com/home.html. Accessed: 1 June 2025.

[39] Peuckert, J. and Kern, F. 2023. How user innovation communities contribute to sustainability transitions. An exploration of three online communities. *Environmental Innovation and Societal Transitions* 49: 100785. doi: 10.1016/j.eist.2023.100785.
Lai, S.-L. and Shu, L. 2014. Do-it-yourselfers as Lead users for Environmentally Conscious Behavior. *Procedia CIRP* 15: 431–436. doi: 10.1016/j.procir.2014.06.078

[40] Lai, S.-L. and Shu, L. 2014.

[41] Peuckert, J. and Kern, F. 2023.

[42] Related practices from the literature: Market Creation in Darroch, J., Miles, M., and Jardine, A. 2015. *Market Creation: A Path to Sustainable Competitive Advantage*: 331.
Creating and Projecting New Sustainable Consumption Needs in Kneipp, J., Gomes, C., Bichueti, R., Frizzo, K., and Perlin, A. 2019. Sustainable innovation practices and their relationship with the performance of industrial companies. *Revista de Gestão* 26 (2): 94–111. doi: 10.1108/REGE-01-2018-0005; Darroch, J., Miles, M., and Jardine, A. 2015. Market Creation: A Path to Sustainable Competitive Advantage: 331.; Market Maker pattern in Lüdeke-Freund et al. (2022).

[43] Breuer, H. & Lüdeke-Freund, F. 2018. Values-Based Business Model Innovation: A Toolkit. In: Moratis, L., Melissen, F. & Idowu, S.O. (Eds.). *Sustainable Business Models*, 395-416. Springer.

[44] Breuer, H. and Freund, F. 2017. *Values-based innovation management*. London: Macmillan Publishers Limited.

[45] Agnew, J. and Henson, S. 2018. Business-Based Strategies for Improved Nutrition: The Case of Grameen Danone Foods. *IDS Bulletin* 49 (1). doi: 10.19088/1968-2018.103.

[46] Agnew, J. and Henson, S. 2018.

[47] Brand, D., Breuer, H., Lüdeke-Freund, F., Ivanov, K. & Heinrich-Fernandes, M. 2020. lab of tomorrow manual for sustainable business co-creation. Federal Ministry for Economic Cooperation and Development. https://www.lab-of-tomorrow.com/docs/default-source/default-document-library/lab-of-tomorrow_manual.pdf. Accessed: 1 June 2025

[48] Related practices from the literature: Innovation Ecosystems in Nylund, P., Brem, A., and Agarwal, N. 2021. Innovation ecosystems for meeting sustainable development goals: The evolving roles of multinational enterprises. *Journal of Cleaner Production* 281: 125329. doi: 10.1016/j.jclepro.2020.125329.. Integration with Local Communities in Kneipp, J., Gomes, C., Bichueti, R., Frizzo, K., and Perlin, A. 2019. Sustainable innovation practices and their relationship with the performance of industrial companies. *Revista de Gestão* 26 (2): 94–111. doi: 10.1108/REGE-01-2018-0005.
Cooperation with Academia in Marques, J., Franco, M., and Rodrigues, M. 2023. International universities-firms cooperation as a mechanism for environmental sustainability: a case study of EdgeWise. *Journal of Applied Research in Higher Education* 15 (4): 966–987. Emerald Publishing Limited. doi: 10.1108/JARHE-05-2022-0170

[49] Zaoual, A. and Lecocq, X. 2018. Orchestrating Circularity within Industrial Ecosystems. Lessons from iconic cases in three different countries. *California Management Review* 60 (3): 133–156. doi: 10.1177/0008125617752693.

[50] Hallingby, H.-S., Gavras, A., Mesogiti, I., Bledow, N., Darzanos, G., Frizzell, R., Breuer, H., Rokkas, T., and Fernandez Vega, L. 2023. 5G and Beyond 5G Ecosystem Business Modelling. White paper. https://www.izt.de/publikationen/5g-and-beyond-5g-ecosystem-business-modelling/. Zenodo. doi: 10.5281/zenodo.7640478. Accessed: 1 June 2025.

[51] Breuer, H. (2023). Sustainability Foresight – Practices and Methods for Future-Oriented Innovation Management. XXXIV ISPIM Innovation Conference, Ljubljana. https://www.uxberlin.com/wp-content/uploads/2024/04/2023_Sustainability_Foresight_ISPIM.pdf. Accessed: 1 June 2025.

[52] Rohrbeck, R. & Kum, M.E. 2018. Corporate foresight and its impact on firm performance: A longitudinal analysis, *Technological Forecasting and Social Change*, Volume 129, pp.105-116, https://doi.org/10.1016/j.techfore.2017.12.013.

[53] See section 2.1.1 and EEA. 2022. The 'Scenarios for a sustainable Europe in 2050' project. https://www.eea.europa.eu/publications/scenarios-for-a-sustainable-europe-2050/the-scenarios. Accessed: 1 June 2025.

[54] Strategic Foresight for Sustainability (SF4S). 2025. Envisioning future mobility with sustainable business models. http://sf4s-project.com/post/envisioning-future-mobility-with-sustainable-business-models. Accessed: 1 June 2025.

[55] Broman, G. and Robèrt, K. 2017. A framework for strategic sustainable development. *Journal of Cleaner Production* 140: 17–31. doi: 10.1016/j.jclepro.2015.10.121.

[56] Lindahl, P., Robèrt, K. and Broman, G. 2014. Strategic sustainability considerations in materials management. *Journal of Cleaner Production* 64: 98–103. doi: 10.1016/j.jclepro.2013.07.015.

[57] Broman, G. and Robèrt, K.-H. 2017.

[58] Lindahl, P., Robèrt, K., and Broman, G. 2014.

[59] Lindahl, P., Robèrt, K. and Broman, G. 2014.

[60] Behrendt, S. 2009. Integriertes Technologie-Roadmapping. In: Popp, R., Schüll, E. (eds) *Zukunftsforschung und Zukunftsgestaltung. Zukunft und Forschung.* Springer, Berlin, Heidelberg. https://doi.org/10.1007/978-3-540-78564-4_19.

[61] Unilever. 2013. Unilever Sustainable Living Plan. Making Progress Driving Change. https://www.unilever.com/files/origin/910902bc7c415bbb6fdd0d9474ccb10da1e7c671.pdf/slp_unilever-sustainable-living-plan-2013.pdf. Accessed: 1 June 2025.

[62] Unilever. 2013.

Chapter 6

[1] Simmel, G. and Rammstedt, O. 2016. *Gesamtausgabe. Band 11.* Frankfurt am Main: Suhrkamp.

[2] Simmel, G. 1994. *Philosophie des Geldes* [Philosophy of Money]. Frankfurt am Main: Suhrkamp, 503, translated from the German edition.

[3] Csikszentmihalyi and Rochberg-Halton point to material artefacts as a shared reference for goal-directed activity and learning experiences. Fuhrer proposes the ideas of a cultured mind and identity as meaning-making practices; *Csikszentmihalyi, M. and Rochberg-Halton, E. 2012. The Meaning of Things.* Cambridge University Press. doi: 10.1017/cbo9781139167611.

[4] Breuer, H. 2001. Kultivation und Imagination in den Neuen Medien. Doctoral dissertation. Magdeburg.

[5] Fuhrer, U. 2004. *Cultivating minds: Identity as meaning-making practice.* New York, N.Y.: Taylor & Francis. P. 119.

[6] Breuer, H., Fichter, K., Freund, F. and Tiemann, I. 2018. Sustainability-oriented business model development: principles, criteria and tools. *International Journal of Entrepreneurial Venturing* 10 (2): 256. doi: 10.1504/IJEV.2018.092715.

[7] Mengering, K. & Hein, C. Gewinne Zukunft Podcast. 2024. #61 ESG-Ziele, Reporting und Datenstrategie vereinen - so macht es die Deutsche Bahn. https://gewinnezukunft.podigee.io/63-esg-datenstrategie. Accessed: 1 June 2025.

[8] Eric Schmidt, formerly chairman of Google, describes the actual impact of the company motto not to do anything evil. In spite of its ambiguity, the good intent served as a criterion to stop and redirect a given course of action: 'The idea was that we do not quite know what evil is, but if we have a rule that says do not be evil, then employees can say, I think that's evil .... So what happens is, I'm sitting in this meeting and we're having this debate about an advertising product. And one of the engineers pounds his fists on the table and says, that's evil. And then the whole conversation stops, everyone goes into conniptions and eventually we stopped the project. So it did work'. Cited from Breuer, H. and Freund, F. 2017. *Values-based innovation management.* London: Macmillan Publishers Limited.

[9] Crofts, P. and van Rijswijk, H. 2020. Negotiating 'Evil': Google, Project Maven and the Corporate Form. *Law, Technology and Humans* 2 (1): 75–90. doi: 10.5204/lthj.v2i1.1313.

[10] Crofts, P. and van Rijswijk, H. 2020.

[11] Loew, T., Clausen, J., Hall, M., Loft, L., Braun, S. 2009. *Case Studies on CSR and Innovation. Company Cases from Germany and the USA.* Berlin: Borderstep Institut.

[12] Boenink, M. and Kudina, O. 2020. Values in responsible research and innovation: from entities to practices. *Journal of Responsible Innovation* 7 (3): 450–470. doi: 10.1080/23299460.2020.1806451.

[13] Ivanov, K. 2022. Values-Based Business Model Innovation–The Case of Ecosia and Its Business Model. *International Journal of Innovation Management* 26 (05). doi: 10.1142/S1363919622400023.

[14] Edmondson, A. and Bransby, D. 2023. Psychological Safety Comes of Age: Observed Themes in an Established Literature. *Annual Review of Organisational Psychology and Organisational Behavior* 10 (1): 55–78. doi: 10.1146/annurev-orgpsych-120920-055217.

[15] Liang, J., Farh, C. and Farh, J. 2012. Psychological Antecedents of Promotive and Prohibitive Voice: A Two-Wave Examination. *Academy of Management Journal* 55 (1): 71–92. doi: 10.5465/amj.2010.0176.

[16] Reay, T. and Hinings, C. 2009. Managing the Rivalry of Competing Institutional Logics. *Organisation Studies* 30 (6): 629–652. doi: 10.1177/0170840609104803.

[17] Hummels, H., van Rensch, M., Heinen, A., Herrebout, E. 2022. Holacracy driving Sustainable Future Winners. A white paper. https://sustainable-finance.nl/upload/researches/Holacracy-driving-Sustainable-Future-Winners_a-white-paper_Jan-2022.pdf. Accessed: 1 June 2025.

[18] The white paper from Deloitte highlights how holacracy contributed to aligning the professional development and everyday practices of individual employees with the corporate sustainability goals of five firms: Hummels, H., van Rensch, M., Heinen, A., Herrebout, E. 2022.

[19] Urbany, J., Reynolds, T. and Phillips, J. 2008. How to Make Values Count in Everyday Decisions 49 (4): 75–80. *MIT Sloan Management Review.*

[20] A respondent in the field study described a situation of a team involved in an innovation project, which did not respond and did not update the project's status. This changed when the *Innovation Impact Assessment* was introduced, and the project was included in the group management report with a remark: 'Information is not available'. The responsible managers immediately reacted, and the project status was updated. However, the involved employees did not feel judged or openly accused of lagging behind.

[21] Related practices from the literature: A clear direction in Geradts, T. & Bocken, N. 2019. Driving sustainability-oriented innovation: a sustainable corporate entrepreneurship approach. *MIT Sloan Review* (Winter 2019) Providing Active Guidance for the Implementation of Normative Statements in Ivanov, K. 2024. Values-Based Barriers and Good Practices in Sustainability-Oriented Innovation Management. https://doi.org/10.1002/csr.3016. *Corporate Social Responsibility and Environmental Management* 1 (19).

[22] R. Montera, A. Monti, M. Rapaccini. 2022. Case of Oil & Gas Corporation in ethnographic study for the IMPACT Erasmus+ project.

[23] European Commission. 2023. Supplementing Directive 2013/34/EU of the European Parliament and of the Council as regards sustainability reporting standards. https://eur-lex.europa.eu/legal-content/en/TXT/?uri=CELEX:32023R2772. Accessed: 1 June 2025.
UNDP. 2023. The Climate Dictionary. Speak Climate Fluently. https://www.undp.org/publications/climate-dictionary. Accessed: 1 June 2025.

[24] Haumer, F., Schlicker, L., Murschetz, P. and Kolo, C. 2021. Tailor the message and change will happen? An experimental study of message tailoring as an effective communication strategy for organisational change. *Journal of Strategy and Management* 14 (4): 426–443. Emerald Publishing Limited. doi: 10.1108/JSMA-08-2020-0207.
Kreuter, M., Lukwago, S., Bucholtz, D., Clark, E. and Sanders-Thompson, V. 2003. Achieving cultural appropriateness in health promotion programs: targeted and tailored approaches. *Health education & behavior: the official publication of the Society for Public Health Education* 30 (2): 133–146. doi: 10.1177/1090198102251021

[25] Lapinski, M., Oetzel, J., Park, S. and Williamson, A. 2024. Cultural Tailoring and Targeting of Messages: A Systematic Literature Review. *Health Communication:* 1–14. doi: 10.1080/10410236.2024.2369340.

[26] Kreuter, M., Lukwago, S., Bucholtz, D., Clark, E. and Sanders-Thompson, V. 2003.

[27] Ye, K. 2024. Using a memetics lens to better understand tailored messages for organisational change toward sustainability. Master's thesis.

[28] Ye, K. 2024.

[29] Related practices from the literature: Positive Reinforcement in Geradts, T. & Bocken, N. 2019.
Eco-friendly Reward System in Islam, M., Tseng, M.-L. and Karia, N. 2019. Assessment of corporate culture in sustainability performance using a hierarchical framework and interdependence relations. *Journal of Cleaner Production* 217: 676–690. doi: 10.1016/j.jclepro.2019.01.259

[30] Alonso, A. 2016. How is sustainability integrated in management bonuses? https://medium.com/@albert.vilarino/how-is-sustainability-integrated-in-management-bonuses-f0f3b07ac4e8. Accessed: 1 June 2025.

[31] See 'The Need for Accountability' in Geradts, T. & Bocken, N. 2019.

[32] Kolk, A. and Perego, P. 2014. Sustainable Bonuses: Sign of Corporate Responsibility or Window Dressing? *Journal of Business Ethics* 119 (1): 1–15. doi: 10.1007/s10551-012-1614-x.

[33] Geradts, T. & Bocken, N. 2019.

[34] Related practices from the literature: Attracting the Right Talent in Geradts, T. & Bocken, N. 2019.
Human Resource Management in Gadomska-Lila, K. 2024. *Changing organisational culture for sustainability*: 206–230. doi: 10.4337/9781035314225.00020
Sustainable Recruitment and Selection in Jepsen, D. and Grob, S. 2015. Sustainability in Recruitment and Selection: Building a Framework of Practices. *Journal of Education for Sustainable Development* 9 (2): 160–178. doi: 10.1177/0973408215588250

[35] Gadomska-Lila, K. 2024.

[36] Mead, T., Jeanrenaud, S. and Bessant, J. 2022. Sustainability oriented innovation narratives: Learning from nature inspired innovation. *Journal of Cleaner Production* 344: 130980. doi: 10.1016/j.jclepro.2022.130980.

[37] Mead, T., Jeanrenaud, S. and Bessant, J. 2022.

[38] Related practices from the literature: Onboarding Training in Geradts, T. & Bocken, N. 2019.
Human Resource Management in Gadomska-Lila, K. 2024

[39] Mao, Y., Roberts, S., Pagliaro, S., Csikszentmihalyi, M. and Bonaiuto, M. 2016. Optimal Experience and Optimal Identity: A Multinational Study of the Associations Between Flow and Social Identity. *Frontiers in Psychology* 7: 67. doi: 10.3389/fpsyg.2016.00067.

[40] Gadomska-Lila, K. 2024.

[41] Geradts, T. & Bocken, N. 2019.

[42] Geradts, T. & Bocken, N. 2019.

[43] See Interpersonal Communication in Islam, M., Tseng, M.-L. and Karia, N. 2019.

[44] Ivanov, K. 2022.

[45] Ivanov, K. 2022.

[46] Rolf, S., Schlachter, S. and Welbourne, T. 2016. Leading

Sustainable Global Change from Within: The Case of Environmental Employee Resource Groups. *Employment Relations Today* 43 (2): 17–23. doi: 10.1002/ert.21564.

[47] Spitzeck, H., Hansen, E., Lenssen, G., Bevan, D. and Fontrodona, J. 2010. Stakeholder governance: how stakeholders influence corporate decision making. *Corporate Governance: The international Journal of Business in Society* 10 (4): 378–391. Emerald Group Publishing Limited. doi: 10.1108/14720701011069623.

[48] Gadomska-Lila, K. 2024.; Islam, M., Tseng, M.-L. and Karia, N. 2019

[49] Lüdeke-Freund, Breuer & Massa, 2022

[50] Spitzeck, H., Hansen, E., Lenssen, G., Bevan, D. and Fontrodona, J. 2010.

[51] Spitzeck, H., Hansen, E., Lenssen, G., Bevan, D. and Fontrodona, J. 2010.

[52] Pfitzner, R. and Lutz, M. 2015. Siemens: Managing Sustainability Along the Value Chain to Benefit Our Customers: 207–225. doi: 10.1007/978-3-319-12142-0_8.

[53] Pfitzner, R. and Lutz, M. 2015.

[54] Pfitzner, R. and Lutz, M. 2015.

[55] ISO 9000. 2015. Quality management systems. Fundamentals and vocabulary. https://www.iso.org/standard/45481.html Accessed: 1 June 2025.

[56] Related practices from the literature: Embedding Values in Organisational Policies: Reficco, E., Gutiérrez, R., Jaén, M. and Auletta, N. 2018. Collaboration mechanisms for sustainable innovation. *Journal of Cleaner Production* 203: 1170–1186. doi: 10.1016/j.jclepro.2018.08.043
Embedding Values in Organisational Controls in Rauter, R., Globocnik, D. and Baumgartner, R. 2023. The role of organisational controls to advance sustainability innovation performance. Technovation 128: 102855. doi: 10.1016/j.technovation.2023.102855; Ronalter, L. M., & Bernardo, M. 2023. Integrated management systems and sustainability–a review on their relationships. *Total Quality Management & Business Excellence* 34 (11-12): 1438–1468.
Adopting Management Systems in Islam, M., Tseng, M.-L. and Karia, N. 2019

[57] Eran, Ö., Ehiorobo, E. and Colin, C. 2023. What are the most effective ways to integrate sustainability management systems in systems management? https://www.linkedin.com/advice/3/what-most-effective-ways-integrate-sustainability-pyoqe. Accessed: 1 June 2025.

[58] ISO 9000. 2015.

[59] ISO 14001. 2015. Environmental management systems. Requirements with guidance for use. https://www.iso.org/standard/60857.html.

[60] ISO 56000. 2020. Innovation management — Fundamentals and vocabulary. https://www.iso.org/obp/ui/es/#iso:std:iso:56000:ed-1:v1:en. Accessed: 1 June 2025.5; ISO 56001:2024 Innovation management system — Requirements. https://www.iso.org/standard/79278.html Accessed: 1 June 2025; ISO 56002:2019 Innovation management — Innovation manage-

ment system — Guidance. https://www.iso.org/standard/68221.html. Accessed: 10 April 2025.

[61] Ronalter, L. M., & Bernardo, M. 2023.

[62] Boonstra, J., and Brillo, J. 2021. Shaping Sustainable Innovation Based on Cultural Values. In: Voinea, C. et al.: Sustainable innovation. *Routledge.*

[63] Garst, J., Maas, K. and Suijs, J. 2022. Materiality Assessment Is an Art, Not a Science: Selecting ESG Topics for Sustainability Reports 65 (1): 64–90. doi: 10.1177/0008125621120692.

[64] Garst, J., Maas, K. and Suijs, J. 2022.

[65] Nielsen, C. 2023. ESG Reporting and Metrics: From Double Materiality to Key Performance Indicators. *Sustainability* 15 (24): 16844. doi: 10.3390/su152416844.

[66] Ilcheong, Y., Bruelisauer, S., Utting, P., McElroy, M., et al. 2022. *Authentic Sustainability Assessment: A User Manual for the Sustainable Development Performance Indicators.* Geneva, Switzerland: UNRISD.

[67] Ilcheong, Y., Bruelisauer, S., Utting, P., McElroy, M., et al. 2022.

[68] United Nations Research Institute for Social Development. 2024. SDPI Community. https://sdpi.unrisd.org/about/sdpi-community/. Accessed: 1 June 2025.

[69] European Financial Reporting Advisory Group (EFRAG) and EU recognised the SDPI as a Key Tool for ESG Measurement aligned with ESRS (European Sustainability Reporting Standard)/CSRD (Corporate Sustainability Reporting Directive), see https://sdpi.unrisd.org/wp-content/uploads/2024/09/20240910_PR_Reference_SDPI_ESRS_-1.pdf. Accessed: 1 June 2025.

[70] United Nations Research Institute for Social Development. 2024.

[71] OECD Development Assistance Committee. 2014. Measuring and managing results in development co-operation. A review of challenges and practices among DAC members and observers. https://www.oecd.org/content/dam/oecd/en/publications/reports/2014/11/measuring-and-managing-results-in-development-co-operation_b71067a7/c7762fac-en.pdf. Accessed: 1 June 2025.

[72] OECD Development Assistance Committee. 2014.

[73] Dembek, K., Lüdeke-Freund, F., Rosati, F. and Froese, T. 2023. Untangling business model outcomes, impacts and value. *Business Strategy and the Environment* 32 (4): 2296–2311. doi: 10.1002/bse.3249.

[74] Dembek, K., Lüdeke-Freund, F., Rosati, F. and Froese, T. 2023. (p. 2301).

[75] Fowler, B. & Strub, F. 2021. Investment Climate Reform Toolbox. https://www.giz.de/de/downloads/giz2021-en-investment-climate-reform-toolbox.pdf. Accessed: 1 June 2025.

[76] Breuer, H. and Ivanov, K. 2022. Case of Inspection Company in ethnographic study for the IMPACT Erasmus+ project. see also Environment and Social Impact Assessment, Health Technology Assessment and Product Impact Tool in Guimarães,

C., Santos, J. and Almeida, F. 2024. Practical tools for measuring and monitoring sustainable innovation. *Innovation and Green Development*, 3(4), 100172.

[77] Laedre, O., Haavaldsen, T., Bohne, R., Kallaos, J. and Lohne, J. 2015. Determining sustainability impact assessment indicators. *Impact Assessment and Project Appraisal* 33 (2): 98–107. Taylor & Francis. doi: 10.1080/14615517.2014.981037.

[78] Breuer, H. and Ivanov, K. 2022.

[79] Cunha, d., Meira, E. and Orsato, R. 2021. Sustainable finance and investment: Review and research agenda. *Business Strategy and the Environment* 30 (8): 3821–3838. doi: 10.1002/bse.2842.

[80] Liang, S., Gu, H. and Bergman, R. 2021. Environmental Life-Cycle Assessment and Life-Cycle Cost Analysis of a High-Rise Mass Timber Building: A Case Study in Pacific Northwestern United States. *Sustainability* 13 (14): 7831. doi: 10.3390/su13147831.

[81] Liang, S., Gu, H. and Bergman, R. 2021.

[82] Atz, U., van Holt, T. and Liu, Z. 2022. Do Corporate Sustainability and Sustainable Finance Generate Better Financial Performance? A Review and Meta-analysis. http://dx.doi.org/10.2139/ssrn.3708495. *Journal of Sustainable Finance and Investment.* doi: 10.2139/ssrn.3708495.

[83] Lüdeke-Freund, F., Froese, T., Dembek, K., Rosati, F. and Massa, L. 2024. What Makes a Business Model Sustainable? Activities, Design Themes and Value Functions. *Organisation & Environment* 37 (2): 194–220. doi: 10.1177/10860266241235212.

[84] HSBC Bank. 2023. Walmart Spurs Suppliers to Cut Carbon With Special Finance Terms. https://www.business.us.hsbc.com/en/insights/sustainability/walmart-and-hsbc-establish-a-sustainable-supply-chain-finance-program. Accessed: 1 June 2025.

PART III

Chapter 7

[1] TÜV SÜD. 2024. Wir erweitern unser Portfolio. https://www.tuvsud.com/de-de/ueber-uns/geschichte. Accessed: 1 June 2025.

[2] TÜV SÜD. 2024. Wir erweitern unser Portfolio. https://www.tuvsud.com/de-de/ueber-uns/geschichte. Accessed: 1 June 2025.

[3] Impartiality is about engaging fairly and objectively to become a trusted third party between technology users and providers, whereas neutrality is about maintaining a non-involved, non-aligned position. Neutrality is about what an entity does not do (i.e. not taking sides), while impartiality is about how an entity conducts itself (i.e. ensuring fairness and equality).

[4] Martin, R. 2023. Strategy in 1000 words. A conversation between Roger Martin and ReD partners Iago Storgaard and Filip Lau. ReD Associates. https://issuu.com/red-associates/docs/red_roger_martin_strategy_in_1000_words_full Accessed: 1 June 2025.

[5] Rather than inspecting the products themselves, some inspection companies had carried out inspections of hip prostheses,

breast implants and financial products by looking at the books. This led to scandals raising questions about the impartiality and quality of their tests when competing for orders; Schmidt, C. 2015. Bezahlte Unabhängigkeit / TÜV zwischen Prüfung und Profit. Deutschlandfunk https://www.deutschlandfunk.de/bezahlte-unabhaengigkeit-tuev-zwischen-pruefung-und-profit-100.html. Accessed: 1 June 2025.

[6] The format involves techniques from Future Search: Weisbord, M. and Janoff, S. 2010. *Future Search: An Action Guide to Finding Common Ground in Organisations and Communities*. Berrett-Koehler Publishers; Breuer, H., Fichter, K., Freund, F., and Tiemann, I. 2018. Sustainability-oriented business model development: principles, criteria and tools. *International Journal of Entrepreneurial Venturing* 10 (2): 256. doi: 10.1504/IJEV.2018.092715; Kawohl, J., Krechting D. & Schilling, R. 2022. Ecosystemize your business: How to succeed in the new economy of collaboration. MVB Marketing- und Verlagsservice des Buchhandels GmbH.

[7] Inspection refers to the approval of a product prototype such as a vehicle, vehicle system or component. Type approval ensures that the prototype meets regulatory standards and specifications before it can be mass-produced and sold (e.g. UN/ECE R101. 2012. Regulation No 101 of the Economic Commission for Europe of the United Nations. https://op.europa.eu/s/zNaG. Accessed: 1 June 2025. Certification is a formal process by which a product, process, system or service is certified to meet specific standards or criteria set by a recognised certification body (e.g. ISO 14001. 2015. Environmental management systems. Requirements with guidance for use. https://www.iso.org/standard/60857.html. Accessed: 1 June 2025.

[8] Breuer, H. 2024. Sustainability Innovation Cards. https://www.uxberlin.com/de/business-innovation-kit/ Accessed: 1 June 2025; based on Schaltegger, S., Lüdeke-Freund, F., Hansen, E. 2012. Business cases for sustainability: the role of business model innovation for corporate sustainability. *International Journal Innovation and Sustainable Development* 6(2):95–119.

[9] Meier-Andrae, R. 2024. TUEV Nord # explore, https://www.tuev-nord.de/explore/de/innovation/wie-hilft-ki-bei-der-hauptuntersuchung/. Accessed: 1 June 2025.

[10] Also in other contexts, TIC Mobility adopted stakeholder integration and innovation practices grounded in customer and user behaviour studies and direct feedback. One notable example is a digital inspection assistant, which leverages voice control to enhance the efficiency of main inspections. This innovation stems from a crucial insight obtained through an ethnographic user study (following the approach outlined in chapter 4). Initial ideas and prototypes have been iteratively refined based on continuous user feedback. This methodology ensures that service products are precisely tailored to user needs, simplify their daily tasks, and maximize the impact and prioritisation of initiatives, thereby optimising resource allocation.

Chapter 8

[1] Newsham, A., Kohnstamm, S., Naess, L. O., & Atela, J. 2018. Agricultural commercialisation pathways. Climate change and agriculture. https://eprints.soas.ac.uk/30551/. Accessed: 1 June 2025.

[2] Intergovernmental Panel on Climate Change. 2022. Global Warming of 1.5°C: IPCC Special Report on Impacts of Global Warming of 1.5°C above Pre-industrial Levels in Context of Strengthening Response to Climate Change, Sustainable Development, and Efforts to Eradicate Poverty. https://www.cambridge.org/core/product/D7455D42B4C820E706A03A169B1893FA. Cambridge: Cambridge University Press. doi: 10.1017/9781009157940.

[3] Saunois, M., Jackson, R., Bousquet, P., Poulter, B., and Canadell, J. 2016. The growing role of methane in anthropogenic climate change. *Environmental Research Letters* 11 (12): 120207. doi: 10.1088/1748-9326/11/12/120207.

[4] Laurance, W., Useche, C., and Rendeiro, J., Kalka, M., Corey, B., et. al. 2012. Averting biodiversity collapse in tropical forest protected areas. Nature 489 (7415): 290–294. doi: 10.1038/nature11318.

[5] Goggins, G., Rau, H., Moran, P., Fahy, F., and Goggins, J. 2022. The role of culture in advancing sustainable energy policy and practice. *Energy Policy* 167: 113055. doi: 10.1016/j.enpol.2022.113055.
Olaya Escobar, D. and Olaya Escobar, E. 2022. Oil and its influence on the creation of a sustainable society: A systematic literature review. *Intangible Capital* 18 (3): 402. doi: 10.3926/ic.1833

[6] Littlewood, G., & Januszewska, M. 2024. Implementing Diversity, Equity and Inclusion Strategy–Learnings for Oil Spill Industry Development. *International Oil Spill Conference Proceedings* (1). Allen Press.
Schoneveld, G. 2020. Sustainable business models for inclusive growth: Towards a conceptual foundation of inclusive business. *Journal of Cleaner Production* 277: 124062. doi: 10.1016/j.jclepro.2020.124062

[7] Mojarad, A. S., Atashbari, V., & Tantau, A. 2020. Developing a strategy process toward sustainability for leading oil corporates in a developing country: A learning organization approach. *International Journal of Business and Management Invention* 9 (11): 49–63.

[8] Simpa, P., Solomon, N., Adenekan, O., and Obasi, S. 2024. Environmental stewardship in the oil and gas sector: Current practices and future directions. *International Journal of Applied Research in Social Sciences* 6 (5): 903–926. doi: 10.51594/ijarss.v6i5.1132.
Joel, O. and Oguanobi, V. 2024. Leadership and management in high-growth environments: effective strategies for the clean energy sector. *International Journal of Management & Entrepreneurship Research* 6 (5): 1423–1440. doi: 10.51594/ijmer.v6i5.1092

[9] European Commission. 2021. EU Emissions Trading System. https://climate.ec.europa.eu/eu-action/eu-emissions-trading-system-eu-ets/what-eu-ets_en. Accessed: 1 June 2025.

[10] Nguyen, H. and Kanbach, D. 2023. Toward a view of integrating corporate sustainability into strategy: A systematic literature review. *Corporate Social Responsibility and Environmental Management*. doi: 10.1002/csr.2611.

[11] The cards are part of a toolkit developed simultaneously in four countries. The overall result is a practitioner card-based toolkit, available for free download at www.uxberlin.com/sustainable-innovation-toolkits and www.impact-project.site/copy-of-community. Accessed: 1 June 2025.

Chapter 9

[1] Katarzyna Matras-Postołek (corresponding author), Cracow University of Technology, Faculty of Chemical Engineering and Technology, Warszawska 24, 31-155 Krakow, Poland, k.matras@pk.edu.pl; Piotr Beńko, Cracow University of Technology, Faculty of Environmental Engineering and Energy, Warszawska 24, 31-155 Krakow, Poland, piotr.benko@pk.edu.pl; Małgorzata Ciesielska, Cracow University of Technology, Center for Technology Transfer, Warszawska 24, 31-155 Krakow, Poland, m.ciesielska@pk.edu.pl; Jacek Kasz, Cracow University of Technology, Center for Technology Transfer, Warszawska 24, 31-155 Krakow, Poland, jacek.kasz@pk.edu.pl; Irena Śliwińska, Department of Market Analysis and Marketing Research, Krakow University of Economics, Rakowicka 27, 31-510 Krakow, Poland, sliwinsi@uek.krakow.pl

[2] Elo, S., & Kyngäs, H. 2008. The qualitative content analysis process. *Journal of Advanced Nursing*, 62(1), 107–115. https://doi.org/10.1111/j.1365-2648.2007.04569.x, accessed 23.03.2025

[3] https://www.astor.com.pl/o-nas/strategia.html Accessed: 5 May 2024

[4] ASTOR. 2021. Social Report 2021. https://www.astor.com.pl/downloads/katalogi/ASTOR_SOCIAL_REPORT_2021.pdf. Accessed: 1 June 2025.

[5] Poreda, R. Fabryki przyszłości a zrównoważony rozwój – jak technologia wspiera sustainable development? https://www.astor.com.pl/biznes-i-produkcja/fabryki-przyszlosci-a-zrownowazony-rozwoj-jak-technologia-wspiera-sustainable-development/. Biznes i Produkcja. Accessed: 1 June 2025.

[6] ASTOR. 2021. Social Report 2021. https://www.astor.com.pl/downloads/katalogi/ASTOR_SOCIAL_REPORT_2021.pdf. Accessed: 1 June 2025.

[7] Wojtulewicz, M. 2020. Finances of Industry 4.0. How to invest and win in the technological revolution? https://www.researchgate.net/profile/Jaroslaw-Gracel/publication/344377764_Finances_of_Industry_40_How_to_invest_and_win_in_the_technological_revolution/links/5f6de783299bf1b53ef0c7bb/Finances-of-Industry-40-How-to-invest-and-win-in-the-technological-revolution.pdf. Kraków. Accessed: 1 June 2025.

[8] Poreda, R. Kapitał technologiczny przedsiębiorstwa i wskaźnik ITA. https://www.astor.com.pl/biznes-i-produkcja/kapital-technologiczny-przedsiebiorstwa-i-wskaznik-ita/ Accessed: 1 June 2025.

Chapter 10

[1] Characteristics of science-based companies are described in the following papers: Setti, A. 2020. Linking science-based firms with performance factors: An integrative systematic review of the literature. *International Journal of Research in Business and Social Science*, 9(2), 9–42; Bruni, D. S., & Verona, G. 2009. Dynamic marketing capabilities in science-based firms: An exploratory investigation of the pharmaceutical industry. *British Journal of Management*, 20, 101–117; De Silva, M., Gokhberg, L., Meissner, D., & Russo, M. (2021). Addressing societal challenges through the simultaneous generation of social and business values: A conceptual framework for science-based co-creation. *Technovation*, 104, 102268

[2] Gangi, F., Daniele, L., Tani, M., and Papaluca, O. 2025. Drivers and impacts of green product innovation as open innovation: Evidence from science-based firms. *Business Ethics, the Environment & Responsibility* 34 (1): 58–68. doi: 10.1111/beer.12583.~
Pavitt, K. 1984. Sectoral patterns of technical change: Towards a taxonomy and a theory. *Research Policy* 13 (6): 343–373. doi: 10.1016/0048-7333(84)90018-0.

[3] Woelders, S. 2020. Unravelling the relationship between organisational inertia, change resistance and (un)learning. http://essay.utwente.nl/82663/.

[4] Bos-Brouwers, H. 2010. Corporate sustainability and innovation in SMEs: Evidence of themes and activities in practice. *Business Strategy and the Environment* 19 (7): 417–435. doi: 10.1002/bse.652.
Varadarajan, R. 2017. Innovating for sustainability: a framework for sustainable innovations and a model of sustainable innovations orientation. *Journal of the Academy of Marketing Science* 45 (1): 14–36. doi: 10.1007/s11747-015-0461-6.

[5] Weisbord, M. and Janoff, S. 2010. *Future Search. An Action Guide to Finding Common Ground in Organizations and Communities.* Berrett-Koehler Publishers.

[6] 'Prouds and sorries' is a workshop facilitation technique that aims to inspire participants to take responsibility and shift to more emotional perceptions of their equal 'humanity, vulnerability and aspiration'. Weisbord, M. and Janoff, S. 2010, 81.

[7] Mousavi, S., Bossink, B., and van Vliet, M. 2019. Microfoundations of companies' dynamic capabilities for environmentally sustainable innovation: Case study insights from high-tech innovation in science-based companies. *Business Strategy and the Environment* 28 (2): 366–387. doi: 10.1002/bse.2255.

[8] Erden et al., 2015

[9] Pattinson, S., & Dawson, P. 2024. The Ties that Bind: How Boundary Spanners Create Value in Science-Based SMEs. *British Journal of Management*, 35(1), 464–486.

[10] Melander, L. 2017. Achieving Sustainable Development by Collaborating in Green Product Innovation. *Business Strategy and the Environment* 26 (8): 1095–1109. doi: 10.1002/bse.1970.

[11] Faller, C. and Knyphausen-Aufseß, D. 2018. Does Equity Ownership Matter for Corporate Social Responsibility? A Literature Review of Theories and Recent Empirical Findings. *Journal of Business Ethics* 150 (1): 15–40. doi: 10.1007/s10551-016-3122-x.

PART IV

Chapter 12

[1] Patagonia. 2025. Our core values. https://www.patagonia.com/core-values/. Accessed: 1 June 2025.

[2] Asphaltgold. 2025. Asphaltgold Blog: Patagonia is revolutionising sustainability in the outdoor industry: This blog post provides an overview of Patagonia's sustainability practices and their commitment to environmental responsibility. https://www.asphaltgold.com/en/blogs/allgemein/wie-patagonia-nachhaltigkeit-in-der-outdoor-branche-revolutioniert. Accessed: 1 June 2025.

3 Orsted. 2017. Green Bonds Investor Letter. https://orsted.com/-/media/www/docs/corp/com/sustainability/orsted_green_bonds_investor_letter_2017. Accessed: 1 June 2025.

4 Lüdeke-Freund, F., Breuer, H., Massa, L. 2022. Sustainable Business Model Design – 45 Patterns. Berlin: Self-Published, 224ff.

5 Lüdeke-Freund, F., Breuer, H., Massa, L. 2022.

6 Leuphana. 2024. EnERgioN. https://www.leuphana.de/en/partners/innovation-incubator-lueneburg/sustainable-energy/energion.html. Accessed: 1 June 2025.

Breuer, H. & Lüdeke-Freund, F. 2017. Values-Based Network and Business Model Innovation, International Journal of Innovation Management, Vol. 21, No. 3, Art. 1750028 (35 pages).

7 Henkel. 2022. Henkel investiert in Innovationsfonds für nachhaltige Verpackungen von Emerald Technology Ventures. https://www.henkel.de/presse-und-medien/presseinformationen-und-pressemappen/2022-03-13-henkel-investiert-in-innovationsfonds-fuer-nachhaltige-verpackungen-von-emerald-technology-ventures-1653688 Accessed: 1 June 2025.

8 Ikea. 2025. Our vision is to create a better everyday life for the many people. https://ikeafoundation.org/ Accessed: 1 June 2025.

9 Breuer, H. & Lüdeke-Freund, F. 2018. Values-Based Business Model Innovation: A Toolkit. In: Moratis, L., Melissen, F. & Idowu, S.O. (Eds.). Sustainable Business Models, 395-416. Springer.

10 Crandall, B. 2015. Interface lifecycle cost analysis: Soft flooring most effective. https://www.fmlink.com/articles/lifecycle-cost-analysis-finds-soft-flooring-most-effective/. Accessed: 1 June 2025.

11 European Medicines Agency (EMA). 2023. ICH Q9 Quality risk management - Scientific guideline. https://www.ema.europa.eu/en/ich-q9-quality-risk-management-scientific-guideline. Accessed: 1 June 2025.

12 Unilever. 2021. Unilever Sustainable Living Plan 2010 to 2020 Summary of 10 years' progress. https://www.unilever.de/files/92ui5egz/production/287881e6e4572af1bc2a1d3c97e3b4abd4e57ea1.pdf Accessed: 1 June 2025.

13 The case description is drawn from an expert interview conducted by the authors with the two managing directors, Marvin Mechelse and Karsten Kührlings, on 23 January, 2025. We used a semi-structured interview guide consisting of sections on personal and organisational background, internal and external sustainability orientation, and sustainable innovation and culture. The interview was recorded, transcribed and analysed to highlight sustainable innovation financing and related practices of the sustainability-oriented investment company.

Chapter 13

1 On the contrary, extractive institutions concentrate power and benefits in the hands of a small elite and thereby tend to stifle participation, entrepreneurship and innovation; Acemoglu, D. & Robinson, J. 2012. Why Nations Fail: The Origins of Power, Prosperity, and Poverty. Crown Publishers, New York.

2 In a large survey on public expectations of business in the United States, fair wages and ethical leadership were ranked as the top two priorities (support of workers' well-being and transparency in communication were ranked third and fourth), which underlines the importance of values-based business development. Tonti, J. 2024. We Asked the American People What They Want From Corporate America – Here's What They Said. https://justcapital.com/news/we-asked-the-american-people-what-they-want-from-corporate-america-heres-what-they-said/. Accessed: 1 June 2025.

3 'All companies should apply a context-based approach to sustainability reporting, allocating their fair share impacts on common capital resources within the thresholds of their carrying capacities' (United Nations Environment Program. 2015. Raising the Bar – advancing environmental disclosure in sustainability reporting. https://wedocs.unep.org/bitstream/handle/20.500.11822/9807/-Raising_the_Bar_-_Advancing_Environmental_Disclosure_in_Sustainability_Reporting-2015UNEP_Raising_the_Bar_2015.pdf.pdf. Accessed: 1 June 2025. For thresholds and allocations and their conceptual development see Baue, B. & Thurm, R. (2018). What Are Thresholds & Allocations, and Why Are They Necessary for Sustainable System Value Creation? https://r3dot0.medium.com/what-are-thresholds-allocations-and-why-are-they-necessary-for-sustainable-system-value-fe127483c407. Accessed: 1 June 2025.

4 UXBerlin. 2018. Business Case Drivers (15 Cards for Download). https://www.uxberlin.com/wp-content/uploads/2023/10/Sustainability_Innovation_Cards_Print.pdf; based on Schaltegger, S.; Lüdeke-Freund, F. & Hansen, E. 2012: Business Cases for Sustainability: The Role of Business Model Innovation for Corporate Sustainability, International Journal of Innovation and Sustainable Development, Vol. 6, No. 2, 95-119.

5 Deal, T. and Kennedy, A. 1982. Corporate Cultures: The Rites and Rituals of Corporate Life. Addison Wesley Publishing Company, Reading.

6 Śliwińska, I., Beńko, P., Breuer, H., Ciesielska, M., Ivanov, K., Kasz, J., Matras-Postołek, K. 2025. The Challenge of Introducing Sustainability-Oriented Innovation: An Ethnographic Study. Sustainable Development. https://doi.org/10.1002/sd.3332; Breuer, H. & Ivanov, K. 2024. Cultural Tensions and Values-Action Gaps in Sustainability-Oriented Innovation: An Ethnographic Inquiry. International Journal of Innovation Management, Vol. 28, No. 01n02 (2024) 2450005

7 Reiter, A., J. Stonig, and K. Frankenberger. 2024. Managing multi-tiered innovation ecosystems. Research Policy 53 (1): 104905. doi: 10.1016/j.respol.2023.104905.

8 Christian, B. 2020. The Alignment Problem: Machine Learning and Human Values. W.W.Norton & Company: New York.

9 Gabriel, I., and Ghazavi, V. 2023. The Challenge of Value Alignment: from Fairer Algorithms to AI Safety. The Oxford Handbook of Digital Ethics. Oxford University Press, 336-355.

10 EU. 2024. Artificial Intelligence Act (Regulation (EU) 2024/1689), Official Journal version of 13 June 2024. https://artificialintelligenceact.eu/the-act. Accessed: 1 June 2025.

11 Marie Francisco, M. & Linnér, B. 2023. AI and the governance of sustainable development: An idea analysis of the European Union, the United Nations, and the World Economic Forum. Environmental Science and Policy 150 (2023) 10359.

[12] Weick, K. E., Sutcliffe, K. M., & Obstfeld, D. 2005. Organizing and the process of sensemaking. *Organization Science*, 16(4), 409-421.

APPENDICES

[1] Baue, B. 2020. From Monocapitalism to Multicapitalism: 21st Century System Value Creation. r3.0 White Paper No.1.

[2] ISO 56000. 2020. Innovation management — Fundamentals and vocabulary. https://www.iso.org/obp/ui/es/ #iso:std:iso:56000:ed-1:v1:en. Accessed: 1 June 2025.

[3] ISO 56000. 2020. Innovation management — Fundamentals and vocabulary. https://www.iso.org/obp/ui/es/ #iso:std:iso:56000:ed-1:v1:en. Accessed: 1 June 2025.

[4] Rimmon-Kenan, S. 2002. Narrative fiction: Contemporary poetics (2nd ed.). London, England: Routledge.

[5] Adapted from Dembek, K., Lüdeke-Freund, F., Rosati, F. and Froese, T. 2023. Untangling business model outcomes, impacts and value. *Business Strategy and the Environment* 32 (4): 2296–2311. doi: 10.1002/bse.3249.
Brundtland, G. 1987. The Brundtland report: 'Our common future'. *Report of the World Commission on Environment and Development* 4 (1).

[6] Adapted from Leonelli, L. 2024. Deliverables, Outputs, Outcomes, and Benefits: A Deeper Dive. https://www.linkedin.com/ pulse/deliverables-outputs-outcomes-benefits-deeper-dive-lorenzo-leonelli-lbisf/. Accessed 1 June 2025.

[7] Meadowcroft, J. 2025. Sustainability. *Encyclopedia Britannica*. https://www.britannica.com/science/sustainability. Accessed 1 June 2025.

[8] Brundtland, G. 1987.

[9] McElroy, Mark. 2008. Social Footprints: Measuring the social sustainability performance of organizations, Dissertation, University of Groningen. pp104-105

[10] Lüdeke-Freund, F., Froese, T., Dembek, K., Rosati, F., and Massa, L. 2024. What Makes a Business Model Sustainable? Activities, Design Themes, and Value Functions. *Organization & Environment* 37 (2): 194–220. doi: 10.1177/10860266241235212.

[11] Breuer, H. and Freund, F. 2017. *Values-based innovation management.* London: Macmillan Publishers Limited. (p. 59).

[12] Brundtland, G. 1987.

[13] Schwartz, S. 2012. An Overview of the Schwartz Theory of Basic Values. *Online Readings in Psychology and Culture* 2 (1). doi: 10.9707/2307-0919.1116.